D1777218

Out of the Shadow of Famine

Other Books Published in Cooperation with the International Food Policy Research Institute

Agricultural Change and Rural Policy: Variations on a Theme by Dharm Narain
Edited by John W. Mellor and Gunvant M. Desai

Crop Insurance for Agricultural Development: Issues and Experience
Edited by Peter B. R. Hazell, Carlos Pomareda, and Alberto Valdés

Accelerating Food Production in Sub-Saharan Africa
Edited by John W. Mellor, Christopher L. Delgado, and Malcolm J. Blackie

Agricultural Price Policy for Developing Countries
Edited by John W. Mellor and Raisuddin Ahmed

Food Subsidies in Developing Countries: Costs, Benefits, and Policy Options
Edited by Per Pinstrup-Andersen

Variability in Grain Yields: Implications for Agricultural Research and Policy in Developing Countries
Edited by Jock R. Anderson and Peter B. R. Hazell

Seasonal Variability in Third World Agriculture: The Consequences for Food Security
Edited by David E. Sahn

The Green Revolution Reconsidered: The Impact of High-Yielding Rice Varieties in South India
By Peter B. R. Hazell and C. Ramasamy

The Political Economy of Food and Nutrition Policies
Edited by Per Pinstrup-Andersen

Agricultural Commercialization, Economic Development, and Nutrition
Edited by Joachim von Braun and Eileen Kennedy

Agriculture on the Road to Industrialization
Edited by John W. Mellor

Intrahousehold Resource Allocation in Developing Countries: Models, Methods, and Policy
Edited by Lawrence Haddad, John Hoddinott, and Harold Alderman

Sustainability, Growth, and Poverty Alleviation: A Policy and Agroecological Perspective
Edited by Stephen A. Vosti and Thomas Reardon

Famine in Africa: Causes, Responses, and Prevention
By Joachim von Braun, Tesfaye Teklu, and Patrick Webb

Paying for Agricultural Productivity
Edited by Julian M. Alston, Philip G. Pardey, and Vincent H. Smith

Out of the Shadow of Famine

Evolving Food Markets and Food Policy in Bangladesh

EDITED BY RAISUDDIN AHMED, STEVEN HAGGBLADE, AND TAWFIQ-E-ELAHI CHOWDHURY

Published for the International Food Policy Research Institute

The Johns Hopkins University Press
Baltimore and London

 Published 2000
Printed in the United States of America on acid-free paper
9 8 7 6 5 4 3 2 1

The Johns Hopkins University Press
2715 North Charles Street
Baltimore, Maryland 21218-4363
www.press.jhu.edu

International Food Policy Research Institute
2033 K Street, NW
Washington, D.C. 20006
(202) 862-5600
www.ifpri.org

Library of Congress Cataloging-in-Publication Data will be found at the end of this book.
A catalog record for this book is available from the British Library.

ISBN 0-8018-6333-3
ISBN 0-8018-6476-3 (pbk.)

Contents

Figures

Tables

Foreword

Bangladesh has suffered from repeated famines in the twentieth century, and memories of these devastating events still haunt the country. In recent years Bangladesh has made important gains in producing food for its people and kept famine at bay, but massive poverty and food insecurity persist. *Out of the Shadow of Famine* describes the evolution of food policy in Bangladesh and sets out guidelines for the future course of the nation's food policies. To eliminate the curse of enormous poverty and ensure food security, Bangladesh must solidify its recent gains in agriculture and strengthen the competitiveness of various sectors of its economy to ensure that economic and social progress are not mired in the forces emerging from globalization. Government has a vigorous but careful role to play in this respect.

This book is the latest product of the long history of policy research in Bangladesh by the International Food Policy Research Institute (IFPRI). In 1977 IFPRI conducted a review of Bangladesh food policies for the World Bank, and since then it has implemented a series of research projects in collaboration with the Bangladesh Institute of Development Studies, focusing on fertilizer policies, Food-for-Work programs, rural infrastructure, the Green Revolution, and policies pertaining to foodgrain markets and the public distribution system. Currently IFPRI and its collaborators are studying food policy issues with a greater emphasis on training in-country collaborators in food policy analysis. This book describes the results of a research project undertaken in collaboration with Bangladeshi institutions in the early 1990s.

It is our hope that the lessons learned from the experiences of Bangladesh will be useful to other developing countries, as indeed lessons from other countries have enriched the authors' development of policy conclusions in Bangladesh.

Per Pinstrup-Andersen
Director General, International Food Policy Research Institute

Acknowledgments

The International Food Policy Research Institute (IFPRI), collaborating informally with the Bangladesh Institute of Development Studies (BIDS) and formally with the government's Ministry of Food, undertook a research project on food policy between 1989 and 1994. Results were immediately communicated to policymakers engaged in food policy reform. After formal completion of the project, we decided to publish this book to synthesize research, document insights, and develop guideposts for emerging food policies. In this task, we received a great deal of help and cooperation from both individuals and institutions. We gratefully acknowledge this help and particularly recognize the cooperation of young officers of the Food Planning and Monitoring Unit of the Ministry of Food.

IFPRI's collaboration with BIDS has always been based on mutual respect and professionalism, and we are grateful for the support of both institutes. We also thank the U.S. Agency for International Development for financial aid in conducting the research that underpins this book. Anonymous reviewers of the manuscript provided invaluable comments that significantly improved on the original. We thank them for their contribution. Finally, we gratefully acknowledge the painstaking support of IFPRI staff members, particularly Elizabeth Daines, Heidi Fritschel, Lisa Grover, Carolyn Roper, and Emma Samman, who processed and monitored the book at various stages.

Out of the Shadow of Famine

1 Introduction

RAISUDDIN AHMED AND STEVEN HAGGBLADE

The transformation in Bangladesh from traditional agriculture to a dynamic and progressively commercial agrarian society is a fascinating process that should interest many developing countries. This change is occurring despite monumental constraints and an adverse natural environment, providing lessons not only for the contemporary leaders of Bangladesh but for actors all across the developing world. By helping shape this transformation, food policy, in Bangladesh and elsewhere, plays a crucial role in addressing complex issues of producer incentives, consumer welfare, and the long-term economic growth necessary to alleviate poverty.

Evolving Food Policy

Food policy commands a position of unusual prominence in Bangladesh. A teeming, densely populated nation astride the fertile but unpredictable confluence of the Ganges (Padma), Brahmaputra, and Meghna Rivers (Figure 1.1), Bangladesh has hosted two of the worst famines of the twentieth century. During the first, the Great Bengal Famine of 1943, at least 1.5 million people died of starvation. The second, in 1974, descended just after independence, compounding the dislocation and pain of consolidating a new nation and leaving behind searing images of poverty, vulnerability, and suffering that still haunt policymakers and color international perceptions of Bangladesh.

Since independence in 1971, foodgrain markets have grown rapidly in Bangladesh, particularly in recent years. Foodgrain production has doubled, while marketed quantities have increased by a factor of six. As a result, Bangladesh has moved from a country chronically in food deficit to one on the brink of self-sufficiency in rice production. Although food policy remains a sensitive and prominent concern, the focus and tone of debate have shifted perceptibly. Debates in the early 1970s focused on high consumer prices and food shortages, while the early 1990s witnessed a surprising shift toward concerns about low rice prices and increased prospects for export. While debates in prior decades focused exclusively on necessary levels of public

FIGURE 1.1 Map of Bangladesh

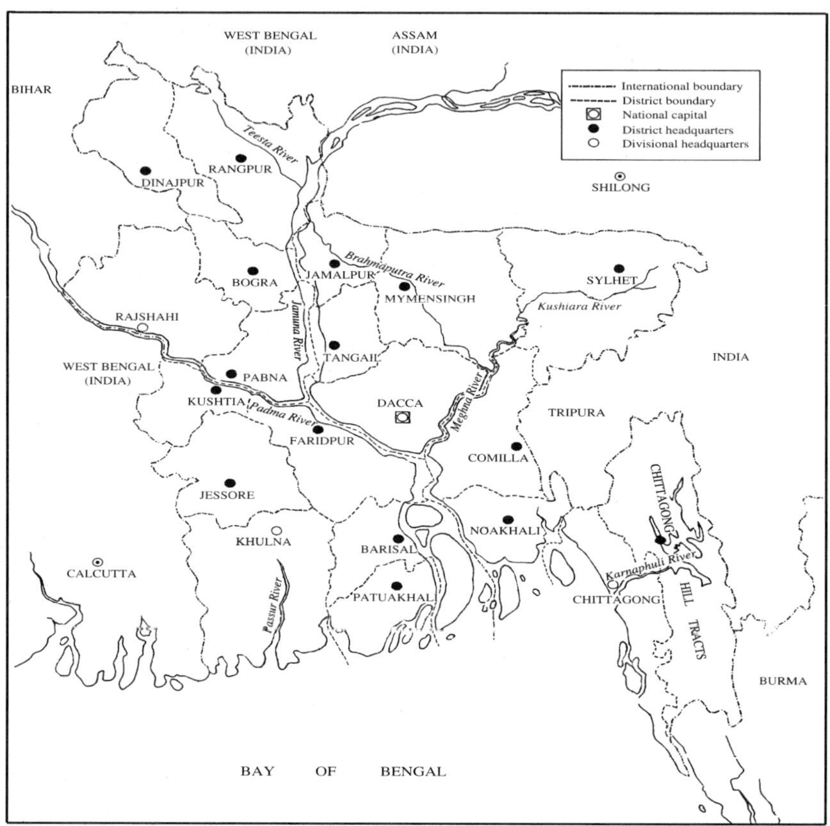

grain import in deficit years, a series of bad harvests in the late 1990s has instead drawn attention to the surprisingly large import response from private traders barred from foodgrain import during the previous five decades.

This book describes how recent increases in foodgrain production have enabled the Government of Bangladesh to dismantle its costly and inefficient public food distribution system and substantially reform domestic food policy. Rooted in the Great Bengal Famine and fueled more recently by the world's second-largest inflow of food aid, Bangladesh's public food distribution system consumed US$300 million, or 17 percent of total government expenditure, at its zenith in 1990.[1] Since then, the government has rapidly dismantled the ration system, privatized foodgrain distribution, lifted restrictions on international trade, and drastically reduced its presence in foodgrain markets.

1. All future references to dollars indicate U.S. dollars.

What spurred this dramatic change? Early and sustained investment in agricultural research, coupled with institutional developments in irrigation and fertilizer markets, laid the necessary foundation for the food policy reforms of the 1990s. In the early 1970s agricultural scientists developed a series of high-yielding rice and wheat varieties (HYVs) that roughly doubled on-farm yields. Then throughout the 1980s a series of reforms in the input market—liberalization of restrictions on tubewell siting, removal of import restrictions on pumps and small diesel engines, and privatization of fertilizer distribution and import—triggered a rapid increase in irrigated dry-season cultivation. The resulting widespread availability of shallow tubewells and fertilizers has enabled Bangladeshi farmers to expand the previously negligible dry-season rice crop (the boro crop) to one that now accounts for 7.5 million metric tons of rice, or about 40 percent of total rice production.[2] Owing to this rapid increase in dry-season production, aggregate foodgrain production has steadily increased at about 2.7 percent per year, exceeding population growth since the early 1970s. In turn, growing production, complemented by infrastructural improvement, a declining population growth rate, and increasing urbanization, has led to major structural changes in foodgrain marketing: dramatically increased marketing volumes, falling real foodgrain prices, and substantial growth in privately held grain stocks.

These structural changes have enabled a series of major adjustments in food policy. Increasing production and marketable surplus have motivated the government to open international trade to private foodgrain traders. Falling real foodgrain prices have allowed the government to prune costly and wasteful ration channels without penalizing the poor. The growth in private rice marketing and privately held rice stocks has allowed the government to reduce its own foodgrain stocks and streamline procurement. Consequently, the cost of government food subsidies has fallen considerably, from taka 3,916 million ($120 million) in 1989 to taka 1,680 million ($42 million) in 1994. The considerable savings from these reforms now permits experimentation with new targeted programs for the poor, such as the government's recently introduced Food-for-Education program.[3] Thus, both food markets and food policy continue to evolve.

Given the vital position that food plays in the national economy, changes in food production and consumption have far-reaching consequences for the overall structure and pace of national economic growth. Rice alone accounts for roughly 25 percent of gross domestic product (GDP) and 30 percent of consumer spending. The evolution of Bangladesh's food policy must be considered in the context of the national economy, for they are inextricably entwined.

---

2. All future references to tons indicate metric tons.

3. Depending on the base year selected, savings range from $65 million to $250 million per year. Using a five-year average of the years preceding 1994/95, one discovers that savings from food subsidies stand at $135 million per year.

Economic Setting

Legacy at Birth

The birth of the nation of Bangladesh in December 1971 was a landmark in the political evolution of the Indian subcontinent. From the beginning, many international observers doubted the economic viability of the new nation. The devastating famine of 1974 reinforced the country's image as a "basket case," a nation in permanent need of food aid.[4] Some observers, more optimistic than the rest, framed the challenge in Bangladesh as a test case for the developing world (Faaland and Parkinson 1976). Yet the pessimistic view dominated and was indeed grounded in several daunting structural features.

Bangladesh's pervasive poverty, its consequently thin margin for generating a surplus for investment, its poor endowment of physical resources and high propensity for natural disasters, and the massive destruction of its infrastructure caused by the war of liberation all supported the perception among many contemporary thinkers that the nation's future was bleak.

In 1971 Bangladesh squeezed a population of 72 million, growing at an annual rate of about 3 percent, into a geographic area of only 143,000 square kilometers. The average density of 504 persons per square kilometer was one of the highest in the world. The average farmer cultivated 1.4 hectares of land, but half of all farms were smaller than 1 hectare in 1977 (Januzi and Peach 1980). Subject to frequent floods, cyclones, and droughts, Bangladesh's deltaic terrain made farming risky. Landlessness in rural areas was high and increasing: about 27 percent of rural households owned no land or fewer than 0.2 hectares of cultivated land. The 1971 war of independence resulted in massive destruction of roads, bridges, and other means of communication, further constraining the normal operation of the economy. Production in agriculture, the dominant economic sector, declined sharply as a result of wartime dislocations. Foodgrain production in 1972/73 fell to about 83 percent of its 1969/70 level, and about 15 percent of the total demand for foodgrains had to be imported, mostly under concessional food-aid programs.

The country's small industrial sector (only about 10 percent of GDP in 1972/73) emerged from the war of independence in no better shape than agriculture did, primarily because most industrial enterprises were owned by Pakistanis who abandoned their enterprises and fled during the chaotic postwar period. This abandonment and the new government's declared policy of socialist development suddenly increased the public share of production.[5] Indus-

4. In a 1971 speech Henry Kissinger originated this memorable but unfortunate phrase.

5. Socialism was one of the government's four principles of political philosophy. Nevertheless, except for nationalizing a few Bangladeshi industries and undertaking all industrial units abandoned by their Pakistani owners, the government took no significant step toward organizing a socialist mode of production.

trial output fell by 23 percent in 1972/73 compared with 1969/70, although most of this loss was regained the following year.

The problems affecting trade and commerce were no less serious. In 1969/70, immediately before independence, roughly one-third of Bangladesh's external trade was directed to West Pakistan (Sobhan 1982). Overnight, Bangladesh had to establish new market relations. Moreover, as they had in the industrial sector, Pakistanis had dominated banking, insurance, foreign and domestic trade, transport, and shipping. Their departure created a vacuum that lasted nearly five years.

Massive poverty and bleak prospects for generating a surplus for investment reinforced Bangladesh's image as a helpless, unviable economic entity. In 1973/74, about 81 percent of the population lived below the poverty line (defined as 2,122 calories intake per capita per day). Even with a poverty line of 1,805 calories, poverty afflicted 41 percent of the population. Per capita annual income was less than $100 at the official 1973/74 exchange rate. With extensive poverty and painfully low incomes, the nation's scope for generating a surplus over consumption was narrow.

Two Decades of Change

Bangladesh has come a long way toward erasing its image as a basket case and projecting an optimistic vision for the future. Development experts now talk of its political leadership and efficient resource management. In place of the old negative stereotypes, they highlight economic assets such as fertile stretches of land that can yield two to three crops a year; a large, hardworking labor force; a huge natural gas deposit; and a vast, replenishable stock of underground water. What has happened since the 1970s to cause this shift?

Changes in key economic and social indicators demonstrate that although Bangladesh has not duplicated the stunning progress of the Asian dragons, its achievements are significant enough to create confidence in its future (Table 1.1). While population density remains a serious concern, the growth rate declined from 2.5 percent (1965–75) to 2.0 percent (1981–91), and it has fallen further in the latter half of the 1990s. GDP has more than doubled, growing on average about 4 percent per year over a 20-year period. Per capita income has grown about 2 percent annually. The share of agriculture in GDP has gradually declined from 56 percent to 30 percent. While the share of manufacturing has stagnated at about 10 percent of GDP, the share of construction and exploitation of natural resources has risen from 2 to 7 percent. The share of services has grown from 34 to 46 percent. Overall, growth in the agricultural sector has barely kept pace with population growth. Except for foodgrains, livestock, and fisheries, other subsectors of agriculture have either declined or grown slowly.

The most disquieting feature of Bangladesh's post-independence economic record is its low level of domestic savings and almost stagnant aggregate

TABLE 1.1 Changes in selected economic and social indicators, Bangladesh, 1973/74–1993/94

				Change (percent)		
Indicators	1973/74	1983/84	1993/94	First Decade	Second Decade	Over Two Decades
Population (million)	76.4	97.6	118.2	27.7	21.1	54.7
GDP (million 1972/73 takas)	49,938	74,245	113,629	48.7	53.0	127.5
Share of agriculture (percent)	56	43	36	–23.2	–16.3	–35.7
Share of industry (percent)	10	16	18	60.0	12.5	80.0
Share of manufactures	8	10.4	10.6	30	1.9	32.5
Share of construction and exploitation of natural resources	2	5.6	7.4	180	33.1	270.0
Share of services (percent)	34	41	46	20.5	12.2	35.5
Per capita income (U.S. dollars)[a]	90	138	230	53.3	66.6	155.6
Rate of gross domestic savings (percent of GDP)[a]	2.0	2.3	7.0	15	204.3	250.0
Rate of aggregate investment (percent of GDP)[a]	11.8	12.3	13.2	4.2	7.3	11.8
Merchandise exports (percent of GDP)	3.2	6.1	12.8	90.6	109.8	300.0
Merchandise imports (percent of GDP)	15.8	16.1	17.9	51.5	70.2	157.8
Exchange rate (takas per dollar)	7.74	26.0	39.5	235.9	51.9	410.3
Average inflation rate (percent)	63.9	15.7	6.8	–48.2	–8.9	–57.1

Infrastructure						
Paved roads (kilometers)	3650	4383	7817	20.0	78.3	114.2
Telephones (number of main connections)	56,200	92,300	258,824	64.2	180.4	360.5
Electricity generating capacity (1,000 kilowatts)	495	990	2720	102.0	174.7	449.5
Irrigated land area (1,000 hectares)	1058	1612	3324	52.4	106.2	214.2
Adult literacy rate	25.8	29.2[b]	32.4[c]	13.1	11.0	25.5
Poverty level (percent of population below 1,805 calories in intake per capita per day)	47.7	37.7	27.5[d]	na	na	na
Life expectancy at birth (years)	50.7	54.0	56.5	6.5	4.6	11.4

SOURCES: Compiled from Khan and Hossain (1989), World Bank (1980, 1988, 1994a, 1994b), IMF (1989, 1994).

NOTE: na indicates not available.

[a]Average of three years.

[b]Relates to 1981.

[c]Relates to 1991.

[d]Relates to 1998/99.

investment. While domestic savings have remained as low as 2 to 7 percent, the inflow of foreign capital has raised overall investment to about 13 percent of GDP. Only since 1993/94 have domestic savings and investment moved up slightly. Despite a stagnant investment rate, GDP appears to have grown consistently with a capital-output ratio of about 3, which implies stagnant capital productivity.

In the area of trade and commerce, merchandise exports have increased remarkably, from about 3 percent of GDP in 1973/74 to about 13 percent in 1993/94. Imports, however, have increased more slowly, from about 16 percent of GDP in 1973/74 to about 18 percent in 1993/94. Food shortages contributed to the high level of imports during the early years of independence. Over the same period the nominal exchange rate depreciated fivefold, and during the 1990s the domestic inflation rate has been cut almost in half.

In the development of infrastructure, the country has made remarkable progress that will enhance its prospects for growth. The length of paved roads has doubled, and telephone connections have more than quadrupled. Electricity generation has increased by about 450 percent, although system loss in electricity is quite high and supply has constantly fallen behind demand. Irrigated land area, crucial to both stability and growth of agricultural production, has increased by about 215 percent.

Indicators of social development (see Table 1.1) show some improvement in the overall quality of life. By 1994/95 about one-third of the country's adult population was functionally literate compared with about one-quarter in 1973/74. The extent of poverty seems to have declined slightly, although the evidence is controversial. Life expectancy at birth has increased by about six years. Taken together, these indicators suggest that the quality of life in Bangladesh has improved since the 1970s. Nevertheless, the nation remains beset by massive poverty: its gains thus far are simply a small dent in a gigantic problem still to be solved in years to come.

Recent Economic Reforms

Bangladesh's food policy reform has proceeded amid general efforts to decontrol major sectors of the economy. In many respects the reforms are interdependent and mutually reinforcing (particularly for food, agricultural inputs, finance, and trade). As Timmer, Falcon, and Pearson (1983) emphasize, because food problems are immersed in the broader problems of economic development, food policies must mesh with overall economic policies.

Like many developing countries, Bangladesh began its post-independence years in a tightly regulated macropolicy environment. The country, however, has made remarkable progress in reforming these policies, particularly since 1989. These changes reflect a striking shift in political philosophy: from the heavy state control that marked the early independence years to a more market-friendly economic regime.

Exchange Rate Policy

Bangladesh maintained a fixed exchange rate during the 1970s. Then in 1979 economic managers instituted a managed, flexible exchange rate in which they pegged the taka to the currencies of the nation's major trading partners. In 1985 they adopted a policy of frequently adjusting the nominal exchange rate as a component of an overall macroeconomic reform under a World Bank–International Monetary Fund program.

By 1990/91 Bangladesh's two-tiered foreign exchange market had been largely unified.[6] The extent of overvaluation of the official exchange rate had decreased from about 28 percent between 1973/74 and 1975/76 to about 8 percent between 1986/87 and 1990/91 (Rahman 1994).[7] By 1995 the degree of overvaluation remained between 5 and 7 percent.

Trade Policy

High tariffs and quantitative restrictions dominated trade policy in the post-independence years. Although the government initiated reforms to liberalize the trade regime in the mid-1980s, it did not take the first major steps toward liberalization until 1989. These reforms were aimed at (1) removing quantitative restrictions, (2) reducing tariff rates, (3) rationalizing the tariff structure, and (4) simplifying trade procedures.

Initially, trade liberalization focused on deregulating trade and removing quantitative restrictions. The positive list (specifying items that could be imported) was changed to a negative list (specifying items that could not be freely imported); any item not on the list could be imported either freely or by fulfilling specified requirements. One survey shows that the index of quantitative restrictions decreased from 47 percent in 1986 to 36 percent in 1990 (Rahman 1994). The decline was more pronounced for banned items. By July–December 1990, 27.5 percent of manufacturing imports were subject to quantitative restriction. The import policy order (IPO) of 1991–93 led to the further reduction of restrictions, and the IPO of 1997–2003 seems poised to completely eliminate quantitative restrictions and move toward a free trade regime.

Bangladeshi imports have faced a series of taxes, including customs duties, sales taxes, development surcharges, and license fees. The overall tariff rate has varied from 10 to 300 percent, and the weighted average tariff rate was 93 percent in 1982/83. Although the average had fallen to about 30 percent by 1994 (World Bank 1994a), some policymakers and donors believe it can decrease still further to between 10 and 15 percent.

---

6. The two-tiered market refers to (a) the government-managed exchange rate and (b) the open market rate based on the trade of remittances.

7. Overvaluation of the official exchange rate was measured in reference to a counterfactual equilibrium exchange rate estimated on the assumption of free trade.

One major objective of exchange rate and trade liberalization is to increase the growth of exports to spur domestic production and stimulate economic growth. Indeed, as a consequence of these reforms, exports have grown rapidly. The total value of exports measured $0.94 billion in 1983/84, increasing to $1.286 billion in 1988/89, $2.383 billion in 1992/93, and $2.975 billion in 1995/96—a compound annual rate of growth of 10.5 percent during these 12 years.[8] Remarkably, the share of nontraditional products has risen in the total value of exports. Traditionally, Bangladesh exported three principal commodities: jute, jute manufactures, and tea. While these traditional products accounted for 61 percent of total export earnings in 1983/84, their share declined to 30 percent in 1988/89 and to 15 percent in 1992/93. Accordingly, the share of nontraditional products has climbed. Three categories—frozen shrimp, fish, and frog legs; ready-made garments; and leather and leather products—accounted for 29 percent of the total value of exports in 1983/84. This share rose to 58 percent in 1988/89, 66 percent in 1992/93, and nearly 75 percent in 1995/96. Exports of specialty and miscellaneous products (primarily handicrafts) increased at a similar pace—from 4 percent in 1983/84, to 15 percent in 1992/93, and to 18 percent in 1995/96.

The combined effect of increased export earnings and low growth in imports has resulted in historically high foreign exchange reserves; gross foreign exchange reserves rose from $0.962 billion in 1988/89 to $2.197 billion in 1992/93 and $3.750 billion in 1995/96. The weak demand for imports, apparently a reflection of the stagnant rate of investment alluded to previously, is emerging as a critical issue that will require attention in coming years.

Fiscal and Monetary Reforms

The objective of Bangladesh's fiscal and monetary reforms has been to reduce the size of the public sector in order to expand the scope of private entrepreneurship in the economy and contain excessive volatility and price increases. Therefore, reducing public expenditure, budget deficits, and money supply was crucial, as was increasing revenue through taxes that do not distort incentives. It is important to recognize, however, that public expenditure for infrastructure, technology, and institutional development remains necessary because the private sector is usually unwilling to finance investments in public goods. In certain circumstances public spending may even increase in these areas to ensure the ultimate success of reform objectives.

The government's reform measures have yielded significant results. For example, government revenue is up: as a percentage of GDP, it increased from an average of 8.5 percent in the mid-1980s to about 12 percent in 1995/96. This was possible even though trade taxes were reduced because of the introduction of a value-added tax in 1991/92. Efficiency in the collection of income tax has

8. Before 1988/89 the value of exports was generally estimated at about $900 million for most of the 1980s.

also contributed to rising public revenue. Together, these measures brought the overall budget deficit down from the equivalent of 9.1 percent of GDP in 1983/84, to 5.4 percent in 1992/93, and to 5.1 percent in 1995/96. Although the share of public spending in GDP remained unchanged between 1984–89 and 1990–93, its composition shifted away from current spending toward developmental spending. The average growth rate of current expenditure fell from 19.6 percent during 1984–89 to 10.6 percent during 1990–93, while the average growth rate of developmental expenditure rose from 7.8 percent to 11.3 percent. The position has not changed much since.

Financial Markets

In contrast to these successes, the financial sector and related policies remain mired in problems. Between 1990 and 1994 commercial banks were trapped in a pool of excess liquidity that they could not lend to productive users because the demand for investment was stagnant. This problem was compounded by the government's unwillingness to reduce interest rates. With inflation brought down to 1.3 percent in 1992/93 and 4.1 percent in 1995/96, the real interest rate needed to be reduced commensurately by the downward adjustment of nominal rates to attract potential investors. Moreover, the government practice of selling bonds and savings certificates at high interest rates while retiring public debt to the banking system has created a vicious circle that limits productive investment.

More recently, the whole banking system has been besieged by bad debts and a general dysfunctional atmosphere in the capital market. Some estimates put the size of defaulted bank loans as high as taka 165 billion, which is equivalent to about 32 percent of total bank credit. Pressure to collect bad debts, efforts to create financial discipline by enacting and enforcing appropriate laws, and the privatization of government-owned commercial banks have created a liquidity crunch, although this may be temporary. Of course, the problem of financial market reforms is enmeshed in the country's fundamental political problems. But without parallel success in the reforms of financial markets, the desired supply response elicited by successful changes in other macropolicies will be constrained.

Sectoral Reforms

Since the early 1980s, the shift from heavy state intervention to more market-oriented philosophies has translated into sectoral policies that support macroeconomic liberalization. A series of sectorally focused liberalization programs emerged in key state-controlled sectors, such as agricultural input markets (particularly fertilizer and tubewells), foodgrains, jute, and textiles.

The government is reducing its involvement in agricultural input markets, particularly in the direct subsidy and distribution of fertilizer and tubewells. These reforms began in the early 1980s and accelerated later in the decade with the complete liberalization of the import of tubewell equipment and a consequent surge in demand for irrigation equipment and fertilizer.

The food policy reforms, which form the core of this book, induced a significant increase in foodgrain production and a surge in marketing that in turn reinforced the momentum of reform. Like the major decontrol of agricultural input markets, reform in the foodgrain market began gradually in the early 1980s, accelerated in the late 1980s, and moved most rapidly in the early 1990s.

Regional Context

Bangladesh shares a common administrative, legal, and economic heritage with its neighbors in the formerly British-ruled subcontinent of India. This common point of departure provides a useful frame of reference against which to gauge progress in Bangladesh, both at a macrolevel and in the food policy arena. Such a comparison, however, must be brief and based on broad indicators to fit within the scope of this book.

Macroeconomic Progress

In 1958, almost a decade after the South Asian countries became independent of Great Britain, their differences in average income were small (Table 1.2). People living in the area now known as Bangladesh earned the smallest income, but no country in the region exceeded Bangladesh's average per capita income by more than 40 percent. India's income was 27 percent higher; and Sri Lanka, the richest nation, earned only 40 percent more income. Twenty-eight years later, in 1986, their relative income positions had changed significantly. Average income in India was about 90 percent higher than in Bangladesh, and the respective levels in Pakistan and Sri Lanka were 2.3 and 2.7 times higher. This disparity in relative income growth is widely known and holds no surprises.

What is revealing, however, is the change in relative income positions during the past 10 years. By 1996 Bangladesh had closed the gap somewhat compared with both India and Pakistan. In that year average incomes in India, Pakistan, and Sri Lanka were respectively about 1.4, 1.9, and 2.9 times higher than in Bangladesh. Components of this improvement in Bangladesh are the increasing application of modern technology in agriculture, higher remittances from abroad, a spur in the production of nontraditional exports made possible by food policy and macroeconomic reforms, and a decline in population growth.

In macropolicy reforms, Bangladesh and Sri Lanka appear to be leading the way, followed by India and Pakistan (although India and Pakistan have recently accelerated the pace of their reforms). While Bangladesh has achieved a higher degree of success in controlling its inflation and budget deficits, other

TABLE 1.2 Per capita income of South Asian countries as a multiple of the per capita income of Bangladesh

Country	1958	1986	1996
Bangladesh	1.00	1.00	1.00
India	1.27	1.93	1.42
Pakistan	1.36	2.30	1.92
Sri Lanka	1.40	2.70	2.91

SOURCE: The 1958 figures are from Khan and Hossain (1989). The country was then known as East Pakistan. Figures for other years are computed using information from World Bank (1988, 1996, 1997).

countries have been more successful in generating domestic savings and making gross investments. Against Bangladesh's stagnant rate of growth in aggregate investment, India and Pakistan each increased their investment at an annual rate of 4.8 percent and Sri Lanka at 3 percent between 1980 and 1990. The ratio of investment to GDP was only 12 percent in Bangladesh compared to 19 to 21 percent in the other countries during the same period.

Food Policy

At independence, all countries in the Indian subcontinent inherited a set of laws, institutions, and practices that provided tight government control of foodgrain production, supply, and distribution. These controls originally emerged in response to the severe supply dislocations that arose during the convergence of a catastrophic famine and World War II. Initially, the Government of India instituted these controls under emergency wartime powers delegated to the central government. From the days of British India, through partition, the years as East Pakistan, and then to Bangladeshi independence, these institutions remained in force through a series of continuing clauses in subsequent legal enactments (see Chapter 7). Thus, the Governments of India, Pakistan, and Bangladesh inherited at independence a common legislative framework for controlling the supply and distribution of foodgrains. Sri Lanka, although not legislatively integrated with British India, adopted broadly similar food controls, including a large public rationing system.

These systems for foodgrain control have evolved differently across the subcontinent. Although India began with the same institutional base as Bangladesh, it retains far tighter control of foodgrain procurement, storage, distribution, and pricing. International trade in foodgrains remains a public monopoly with limited privatization of rice exports. The government purchases 12 to 15 percent of total annual foodgrain production through an elaborate system of procurement at administratively fixed prices. To facilitate public procurement, the government once cordoned off surplus areas; however, these movement restrictions have been relaxed in recent years. The government distributes the procured grain at subsidized prices to consumers through about 400,000 fair-price shops spread throughout the country (Tyagi 1990). India retains a buffer stock of 15 to 20 million tons of foodgrain. In a time-honored system developed to ensure wartime foodgrain control during World War II, interstate differences in supply and demand continue to be smoothed through public distribution. Likewise, as in agricultural output markets, an elaborate subsidy mechanism still exists in India's input markets. Subsidies for fertilizer, canal irrigation, credit, and electricity supply to agriculture were estimated at about 45 percent of the total plan expenditure on agriculture in 1983/84. This estimate increased to about 82 percent in 1989/90 (Rao and Gulati 1994). Although India's overall economic reform program has so far remained focused on the manufacturing sector, many observers expect that the government will move next to agricultural policy reform (Pursell and Gulati 1993).

Pakistan has likewise not proceeded far on food and agricultural policy reforms, although it did abolish the wartime rationing system in 1987 (Pinckney 1987; Faruqee 1995). In the market for wheat, Pakistan's major foodgrain, the government maintains a remarkable presence, procuring between 20 and 30 percent of total production and supplying about 35 percent of public wheat stock at fixed prices to mills every year for processing (Goletti et al. 1994). Although in theory farmers are free to sell wheat to either the private sector or the public procurement agency, in practice restrictions on the movement of wheat during harvest time force farmers to sell to the public sector. Import and export of foodgrains remain government monopolies. The extent of subsidy and the involvement of parastatals in the distribution of fertilizers, seeds, and irrigation water is huge, with little sign of fundamental change in input markets (Faruqee 1995). The burden of these public interventions is taking its toll on the Pakistani economy.

In contrast, Sri Lanka and Bangladesh have moved further along in food and agricultural policy reforms. Sri Lanka abolished its rationing system in 1979 and introduced instead a food stamp scheme (Edirisinghe 1988). In recent years it has sharpened that scheme to better reach the poor and to reduce costs. The country has also significantly reduced input subsidies—for example, eliminating the subsidy on fertilizer. Sri Lanka, like Bangladesh, has liberalized domestic marketing as well as the international foodgrain trade.

Bangladesh has likewise moved rapidly to reduce public presence in foodgrain procurement and distribution. It has liberalized the import of foodgrains so that private licensed import is allowed. It has also dismantled prior restrictions on private stockholding and marketing and withdrawn urban and rural consumer ration subsidies in favor of targeted, in-kind, often "for work" programs. Unlike many countries, Bangladesh has conducted its food market reforms without provoking violence or food riots. Rarely has a major food policy reform proceeded so smoothly. In contrast, countries such as Egypt,

Liberia, Sudan, and Tunisia have all experienced violent popular reactions to incipient food policy reforms.

Objectives and Organization of the Book

Against this background, the following chapters examine how Bangladesh, despite an unpromising outlook at independence, has managed to overhaul its food policy, an arena in which so many governments have faltered. Part I provides an overview of broad changes in foodgrain production, import, prices, consumption, and marketing; for it is the maturing of these markets that, in large measure, laid the foundation for the decisive food policy reforms of the early 1990s. The focus on foodgrains, as opposed to all foods, stems from their historical dominance as the centerpiece of Bangladesh's food policy. Forward-looking sections of the book, however, broaden the discussion to include non-foodgrains since these emerge as important elements of future domestic food policy. The discussion of foodgrain supply in Part I highlights major recent changes in production and production technology and consequent implications for imports (Chapter 2). It also addresses the importance of recent liberalization in agricultural input markets for fertilizer, pesticides, and irrigation equipment (Chapter 3). For a number of reasons, the spread of the Green Revolution began in Bangladesh 15 years after it reached the rest of the Indian subcontinent. The resulting spurt in foodgrain production triggered an expansion of far greater proportions in trade and marketing networks (Chapter 4). Since distrust of private traders forms the bedrock on which government food market intervention is founded, the major expansion and change in private marketing systems harbor potentially important implications for the magnitude and scope of government intervention. Part I concludes with a review of evolving patterns of food consumption and poverty (Chapter 5) to highlight a key objective of food policy—the development of sustainable systems for ensuring adequate nutrition among vulnerable groups.

Structural changes in production, consumption, and private marketing paved the way for a major overhaul of tight controls on foodgrain markets in the early 1990s. Part II launches a review of these reforms by looking back through time—as much as 50 years—at long-term changes in food policy in Bangladesh (Chapter 6). This retrospective lays the groundwork for a detailed examination of the recent evolution in the political economy of food, the central theme of Part II. Both historically and today, government food marketing controls have derived their legal authority from a voluminous and intricate body of legislation emanating from the Bengal Famine of 1943. Thus, the status and evolution of these legal enactments remain central to an understanding of recent reforms as well as the legal requirements for future change (Chapter 7). Not surprisingly, given the scale and longevity of public food distribution and controls, the history of food policy in Bangladesh involves many domestic and international actors. Because an array of food-aid donors historically has financed about half of all public food distribution, these donors have played a major role in shaping and reshaping the Bangladeshi public food distribution system over time (Chapter 8). Concluding this historical discussion, Part II ends with an in-depth review of the food policy reforms of the early 1990s (Chapter 9), offering a strategic review of reform efforts and of counterthrusts from those resisting change and drawing a number of important lessons about how reforms have been sustained.

Looking forward, Part III examines the diminishing case for direct government intervention in Bangladesh's foodgrain markets. It reviews each of the classic short-run objectives of Bangladesh food policy: price stabilization, maintenance of emergency stocks to cope with natural disasters (Chapter 10), and targeted food distribution to vulnerable groups (Chapter 11). These chapters reveal that recent changes in foodgrain markets have considerably reduced the need for direct government involvement in stabilizing prices and holding security stocks. Nevertheless, the need for targeted distribution to vulnerable groups remains strong. In the face of declining resources, rigorous targeting will become even more necessary in the future. In the long run, food policy must balance production and income growth with food availability and the purchasing power of vulnerable groups. In Bangladesh, key elements of a long-run food strategy will probably involve agricultural diversification (Chapter 12) and possibly rice export (Chapter 13), particularly of high-value varieties that will enable the import of lower-cost foodgrains such as wheat and lower-quality rice.

Chapter 14 concludes the book by synthesizing the major themes emerging from this broad historical panorama. It looks forward, anticipating likely key policy issues for agriculture in the future, and summarizes lessons learned from recent food policy reforms, highlighting lessons for Bangladesh and other countries that are attempting to improve the food security of their population.

References

Edirisinghe, N. 1988. Food subsidy changes in Sri Lanka: The short-run effects on the poor. In *Food subsidies in developing countries,* ed. P. Pinstrup-Andersen. Baltimore: Johns Hopkins University Press.

Faaland, J., and J. R. Parkinson. 1976. *Bangladesh: The test case of development.* Boulder, Colo., U.S.A.: Westview Press.

Faruqee, R. 1995. *Government's role in Pakistan agriculture: Major reforms are needed.* Working Paper 1468. Washington, D.C.: World Bank.

Goletti, F., A. Salam, N. Sultana, and K. Mahammed. 1994. Integration of wheat markets in Pakistan. Final report to the U.S. Agency for International Development (USAID), Islamabad, Pakistan, under Grant 391-0492-G-00-1791-00. Washington, D.C.: International Food Policy Research Institute. Mimeo.

International Monetary Fund (IMF). 1989 and 1994. *International financial statistics year books.* Washington, D.C.: International Monetary Fund.

Januzi, F. T., and J. T. Peach. 1980. *The agrarian structure of Bangladesh: An impediment to development.* Boulder, Colo., U.S.A.: Westview Press.

Khan, A. R., and M. Hossain. 1989. *The strategy of development in Bangladesh.* London: Macmillan.

Pinckney, T. C. 1987. The effects of wheat pricing policy on fiscal cost and private seasonal storage. Washington, D.C.: International Food Policy Research Institute. Mimeo.

Pursell, G., and A. Gulati. 1993. *Liberalizing Indian agriculture: An agenda for reform.* Working Paper 1172. Washington, D.C.: World Bank.

Rahman, S. H. 1994. The impact of trade and exchange rate policies on economic incentives in Bangladesh agriculture. Working Paper 8. Washington, D.C.: International Food Policy Research Institute. Mimeo.

Rao, C. H., and A. Gulati. 1994. Indian agriculture: Emerging perspectives and major policy issues. Washington, D.C.: International Food Policy Research Institute. Mimeo.

Sobhan, R. 1982. *The crisis of external dependence.* Dhaka, Bangladesh: University Press.

Timmer, C. P., W. P. Falcon, and S. R. Pearson. 1983. *Food policy analysis.* Baltimore: Johns Hopkins University Press.

Tyagi, D. S. 1990. *Managing India's food economy.* New Delhi, India: Sage Publications.

World Bank. 1980. *Bangladesh: Current economic position and short-term outlook.* South-Asia Department Report 2870-BD. Washington, D.C.: World Bank.

———. 1988. *World development report 1988: Public finance.* New York: Oxford University Press.

———. 1994a. Bangladesh: From stabilization to growth, South-Asia Department Report 12724-BD. Washington, D.C.: World Bank.

———. 1994b. *World development report 1994: Infrastructure for development.* New York: Oxford University Press.

———. 1996. *World development report 1996.* New York: Oxford University Press.

———. 1997. *World development report 1997.* New York: Oxford University Press.

PART I

Shifting Structure of Foodgrain Supply and Demand

2 Foodgrain Production and Imports: Toward Self-Sufficiency in Rice?

PAUL DOROSH

Bangladesh faces huge obstacles in its efforts to increase foodgrain production, raise rural incomes, and reduce food insecurity. In this country of nearly 125 million people living in an area of approximately 143,000 square kilometers, there is immense population pressure on the available cultivable land. Average farm size is only 0.8 hectare, and there is virtually no scope for expansion of cultivated land (although some expansion in multiple cropping is possible). Moreover, agricultural production is susceptible to the vagaries of the weather: floods, droughts, and cyclones frequently cause substantial damage.

After the massive food shortages of the early 1970s, the Government of Bangladesh made substantial investments in the rice sector in an effort to overcome these constraints. During the 1980s these efforts paid off. Rice production increased substantially through the introduction of a Green Revolution technology package consisting of high-yielding varieties (HYVs), irrigation, and fertilizers. Wheat production expanded considerably during the 1970s, from fewer than 100,000 metric tons per year at independence to more than 1 million per year through most of the 1980s.[1] Thus, in the early 1990s Bangladesh seemed to be approaching self-sufficiency in rice, with domestic production of foodgrains (rice and wheat) accounting for 93 percent of national foodgrain supply and import of rice virtually nil during 1991–93.

Several poor harvests in the mid- and late 1990s have dampened the optimism of the first half of the decade. Average yields of HYV rice have stagnated, and production has fluctuated widely around a slower growth trend. Private sector imports, permitted only since liberalization of the private sector international trade in foodgrains in the early 1990s, have to a large extent offset these variations in production. As Bangladesh approaches the twenty-first century, considerable uncertainty surrounds the medium-term outlook for foodgrain production and available supplies. Is a period of sustained growth in production similar to that of the 1980s feasible? If not, to what extent do private trade and international markets help reduce food insecurity?

1. All further references to tons indicate metric tons.

Foodgrain Production Systems and Technical Change

Rice dominates the crop production landscape of Bangladesh. Nearly three-quarters of total gross cropped area in Bangladesh is planted to rice (Table 2.1).[2] Rice is grown in three different seasons, although not more than twice per year on any given plot of land. Traditionally, the major rice crop has been the aman crop, harvested after the monsoon rains.[3] Aman rice alone accounts for 42 percent of gross cropped area. Two smaller rice crops, aus and boro, are also cultivated, often in a crop rotation that includes aman. More than 90 percent of boro rice is irrigated, although overall only 26 percent of gross cropped area is irrigated. Thus, boro rice accounts for 71 percent of total irrigated gross cropped area. Wheat accounts for only 5 percent of the 33 million acres planted with crops.

Except for hill areas along the northern and northeastern borders and the Chittagong hill tracts in the southeast, Bangladesh is a flat alluvial plain spotted with small terrace areas in the central and northwestern regions (the Madhpur and Barind tracts) (see Hossain 1991:18–19). The monsoon (kharif) rains, beginning in April or May, provide water for planting the aus rice crop and jute and swell the rivers. Floodwaters cover much of the alluvial plain during parts of July, August, and September. Weather outside Bangladesh, however, greatly influences the extent and duration of the flooding since approximately 90 percent of the catchment area of the major rivers (the Ganges [Padma], the Brahmaputra, and the Meghna) lies outside the country.[4]

The main rice crop, aman, is generally sown between June and August. Seeds of broadcast aman are sown before the floods, and if the floods are not too severe, plants are typically harvested in November or December after the floodwaters have receded. For transplanted aman, seedlings are transplanted in the fields in late July or August and harvested three to four months later. Because most traditional aman varieties are sensitive to photoperiod, transplanting must occur before mid-September to ensure flowering of the rice plants. During the winter, or rabi season, a wider variety of crops is grown, including boro rice (mainly on irrigated land), wheat, pulses, and vegetables.

There are many crop rotations, most involving at least one crop of rice and depending largely on the depth of flooding in the monsoon (kharif) season and the availability of water during the winter (rabi) season. On lowlands that are

---

2. Gross cropped area counts two or more crops grown sequentially on the same piece of land as separate crops. Net cropped area measures the total amount of land cultivated during a period. The ratio of gross cropped area to net cropped area is the cropping intensity. From the early 1970s to the early 1990s, the cropping intensity in Bangladesh remained at about 1.6 (Zohir 1995: 81).

3. There are three major rice harvests in Bangladesh: aus (July–August), aman (November–January), and boro (April–June). These same terms are often used to designate varieties of rice typically grown in these seasons.

4. See Novak 1992 for a fuller description of the rivers and their influence on village life in Bangladesh.

TABLE 2.1 Distribution of cropped area in Bangladesh, 1995/96

Crop	Cropped Area		Irrigated Area		Cropped Area That Is Irrigated
	(thousand hectares)	(percent of cropped area)	(thousand hectares)	(percent of irrigated area)	(percent)
Rice	9,954.3	73.6	2,940.5	82.7	29.5
Aus	1,554.0	11.5	114.9	3.2	7.4
Aman	5,646.7	41.8	295.4	8.3	5.2
Boro	2,753.5	20.4	2,530.1	71.1	91.9
Wheat	700.9	5.2	299.9	8.4	42.8
Minor cereals	93.1	0.7	3.6	0.1	3.9
Pulses	698.5	5.2	1.6	0.0	0.2
Oilseeds	554.8	4.1	19.0	0.5	3.4
Potato	132.3	1.0	100.8	2.8	76.1
Vegetables	191.0	1.4	82.2	2.3	43.0
Sugarcane	174.4	1.3	22.7	0.6	13.0
Cotton	36.8	0.3	10.5	0.3	28.6
Others	985.8	7.3	76.1	2.1	7.7
Total[a]	13,522.1	100.0	3,556.9	100.0	26.3[b]

SOURCE: BBS (1997).

[a]Totals may not be precise owing to rounding.

[b]Average.

heavily flooded in the monsoon season (known as F3 areas), land is fallow at the beginning of the crop year (April), and generally only one crop is grown; typically this is broadcast aman or, on irrigated land, modern-variety boro. On medium lowlands (F2), land is also usually fallow at the start of the crop year, but two crops are then grown: broadcast or local transplanted aman, followed by wheat or other rabi crops. On irrigated F2 land, aman rice is followed by boro rice. On medium highlands (F1) and highlands (F0), transplanted aman is a common factor in most rotations, with large variations in winter crops sown. After the onset of the monsoons, the land is typically fallow or planted with aus, followed by transplanted aman, and then either left fallow or planted with pulses (on nonirrigated land) or boro, wheat, or potatoes (on irrigated land) (see Zohir 1995:89, tab. A.2).

According to the 1991 Bangladesh Institute of Development Studies (BIDS)–IFPRI survey of 88 villages representing the various agro-ecological zones of Bangladesh, 28 percent of net cropped area was planted with only a single crop of rice or wheat (Zohir 1995). Another 34 percent was planted with a double crop of rice or rice and wheat. In all, 62 percent of net cropped area was planted only with foodgrains, predominantly rice.

Production Trends and Variability

Bangladesh achieved impressive gains in wheat production in the 1970s and in rice production in the 1980s through investments in irrigation, increased fertilizer use, and the adoption of new seeds, especially in the boro season. Rice production grew by an average of 1.76 percent annually during 1973/74–1983/84, 2.78 percent during 1983/84–1993/94, and 1.89 percent during 1993/94–1997/98 (Table 2.2). Average rice yields rose in all three seasons, with total yields rising from 1.20 tons per hectare to 1.82 tons per hectare from the early 1970s to the late 1990s (Table 2.3). During this period areas cultivated with HYVs rose rapidly, from an average of 15 percent of rice area in 1974–76 to 51 percent in 1996–98. At the same time irrigation spread rapidly, increasing from 12 percent to 28 percent of total rice area. By the late 1990s, 91 percent of boro area was irrigated, and 92 percent was cultivated with HYVs as boro's share in rice production rose from 19 percent in the early 1970s to 41 percent in 1996–98.

The increase in boro's share of total production has contributed to a decline in variability of total annual rice production. Between 1974–84 and 1984–94, the variability of production (as measured by the standard deviation of the residuals from a semilogarithmic trend line) declined from 4.17 to 3.31 percent (Table 2.2). In addition, the variability of the boro harvest itself decreased from 14.69 percent in 1974–84, to 8.49 percent in 1984–94, and to only 3 percent in 1994–98. This decline is due mainly to the reduced variability of boro production as more boro land has come under controlled irrigation. A second factor is the negative correlation between variations in boro

TABLE 2.2 Growth rates and variability of foodgrain production, 1974–98

Rates	Aman	Aus	Boro	Total Rice	Wheat	Total Foodgrains
				(percent)		
Growth rates						
1973/74–1997/98	1.25	−2.71	6.72	2.02	8.72	2.25
1973/74–1983/84	1.18	0.25	5.26	1.76	30.17	2.62
1983/84–1993/94	2.10	−4.88	8.18	2.78	−1.34	2.50
1993/94–1997/98	−0.08	0.70	4.71	1.89	11.48	2.55
Variability						
1973/74–1997/98	6.84	11.61	12.96	4.47	51.20	4.10
1973/74–1983/84	5.75	6.54	14.69	4.17	23.28	4.03
1983/84–1993/94	7.57	7.53	8.49	3.31	12.29	3.04
1993/94–1997/98	4.93	4.46	3.00	3.55	3.86	3.29

SOURCES: FPMU, Hamid (1991), and author's calculations.

NOTE: Growth rates are computed with a semilogarithmic trend. Variability of production is measured by the standard deviation of percentage differences between production figures and the fitted value derived from the semilogarithmic line.

TABLE 2.3 Rice yields and prevalence of HYVs and irrigated area by season

	Aus	Aman	Boro	Total Rice
Average rice yield (metric tons per hectare)				
1973/74–1975/76	0.93	1.18	2.05	1.20
1983/84–1985/86	0.99	1.38	2.42	1.42
1995/96–1997/98	1.15	1.58	2.69	1.82
Average proportion of HYV area in respective rice crops (percent)				
1973/74–1975/76	8	11	56	15
1983/84–1985/86	16	12	79	27
1995/96–1997/98	29	37	92	51
Average proportion of irrigated rice area in respective total rice area (percent)				
1973/74–1975/76	2	2	93	12
1983/84–1985/86	5	3	82	15
1993/94–1995/96	8	5	91	28
Average shares of seasonal rice crop in total rice production (percent)				
1973/74–1975/76	25	56	19	100
1983/84–1985/86	20	55	25	100
1995/96–1997/98	10	49	41	100

SOURCES: FPMU, Hamid (1991), and author's calculations.

TABLE 2.4 Growth rates of modern and local rice varieties by season, 1973–98

	Total Rice			Modern Varieties			Local Varities		
	Output	Area	Yield	Output	Area	Yield	Output	Area	Yield
1973–98									
Annual	2.34	0.09	2.25	7.58	7.43	0.27	−1.52	−2.63	1.14
Aus	−2.09	−3.22	1.17	1.57	3.59	−1.95	−2.64	−3.72	1.12
Aman	1.62	−0.05	1.68	8.41	8.38	0.03	−0.96	−2.07	1.13
Boro	6.62	5.22	1.33	8.81	8.74	0.06	−3.08	−3.32	0.25
1973–87									
Annual	2.66	0.57	2.08	7.11	8.21	−1.02	0.34	−1.06	1.41
Aus	0.83	−0.51	1.35	7.45	10.39	−2.67	−0.79	−1.58	0.80
Aman	2.30	0.47	1.82	7.11	7.72	−0.56	1.10	−0.58	1.68
Boro	5.59	3.71	1.81	7.81	8.85	−0.96	−2.38	−3.47	1.12
1987–98									
Annual	1.65	−0.38	2.04	7.87	5.70	2.06	2.34	0.57	0.43
Aus	−5.44	−6.11	0.72	−2.37	−2.11	−0.26	−2.09	−8.73	−0.58
Aman	1.47	0.19	1.28	12.56	8.15	4.08	1.62	−3.35	0.28
Boro	4.95	3.75	1.15	6.00	5.66	0.32	6.62	3.71	0.64

SOURCES: BBS (various), FPMU, and author's calculations.

NOTES: For modern and local variety figures data are available up to 1995–96, and all figures have been calculated from a semilogarithmic equation: $\ln q = a + b \times \text{time}$.

production and variations in aus and, to a lesser extent, aman production.[5] Particularly in very poor aman production years, such as 1997/98 or the flood years of 1988/89 and 1998/99, high rice prices after the aman harvest have increased incentives for fertilizer and other inputs in the boro season.

The production growth rates of the 1980s have not been matched in the 1990s, however, leading to concerns about long-term production trends. As Table 2.4 shows, almost all of the growth in rice production achieved in the 1970s, 1980s, and 1990s was the result of increases in average yields.[6] For 1972/73–1997/98, the area harvested increased by only 0.09 percent per year, while production increased by 2.34 percent per year. The increases in average yields, however, do not reflect increases in productivity of either HYVs or local varieties but rather a switch from local varieties to HYVs. Yields of modern varieties have remained essentially unchanged in aggregate and have actually declined for aus. Thus, three-quarters of the total growth of rice production in Bangladesh resulted from this change in cropping patterns from local aus and boro to HYV boro rice and to the change from local to modern

5. The correlation coefficient of the residuals from the trend growth regressions are −0.52 for aus-boro and −0.61 for wheat-boro, reflecting direct competition for available land. The correlation coefficient for aman-boro is −0.45, reflecting the relatively weaker effects of aman production on boro through market prices.

6. This section draws heavily from chapter 2 of Del Ninno and Dorosh (1998).

varieties in the aman season (Baffes and Gautam 1996). Increases in local-variety aman yields account for much of the residual growth.

The area cultivated with aman rice has remained essentially constant, declining slightly from 5.91 million hectares in 1983–85 to 5.76 million hectares in 1996–98 (Table 2.5). This constancy of aman area is explained largely by the overall land constraint and the lack of water control during this season, which results in high soil moisture and poor drainage, limiting the possibilities for substituting other crops.

Substantial shifts have occurred, however, in the area cultivated in the overlapping boro and aus seasons. Area planted with boro rice increased by an average of 5.55 percent per year between 1973–75 and 1992–94, a change made possible by an expansion of controlled (groundwater) irrigation through tubewells. An increase in boro area led to a decline in aus area as aus-aman-fallow cropping sequences were replaced by fallow-aman-boro and rotations involving boro with various rabi crops. Over the 24-year period, aus area (which was mostly rainfed) fell by an average of 2.71 percent per year. This switch from aus to boro has also raised average yields since HYV boro yields (2.73 tons per hectare) are higher than those of local aus (0.87 tons per hectare).

Similarly, yields of modern wheat varieties have remained essentially unchanged. The large 25.5 percent annual average increase in wheat production in Bangladesh between 1973 and 1987 was due mainly to rapid area expansion (by 16.6 percent per year) and a shift from local to modern varieties. Between 1987 (when 100 percent of area cultivated was sown with modern varieties) and 1994, however, wheat production increased by only 1.28 percent per year.

Although the national average rice yield increased by about 50 percent between 1975 and 1995, yields of modern varieties almost stagnated. This suggests that, without further technical change, foodgrain production in Bangladesh may soon reach a plateau unless the proportion of HYVs in the total rice area can be raised from its present 51 percent to 70 percent or more by investment in irrigation and water control and the improved use of fertilizers and other inputs. Although the growth rate of yields of modern rice varieties was almost stagnant (that is, only 0.27 percent per year) during 1973–98, this was the average result of an annual decline of growth rate (–1.02 percent) during 1973–87 and an increase in growth rate (2.06 percent) during 1987–98, when the level of fertilizer use increased faster than it had during the earlier period. This points to the possibility of sustained higher yields of modern varieties through better use of fertilizer.

Bangladesh's average rice yield of 1.77 tons per hectare (equal to approximately 2.64 tons of paddy per hectare) is still low compared with average Asian paddy yields of 4 tons per hectare in Indonesia and 5 to 6 tons per hectare in China and Korea. Average yields during the boro season, however, during which 90 percent of the rice area is planted with modern varieties, are 2.73 tons

TABLE 2.5 Production of modern and local rice varieties by season, 1973–98

	Total Rice			Modern Varieties			Local Varieties		
	Output[a]	Area[b]	Yield[c]	Output[a]	Area[b]	Yield[c]	Output[a]	Area[b]	Yield[c]
1973/74–1975/76									
Annual	12,357	10,000	1.23	3,681	1,515	2.43	8,116	8,485	0.96
Aus	3,124	3,236	0.97	645	256	2.52	2,319	2,980	0.78
Aman	6,946	5,644	1.23	1,412	628	2.25	5,169	5,016	1.03
Boro	2,287	1,120	2.02	1,624	630	2.58	628	490	1.28
1983/84–1985/86									
Annual	14,723	10,390	1.42	6,292	2,759	2.27	8,431	7,631	1.11
Aus	2,944	2,974	0.99	930	483	1.93	2,014	2,492	0.81
Aman	8,136	5,913	1.38	2,229	1,107	2.01	5,907	4,806	1.23
Boro	3,643	1,503	2.42	3,133	1,170	2.68	510	333	1.53
1995/96–1997/98									
Annual	18,475	10,139	1.82	13,021	5,194	2.51	5,454	4,748	1.15
Aus	1,807	1,571	1.15	702	419	1.68	974	1,123	0.87
Aman	9,064	5,761	1.57	5,467	2,269	2.41	4,110	3,379	1.22
Boro	7,604	2,807	2.71	6,852	2,507	2.73	370	247	1.50

SOURCES: FPMU, BBS (various), and author's calculations.

NOTES: For modern and local varieties data for 1997 and 1998 are not available. Figures shown for modern and local varieties for 1995/96–1997/98 are the figures from 1996/97. Rice production figures are in milled rice.

[a]In thousand metric tons.

[b]In thousand hectares.

[c]Metric tons per hectare.

per hectare (4 tons per hectare of paddy). Achieving substantial further average yield gains is likely to require substantial investments in research, extension, and irrigation (for increased water control) as well as adequate price incentives for producers. In the long run, maintenance of the natural resource base is also crucial.

Soil nutrient status may already be deteriorating in Bangladesh (Zaman 1987). Sources of this degradation are not entirely clear, nor do observers know if this trend can be reversed by balanced and increased use of fertilizers. Degradation of nutrient status implies that yield rates will drop without enhanced levels of nutrient application. Recent agronomy trials suggest that high yields may be sustained with balanced chemical fertilizer applications. The availability of water for two rice crops per year may also become an issue in the long term, especially since efficiency of water use is low at present.

Imports, Total Foodgrain Supply, and Price

Increases in production have helped transform the foodgrain economy in Bangladesh by reducing dependence on food aid and government commercial imports and contributing to a long-term decline in real prices. Production as a share of total availability of foodgrains increased from 83.5 percent in 1973–75 to 93 percent in 1991–93 as production per capita rose from 132.2 kilograms to 152.7 kilograms. In the same period imports per capita fell from 27.4 to 12.8 kilograms, while the total availability of foodgrains rose on average from 158.4 to 165.3 kilograms per capita (Table 2.6 and Figure 2.1).

Nevertheless, aggregate foodgrain production and import figures obscure the vastly different roles of rice and wheat in foodgrain markets and policy in Bangladesh. As discussed, in spite of substantial increases in wheat production since the early 1970s, rice still accounted for 94 percent of national foodgrain production in the late 1990s. It also constituted the bulk of government commercial imports; private commercial imports of foodgrain were banned until 1991. Yet wheat dominates foodgrain imports, largely because of food aid but also because of increased demand related to rapid urbanization. Food aid flows, which began in East Pakistan in the 1960s, have been almost entirely in the form of wheat, reflecting production and excess stocks in donor countries. At the same time, scarcity of fiscal resources and foreign exchange placed tight constraints on the government's ability to import rice, particularly in the 1970s.

The quantity of food aid wheat flows has been determined by both supply and demand. On the supply side, the level of stocks and prices in donor countries (reflecting production and world market conditions) determine total worldwide food aid availability, with donor political objectives and conditions influencing allocations to Bangladesh. The demand or need for food aid is framed in terms of foodgrain requirements, which are calculated as target level of per capita food consumption minus expected levels of domestic net produc-

TABLE 2.6 Foodgrain availability and requirements in Bangladesh, 1972–98

Year (1)	Domestic Production Rice (2)[a]	Wheat (3)[a]	Total (4)[a]	Net Production (5)[a]	Mid-Year Population (6)[b]	Foodgrain Consumption Requirement (7)[a]	Food Gap (7) – (5) (8)[a]	Private Imports (9)[a]	Public Distribution (10)[a]	Internal Procurement (11)[a]	National Availability (5) – (9) + (10) – (11) (12)[a]	Per Capita Availability (13)[c]	Net Production/ Availability (14)[d]
1971/72	9,931	115	10,046	9,041	73	12,020	2,979		1,763	10	10,794	148.7	83.8
1972/73	10,090	91	10,181	9,163	74	12,301	3,139		2,660	1	11,822	159.1	77.5
1973/74	11,909	111	12,020	10,818	76	12,649	1,831		1,755	71	12,502	163.6	86.5
1974/75	11,287	117	11,404	10,264	78	12,947	2,684		1,785	129	11,920	152.4	86.1
1975/76	12,763	218	12,981	11,683	80	13,245	1,562		1,722	422	12,983	162.3	90.0
1976/77	11,753	105	11,858	10,672	82	13,560	2,887		1,486	319	11,839	144.6	90.1
1977/78	12,970	356	13,326	11,993	84	13,891	1,897		1,908	560	13,341	159.0	89.9
1978/79	12,849	494	13,343	12,009	86	14,222	2,213		1,854	361	13,502	157.2	88.9
1979/80	12,740	823	13,563	12,207	88	14,537	2,330		2,498	355	14,350	163.4	85.1
1980/81	13,880	1,092	14,972	13,475	90	14,884	1,409		1,542	1,017	14,000	155.7	96.2
1981/82	13,629	967	14,596	13,136	92	15,215	2,079		2,067	303	14,901	162.1	88.2
1982/83	14,215	1,095	15,310	13,779	94	15,546	1,767		1,935	192	15,522	165.3	88.8
1983/84	14,509	1,211	15,720	14,148	96	15,894	1,746		2,051	266	15,933	166.0	88.8
1984/85	14,623	1,464	16,087	14,478	98	16,242	1,764		2,562	349	16,692	170.1	86.7
1985/86	15,038	1,042	16,080	14,472	100	16,606	2,134		1,541	349	15,664	156.2	92.4

1986/87	15,406	1,091	16,497	14,847	103	16,970	2,123		2,120	188	16,779	163.7	88.5
1987/88	15,413	1,048	16,461	14,815	105	17,335	2,520		2,503	375	16,943	161.8	87.4
1988/89	15,544	1,021	16,565	14,909	107	17,682	2,774		2,941	416	17,433	163.2	85.5
1989/90	17,856	890	18,746	16,871	109	18,030	1,159		2,164	960	18,075	166.0	93.3
1990/91	17,852	1,004	18,856	16,970	111	18,378	1,407		2,372	783	18,559	167.2	91.4
1991/92	18,252	1,065	19,317	17,385	113	18,709	1,323		2,345	1,016	18,714	165.6	92.9
1992/93	18,341	1,176	19,517	17,565	115	19,040	1,475	355	1,073	233	18,761	163.1	93.6
1993/94	18,041	1,131	19,172	17,255	117	19,371	2,116	312	1,376	166	18,777	160.5	91.9
1994/95	16,833	1,245	18,078	16,270	119	19,702	3,432	1,013	1,573	277	18,579	156.1	87.6
1995/96	17,687	1,369	19,056	17,150	121	20,033	2,883	850	1,795	422	19,373	160.1	88.5
1996/97	18,883	1,454	20,337	18,303	123	20,364	2,061	237	1,392	616	19,316	157.0	94.8
1997/98	18,824	1,803	20,627	18,564	125	20,696	2,131	1,133	1,621	617	20,701	165.6	89.7

SOURCES: BBS (various) and Hamid (1991).

NOTE: Food grain consumption requirement is calculated using the Government of Bangladesh's standard 16 ounces per person per day. Before 1985/86, however, the official food requirement was calculated using 15.5 ounces per person per day. Before 1991/92 private imports of foodgrain were not allowed.

[a]In thousand metric tons.

[b]In millions.

[c]Kilograms per person.

[d]Percent.

FIGURE 2.1 Total rice production and availability in Bangladesh

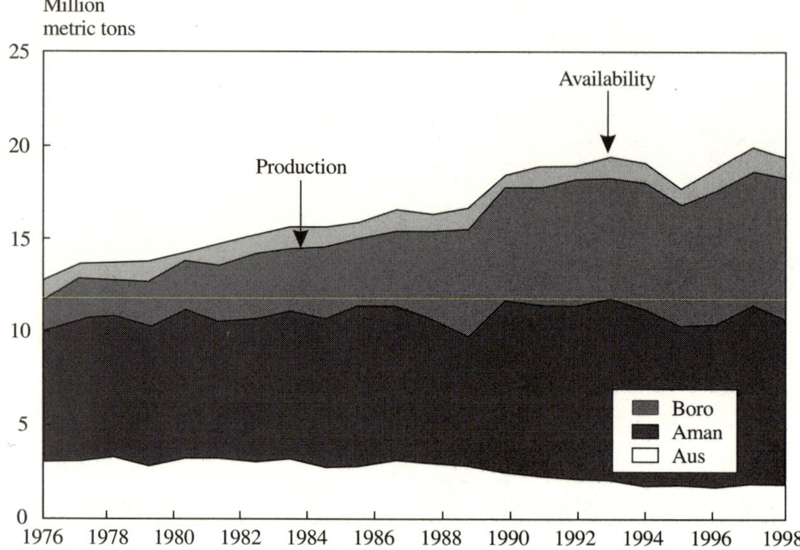

SOURCES: FPMU and MOF.

tion, changes in government stock, and commercial imports. Floods, cyclones, and droughts have increased the need for food aid to offset loss of domestic production or to provide emergency food relief. (See Chapter 8 for a detailed discussion of food aid flows to Bangladesh.)

Increases in domestic production, increased government capacity to import foodgrains commercially, and declining availability have reduced the share of food aid imports in total foodgrain supply over time. With increases in rice production, government rice imports fell somewhat during the 1980s. Nonetheless, this decline did not offset the gains in production, meaning that overall rice supplies per capita increased and market prices fell.

Real prices of rice in Bangladesh declined considerably from the mid-1970s to the early 1990s (Figure 2.2). Using the Dhaka middle-income consumer price index (CPI) as a deflator, a measure of overall inflation, the decline in rice prices between 1977–79 and 1991–93 was 34 percent. Using only the nonfood component of the CPI as a deflator, the decline in real prices of rice relative to the average price of nonfood consumer goods was 43 percent.[7] Over the same period, rice consumption per capita (proxied by net availability per capita) rose by 1.6 percent, from 137.6 to 145.4 kilograms per

7. These calculations are based on a December-to-January marketing year since the aman rice harvest occurs in November and December.

FIGURE 2.2 Real prices of coarse rice, 1977–98 (December–November marketing year)

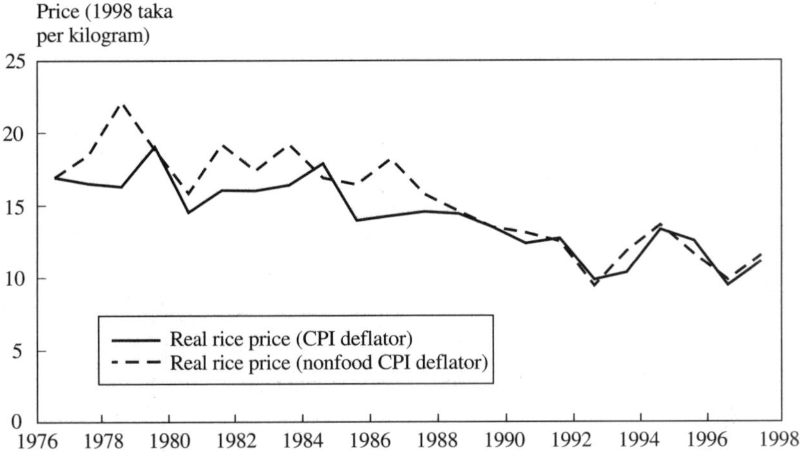

SOURCES: DAM, BBS (various), and author's calculations.

capita per year in 1991–93. With no effect or a negative income effect on demand combined with an inelastic demand curve, a modest increase in supply translated into a steep decline in the real price of rice. A worsening income distribution may have also contributed to the fall in real prices (see Appendix).

Because private trade was not allowed during this period, these rice prices reflected the balance between total domestic supply (including net government market injections) and demand. Beginning in 1994, however, in periods following poor harvests, domestic prices have risen only to import parity levels because of private sector imports from India.

Rice Prices and Imports after Trade Liberalization

Since the liberalization of international rice trade in 1994, the variation in rice prices in Bangladesh has increased, and substantial quantities of rice were imported following poor harvests in 1995/96 and in 1997/98 (Figure 2.3 and Table 2.7). In the first few months after liberalization, from April to November 1994, normal aman (November/December 1993) and boro (May/June 1994) harvests were sufficient to bring domestic supply to levels approximately equal to domestic demand at import parity prices of rice from India. As a result, even though private import trade was liberalized, only small amounts of rice were imported.[8]

8. At least 10,100 tons of the 34,000 tons of rice imports for which letters of credit were opened between July and September 1994 were from Pakistan. No country of origin was specified on most of the letters of credit in this period (see Dorosh 1999: tab. 3.1).

FIGURE 2.3 Import prices (exported from India) and quantity of private rice imports, 1993–98

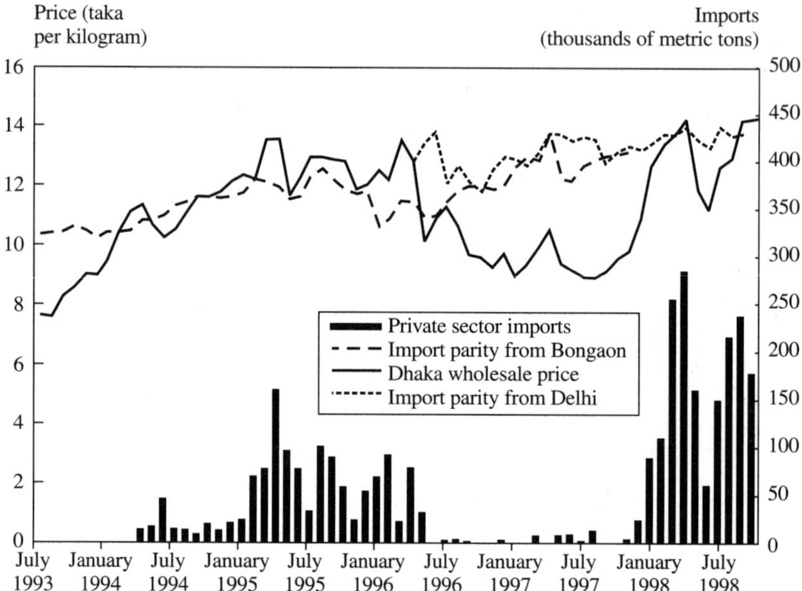

SOURCES: Baulch et al. (1998), FPMU, and author's calculations.

Imports surged in 1995 and early 1996, however, due to a sequence of below-average harvests in Bangladesh and India's liberalization of rice exports in October 1994. Bad weather reduced the size of the 1994/95 aman harvest, fertilizer shortages reduced the size of the 1995 boro crop, and more bad weather reduced the 1995/96 aman crop as well.[9] Moreover, India's removal of its quantitative restrictions on rice trade freed the country's private sector to export large quantities of rice to Bangladesh. Given the poor harvests in Bangladesh, there was a substantial excess of demand over supply at import

9. The 1994/95 aman crop was small, leading to increased market prices and greater incentives for producers in the following boro season. The Ministry of Agriculture, however, authorized a large level of fertilizer exports based on projections of normal price and weather conditions. Responding to high paddy prices in the boro planting season, farmers increased their demand for fertilizer. Fertilizer shortages ensued, the open market price of fertilizer rose, and the production of boro rice was only 6.54 million tons (3.5 percent below the previous year's harvest). After the poor aman harvest in 1994/95, the government attempted to import 800,000 tons of rice through open tenders in February 1995. Contract problems involving specification and inspection delayed import arrivals, and subsequent increases in world rice prices made the export sales less attractive to exporters. As a result, only 350,000 tons of rice had arrived within eight months, with final deliveries not arriving until April 1996.

TABLE 2.7 Bangladesh foodgrain imports, 1980–98

	Rice				Wheat				Total Foodgrain
Year	Food Aid	Government	Private	Total	Food Aid	Government	Private	Total	Imports
	(thousand metric tons)								
1980	24	688	0	712	1,136	734	0	1,870	2,582
1981	19	65	0	84	732	260	0	992	1,076
1982	30	114	0	144	1,111	0	0	1,111	1,255
1983	131	186	0	317	845	682	0	1,527	1,844
1984	117	62	0	179	1,324	553	0	1,877	2,056
1985	125	570	0	695	1,181	717	0	1,898	2,593
1986	27	10	0	37	1,060	103	0	1,163	1,200
1987	108	150	0	258	1,317	192	0	1,509	1,767
1988	192	398	0	590	1,595	732	0	2,327	2,917
1989	40	21	0	61	1,316	759	0	2,075	2,136
1990	41	258	0	299	908	326	0	1,234	1,533
1991	10	0	0	10	1,530	37	0	1,567	1,577
1992	39	0	0	39	1,375	150	0	1,525	1,564
1993	19	0	0	19	716	93	355	1,164	1,183
1994	0	0	74	74	654	0	238	892	966
1995	0	230	583	813	935	390	430	1,755	2,568
1996	1	487	650	1,138	737	352	200	1,289	2,427
1997	10	9	15	34	608	103	222	933	967
1998	0	98	993	1,091	549	155	142	846	1,937
Average									
1980–84	64	223	0	287	1,030	446	0	1,475	1,763
1985–89	98	230	0	328	1,294	501	0	1,794	2,123
1990–92	30	86	0	116	1,271	171	0	1,442	1,558
1994–98	2	165	463	630	697	200	246	1,143	1,773

SOURCE: FPMU.

parity prices, so the private sector imported 1.127 million tons (an average of 66,000 tons per month) while the government imported 704,000 tons. Most of this rice came from India in small lots.[10]

Fortunately, favorable weather and stable input supplies contributed to three consecutive good rice harvests: boro 1996, aman 1996/97, and boro 1997. Increased domestic supply reduced market prices to below import parity levels. As a result, private imports were no longer profitable and thus essentially stopped. Real prices during this 1.5-year period were on average slightly below the long-term declining trend (Figure 2.4). In fact, prices even fell below export parity with India, suggesting that Bangladeshi rice exports would have been competitive with Indian exports in the world market. As Rahman (1998) discusses, however, lack of established market links and appropriate grading standards prevented such exportation.[11]

A poor aman harvest in November/December 1997 led to high domestic prices and large-scale imports. Within two months after the start of the aman harvest, Bangladeshi prices rose to the import parity price. Although some groups called for immediate large-scale foodgrain imports, the Ministry of Food opted for a cautious strategy involving only moderate increases in government imports of rice and wheat. Instead, the government encouraged private sector food imports by removing a surcharge on rice imports and increasing open market sales (OMS) and distribution to poor households while maintaining adequate foodgrain stock levels.

Given the price incentives for imports and the large gap between domestic supply and demand, substantial flows of private sector rice imports from India followed. Between December 1997 and May 1998, 916,000 tons of rice were imported through officially approved private channels. As in 1994/95, most of this trade was in small lots. Letter of credit data from January–March 1998 show that the average quantity was only 167.5 tons per letter of credit for the 1,022 letters issued (Dorosh 1999). Moreover, these letters of credit were opened by 387 different traders, who imported an average of only 896 tons of rice each. The largest ten traders (in terms of total imports) imported 69,567 tons, 20 percent of the total. Given this broad participation in the rice import trade and the small share of the largest supplier, there apparently has been little scope for individuals or small groups of traders to significantly affect market prices by restricting market supply.

Wheat Prices, Food Aid, and Commercial Imports

Before the liberalization of foodgrain trade in the early 1990s, domestic wheat prices were determined largely by the amount of food aid, the timing of

10. Letter of credit data indicate that the average size of the 1,251 shipments of rice in 1994/95 was only 707 tons (Dorosh 1999: tab. 3.1).

11. India was exporting non-basmati rice to other countries during this period. Bangladeshi rice could not be imported legally by India (for domestic consumption or transshipment) because of a rice import ban.

FIGURE 2.4 National average real wholesale price of rice and wheat, 1987–88

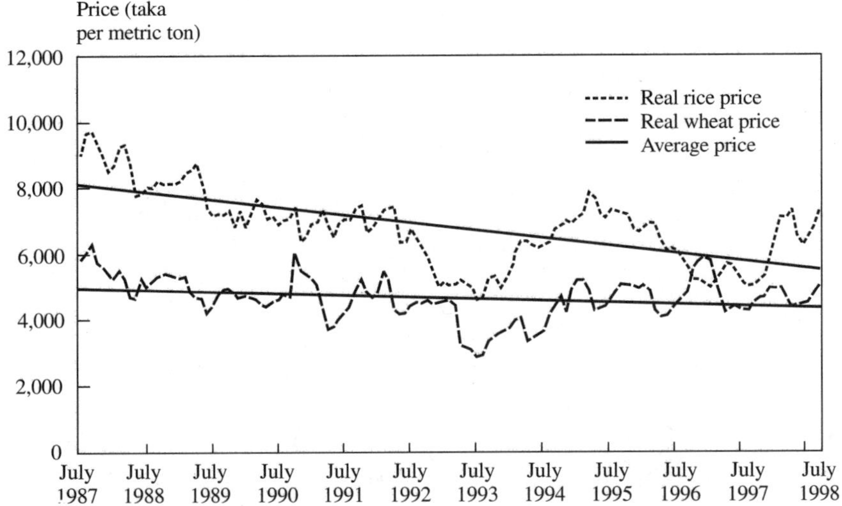

SOURCES: FPMU and author's calculations.

distribution, the level of domestic wheat production, and conditions in the rice market in a given year. Government interventions in the wheat market were limited mainly to distributing food aid through various channels. During the 1980s wheat procurement averaged only 8.7 percent of domestic production, and food aid inflows were on average 2.5 times larger than government commercial wheat imports at 1,162,000 tons of food aid and 473,000 tons of commercial imports. Unlike rice prices, however, real prices of wheat experienced only a slight downward trend in this period (Figure 2.4).

Liberalization of the foodgrain trade opened domestic markets to private sector imports of wheat. Such imports, however, have been on average less than rice imports. Between 1994 and 1998, private wheat imports have averaged 246,000 tons per year, compared with 463,000 tons of rice and 697,000 tons of food aid wheat. Unlike food aid imports (and domestically produced wheat), which are almost exclusively soft wheat varieties, a large share of commercial wheat imports have been more expensive hard wheat varieties better suited for baking bread, biscuits, and pastries.

Figure 2.5 shows the levels of domestic and import parity prices for wheat from 1993 to 1998. Since liberalization of trade in 1993, wheat prices have been near import parity border prices (measured on the basis of the FOB price at Gulf of Mexico ports for U.S. hard red winter wheat plus shipping costs) in most years.[12] The major exception was between September 1995 and Septem-

12. Import parity prices were in fact lower than those for 1993 due to the U.S. Export Enhancement Program, which subsidized wheat exports.

FIGURE 2.5 Import parity prices and quantity of private wheat imports, 1993–98

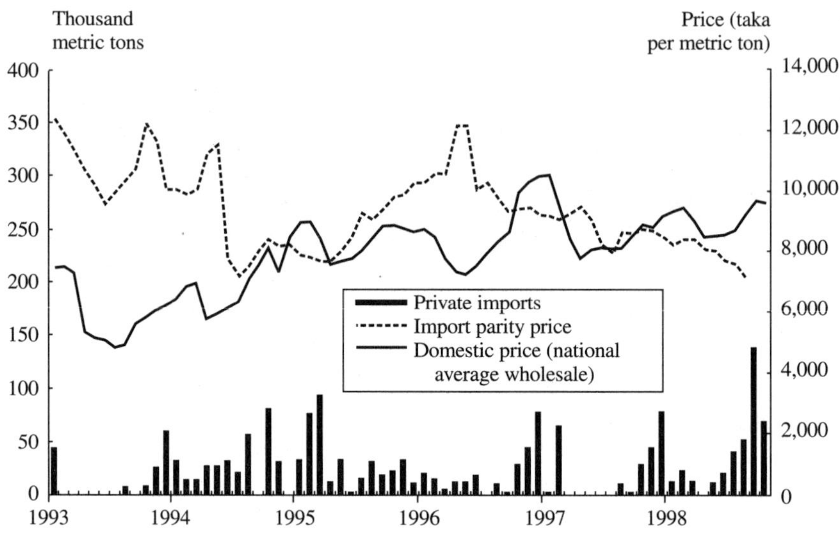

SOURCES: FPMU and author's calculations.

ber 1996, when world prices rose sharply while domestic prices fell, leading to a large gap in April and May 1996. This divergence between domestic prices and border prices is largely due to imports of lower-quality wheat from India, large amounts of Food-for-Work (FFW) wheat distributed in early 1996, and good boro rice and wheat harvests in April–June 1996.

Producer Disincentive Effects

To avoid depressing market prices below import parity prices, the total level of food aid must not exceed the amount of wheat that would be imported by the private sector under free trade. If wheat imports (in the form of food aid) exceed the free-trade level of imports, the domestic price of wheat will fall below import parity, encouraging more wheat consumption. Unfortunately, the lower price also discourages domestic wheat production and lowers farmer incomes. How much wheat would be imported under free trade depends on the import price of wheat and the responsiveness of domestic production and demand to changes in the wheat price, as reflected in the own-price elasticities of supply and demand.

Assuming probable values of supply and demand elasticities, Table 2.8 shows estimates for the levels of wheat imports that would have resulted without food aid in 1996/97. These estimates also represent the maximum amount of food aid wheat that could be released on the domestic market during the year without depressing market prices below import parity levels. At

1996/97 world prices of $221 per ton CIF Chittagong (equal to an import parity price of taka 10.2 per kilogram), only 710,000 tons of wheat would have been imported under free trade (compared with the 933,000 tons actually imported). Thus, without food aid, wheat prices in 1996/97 would have been an estimated 12.9 percent higher and imports 223,000 tons less.[13]

Sensitivity analysis using different world prices and alternative elasticity estimates gives similar results. For calculations of price incentives, it makes sense to use an estimate of the medium-term border price to correct for temporary fluctuations in world markets. With a lower world price of $208 per ton (approximately equal to the five-year average of world prices), domestic prices would rise by only 9.1 percent to taka 9.8 per kilogram, and imports would equal 773,000 tons. According to alternate elasticities of supply and demand of 0.2 and –0.4, respectively (which models less price-responsiveness of supply and demand to changes in prices), imports would be 839,000 tons.

Thus, these rough calculations suggest that, with no commercial imports, 700,000–840,000 tons of food aid, distributed evenly over a year, could be imported without depressing domestic prices below import parity. Other factors left out of the current analysis would increase the amount of food aid wheat that could be imported without depressing market prices. Direct distribution of wheat to the poor increases demand for wheat, even apart from any reduction in market prices, by increasing their purchasing power. Earlier studies suggest that the marginal propensity to consume (MPC) wheat out of wheat payments in kind in FFW programs is larger than the MPC out of cash purchase by about 0.3. In other words, for each 1 kilogram of wheat given to FFW participants, their total wheat consumption increases by 0.3 kilograms more than the usual market-based consumption of wheat. If half of wheat food aid were distributed in a like manner, total wheat demand would increase by a further 105,000 tons (that is, 700,000 tons × ½ × 0.3).

Another important factor is domestic rice prices. In years when rice prices are high, wheat demand increases. Econometric estimates of the cross-price elasticity of demand for wheat given a change in the rice price vary, and further analysis is required.[14] Average rice prices in 1996/97, however, were somewhat below medium-term average prices. These lower prices reduce demand for wheat. In contrast, if rice prices were higher, wheat demand would increase.

Further sensitivity analysis could be done according to various scenarios for rice prices (which have cross-price effects on wheat demand and supply)

13. Why then did private traders import wheat? That answer is that they imported primarily hard wheat for biscuits and breads. They may also have misjudged the market for wheat, guessing wrongly about future prices, a complicated calculation that depends on the size and timing of food aid disbursements on the local market, the size of the wheat harvest, and movements in rice prices. Note, too, that the calculation in this chapter of projected wheat imports does not take into account fluctuations in the world price of wheat during the 1996/97 fiscal year.

14. The cross-price elasticity of demand is the percentage change in the demand for rice for a 1 percent change in the price of wheat.

TABLE 2.8 Estimated production, demand, and supply of wheat with alternative parameter values and world prices

	Base 1996/97	Current World Price	Low World Price		Medium World Price	
			Base	Inelastic	Base	Inelastic
Production (MMT)	1.454	1.566	1.486	1.464	1.534	1.480
Domestic procurement (MMT)	0.103	0.103	0.103	0.103	0.103	0.103
Offtake (MMT)	0.653	0.653	0.653	0.653	0.653	0.653
Food aid (MMT)	0.608					
Government commercial imports (MMT)	0.103					
Private imports (MMT)	0.222					
Total imports (MMT)	0.933	0	0	0	0	0
Supply (MMT)	2.081	1.959	1.887	1.868	1.930	1.882
Demand (MMT)	2.081	1.959	1.887	1.868	1.930	1.882
CIF price (dollars per metric ton)	220.500	220.500	197.000	197.000	208.000	208.000
Import parity (takas per kilogram)	10.152	10.152	9.315	9.315	9.810	9.810
Domestic price (takas per kilogram)	8.990	10.152	9.315	9.315	9.810	9.810
Percent change in price	0	12.925	3.615	3.615	9.121	9.121
Percent change in production	0	7.697	2.190	0.713	5.469	1.761
Percent change in demand	0	–5.897	–1.760	–1.410	–4.271	–3.431
Elasticity of supply	0.610	0.610	0.610	0.200	0.610	0.200
Elasticity of demand	–0.500	–0.500	–0.500	–0.400	–0.500	–0.400

SOURCE: Author's estimations as explained in the text.

NOTES: MMT indicates million metric tons. The import parity price is calculated as the CIF price in takas plus 0.45 takas per kilogram for handling and transport costs. The exchange rate is 45 takas = US$1.

and disaggregating wheat import demand by type of wheat.[15] Effects of a further devaluation of the taka, which would raise the border price of wheat but also might have major effects on the rice market, could be analyzed as well. Nonetheless, these rough calculations suggest that a moderate level of food aid, on the order of 700,000–840,000 tons of wheat, is consistent with a policy of keeping producer incentives in line with long-run import parity prices.

Timing of Food Aid Distribution and Sales

Large-scale distribution of FFW wheat occurs between January and April, after the monsoon rains and the aman rice harvest, when drier weather and soils permit road building. When the FFW programs began in the mid-1970s, there was almost no domestic production of wheat. Today, however, the major wheat harvest occurs in March and April, and distribution of FFW wheat (much of which is resold in the market) significantly depresses farmgate prices at harvest. Dorosh and Haggblade (1997) show that the price-depressing effects of FFW wheat could be minimized if the wheat food aid were monetized at other times of the year and FFW was replaced by Cash-for-Work (as CARE has done with the Integrated Food for Development [IFFD] program). Monetization of the wheat later in the year could benefit the urban poor as well, lowering prices during the months before the aman rice harvest (the September/October lean season). Alternatively, other types of work could be included in FFW programs so that direct distribution of wheat is spread out more evenly through the year.

The previous calculations show that, barring unforeseen changes in technology or a large increase in the price of wheat relative to rice, Bangladesh will likely remain a net importer of wheat in the medium run. Thus, moderate levels of food aid can substitute for commercial imports without adversely affecting producer price incentives as long as most of the imported wheat is not released on the market immediately before and after the harvest. Although theoretically other aid can be substituted for food aid on a dollar-for-dollar basis, food aid has more political support in donor countries (farm lobbies and public approval for donations of food) than does other aid. The implication is that cuts in food aid would likely mean cuts in total public resource flows to Bangladesh, to the detriment of the country's poor.

Summary

Rapid increases in foodgrain production in the 1980s, achieved through adoption of Green Revolution technology, significantly reduced Bangladeshi de-

15. In recent years the private sector has imported about 200,000 tons of hard wheat annually, mainly for use in biscuits and bread. Even with the severe assumption that hard and soft wheat cannot be substituted for one another, the total amount of soft wheat imports would be only about 200,000 tons less than the analysis here suggests.

pendence on food aid and commercial imports. The slower growth rates in the 1990s and the higher variability of output, largely due to weather, have replaced earlier optimism with pessimism about the medium-term prospects for rice production. Moreover, wheat production still accounts for only about 60 percent of domestic wheat supply in the late 1990s so that wheat self-sufficiency is unlikely to be achieved if large-scale distribution of wheat continues.

Neither rice nor total foodgrain self-sufficiency is a necessary condition for food security at the national level, however, provided that sufficient resources are available for the purchase of foodgrains in reliable international markets. Food aid and government commercial imports boosted foodgrain availability in Bangladesh in the 1970s and 1980s. Since liberalization of private trade, however, private sector imports of rice in the 1990s have several times contributed significantly to market food supplies after poor rice harvests.

As discussed later in this book, changes in production and trade policy have had profound effects on the entire foodgrain economy by influencing availability, price levels, and price variability. Future changes are certain to be major determinants of the structure of the foodgrain economy as well as the welfare of the more than 125 million people in Bangladesh.

Appendix: Determination of Rice Prices in Bangladesh

In price theory, prices are determined by the interplay of forces of supply and demand. Forces underlying demand consist of income, income distribution, the price of substitutes, taste, and the price of the commodity itself. Forces underlying supply consist of production, supply from imports and stocks, and the price of the commodity itself. Speculative activities of traders can influence price, but such speculations would affect market price through stock changes. Public procurement and distribution can also influence price: procurement from the domestic market reduces market supply from domestic production, and distribution from imported grains augments market supply. Empirical analysis of the determinants of rice price incorporating all these factors is complex and constrained by the unavailability of accurate data for some of them.

The available rice price data we have are annual average prices of rice based on the average of monthly prices (see Table A2.1). Thus, determining the annual average price involves determination of monthly prices. Such prices are the results of the interaction of demand forces with given levels of supply. Determination of the demand forces therefore constitutes the primary task of the determination of rice prices, although actual consumption or demand is not known. Conventionally, an indirect estimate of actual consumption is obtained by measuring total availability as defined in the chapter. Comparison of this per capita availability with actual per capita consumption of rice, as found through a few household survey estimates (HSE), indicates that per capita availability was quite close to HSE (the ratio of availability to HSE consumption varying from 1.11 to 0.93 in 1973/74–1983/84). For four years beginning in 1985/86, however, this ratio fell to about 0.83. The divergence could be due to errors in production or consumption estimates. In spite of the difference, it is appropriate to see how estimates of demand functions behave using per capita availability as equivalent to per capita consumption. With this assumption, the demand function is formulated as

$$Qd = f\,(\text{Price}, P_{\text{other}}, Y_h, \text{Distrib}) \qquad \text{(A2.1)}$$

where
Qd = quantity demanded,
Price = price of coarse-quality rice,
P_{other} = price of other commodities in the consumption basket,
Y_h = income, and
Distrib = public distribution of rice.

Distrib is included in the demand function for its income effect arising from food subsidy and following past studies on prices (Ahmed and Bernard 1989; Shahabuddin 1992). Quantity of rice and income are taken in per capita terms. Prices and income are in real terms, using CPI as a deflator. Deflating nominal prices of rice by CPI is presumably sufficient for the exclusion of P_{other} directly in the demand function. This function is estimated following OLS methods and in a logarithmic form. Results of the regressions are presented in Appendix Table A2.2.

The results show that the own-price elasticity of demand for rice is significant in almost all cases and varies from –0.11 to –0.15, and that the coefficient of the logarithm of public rice distribution per capita is positive but not significant at an acceptable level. The income elasticity of demand is not significantly different from zero, suggesting that changes in real income have little effect on national rice consumption.

Neither including a time trend nor extending the observations to include years in the late 1970s in the regression produced any significant differences in the results (see Appendix Table A2.2).

Other empirical studies show widely varying own-price elasticities of demand and a declining trend in income (expenditure) elasticity, still with a positive sign (Dorosh 1999). In general, own-price elasticity of demand estimated from cross-section data is larger in absolute terms than the estimate from time-series data. Similarly, a cross-section estimate of expenditure (income) elasticity is generally small (0.15–0.40) but positive, while the time-series regressions yield a coefficient not significantly different from zero.

In the light of the demand parameters estimated through time-series regression, it is reasonably clear that the modest increase in per capita supply of

APPENDIX TABLE A2.1 Rice production, availability, and prices, 1977–98

							CPI Deflated (national aveage) Rice Price	
Year	Midyear Population	Rice Production	Rice Procurement	PFDS Distribution	Rice Availability	Availability per Capita	June–July Coarse	Dec.–Nov. Coarse
	(million)	(thousand metric tons)	(thousand metric tons)	(thousand metric tons)	(thousand metric tons)	(kilograms per person)	(1997 taka per kilogram)	(1997 taka per kilogram)
1976/77	81.8	11,753	317	750	11,011	134.6	18.0	16.9
1977/78	83.7	12,969	548	600	11,724	140.1	20.6	16.4
1978/79	85.6	12,849	306	570	11,828	138.2	16.8	16.4
1979/80	87.7	12,740	228	695	11,934	136.1	24.6	19.1
1980/81	89.9	13,880	841	514	12,165	135.3	16.0	14.5
1981/82	91.9	13,629	290	772	12,748	138.7	14.5	16.0
1982/83	93.9	14,215	168	496	13,121	139.7	16.7	16.0
1983/84	96.0	14,509	145	503	13,416	139.7	16.1	16.4
1984/85	98.1	14,623	133	399	13,426	136.9	18.2	17.8

1985/86	100.3	15,038	219	372	13,687	136.5	14.5	13.9
1986/87	102.5	15,406	137	495	14,223	138.8	15.3	14.2
1987/88	104.7	15,413	288	468	14,052	134.2	15.4	14.5
1988/89	106.8	15,544	364	690	14,316	134.0	14.2	14.4
1989/90	108.9	17,856	918	675	15,827	145.3	13.0	13.5
1990/91	111.0	17,852	727	971	16,311	146.9	12.8	12.3
1991/92	113.0	18,252	939	759	16,246	143.8	13.3	12.7
1992/93	115.0	18,341	233	476	16,750	145.7	12.9	9.8
1993/94	117.0	18,041	148	350	16,438	140.5	9.1	10.3
1994/95	119.0	16,833	246	329	15,233	128.0	12.4	13.2
1995/96	121.0	17,687	353	593	16,158	133.5	13.7	12.5
1996/97	123.0	18,753	513	739	17,104	139.1	11.4	9.4
1997/98	125.0	18,424	430	555	16,707	133.7	9.5	11.0

SOURCES: BBS (various), FPMU, and author's calculations.

APPENDIX TABLE A2.2 Time-series estimates of rice demand parameters in Bangladesh
Dependent Variable: Natural Logarithm of Rice Availability per Capita

Sample	Constant	In Price	Dist Dum	In Income	Time	Durbin-Watson Statistic	R^2	Adjusted R^2
1. 1980–98	5.051*	–0.127*	0.037	0.023		1.699	0.348	0.217
19 observations	(4.464)	(–2.121)	(1.508)	(0.186)				
2. 1980–98	5.117	–0.127*	0.037	0.014	0.0002	1.697	0.348	0.161
19 observations	(1.682)	(–2.010)	(0.028)	(0.039)	(0.024)			
3. 1980–98	7.349*	–0.110		–0.258	0.0038	1.476	0.265	0.118
19 observations	(2.189)	(–1.742)		(–0.819)	(0.572)			
4. 1977–98	5.820*	–0.109*		–0.071		1.457	0.249	0.169
22 observations	(6.705)	(–1.891)		(–0.817)				
5. 1977–98	5.140*	–0.127*	0.036	0.012		1.721	0.348	0.240
22 observations	(5.551)	(–2.257)	(1.661)	(0.124)				
6. 1977–98	5.311*	–0.153*	0.041	–0.000		1.637	0.361	0.201
16 observations	(3.966)	(–2.257)	(1.440)	(–0.002)				

SOURCE: Author's calculations.

NOTE: Values of *t*-statistics appear in parentheses.

*Significance at 95 percent confidence level.

rice during the past 15 to 18 years has caused a significant decline in the real price of rice because of a price-inelastic demand curve and a zero or negative income effect on demand for rice. Nevertheless, in light of only a modest increase in per capita supply and a sharp fall in real prices of rice, some economists have speculated that income distribution was worsening, adversely affecting demand for rice. This is an area in need of further research.

References

Ahmed, R., and A. Bernard. 1989. *Rice price fluctuation and an approach to price stabilization in Bangladesh.* Research Report 72. Washington, D.C.: International Food Policy Research Institute.

Baffes, J., and M. Gautam. 1996. *Is growth in Bangladesh's rice production sustainable?* Policy Research Working Paper. Washington, D.C.: World Bank, International Economics Department, Commodity Policy and Analysis Unit.

Bangladesh Bureau of Statistics (BBS). Various. *Statistical yearbook of Bangladesh.* Dhaka, Bangladesh.

Baulch, B., J. Das, W. M. H. Jain, N. Farid, and S. Zohir. 1998. The spatial integration and pricing efficiency of the private sector grain trade in Bangladesh: Phase II report. Bangladesh Institute of Development Studies, Bureau of Socioeconomic Research and Training, Bangladesh Agricultural University, Institute of Development Studies at the University of Sussex, U.K., May.

Del Ninno, C., and P. Dorosh. 1998. Government policy, markets and food security in Bangladesh. Food Management and Research Support Project, International Food Policy Research Institute, Dhaka, Bangladesh. Mimeo.

Dorosh, P. 1999. The determination of rice prices in Bangladesh: Supply shocks, trade liberalization and cross-border trade. Food Management and Research Support Project, Working Paper 2. International Food Policy Research Institute, Dhaka, Bangladesh.

Dorosh, P., and S. Haggblade. 1997. Shifting sands: The changing case for monetizing project food aid in Bangladesh. *World Development* 25, no. 12: 2093–2104.

Hamid, M. A. 1991. A data base on agriculture and foodgrains in Bangladesh (1947/8–1989/90). Dhaka, Bangladesh.

Hossain, M. 1991. *Agriculture in Bangladesh: Performance, problems and prospects.* Dhaka, Bangladesh: University Press.

Novak, S. 1992. *Hydrological features of the Ganges Basin.* New Delhi, India: Oxford University Press.

Rahman, M. 1998. Turning the full circle: Rationale and mechanics of rice exports from Bangladesh. Food Management and Research Support Project, International Food Policy Research Institute, Dhaka, Bangladesh, June. Mimeo.

Shahabuddin, Q. 1992. Disaggregated model for stabilization of rice prices in Bangladesh. *Bangladesh Development Studies* 20 (March): 1–41.

World Bank. 1998. *From counting the poor to making the poor count.* Poverty Reduction and Economic Management Network, South Asia Region, Washington, D.C.

Zohir, S. 1995. Problems and prospects of crop diversification in Bangladesh. *Bangladesh Development Studies* 21 (September): 73–90.

Zaman, S. M. H. 1987. Agronomic and environmental constraints on fertilizer effectiveness. In *Fertilizer pricing policies in Bangladesh,* ed. B. Stone. Washington, D.C.: International Food Policy Research Institute; Dhaka: Bangladesh Institute of Development Studies.

3 Liberalization of Agricultural Input Markets in Bangladesh

RAISUDDIN AHMED

As recommended by the Agricultural Commission of 1960, the East Pakistan Agricultural Development Corporation was established in 1963. Later known as the Bangladesh Agricultural Development Corporation (BADC), this public parastatal was responsible for procuring and distributing agricultural inputs such as fertilizers, seeds, agricultural equipment, and pesticides (Ahmed 1978a). BADC soon developed an elaborate national organization for delivering goods and services to farmers, establishing a virtual monopoly over fertilizer and agricultural equipment markets while conforming to government pricing and related policies. The corporation has since been replaced by liberalized and deregulated input markets. This chapter chronicles the process of liberalization, examines its impact, and draws lessons from the change.

Liberalization of Input Markets

The step-by-step liberalization of markets for modern inputs in agriculture was carried out under pressure from foreign donors and with the realization that various direct interventions were fiscally unsustainable and unproductive in the long run.

The Structure of Markets before Liberalization

FERTILIZER MARKET. In 1959/60, about 11,400 nutrient metric tons of chemical fertilizers were used in Bangladesh, primarily on tea estates.[1] The use of fertilizers spread incrementally to peasants about the time when BADC was established. By 1977/78, the corporation had sold 354,000 nutrient tons of fertilizers (equivalent to 725,000 material tons), consisting of 65 percent nitrogen, 25 percent phosphorus, and 8 percent potassium.

BADC was the sole organization procuring fertilizers from domestic factories and foreign sources. Fertilizers were first shipped to transit warehouses, then to intermediate warehouses at strategic points, and finally to *thana* sales centers (TSCs).[2] These intermediaries functioned as both wholesale and retail

1. All further references to tons indicate metric tons.

2. A *thana* is an administrative unit consisting of 80 to 90 villages.

points, selling fertilizer to licensed private dealers and directly to farmers. Between 1963 and 1978, there were 67 intermediate warehouses and 423 TSCs. The other category of wholesaler was the Thana Central Cooperative Association, which sold fertilizer to private dealers and village cooperatives for retail sales to farmers. The share of cooperatives in total sales was small, accounting for only 12 to 17 percent. Three or four private dealers would serve 7 to 10 villages. Dealers were not supposed to sell outside a defined area, procuring their fertilizers from specified TSCs and selling at government-fixed prices. The fixed price included a commission based on the distance from the TSC to the operation center. Dealers were required to maintain registers, which were subject to occasional inspection by BADC officers. Excluding the commission, fertilizer prices were supposed to be uniform throughout the country. The system suffered from numerous problems arising from excessive bureaucratic control.

IRRIGATION EQUIPMENT. BADC changed public irrigation policy from expensive, large-scale projects to low-cost, small-scale ones. It initiated low-lift pump irrigation (lifting water from surface sources to adjoining fields) using diesel engines and distribution pipes, mainly to reclaim the *haor* areas of the Sylhet and Mymensingh districts.[3] Most of these engines had a capacity of 0.0566 cubic meters per second. Initially, BADC owned, maintained, and operated these pumping sets to supply water to groups of farms using a flat charge per hectare, a system that covered only about 60 percent of the operating cost. Rapidly expanding from the *haor* areas, the scheme spread throughout the country along riverbanks, large ponds, and lakes, eventually making operations unwieldy and expensive. Therefore, by the end of the 1960s BADC introduced some reforms. Farmers were required to organize into irrigation groups, supply all diesel fuel costs, and pay a share of the maintenance cost at flat rates per hectare of irrigated land. Farm groups were responsible for water management, obtaining diesel fuel, and collecting charges. By the mid-1970s a rental system was introduced so that BADC's only responsibility was to make available well-functioning pumping sets. Farm groups had to meet all costs of the service, including the wages of pump operators.

Tubewell irrigation is suitable for areas in which surface water is not available and underground water is the next best source. In the early 1960s the Bangladesh Water Development Board initiated the first tubewell program, drilling 90 tubewells, each with 0.0566 to 0.0849 cubic meter per second capacity engines, in northern Bangladesh. For many years, however, the project did not attract farmers, even with a 100 percent subsidy. BADC began a deep tubewell experiment (0.0566 cubic meter per second capacity) at about the time when its low-lift pump program had reached saturation. In the meantime, using cooperative societies, the Comilla Academy for Rural Develop-

3. A *haor* is a lake-like depression in a low-lying, marshy stretch of land.

ment was successfully experimenting with shallow tubewells with a capacity equivalent to one-eighth to one-half of BADC tubewells, drilling them at a price much cheaper than BADC's. The academy also implemented a training program to develop private-sector tubewell installation capacity. In 1970 BADC started a modest tubewell irrigation program for farmers based on engines with a 0.0566 cubic meter per second capacity, initially operating these wells on the same principles as low-lift pumps. In about 1978 the corporation was asked to install tubewells for farmers at subsidized (20–30 percent) rates. Except for these publicly initiated programs, however, there was hardly any private initiative in the development of modern irrigation until the mid-1970s.

Irrigation equipment (engines, pumps, and so on) had always been part of a small, private, nonagricultural market. Because domestic capacity for producing diesel engines and pumps was small, most of BADC's equipment was imported using foreign aid. Therefore, liberalizing the import trade became the key element of market liberalization in agricultural equipment. Before the mid-1980s, two import restrictions were in effect:

1. Private import of diesel engines for irrigation was not allowed except for makes and models approved by a standardization committee in the Ministry of Agriculture (MOA) and with special permission from the ministry.
2. Private import of pumps for irrigation was not allowed except with MOA permission, foreign exchange through a donor-funded project, and no objection from the Ministry of Industries.

CULTIVATION EQUIPMENT. At its inception BADC began a mechanized cultivation scheme based on tractors, but such experiments had limited success. In about 1968 the Pak-Japan (later known as Bangladesh-Japan) Cooperative Scheme on Agricultural Machineries successfully introduced power tillers for plowing. Nevertheless, no special public agency was created to market and distribute the tillers, as had been the case for other inputs. Instead, private importers and distributors performed this function. Medium to large farms purchased power tillers to meet their own requirements and rent to neighbors. While the domestic market was not publicly controlled, the import market was constrained. Before the mid-1980s, MOA had to approve the make and model of all power tillers to be imported (Guisselquist 1992).

PESTICIDES. BADC was given the task of procuring plant protection materials, while the Agricultural Extension Department was supposed to implement crop protection schemes. By the end of the 1960s, however, procurement and distribution were liberalized for several reasons. There were numerous complexities in storing and handling the poisonous materials and in dispensing them to farmers. Moreover, the government recognized that a bureaucratic agency was not well suited to take timely measures against pests. Private importers began to import and distribute pesticides through private dealers and general retailers of consumer goods, but such import was allowed only for brands and dealers approved by MOA. This approval process might have implied hidden costs for traders, and import only by brand names was potentially oligopolistic. Canada's agricultural sector team in Bangladesh found pesticide prices in 1991 to be as much as double the prices in Pakistan despite the absence of tariffs (CIDA 1991).

SEEDS. Traditionally, Bangladeshi farmers produce seed for their own use and sale to markets. Those who need seeds buy from the market, and it is common for some farmers to specialize in seed production. These traditional markets have been the primary distribution channel not only among farmers within the country but also between those in Bangladesh and India. To supplement traditional seed markets, since the late 1960s BADC has been operating 19 seed multiplication farms to produce and distribute improved seeds of various crops. The government has developed a seed certification mechanism to ensure quality. Nonetheless, complaints that publicly produced seeds are of poor quality and unavailable when needed are common.

In the past BADC has imported seeds to introduce high-yielding varieties (HYVs) of crops, such as Dutch potatoes and Mexican wheat. Liberalizing seed markets, aimed at promoting free and competitive international trade in seeds, would be a potent mechanism of technological progress in Bangladeshi agriculture.

Reforms in Input Markets

FERTILIZER. The chronology of reforms in the agricultural input markets is summarized in Table 3.1. The liberalization of the fertilizer and irrigation equipment markets was the dominant reform that boosted production. The fertilizer trade expanded rapidly, and by 1988 nearly 8,000 wholesalers and 50,000 retailers operated competitively in the fertilizer market (Infanger, Samad, and Hooker 1988). The share of private trade climbed quickly to 75 percent in 1989 and nearly 100 percent by 1992. The import trade was partially privatized, although there is an underlying fear that it may ultimately turn into an oligopoly because of economies of scale and differential access of traders to capital markets. Throughout the time of reform each process was monitored to identify problems and solve them as they emerged. The International Fertilizer Development Center (IFDC), through a network of field investigators, provided a useful service in this regard.

Although the distribution of fertilizers was privatized, most urea production stayed in the public sector. Between December 1994 and March 1995, a serious urea shortage shocked the fertilizer market, resulting in a partial reversal of the reform process that had worked so well before the crisis. Farmers reacted violently, and 17 died before order was restored. There are divergent views about what caused the crisis. The government believes that it resulted from the wholesale privatization of the fertilizer distribution system, arguing that the private sector created an artificial shortage by hoarding and selling at

TABLE 3.1 Step-by-step liberalization of agricultural input markets in Bangladesh

Actions	Time Span	Remarks
Fertilizer market		
1. BADC withdrew from retail and wholesale markets at *thana* levels, the primary distribution points.	1978–83	Done first at Chittagong Division, with vigorous response from traders
2. Licensing requirement was abolished and restriction on movement removed (except for eight-kilometer border zones with India).	1982–83	
3. Deregulation of fertilizer price took place.	1982–84	Beginning of real competition
4. Private traders directly purchased from factory gates and port points.	1987	Vigorous response from traders
5. Free import from world market began.	1992	Good response but persistent fear of oligopoly
6. Fertilizer crisis took place, with partial reversal of reform.	1994/95	Too early to assess full implications; large subsidy returns
Irrigation devices		
1. BADC sold all its low-lift pumps to private parties backed by special credit arrangement for purchasers.	1980–82	Good response from farmers
2. BADC sold all its tubewells for irrigation to farmers and cooperatives; sale was supported by special credit arrangement for purchasers.	1983–85	Good response from farmers
3. Restriction on import of engines and pumps was withdrawn.	1988	Drastic fall in prices of engines
4. Standardization restrictions limiting makes and models were removed.	1988	Drastic fall in prices of engines
Power tillers, pesticides, and seeds		
1. Restriction on power tiller import and the standardization requirement were removed.	1989	Modest response
2. Restriction on import by brand names was liberalized for pesticides.	±1989	Modest response
3. Except for rice and wheat, all seed imports were liberalized.	1990	Modest response

SOURCES: Computed from information in Mudahar (1984), Sidhu (1992), Guisselquist (1992), ADB (1990), Bangladesh Establishment Division (1992), and personal communications.

higher prices, smuggling across borders, and deliberately manipulating the allotment orders and lifting schedules formulated by the public production agency. The private fertilizer traders contend that the crisis erupted because the government took two contradictory steps at the same time: (1) reducing fertilizer prices in the domestic market (perhaps a preelection strategy), which boosted domestic demand, and (2) exporting fertilizer without considering the newly inflated demand. Moreover, the private traders believe that resorting to administrative controls worsened the market situation. A number of studies concluded that the crisis stemmed from the culmination of several factors. First, it occurred at peak seasonal demand. Second, the export of 554,000 tons of urea between June 1994 and January 1995 drastically reduced domestic availability during this peak period. Third, the introduction of administrative controls during the crisis destabilized the distribution system and hurt crisis management. There seems to be little evidence of private smuggling across borders.

EQUIPMENT. Perhaps the most significant effect of reform was realized in the case of irrigation equipment. By early 1989 the cost of a shallow tubewell (complete with sinking, pipe, pump, and engine) to irrigate four to five hectares of land had fallen below taka 20,000 (US$600), which is about 60 percent of the subsidized price for such equipment through BADC.[4] As a result, between 1988 and 1996 irrigated area expanded at a rate roughly twice as quickly as had been achieved between 1978 and 1986. Although the practice of using power tillers for cultivation was still uncommon, the price of a tiller had decreased to $1,500 in 1989 from $2,500 only a few months earlier, before the liberalization of imports (Guisselquist 1992). The use of power tillers is spreading faster now due to the removal of import restrictions. Thus far, the liberalization of markets for seeds and pesticides has had only a modest impact. In the long run, however, that impact, particularly for seeds, is likely to be large.

The Impact of Liberalization

The impact of liberalization is twofold, consisting of (1) its direct influence on agricultural production owing to changes in the level of input use and (2) its indirect influence on the production of both agricultural and nonagricultural products arising from reallocating budgetary savings achieved by reducing or eliminating input subsidies. These savings are likely to lower budget deficits and affect the price of foreign exchange, which in turn may influence production of tradable agricultural products. Measurement of the indirect impact warrants economy-wide modeling that is not attempted here. Nevertheless, this section considers some of the fiscal impact relating to the magnitude of the subsidies eliminated from the budget.

---

4. All further references to dollars indicate U.S. dollars.

Detailed calculations indicate that the budgetary subsidy on fertilizers dropped from taka 1,286 million ($83 million) in 1979/80, to taka 1,426 million ($57 million) in 1983/84, to taka 1,273 million ($40 million) in 1988/89, to only about taka 25 million ($0.6 million) in 1992/93 (Ahmed 1987; Renfroe 1991; and personal contacts in the Bangladesh Ministry of Agriculture). The small subsidy in 1993 was meant to correct minor and trace-element deficiencies in certain soils. In 1995/96, however, the new government reversed the subsidy policy so that the direct subsidy on fertilizer in 1996/97 is estimated at taka 4,725 million ($105 million). The 1983/84 figure was equivalent to about 14 percent of total public development expenditure on agriculture and rural development, while the 1979/80 figure was equivalent to 28 percent of such expenditure (IFPRI 1985).

Although budgetary savings arising from liberalization of the fertilizer market are significant, comparable estimates of irrigation subsidies are not available. Nevertheless, the budgetary subsidy on BADC's low-lift and tubewell irrigation program was estimated at taka 1,035 million ($66.7 million) in 1979/80 and taka 830 million ($33 million) in 1983/84 (Rashid 1986). By 1986 almost the entire subsidy had been eliminated. These subsidies are indeed budgetary losses, but they also contributed to social gains. Their role in the development of markets for modern inputs and as a foundation for larger growth in production in the post-liberalization period cannot be ignored (Ahmed 1978b; Osmani and Quasem 1985).

Methodology

Model for Measuring Direct Impact on Rice Production

The impact of market reform on the use of inputs and the production of agricultural products depends on farmers' response to changes in prices and the availability of inputs resulting from reform. Although farmers' responses are rooted in household-level resource allocation decisions and motivation, price formation takes place at the aggregate level. Therefore, a model to determine the nationwide impact of reform on agricultural production should reflect farm-level behavior.

Consider a typical farm with a production function,

$$V = F(X_1 \ldots X_m; Z_1 \ldots Z_n), \tag{3.1}$$

where V represents output, X variable inputs, and Z fixed inputs and other shifter variables of the function. The farm is seeking maximization of profit,

$$\Pi = PF(X_1 \ldots X_m) - \sum_{m}^{j} q_j x_j \tag{3.2}$$

where P is the unit price of output and q_j is the unit price of the jth variable input. Fixed costs are conveniently ignored. The profit maximizing level of input use is given by

$$\partial F / \partial X_j = q_j / P. \tag{3.3}$$

Equation (3.3) can be solved for optimal quantities of variable inputs denoted as a function of prices and Z:

$$X_j^* = F_j(P, q, Z). \tag{3.4}$$

Substituting equation (3.4) into equation (3.2), the restricted profit function becomes

$$\Pi = G(P, q_1 \ldots q_m; Z_1 \ldots Z_n). \tag{3.5}$$

This general function gives maximized values for the optimal sets of ($q_1 \ldots q_m$) so that

$$\Pi = G^*(P, q_1 \ldots q_m; Z_1 \ldots Z_n). \tag{3.6}$$

It is possible to derive output supply and input demand functions from equation (3.6) via Shepard's (1970) lemma. The output supply function is

$$V^* = \Pi(P, q, Z), \tag{3.7}$$

and input demand function is

$$X_j^* = F_j(P, q, Z). \tag{3.8}$$

The function is negative in input prices. Note that P and q can be expressed in relative terms, collapsing the two vectors into one of relative output and input.

The values of V^* and X_j^* relate to a typical farm: if there are n number of such farms (measured in efficiency units) in an economy, then aggregate values can be obtained by multiplying V^* and X_j^* by n:

$$\text{aggregate } V_a^* = nV^* \tag{3.9}$$

and

$$\text{aggregate } X_a^* = nX_j^*. \tag{3.10}$$

At the household level farms are assumed to be price takers. At aggregate levels the prices of outputs and inputs are determined in markets. The theoretical logic in the previous equations and the process of aggregation indicate the pace of adjustment at farm level and aggregate impact on production arising from a change in the incentive environment (such as market reform). Given a technical condition of production, and assuming that all farms are alike and there are no credit constraints, the adjustment and impact arising from a change in incentives occur faster and may appear to be one-shot affairs. In the real world, however, farms are not all alike, and there are constraints. Therefore, the aggregate impact takes some time. The time span within which all adjustments are completed is primarily an empirical issue.

The household-level model just described could be used directly to measure the impact of liberalization if necessary data at household levels were available for all pre- and post-liberalization years—which is not the case. Nevertheless, models based on time-series aggregate data rooted to the behavioral logic at household levels can be formulated. Grounded in the microeconomics of production, an empirical aggregate model can be developed that simultaneously determines input use and crop production:

$$FC_t = (PFR_t/PR_t, AGR_t, NAR_t, CDS_t/P_t, D) \tag{3.11}$$

$$(PFR_t/PR_t) = f(PFD_t/PR_t, HYV, PFM_t/PR_t, D) \tag{3.12}$$

$$AGR_t = f(PD_t/PR_t, EG_{t-1} \neq P_{t-1}, CDL_{t-1}/P_{t-1}) \tag{3.13}$$

$$DAR_t = f(AGR_t, PR_t/PO_t, D) \tag{3.14}$$

$$QR_t = f(FC_t, AGR_t, DAR_t, D) \tag{3.15}$$

The algebraic symbols are defined as

FC_t = consumption of fertilizers (urea, triple superphosphate, and murate of potash) in year t (measured in thousands of tons),

PFR_t, PFD_t, PFM_t = respectively, retail, domestic factory gate, and border prices of fertilizer in year t, measured in taka per ton (with prices a weighted average of three types of fertilizer),

PR_t = wholesale price of rice in year t (taka per ton),

AGR_t = total irrigated area of rice in year t (thousands of acres),[5]

NAR_t = other crop area in year t (thousands of acres),

CDS_t = short-term crop loan advanced to farmers from banking institutions and public agencies in year t (10 × taka 1 million),

P_t = general price index

PD_t = price of diesel fuel in year t (taka per ton),

D = dummy variable that takes a value of 0 for 1975/76 to 1988/89 and 1 for 1989/90 to 1996/97,

EG_{t-1} = public expenditure on water control and irrigation development in year t–1 (10 × taka 1 million),

CDL_{t-1} = long-term loan to farmers from banks and public agencies in year t–1 (10 × taka million),

DAR_t = dry-land rice area in year t (thousands of acres),

HYV = area planted in high-yielding varieties of rice (thousand of acres),

5. The multiequation model, employing simultaneous system estimation, was estimated with acreage rather than hectorage as a land measure. Changing the measurement unit from acres to hectares may involve nonlinear transformation; therefore, this change was not made. It is not expected to make any difference, except in some nonuniformity of style.

PO_t = price of mustard oil seeds (taka per ton) as proxy for crop prices other than rice, and
QR_t = production of rice.

The impact of reform on rice production was chosen because of its importance to the economy. Rice contributes about 73 percent of GDP (gross domestic product) in the crop sector; 85 percent of fertilizers and 95 percent of irrigated areas are used to produce rice (Chowdhury 1993).

The following hypotheses are plausible in light of evidence from previous studies (Hossain 1988; Ahmed 1978a; Stone 1987):

1. Change in fertilizer consumption
   - due to increase in real price of fertilizer: negative
   - due to increase in irrigated area: positive
   - due to increase in other crop area: zero or positive
   - due to increase in volume of short-term credit: positive
2. Change in irrigated area
   - due to increase in real price of diesel fuel, which is critical for tubewells and low-lift pumps: negative
   - due to public expenditure on water control and irrigation: positive or zero
   - due to long-term credit to agriculture: positive
3. Change in retail price of fertilizer
   - due to increase in domestic factory-gate price: positive
   - due to increase in world price and exchange rate: positive
   - due to increase in HYV: positive
4. Change in dry-land rice area
   - due to irrigation expansion: negative or zero
   - due to increase in relative price of rice: positive
5. Change in rice production
   - due to increase in fertilizer use: positive
   - due to increase in irrigated area: positive
   - due to increase in dry-land rice area: positive

Most of these hypotheses may appear intuitive except for the effects of (1) other crop area on fertilizer consumption, (2) public expenditure for water control and irrigation on irrigated area, and (3) long-term credit to agriculture on irrigated area. Fertilizer use in nonrice crops, particularly nonirrigated ones, is patchy due to various risks associated with such land and underdeveloped technology for nonirrigated crops. In the case of public expenditure for water control and irrigation, the effect is hypothesized to be either zero or positive for two main reasons. First, the bulk of such expenditure is meant for flood control that does not influence irrigation. Second, the part of this expenditure that goes for irrigation is meant for large tubewells and surface irrigation structures.

Although farmers are unlikely to participate in either scheme, the indirect impact of such expenditures on tubewell irrigation could be significant. With the expansion of tubewell irrigation, the most suitable areas are covered first. Subsequent expansion may depend on the scope of flood-protected areas that such water-control projects tend to create. Long-term credit for agriculture in Bangladesh is largely meant for modern farm equipment—primarily tubewell and low-lift pump equipment for irrigation and power tillers for cultivation.

The most important and relevant hypothesis in the context of this analysis is the effect of the dummy variable *D*, which is designed to capture the complex effects of various changes induced by the liberalization measures on the levels of input use and production. There is no a priori presumption that the effect of the dummy will be positive or negative except that the coefficient of the dummy in equation (3.15) is expected to not differ significantly from 0. This is because the impact on production occurs through the impact on the levels of use of inputs, particularly the technology-embodied fertilizers, and irrigation. In equation (3.15) the actual levels of these inputs include any effect of market reform. A change in productivity may, however, influence the parameters of the production equation. The productivity of these inputs is not expected to be influenced by the liberalization measures because shifts in productivity are a function of technological change that does not pertain directly to liberalization measures, at least in the short term.

Using a dummy to capture the effect of unusual phenomena, structural change, spatial differences, and so on is not a new approach. Many researchers have adopted it for measuring the effect of structural reforms, particularly when direct and relevant data are difficult to obtain (Harris, Schiantarelli, and Sireger 1994; Alderman and Shively 1996; Devarajan, Swaroop, and Zou 1996; Khan 1996). Researchers have long faced the problem of impact measurements that require counterfactual information. Depending on their objectives and the degree of empirical problems, they have tried economy-wide, sectoral, or multimarket models that are capable of generating such information using "before and after" and "with and without" scenarios. None, however, has been completely satisfactory. Regardless of a model's dimensions, its central challenge is to develop appropriate relationships that link the factors affected by reform to the defined objectives of analysis. The use of dummy variables in econometric models is one such way to attempt to capture "with and without" effects. Nevertheless, it is essential that the number of years in pre- and post-reform periods does not differ widely so that random effects have an equal chance of distribution between the two periods (Mill 1990).

In the case of fertilizers the complex changes induced by liberalization measures that are not explicitly included as explanatory variables concern real costs of fertilizer to producers and availability of the input at the right time and place because of a greatly enhanced competitive market after privatization, deregulation of the market, and decontrol of prices. The price of fertilizer included as an explanatory variable does not include various discounts that the dealers are known to provide to purchasers to reap quick profits through high turnover. Similarly, fertilizer dealers sometimes resort to sales on informal credit to their subordinate retailers and farmers (Chowdhury 1993; World Bank 1992). Moreover, increasing the access of fertilizer dealers to factory-gate deliveries instead of controlled delivery from BADC stores must have enhanced the speed and volume of overall supply in the market. As discussed, in the case of irrigation the price and supply of low-lift pump and tubewell engines suddenly changed (price decreased and supply increased) because of market reforms, which included the withdrawal of import restrictions. These price and supply data are not systematically recorded and therefore cannot be used as explanatory variables in the model; the dummy variable is designed to pick up these effects.

Three other considerations also need a brief explanation. The first concerns the selection of 1988/89 as the splitting point between the pre- and post-liberalization periods.[6] The process of liberalizing fertilizer markets proceeded gradually; deregulation and privatization of the market and decontrol of prices were effectively completed by 1984 but partially reversed in 1995. A crucial event occurred in 1988: the deregulation and withdrawal of all restrictions on the import of irrigation equipment. Since irrigation is the leading factor for growth based on seed-fertilizer technology, this year was selected as the effective separating point between the pre- and post-liberalization production periods (see Table 3.1). Cheaper irrigation equipment fueled the process of expansion in tubewell irrigation.

The second consideration concerns the fact that HYVs of rice do not appear in any equation that also includes irrigated rice area. Analysis of HYV area and irrigation indicated that the correlation between the changes in HYV area and changes in irrigated area was very high (0.91). Thus, the effect of irrigation must be viewed as inclusive of the effect of HYVs. Although fertilizer and irrigation are also positively correlated, the correlation is not as strong as between irrigation and HYVs.

The third consideration is that the variable *NAR* and a few others have not been endogenized in the model because the type of information (for example, the relative profitability of crops in a time-series framework) was not available. Moreover, given the known high profitability of irrigated rice crops, *NAR* remains primarily a function of weather conditions (rainfall, drought, and so on). *CDS, PD,* and *CDL* were not endogenized because they are hardly influ-

---

6. A simple comparison of growth rates in production between the two periods may give misleading conclusions about the impact of modern inputs and liberalization of their markets. Splitting the years from 1975/76 through 1996/97 into two periods, each with an equal number of years, shows that in the first period the annual logarithmic growth rate in rice production is 2.1 percent—the result of 1.6 percent growth in yield and 0.5 percent growth in rice area. In contrast, the 1.7 percent logarithmic growth rate in production in the second period is caused by a 2.3 percent growth rate in yield and 0.5 percent annual decline in rice area.

enced directly by input market liberalization and because such an extension of the model would ultimately devolve into a general equilibrium framework that is beyond the scope of this chapter.

The final consideration relates to the labor market. No variables on supply and demand for labor are included in the model. In a generally labor-surplus economy such as Bangladesh, and with a relatively undistorted rural labor market, the exclusion of labor from the model is not likely to influence the measurement of the contribution of input market reform to production. Rural labor markets are generally not as distorted as urban labor markets are. Moreover, annual data on labor services (as opposed to stock of labor) used in production are not available to incorporate such variables as explanatory factors in the equations. Therefore, the effect of reforms in fertilizer and agricultural equipment on labor use in agricultural production remains a primary concern. In terms of labor's contribution to production in equation (3.15), the implication is that such a contribution is mixed with the contribution of land and other inputs.

Data

The data set used to estimate the model is presented in Table 3.2. These time series data were collected from various sources, mostly government organizations. Certain data, such as credit, production and areas of nonrice crops, and even the use of major inputs, have certain degrees of unreliability. Even rice production statistics, once considered to be the most reliable, have been questioned (see Mitchell 1998). Although such skepticism tends to weaken this type of analysis, the conclusions derived here should hold, if not in precise magnitude at least in approximate order and direction.

Estimation and Results

The system of equations (3.11) through (3.15) was estimated using Zellner's Seemingly Unrelated Regression (SUR) model, with annual data from 1975/76 to 1996/97. This model is efficient in situations in which the equations are closely interrelated, with the possibility of the error term of one equation being correlated with the error term of another. Before using the SUR model, the equations were estimated using the simple Ordinary Least Squares (OLS) model. The adjusted R^2s were generally high.

As Table 3.3 shows, results indicate that most of the hypotheses about input use are true, with the overall conclusion that the story of market liberalization is primarily one of irrigation-driven success in rice production. Liberalization of markets for irrigation equipment had both a direct and indirect impact on not only irrigated rice but also fertilizer use and rainfed rice area—hence, total rice production.

TABLE 3.2 Time-series data used to estimate models for measuring the impact of liberalization

Year	FC	PFR	PFD	PFM	PR	P	PO	PD	AGR	NAR	HYV	EG	CDS	CDL	DAR	QR
1975/76	451	1,361	1,368	2,222	3,382	160	6,650	2,075	3,008	9,851	3,833	608	625	795	22,516	12,763
1976/77	509	1,633	1,437	1,711	3,023	167	5,920	2,107	2,242	10,864	3,162	716	687	1,205	22,175	11,752
1977/78	725	1,633	1,437	1,843	3,877	188	7,330	2,164	2,868	10,122	2,975	851	1,085	1,539	21,291	12,970
1978/79	698	1,905	1,749	2,268	4,216	201	7,160	2,164	2,916	10,111	3,392	1,028	967	747	22,075	12,849
1979/80	797	2,450	2,147	2,719	5,657	237	7,840	2,776	3,038	7,166	4,936	1,423	1,354	1,415	21,769	12,740
1980/81	820	2,994	2,537	3,592	4,770	258	8,920	5,043	3,110	7,048	5,421	1,632	1,976	2,092	22,363	13,882
1981/82	772	3,605	3,328	3,828	6,060	298	8,370	5,499	3,309	6,786	5,745	2,016	2,186	2,710	22,542	13,631
1982/83	885	3,945	3,594	3,409	6,700	327	9,130	7,574	3,607	6,746	6,498	1,989	3,511	4,008	22,552	14,215
1983/84	1,032	4,007	3,658	3,599	7,450	355	12,040	7,574	4,711	6,677	6,499	2,840	5,110	3,749	21,354	14,508
1984/85	1,247	4,749	4,020	3,940	8,250	395	12,210	7,575	3,909	7,233	6,860	3,508	5,148	3,432	21,354	14,622
1985/86	1,152	4,995	4,399	3,693	6,620	439	11,680	7,643	3,987	7,764	7,126	3,571	1,247	2,344	21,708	15,041
1986/87	1,317	4,931	4,530	3,609	9,160	487	12,550	8,828	4,244	8,668	7,738	3,311	2,527	1,944	21,971	15,456
1987/88	1,505	4,924	4,557	4,405	9,970	532	13,890	8,192	4,835	9,987	8,239	4,459	2,743	1,525	20,156	15,661
1988/89	1,645	4,639	4,320	4,394	9,810	571	15,170	8,245	4,958	7,333	9,645	5,187	3,537	1,992	21,516	15,794
1989/90	1,968	4,648	4,197	5,013	9,600	616	15,090	8,064	5,944	8,859	10,549	5,328	3,571	1,668	19,947	17,462
1990/91	1,984	4,725	4,150	5,937	10,650	668	15,940	8,572	6,124	8,794	11,358	5,932	3,199	1,085	19,462	17,852
1991/92	2,124	5,004	4,194	5,806	9,720	701	15,970	8,715	6,681	9,436	12,003	6,376	4,464	1,528	18,633	18,252
1992/93	2,234	5,390	5,039	4,854	9,637	708	16,410	8,802	6,690	9,859	12,488	7,010	4,821	1,309	18,461	18,495
1993/94	1,921	5,679	4,869	5,021	9,719	735	17,280	9,845	6,709	10,322	12,347	6,330	5,151	2,161	17,954	18,041
1994/95	2,368	5,972	4,975	7,041	12,371	772	17,910	9,245	7,011	10,158	12,283	5,650	5,912	4,345	17,506	16,833
1995/96	2,305	5,821	4,711	8,294	12,172	799	18,040	8,317	7,266	9,768	12,182	6,279	6,505	4,005	17,291	17,687
1996/97	2,414	5,659	4,739	7,157	9,935	809	17,950	8,325	7,492	9,866	12,622	8,498	7,416	3,074	17,657	18,883

SOURCES: BBS (1991, 1993), Khalil (1989), IFDC, DAM, and Planning Commission of Ministry of Planning.

TABLE 3.3 SUR estimates of fertilizer consumption, fertilizer price, irrigated area, and rice production

	Model 1			Model 2		
Function	Coefficient	*t*-Statistic	R^2	Coefficient	*t*-Statistic	R^2
Fertilizer consumption (*FC*)			0.95			0.95
Intercept	−145.432	−0.351		−501.636	−1.224	
Fertilizer price (*PFR/PR*)	−162.551	−0.395		−133.460	−0.310	
Irrigated rice area (*AGR*)	0.435	9.223		0.410	8.873	
Other crop area (*NAR*)	−0.023	−0.823		0.007	0.241	
Short-term credit (*CDS/P*)	−26.383	−2.079		—	—	
Dummy (*D*)	−129.134	−0.782		−92.184	−0.545	
Retail fertilizer price (*PFR/PR*)			0.92			0.92
Intercept	−0.087	−2.158		−0.086	−2.111	
Factory-gate price (*PFD/PR*)	1.120	15.726		1.122	15.662	
HYV area (*HYV*)	0.000	0.805		0.000	0.765	
World price (*PFM/PR*)	0.125	2.493		0.123	2.379	
Dummy (*D*)	−0.001	−0.035		0.000	0.002	
Irrigated rice area (*AGR*)			0.87			0.87
Intercept	886.791	1.275		936.504	1.346	
Diesel price (*PD/PR*)	−760.518	−0.693		−829.307	−0.755	
Public expenditure (*EG/P*), lagged one year	509.050	3.264		524.341	3.363	
Long-term credit (*CDL/P*), lagged one year	79.241	1.251		66.641	1.059	
Dummy (*D*)	2,024.292	4.32		1,943.962	4.166	

(continued)

TABLE 3.3 *Continued*

	Model 1			Model 2		
Function	Coefficient	*t*-Statistic	R^2	Coefficient	*t*-Statistic	R^2
Dry-land rice area (*DAR*)			0.89			0.89
Intercept	22,840.000	22.221		22,869.000	22.198	
Irrigated rice area (*AGR*)	−0.626	−3.462		0.622	−3.440	
Rice price (*PR/PO*)	1,968.157	1.257		1,900.933	1.211	
Dummy (*D*)	−1,484.394	−2.369		−1,495.939	−2.386	
Rice production			0.95			0.95
Intercept	−1,903.471	−0.421		−1,916.240	−0.422	
Fertilizer (*FC*)	1.661	2.142		1.536	1.974	
Irrigated rice area (*AGR*)	0.993	2.881		1.039	3.003	
Dry-land rice area (*DAR*)	0.490	2.646		0.488	2.633	
Dummy (*D*)	553.040	0.978		556.235	0.983	

SOURCE: Author's estimations.

NOTE: R^2 relates to separate OLS estimation.

The results in Table 3.3 represent two models: one with a short-term credit variable (*CDS*) in the fertilizer consumption function, the other without this variable. Contrary to the hypotheses, the variable *CDS* produced a significantly negative coefficient. This perverse relation was puzzling, but it appears to be due to a failure to endogenize *CDS*. Short-term credit supply from public institutional sources is often driven by political concern about helping farmers in bad crop situations. Therefore, a negative correlation between fertilizer use and credit becomes germane in the time-series data. Endogenizing *CDS* was not possible because of inadequate data, so *CDS* was dropped to show whether the omission affected R^2 and coefficients of other variables of interest. As the comparison shows, the results are not substantially distorted. The fertilizer function demonstrates that irrigated rice area is the dominant influence in fertilizer consumption. The relative price of fertilizer has the right sign, but the coefficient is not significantly different from 0, implying that the price effect on demand falls within the margin of error. The coefficient of the dummy variable in the fertilizer consumption function is also not significant, implying that liberalizing the fertilizer market did not make any significant difference in consumption. This liberalization began much earlier than that of irrigation equipment and was completed by 1984/85. Any effect should have been fully realized within six to seven years. Accordingly, a separate regression treating 1975/76 through 1984/85 as the pre-liberalization period and 1985/86 through 1992/93 as a post-liberalization period yielded results that showed a modestly positive impact of liberalization: that is, the coefficient of the dummy was significant at the 10 percent level. The size of the dummy coefficient and that of the production coefficient implies that the liberalization of the fertilizer market contributed only 280,000 tons of rice. Squeezing the adjustment period further by one year (that is, taking data up to 1991/92) produced a significant coefficient of the dummy and a larger impact (350,000 tons) of liberalization. It may be possible to conclude that fertilizer market liberalization did not create any negative impact on rice production. Moreover, the positive impact that may have been realized during the late 1980s and early 1990s was of a small order of magnitude. This conclusion does not, however, deny the considerable budgetary savings that occurred due to liberalization of the fertilizer market.

The fertilizer price equation demonstrates that the supply-side factors, particularly the pricing policy at the factory gate (which is administratively determined) and world price levels, dictate the retail prices. This is not surprising. But given the present composition of various fertilizers, particularly of domestic versus import, a taka increase in factory-gate prices seems to raise the average retail price by taka 1.12. On the other hand, a world price increase of the same magnitude causes the average retail price to increase by taka 0.13. This reflects the small share of imports in the total fertilizer consumption rather than the extent of transmission of world price to retail levels. The dummy variable in the price equation is not, as expected, significant.

The equation with irrigated rice area (*AGR*) as an independent variable indicates that the price of diesel fuel relative to rice has the correct negative sign but is significant only at the 30 percent level, which is traditionally a case of not being significantly different from 0. The statistical significance improves substantially, however, when the regression is run with data up to 1992/93 and the breaking point for the dummy is 1984/85. This could reflect the fact that, during the 1990s, irrigation tubewells have been partly electrified; therefore, the price of diesel may be of lesser consequence. Interestingly, the coefficient of annual public expenditures on water development measures is significant in influencing the change in irrigated area. This is surprising because such public projects are generally considered to be ineffective, a perception that seems to be erroneous. The flood protection, drainage, and other activities may indeed create congenial conditions for the expansion of tubewell irrigation. Long-term credit (*CDL*) does appear to have a positive but weakly significant influence on irrigated rice area.

Perhaps the most important coefficient in this equation is that of the dummy variable. It is significant and positive, and the underlying effect of forces is large. Without liberalization of the market for agricultural equipment, deregulation, and the privatization of tubewell installations, the irrigated area could have been about 0.81 million hectares smaller than its size in 1996/97. As in the case of fertilizer, repeated estimations of parameters and shortening the time period indicate that most of the effects of liberalization, as proxied by the size and significance of the dummy variable, have been realized in the 1990s.

The equation on rainfed rice area yields some interesting results that were previously overlooked. Changes in the rainfed rice area are negatively influenced by irrigation and positively by price factors—the former influence being significant, the latter moderately so. An increase of 1 hectare of irrigated rice area decreases rainfed rice area by about 0.6 hectare. This is the direct effect of irrigation and supports the general perception that an increase in irrigated rice comes at the cost of local varieties of rainfed rice and other crops. Similarly, a higher rice price relative to other prices tends to increase hectares of rainfed rice. The indirect effect of irrigation, in addition to the direct and price effects, is especially interesting and is captured by the coefficient of the dummy variable, which is highly significant, has a negative sign, and is large. Even though market liberalization has directly contributed to increased irrigated area, it generated a large negative impact indirectly on the area of rainfed rice. What might the underlying forces for this effect be, which are independent of direct effects of irrigation and price factors? Initially, this result appeared to be a misleading correlation, but discussion with a few agronomists and knowledgeable persons corrected that perception. The rapid expansion of irrigation and HYV rice has forced farmers to change the crop rotation involving all crops. Because irrigated rice is of longer duration (about 120–140 days compared to

60–100 days in other crops) and because of labor constraints in the peak season, farmers generally make changes by cutting down on area of rainfed rice. Farmers often produce other short duration crops on the rainfed rice area that has been dropped from rotation. Further research on this subject would contribute to our understanding of Bangladesh's crop agriculture.

Finally, the production equation seems to be well behaved in all respects. The coefficients of all variables (except the dummy) are significant, of the right sign, and of appropriate magnitude. The coefficient of the dummy is not, as expected, statistically significant. This implies that the measure of the contribution of market liberalization is not distorted by effects of unusually good weather or similar extraneous forces. The coefficient values seem close to what is generally perceived as marginal contributions of factors. Thus, adding a unit of fertilizer generates an additional 1.7 units of rice. Similarly, adding an area equivalent to 0.40 hectare of irrigated rice area results in an additional ton of rice production, but the same increase in rainfed area yields only half a ton of rice.

Net Effect on Rice Production

The net impact of input market liberalization on rice production between 1976 and 1997 is shown in Table 3.4. The effects consist of two factors: irrigation and rainfed rice. The effect of fertilizer market liberalization is small (about 300,000 tons of rice) and realized mostly before 1992/93 and coming to a steady state at about that time.[7]

The gross effect of the liberalization of agricultural equipment markets appears to be large—about 2 million tons. But the indirect effect of expansion of irrigated rice on rainfed rice via the change in crop composition also appears to be large and negative. This effect of irrigation has been realized mostly during the 1990s. It was not possible to infer whether the effect had reached a steady state by 1996/97. The net effect of irrigation-related changes is about 1.3 million tons of rice, meaning that the rice production during the post-liberalization period would have been 1.3 million tons less had market reforms not been undertaken. Another way of expressing the result is to note its impact on the growth rate of rice production or the share of the net effect of total increase in production. Based on the comparison of estimated trend production levels in 1988/89 and 1996/97 (15.67 and 19.09 million tons), the annual average growth rate in production was 2.5 percent and the absolute amount of

7. The dummy variable captures the difference between the average levels of fertilizer use in post- and pre-liberalization periods. This difference seemed to peak positively in about 1992/93 and then fell back to pre-liberalization levels. It has, however, not become negatively significant. The steady state, therefore, means a steady state in reference to the pre-liberalization period. The fall in the significance of the dummy variable after 1992/93 may imply a negative impact of reversals in some liberalization measures, an exhaustion in the scope of incentives for fertilizer use originally created by the liberalization, or a mixed effect of both factors.

TABLE 3.4 Estimated contribution of liberalization to rice production, 1976–97

Significant Factors	Coefficient of Dummy Variable		Production Coefficient		Contribution (thousand metric tons)	
	Model 1	Model 2	Model 1	Model 2	Model 1	Model 2
Irrigated area (*AGR*)	2,024.29	1,943.92	0.993	1.039	2,010	2,020
Dry-land area (*DAR*)	–1,484.39	–1,495.94	1.490	0.498	–727	–730
Net contribution					1,283	1,290

SOURCE: Computed from Table 3.3.

NOTE: Model 1 includes short-term credit as an explanatory variable. Model 2 does not.

increase 3.42 million tons. The net effect of 1.3 million tons implies that the net effect is 38 percent of total incremental production and suggests that the growth rate would have been 0.9 percentage points lower without liberalization.

These conclusions warrant a few cautionary words lest the results are interpreted wrongly to suit various purposes. First, market reform is not a substitute for sustained growth in foodgrain production. For sustained growth the continual development of technology, institutions, and infrastructures (the shifter variables in the equations) is essential. Second, the focus of the impact measurement in the chapter was on rice production. The impact on income distribution and consumer welfare was not the focus, even though these are important. Third, the approach adopted is not comprehensive enough to include crops other than rice. The impact on other crops might augment or reduce the overall impact. For example, the reduction in rainfed rice area shown in the analysis might have caused an increase in areas of other crops so that the net gain in the crop sector might have been larger than that indicated by rice alone.

Finally, attributing success entirely to market liberalization would be shortsighted. While the measurement of the impact of liberalization warrants a distinction between pre- and post-reform periods, the government's role in the pre-liberalization period (creating fertilizer and irrigation markets and nurturing them to maturity) must not be underrated. The efforts of research and extension departments and the construction of rural infrastructure accumulated over time to build a foundation for growth in agricultural productivity. The impact of market liberalization could have been smaller or even negative without the cumulative effects of market development in the pre-liberalization period, as is observed in many developing countries, particularly in Africa.

Conclusions and Lessons

Although BADC contributed markedly to the infusion of modern inputs into Bangladesh's traditional agriculture, a competitive distribution system eventually became necessary for efficiency and effectiveness. Liberalization and privatization of input markets began gradually but have substantially influenced the growth of rice production; about 1.3 million tons of rice (about 38 percent of the trend incremental production between 1988/89 and 1996/97) may be credited to market liberalization. Without it the growth rate could have been 0.9 percent lower. This net effect, however, is mostly the result of irrigation-related development and the influence of irrigation on fertilizer use, which the liberalization process induced. The effect of fertilizer market liberalization was small (about 300,000 tons)—realized before 1992/93 and achieving a steady state at about that time.

Many developing countries are also attempting to liberalize their input markets. Therefore, lessons from Bangladesh may have international relevance, except perhaps for former Communist countries.

1. At first farmers are generally unfamiliar with modern inputs such as fertilizer, power-driven equipment, HYV seeds, and pesticides. Such markets do not exist and need to be created. This initial period of market failure is quite different from when modern inputs become reasonably well known and market size becomes adequate for a viable competition. The "one-size-fits-all" principle frequently pushed by donors can be harmful, as can wholesale condemnation of public parastatals such as BADC, whose role in the development of infant and missing markets is a remarkable success story.
2. Consider the evolution of the forces that drove public marketing out of circulation in Bangladesh. Donor conditionality was a powerful force but so were other compelling factors, such as budgetary burden and political will. The rapid removal of subsidies followed by privatization and liberalization of import restrictions demonstrates the government's eagerness to change its mode of agricultural development. But as the fertilizer crisis of 1994/95 has shown, unless the process of change is closely watched for problems, setbacks are likely to imperil reforms.
3. Sudden liberalization of markets (the shock therapy approach) and liberalization in phases (the gradual approach) have been much debated in both the literature and policy circles. Because one-shot approaches are rare, the sequencing of reform measures generally plays a strategic role in liberalization. If phasing is unavoidable, the question of how to sequence becomes relevant. One order is to introduce competitive trading in various layers of the marketing channel involving external trade: from grass-roots retailing, to wholesaling. Generally, the public sector gains efficiency as it withdraws from retail, to wholesale, to the apex; it loses efficiency as it moves in the reverse order. In contrast, the degree of competition in private trade generally diminishes as one moves from retail, to wholesale, to the apex. Thus, the best strategy of sequencing is to privatize the retail market first and then gradually move to the apex level—the sequence followed in Bangladesh (see McKinnon 1993).

   Another order might be gradual geographical coverage of markets by reform measures, as in the case of the privatization and price decontrol of fertilizers in Bangladesh. This sequence is generally chosen to avoid a risky failure at the beginning in the event that country-wide privatization and liberalization create turmoil or have unforeseen side effects that a weak administration cannot handle. If no side effects are observed, then reform measures can be extended to all regions. Such gradual coverage, however, should be considered only when the risk of failure is high and vested interests seem to be working against reform. When adopting this approach, reformers should begin with the region that has a relatively strong demand for the input in question.

4. Complementary support for the principal program of liberalization is almost always critical for success. Monitoring changes in supply, demand, prices, and emerging situations is essential. Without a well-considered support plan, the process often falters. In the case of fertilizer in Bangladesh, IFDC's monitoring role has been a profound factor in the success of liberalization.

References

Ahmed, R. 1978a. *Foodgrain production in Bangladesh: An analysis of growth, its sources, and related policies.* Dhaka: Bangladesh Agricultural Research Council; Washington, D.C.: International Food Policy Research Institute.

———. 1978b. Price support versus fertilizer subsidy for increasing rice production in Bangladesh. *Bangladesh Development Studies* 6 (Summer): 119–138.

———. 1987. Structure and dynamics of fertilizer subsidy: The case of Bangladesh. *Food Policy* 12 (February): 63–75

Alderman, H., and G. Shively. 1996. Economic reform and food prices: Evidence from markets in Ghana. *World Development* 24 (March): 521–534.

Asian Development Bank (ADB). 1990. Food crops development program loan (FDPL). Dhaka: Bangladesh Ministry of Agriculture. Mimeo.

Bangladesh Bureau of Statistics (BBS). 1991. *Statistical yearbook, 1990.* Dhaka: Bangladesh Bureau of Statistics.

———. 1993. *Monthly statistical bulletin.* Dhaka: Bangladesh Bureau of Statistics, April.

Bangladesh Establishment Division. 1992. *The Dhaka gazette.* Dhaka: Bangladesh Establishment Division, October.

Canadian Agency for International Development (CIDA). 1991. Agricultural sector study of Bangladesh. Report submitted to the Bangladesh Ministry of Agriculture, Dhaka. Mimeo.

Chowdhury, N. 1993. Credit relations and Bangladesh's rice market: Where sharing is the currency. Washington, D.C.: International Food Policy Research Institute. Report submitted to the U.S. Agency for International Development (USAID), Dhaka. Mimeo.

Devarajan, S., V. Swaroop, and H. Zou. 1996. The composition of public expenditure and economic growth. *Journal of Monetary Economics* 37 (April): 313–344.

Guisselquist, D. 1992. Empowering farmers in Bangladesh: Trade reforms open door to new technology. Paper presented at the annual conference of the Association for Economic Development Studies on Bangladesh, November 21–22, World Bank, Washington, D.C.

Harris, J., F. Schiantarelli, and M. G. Sireger. 1994. The effect of financial liberalization on the capital structure and investment decisions of Indonesian manufacturing establishments. *World Bank Economic Review* 8 (January): 17–47.

Hossain, M. 1988. *Nature and impact of the Green Revolution in Bangladesh.* Research Report 67. Washington, D.C.: International Food Policy Research Institute.

Infanger, C. L., A. Samad, and R. W. Hooker. 1988. *Final evaluation: Bangladesh fertilizer distribution project.* Dhaka: International Fertilizer Development Center.

International Food Policy Research Institute (IFPRI). 1985. *Report on fertilizer pricing policies in Bangladesh.* Washington, D.C.: International Food Policy Research Institute. Report submitted to the Bangladesh Ministry of Agriculture, Dhaka.

Khalil, M. 1989. *Agricultural statistics of Bangladesh.* Dhaka: U.S. Agency for International Development (USAID).

Khan, M. S. 1996. Government investment and economic growth in the developing world. *Pakistan Development Review* 35 (Winter, Part I): 419–439.

McKinnon, R. I. 1993. *The order of economic liberalization: Financial control in the transition to a market economy,* 2d ed. Baltimore: Johns Hopkins University Press.

Mill, T. C. 1990. *Time series techniques for economists.* Cambridge: Cambridge University Press.

Mitchell, D. 1998. Promoting growth in Bangladesh agriculture. Washington, D.C.: World Bank, Development Prospects Group, Development Economics, May 25. Mimeo.

Mudahar, M. S. 1984. *Fertilizer price deregulation and public policy: The case of Bangladesh.* Muscle Shoals, Ala., U.S.A.: International Fertilizer Development Center.

Osmani, S. R., and M. A. Quasem. 1985. Pricing and subsidy policies for Bangladesh agriculture. Dhaka: Bangladesh Institute of Development Studies. Mimeo.

Rashid, H. 1986. Irrigation development and policies for Bangladesh. Paper written for the United Nations Development Programme, Agricultural Sector Study, Dhaka. Informal seminar of the Association of Economic Development Studies of Bangladesh (AEDSB).

Renfroe, R. 1991. *Fertilizer price and subsidy policy in Bangladesh.* Dhaka: U.S. Agency for International Development (USAID).

Shepard, R. W. 1970. *Theory of cost and production functions.* Princeton, N.J., U.S.A.: Princeton University Press.

Sidhu, S. S. 1992. Development of competitive free market structure for fertilizers in Bangladesh: IFDC experience. Muscle Shoals, Ala., U.S.A.: International Fertilizer Development Center. Mimeo.

Stone, B., ed. 1987. *Fertilizer pricing policies in Bangladesh.* Occasional Paper. Washington, D.C.: International Food Policy Research Institute.

World Bank, Agricultural Operations Division. 1992. Project identification report. Washington, D.C.: World Bank, Rural Trade Credit Project, Agricultural Operations Division. Mimeo.

4 Evolving Rice and Wheat Markets

NUIMUDDIN CHOWDHURY AND STEVEN HAGGBLADE

Bangladesh's Green Revolution in foodgrain production has triggered a marketing revolution of far greater proportions. While production has doubled since the 1960s, marketings (the proportion of harvest a farmer sells) have increased by a factor of six. Yet rice and wheat markets remain different in scale, structure, and performance.

Historically, the performance and conduct of private marketing agents have been central to the case for direct public control of foodgrain marketing. During the great famines of 1943 and 1974, widespread concern about market malfunction and trader misconduct motivated the introduction of broad public marketing controls as well as large-scale direct public marketing of foodgrains (see Chapters 6, 7, and 11). Consequently, any major shifts in market structure or behavior will alter the fundamental premises on which large-scale public intervention was founded. To set the stage for later discussion of evolving public policy (in Chapters 6, 7, 8, 10, and 11), this chapter traces the broad changes occurring in the structure, conduct, and performance of Bangladesh's rice and wheat markets.

Rice Markets

Growing Scale

Since the 1960s, rice marketing has grown far faster than production has. Driven by high-yielding varieties (HYVs), irrigation equipment, and fertilizer, rice production has doubled. But over the same period farmers' marketed share of production has jumped from 10 to 14 percent to nearly 50 percent in the 1990s (Table 4.1).

Marketed share has increased so greatly for a variety of reasons. On the supply side, growing crop intensity and overall yield rates have substantially increased the number of farmers with surplus. New HYV rice packages yield more than traditional varieties by roughly a factor of two (Hossain et al. 1990). For example, 20 years ago a farmer growing only a local-variety aman crop

TABLE 4.1 Broad changes in Bangladeshi rice markets

Variable	1960s	1970s	1980s	1990s
Production				
Total (million metric tons)	10	12	15	18
Boro share	7%	18%	26%	38%
HYV share	1%	23%	36%	63%
Marketings				
As share of production	12%	27%	34%	49%
Total marketed (million metric tons)	1	3	5	9
Marketings per capita (kilograms)	20	41	51	76
Distribution				
Public share of rice marketed	30%	15%	11%	7%
Share marketed in the three largest urban centers	na	40%	na	20%
Share sold on the farm to itinerant traders	28%	na	na	66%
Number of marketing agents				
Itinerant traders	4,000	na	na	48,000
Millers				
Automatic	0	3	66	88
Major	106	152	251	480
Small huller	6,049	11,437	43,374	50,300
Total	6,155	11,592	43,691	50,868
Private rice stocks				
Number of months consumption requirements	1	na	na	3
Average storage time for trader stocks (months)	4	na	na	1

SOURCES: Production figures from BBS, computed as decennial averages through 1997/98. Marketed share from Raquibuzzaman (1968), Farruk (1972), BBS (1969) (1960s); Dey (1988), DAM (1974), Ahmed (1979) (1970s); Dey (1988), Islam et al. (1985), Ahmed and Hossain (1990) (1980s); Chowdhury (1992) (1990s). Public distribution shares computed from MOI statistics. All others from Ahmed (1979) and Chowdhury (1992).

NOTE: na indicates not available.

required 0.49 hectare to feed a family of six. Today, however, with HYV boro and the same transplanted aman a similar family can satisfy its foodgrain needs with only 0.16 hectare of land. Given widespread HYV adoption by farms of all sizes, a large proportion of even marginal farms (those owning up to 0.2 hectare of land) have now become net sellers of paddy in good harvest years (Chowdhury 1994).[1] Even deficit farmers now market some rice, particularly

1. Adoption rates range from 60 percent for marginal farms (0.5 acres or less) to 75 percent

in the boro season, when the keeping qualities of HYVs make them difficult to store.

In fact, the poorer keeping quality of HYV paddy accentuates the inclination of all farmers to sell at least some of their output. Because most HYV paddy retains more moisture than do local varieties at harvest time, it stores poorly in comparison. The advent of a large boro season harvest compounds the storage problem because farmers harvest boro rice in May and June, just at the onset of the monsoon season, when humidity is high and open-air drying difficult. Although aman paddy, harvested at the beginning of the dry season, will last several years in on-farm storage, farmers must dispose of their boro paddy over the course of a single four-month marketing season. For this reason, they market only one-third of their aman crop but fully two-thirds of their boro (Chowdhury 1992).

The rise of a major boro rice crop has also radically altered patterns of price seasonality. During the 1960s a single deep price trough following the principal aman harvest gave way to a gradual seven-month price rise and sustained high peak before the subsequent aus and aman harvests. But by the 1990s the emergence of a large dry-season boro crop had shifted the timing of price peaks, introduced a second peak, dampened the price trough, and shortened the trough-to-peak time spread to about four months (Figure 4.1).

The demand side of the rice market has likewise contributed to a higher share of marketings in total consumption. Structural changes in the Bangladeshi economy—in particular, growing nonfarm income and rapidly advancing urbanization—contribute to a growing share of nonproducers who necessarily become net purchasers of rice and other foods.

The ability of private markets to supply this growing urban and nonfarm demand has been facilitated by two decades of public investment in rural infrastructure. Since independence, Bangladesh's network of rural roads has expanded at a rate of 14 percent per year, rural electrification has grown just as rapidly, phone lines have increased by 9 percent per year, and water transport has grown at an annual rate of 5 percent. This expansion has made it possible to process and transport growing volumes of rice quickly and at lower cost. As a result, public investments in rural infrastructure have facilitated the emergence of a rice market of national scope and enhanced rice's attractiveness as a cash crop.

Changing Market Structure

PADDY TRADE. To handle these increasing volumes, rice and paddy markets have attracted a growing body of traders and millers (Table 4.1). The

---

for large farms (those cultivating more than five acres). But smaller farms adopt HYVs more intensively, allocating 54 percent of cultivated area to modern varieties compared with 35 percent by large farms (Hossain et al. 1990). After good aman and boro harvests during the 1989/90 crop year, an estimated 70 percent of all farms were net sellers of rice (Chowdhury 1992).

FIGURE 4.1 Changes in rice price seasonality (price over 12-month moving average)

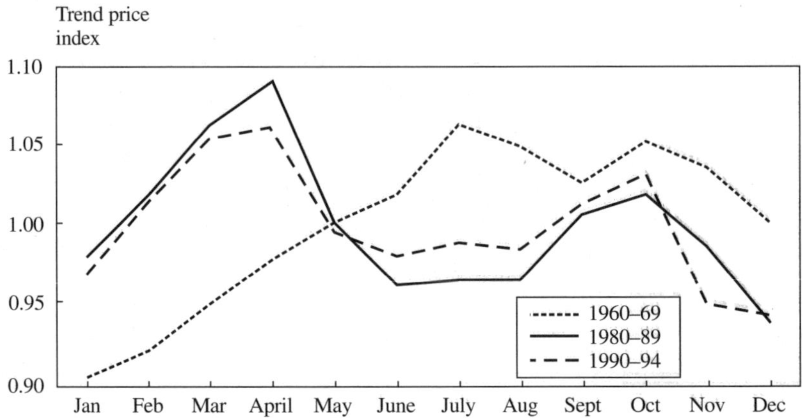

SOURCE: Monthly price data from DAM.

first link in the marketing chain, itinerant paddy traders (*bepari* and *faria*), has swelled in number by a factor of 12 to 15 since 1973 (Chowdhury 1992; see Figure 4.2). This increased competition enables farmers to sell more than two-thirds of their marketings at farm gate rather than in nearby markets (Table 4.2). In contrast, 30 years ago they sold only 28 percent from their farms (Ahmed 1979). Currently, farmers of all size holdings prefer selling from the homestead, where they receive similar prices regardless of their size (Table 4.2, Figures 4.3a and b).

Over time expanded marketing options accompany the widespread adoption of HYVs. As a result, access to itinerant paddy *bepari* proves more prevalent in progressive districts, where 68 percent of small and marginal farms sell from the farm gate compared with only 46 percent in nonprogressive areas (Table 4.2).[2]

RICE MILLING. Parboiling of rice, which accounts for more than 90 percent of total production, takes place in a growing array of small and large mills.[3] About 20,000 small, full-service rice mills process the bulk of marketed paddy—close to 50 percent in 1990 (Figure 4.2). The typical small rice mill employs 10 to 15 workers, who first parboil the paddy in simple oil-drum steam units, then spread it to dry on open-air floors. After drying they transfer the parboiled paddy by hand to Engleberg friction dehullers with a capacity of

2. These data come from Chowdhury (1992), who defines progressive districts as those with surplus per capita foodgrain production or high use of modern agricultural inputs.

3. Among Bangladeshis only Chittagonians and Sylhetis prefer nonparboiled rice.

FIGURE 4.2 Rice marketing sector map, 1990

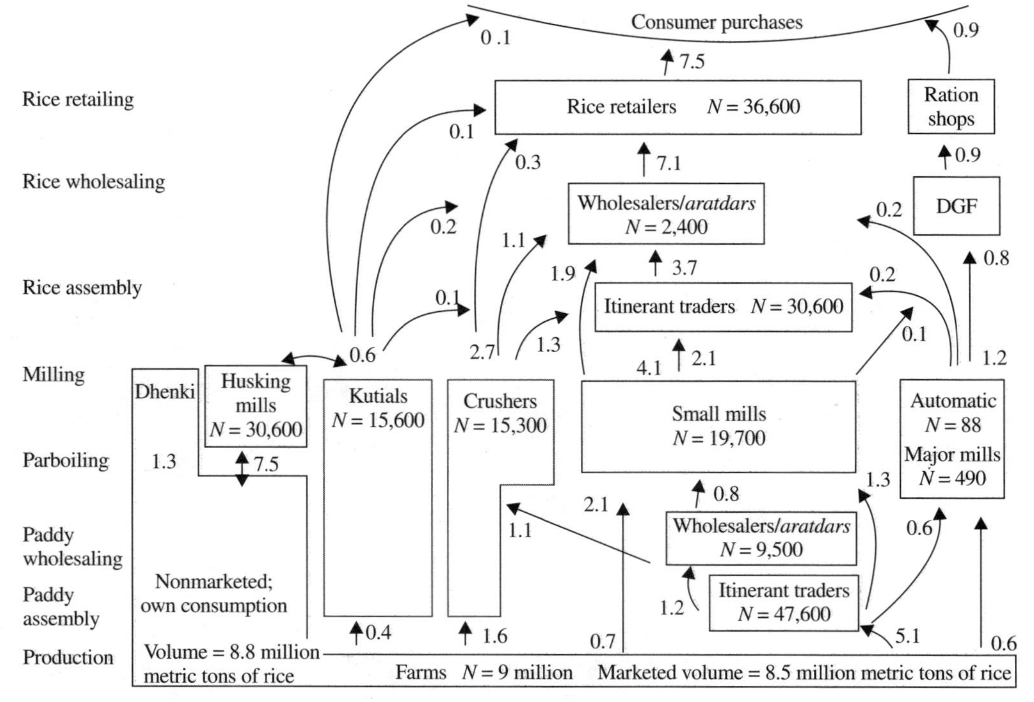

SOURCE: Based on FPMU/IFPRI (1992).

NOTE: Figures for volume of rice are in million metric tons.

TABLE 4.2 Rice marketing by farm size, 1989/90

	Progressive Districts	Nonprogressive Districts	Progressive/ Nonprogressive
Marketings (tons per farm per year)			
Small farms	7.2	3.7	1.9
Medium farms	4.3	3.5	1.2
Large farms	11.7	7.1	1.7
Quantity sold from home (tons per farm per year)			
Small farms	4.9	1.7	2.9
Medium farms	2.9	2.1	1.4
Large farms	7.5	4.3	1.8
Share of marketings sold from home (percent)			
Small farms	68	46	1.5
Medium farms	68	61	1.1
Large farms	64	60	1.1
Price received at home for coarse rice (taka per kilogram)			
Small farms	5.8	5.9	1.0
Medium farms	5.7	5.7	1.0
Large farms	5.8	5.8	1.0
Home price/market price			
Small farms	0.97	0.97	1.0
Medium farms	0.99	0.98	1.0
Large farms	0.99	0.98	1.0

SOURCE: Chowdhury (1992).

NOTES: Small farms = 0.5 to 2.49 acres.
Medium farms = 2.5 to 4.9 acres.
Large farms = 5.0 acres or more.
Progressive districts have a surplus per capita cereal production and use a high proportion of modern agricultural inputs. Nonprogressive districts are all others.

about 0.6 metric tons per hour.[4] The venerable Engleberg dehullers, developed at the turn of the twentieth century by a German railway engineer, remove the husk and polish the rice, all in one unit.[5]

Similar in scale and technology are Bangladesh's 30,000 husking mills, which furnish a second major source of milling capacity. Using the same 0.6-ton-per-hour Engleberg dehullers as the small full-service mills, the husking mills have no parboiling units or drying yards. Instead, they run purely custom milling operations for households and for two groups of paddy entrepreneurs without their own milling equipment: the *kutials* (home-based) and crushers (itinerant paddy entrepreneurs). With the advent of inexpensive small diesel

4. All further references to tons indicate metric tons.

5. See Rahman (1988) and Ahmed (1988) for detailed technical descriptions of alternative rice milling technologies currently in use in Bangladesh.

FIGURE 4.3a Quantity marketed by farm size (aman HYV paddy), 1993/94

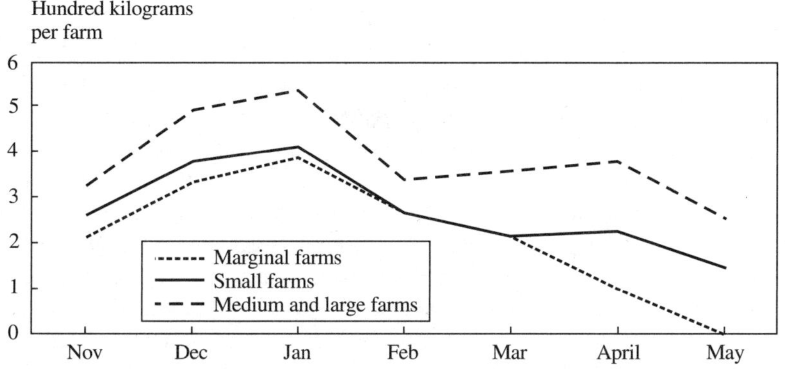

SOURCE: IFDC (1994).

FIGURE 4.3b Average price received (aman HYV paddy), 1993/94

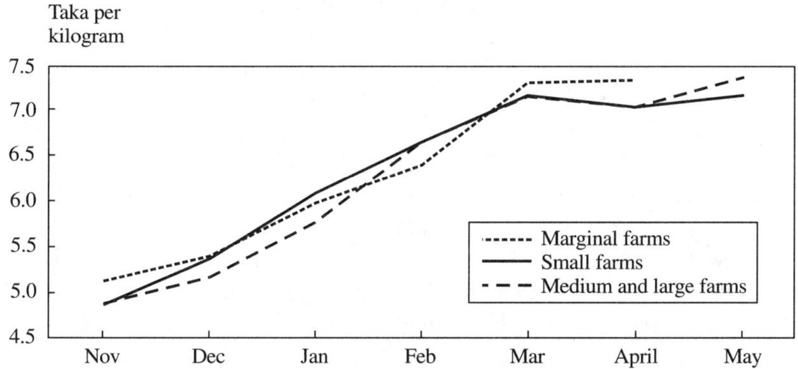

SOURCE: IFDC (1994).

engines in rural areas, particularly since the import liberalization of the input markets (see Chapter 3), the husking mills have largely supplanted the traditional foot-powered dehullers known as *dhenkis*. Today, *dhenkis* dehull only about 8 percent of total paddy production and virtually none of the marketed share (Chowdhury 1992).

At the other extreme, representing the pinnacle of modern technology in the Bangladesh rice market, nearly 90 large-scale automatic mills emerged during the 1980s, integrating steam-pressure parboiling, mechanical forced-air dryers, rubber roller shellers, and polishing machines in a single conveyer-driven, flow-through facility (Ahmed 1988). Financed largely through donor grants, the automatic rice mills can operate at a capacity of about 2 tons per hour (Rahman 1988).

Filling out the lineup of milling establishments are Bangladesh's nearly 500 major rice mills. Veterans of the rice trade, about 100 of them, have operated since Bangladesh was known as East Pakistan, while roughly 400 newcomers have set up operation since independence. With a capacity of 1 ton per hour, they integrate steam-boiler parboiling units, large open-air drying yards, and hand transfer to dehuller units. Unlike the automatics, which use rubber roller shellers followed by polishing machines, the major rice mills (like all the small and husking mills) operate abrasion-based Engleberg dehullers. But unlike the smaller mills, major mills typically operate a series of hullers with progressively finer milling clearances. By transferring the paddy though this sequence of dehullers, the major mills dehusk and then polish more gradually than do the small mills, thus improving milling recovery, reducing broken grains, and improving product quality. Employing about 25 workers each, the major mills today process about 3 percent of Bangladesh's paddy.

Overall, the newer and smaller units—the small, full-service rice mills, the husking mills, and the crushers—dominate Bangladesh's now-mechanized paddy processing. Veritable icons of the emerging rice markets, these small millers and itinerant entrepreneurs have grown most rapidly of all the milling classes. Currently, they process about 85 percent of Bangladesh's paddy. Invariably with small capitalization, these agents have no option but to compete vigorously on price and delivery—one of the keys to the competitive health of this market. Progress in the development of processing capacity has been impressive, yet the system lacks sophistication in the processing generally needed for trade in international markets.

RICE WHOLESALING. Large rice wholesalers and *aratdars,* widely reviled during the famines of 1943 and 1974 for alleged market manipulation and hoarding, have likewise grown in number.[6] The Badamtoli rice market in Dhaka, the largest in Bangladesh, opened with only four wholesalers in 1968. It now houses more than 300. Meanwhile, rival markets have sprung up in Mohamadpur, Savar, and other surrounding areas.

The dominance of these terminal market wholesalers has likewise eroded with the shifting pattern of regional flows. During the 1950s and 1960s long-distance paddy shipments—mostly from Dinajpur, Barisal, and the *haor* areas in Mymensingh and Sylhet to Dhaka and nearby Narayanganj—dominated interdistrict flows.[7] But during the 1970s and 1980s an evolving patchwork of

6. *Aratdar* translates most directly as "commission agent." Today, because of historic government restrictions on individual stockholding, many large wholesalers find it convenient to describe themselves as mere commission agents holding other traders' stocks. Although *aratdars* do sell stocks on commission for others, they also buy and sell on their own account as any large-scale wholesaler would.

7. *Haor* are low-lying swampy areas.

HYV adoption across Bangladesh led to a shifting sequence of surplus zones and a welter of cross-district movements (Goletti 1993a; Chowdhury 1992). Once, major urban centers such as Dhaka, Chittagong, and Khulna accounted for about 40 percent of marketings in the 1970s; now they account for only 20 percent (Chowdhury 1992). As a result, the bulk of Bangladesh's rice trade has become geographically decentralized.

Because Bangladesh grows more than 500 varieties of paddy, rice grading, varietal classification, and quality control demand considerable attention from traders. Yet no generally agreed-on quality standards exist in the rice and paddy trade other than the directorate general of food's (DGF) single, longstanding grade, Fair Average Quality (FAQ), the single standard applied in government procurement.[8] In the absence of a broader system of clearly accepted grades and standards, 90 percent of all sales take place by visual inspection in both paddy and rice markets. This inspection warrants labor input and travel from retail to wholesale or assembly centers. Costs involved in this process could be reduced by the introduction of objective standards and grades to replace the prevailing subjective procedure of grading in reference to FAQ.

DIRECTORATE GENERAL OF FOOD. The DGF rounds out the roster of the major players in Bangladeshi rice markets. Historically, the scale of its direct purchasing in rice markets has ebbed and flowed. During two periods, the mid-1960s and the late 1980s to the early 1990s, the DGF traded intensively in rice and paddy markets, primarily in an effort to support farm prices (see Chapter 6). But given high fiscal costs and difficulties in managing subsequent stock disposal, the directorate has pulled back once again. Thus, the government's share in marketed surplus has varied from highs of 30 percent in the mid-1960s to about 7 percent in the first half of the 1990s (Table 4.1). By 1998 that share had fallen closer to 5 percent of total marketings.

As government procurement has diminished, so has its share of domestic rice stocks. Derivatives of large procurement programs, government rice stocks have dwindled in the mid-1990s after peaking at slightly more than 800,000 tons in 1990. By 1998 year-end government rice stocks stood at about 400,000 tons.

This reduction in public stocks, coupled with gradually rising private holdings, has led to a growing reliance on privately held rice and paddy stocks. Since the Great Bengal Famine of 1943, government antihoarding laws have restricted private stockholding of foodgrains. As recently as December 1989, these laws made it illegal for traders or other private citizens to hold more than 750 kilograms of rice. But in the early-1990s a succession of good harvests and an obviously growing private trade led to relaxed law enforcement, although

8. In 1992 the DGF began to introduce a series of multiple grades in connection with rice-tendering procedures. But as government procurement dwindled, so did efforts to standardize a broader range of rice grades.

TABLE 4.3 Key holders of foodgrain stocks, 1990–93

Foodgrain	Private Stocks			Public		
	Farm	Trade	Total	Stocks	Total Stocks	
	(percent)			(percent)	(percent)	(million metric tons)
Rice						
Lean season	59	20	79	21	100	2.67
Post-aman harvest	68	25	93	7	100	7.79
Post-boro harvest	64	26	90	10	100	6.09
Wheat						
Lean season	13	7	20	80	100	0.75
Post-aman harvest	0	15	16	84	100	0.69
Post-boro harvest	26	7	34	66	100	0.75
Total foodgrains						
Lean season	49	17	66	34	100	3.42
Post-aman harvest	63	24	87	13	100	8.48
Post-boro harvest	60	24	84	16	100	6.84

SOURCES: Ahsan et al. (1994), Chowdhury (1993a).

NOTE: Lean season figures average October 31 carryout stocks for 1989–93. Post-aman harvest figures average January 31 carryout stocks for 1990–93. Post-boro harvest stocks average June 30 figures for 1990 and 1993.

not outright repeal (see Chapter 7). As production and trader confidence in nonconfiscation have grown, so have private foodgrain stocks. Private rice and paddy stocks per capita have roughly doubled since the late 1960s (Chowdhury 1992). Perhaps most striking is the dominance of on-farm stocks, which throughout the year systematically account for more than three-fourths of all private stocks. Although they have varied considerably over time, public rice stocks averaged 10 percent of midyear, economy-wide rice stocks during the early 1990s. In the lean season, just before the aman harvest, private rice stocks typically exceed those held in government storage by about a factor of four (Table 4.3).

Conduct

GOVERNMENT. Since at least World War II, governments in Bangladesh have regarded rice traders with distrust. Long memories and stiff regulations on foodgrain movement and stockholding have only slowly and gradually softened (Chapter 7). Given its historic penchant for limiting and regulating private sector foodgrain trade as well as its periodic large-scale forays into rice and paddy markets, the government's stock levels and conduct remain closely watched determinants of other participants' behavior.

Among rice traders the level of government rice stocks has been a topic of constant interest and concern, for government has proven an unpredictable player in the markets. Recent econometric estimates quantify what traders suggest—that public rice stocks crowd out private trader stocks, although they do not affect on-farm holdings. Chowdhury (1993b) estimates that a 100-ton increase in public rice stocks will reduce private trade stocks by about 83 tons. This estimate must be considered as tentative, however, given several limitations affecting the analysis.[9]

PRIVATE TRADE STOCKS. Partly because of the fluctuating presence of government in the market and partly because of the more even flow of paddy onto the market throughout the year, private traders no longer hold long-term, year-to-year carryover stocks.[10] Instead, they now engage primarily in spatial rather than temporal arbitrage (Chowdhury 1992). Unlike the 1960s, when traders kept stocks four months on average (Farruk 1972), they now retain stocks only one month on average (Chowdhury 1992).

COLLUSION? Do rice traders collude? Certainly popular wisdom suggests that they do—or at least that they once did. In the 1960s and 1970s, when a handful of *aratdars* dominated key urban markets, which in turn served as final destinations for most marketed surplus, this may have been possible.[11] Indeed, evidence suggests that even today, in remote or inaccessible areas, small numbers of traders may collude to extract low prices from vulnerable marginal farmers (Crow and Murshid 1993). Overall, however, collusion seems much less likely given the rapid growth in rural infrastructure (particularly roads and telephones), greatly increased numbers of traders at all levels, and a clear deconcentration of marketing flows. Most students of Bangladeshi rice markets now conclude that rice traders compete rather than collude (Islam et al. 1985; Chowdhury 1992). Even skeptics note that in less-developed areas the arrival of Green Revolution technologies and improved rural infrastructure have broken collusive monopolies and improved competition (Crow and Murshid 1990, 1993).

Traders certainly organize, however, and collectively lobby to protect their interests. The Badamtoli rice *aratdars* have formed a trade association, as have the automatic mill owners. Even the more numerous small mills organize

9. Data constraints limit our ability to generalize about the relationship between public and private stocks. First, the analysis was based on data for 12 months in 1989/90, when production was very good. Whether the results would adequately capture the behavior of traders in dissimilar years is an open question. Second, given the short data series available, the estimate must be considered primarily a reflection of a short-run relation. In spite of these unavoidable shortcomings, the effort is a pioneering one. Replication of similar studies, covering a wide spectrum of conditions, could shed light on the relation between public and private stocks.

10. Many observers now refer to the blurring together of boro and HYV aus crops as the "braus" season, which effectively extends rice harvesting from May through August.

11. An early study by Farruk (1972) notes instances of high concentration, with as much as "75–80 percent of supplies controlled by small groups of aratdars." Although he indicates this could "undercut the elements of competition," he finds "no solid evidence of collusive behavior" (37).

lobbying groups when they perceive a need. During 1992 and 1993, when the government simultaneously reduced rice procurement and began to experiment with procurement through tenders, many regional millers organized to launch newspaper campaigns, blockade roads, and otherwise voice strong preference for renewed large-scale government procurement through the mills (*Morning Sun,* November 1 and 4, 1992; *Daily Ittefaq,* November 17, 1992).

TIED CREDIT. Recently, researchers have argued that large rice traders and millers control markets subtly through onerous trade credit to *bepari* and preharvest lending to small farmers (Crow 1989; Crow and Murshid 1990, 1993). Apparent competition among itinerant traders, they suggest, may really mask a dance of marionettes all controlled upstream by a handful of large *aratdars.*

Implicit in this argument is the belief that most of the credit in the rice economy is largely one way, top down. Chowdhury's comprehensive studies (1992, 1994) of rice markets during 1989/90 sheds light on this important question. He is able to bring together receivables and payables on a comprehensive basis to and from all destinations and document which proportion of the traders disbursed and received credit during the same interval. Further, he is able to enlarge the analysis from sample to population estimates. Like the two other major rice marketing studies that preceded his (Farruk 1972; Islam et al. 1985), Chowdhury finds that virtually all traders, large and small, receive credit. More important, he finds that most also disburse credit. In fact, the largest issuers of trade credit are also the largest recipients (Table 4.4). Note that the rice wholesalers and *aratdars* offer taka 1.7 billion in net trade credit while suppliers, the lowly rice *bepari,* offer nearly as much (taka 1.1 billion) in return.

What does the mutual lending and borrowing among traders suggest about market competition? Why do they do so, and how does it affect competition in the rice market? In all businesses, information, access to capital, and insurance against risk play important roles in determining the extent of profit. Without any institutional source of cheap and easy information about a supplier's ability to supply in time, the reliability of trading partners, or quality of grains and with poor and costly facilities for enforcing contracts, traders develop a personal equation of trust among themselves (Fafchamps and Minten 1998). Such personal trust also lends itself to helping each other with short-term credit in a situation of fluctuating liquidity and difficult and costly access to institutional credit. Whether these personal relations are exploitative in any direction cannot be ascertained without knowing the extent of such transaction costs and the benefits players derive from these relations. But if the numbers of players are large and options are many, as seems to be the case in the Bangladeshi rice market, the chances of exploitative relations are small. Nevertheless, these personal relations reflect a barrier to entry. Competition in rice marketing would be more impersonal and stronger with the institutional

TABLE 4.4 Trade credit among rice and paddy traders, 1989/90 (billion taka)

	Trade Credit					
			Net Disbursement			
Trader Type	Disbursed	Received	Billion Taka	Percent	Other Credit Received[a]	Total Credit Received
Paddy traders						
Itinerant	729	592	137	2.3	384	976
Wholesalers	2,534	642	1,893	32.3	546	1,188
Millers						
Automatics	22	9	13	0.2	112	120
Major	38	29	8	0.1	212	241
Small	1,527	782	746	12.7	2,261	3,043
Kutials	132	32	100	1.7	27	58
Crushers	570	412	158	2.7	283	695
Rice traders						
Itinerant *bepari*	1,624	556	1,068	18.2	634	1,190
Wholesalers and *aratdars*	2,291	565	1,727	29.5	312	877
Retailers	160	149	11	0.2	101	249
Total	9,626	3,765	5,861	100.0	4,487	7,660

SOURCE: Chowdhury (1994).

[a]Other sources of credit include banks, the government, and noninstitutional lenders.

provision of information on traders and trading and with easier access to institutional credit.

Farm credit remains much larger in absolute size, accounting for about taka 190 billion in 1989/90 compared with taka 9 billion in trade credit (Chowdhury 1992; Table 4.5). Preharvest lending, to be repaid at harvest time at a fixed and usually below-market price, has caused the most concern. Known as *dhaner upore* (DU), this form of lending accounts for about 9 percent of total farm credit and is used by about 4 percent of total farms. It is most common among marginal and small farmers, 9 percent of whom contracted DU loans during the study year (Table 4.5). Unlike farmers with medium-sized and large holdings, the marginal and small cultivators depend heavily on these loans, which account for more than one-third of their total borrowing. DU lending likewise proves more prevalent in remote, low HYV adopter districts and less common in progressive districts. Conditions improve considerably in the progressive districts, where both volume and duration of informal borrowing falls, as do interest rate charges (Table 4.5). Noting similar differences, Crow and Murshid (1990) find that lending flows actually reverse direction: while merchants lend to farmers in the backward areas, prosperous farmers finance merchants in the progressive zones.

For small traders and farmers, credit conditions improve considerably with the advent of improved roads, telephones, irrigation, and HYV foodgrain technologies that bring increased output and market competition to formerly isolated regions (Chowdhury 1992; Crow and Murshid 1990, 1993). Therefore, as HYV use and rural infrastructure continue to spread, the prevalence of preharvest lending to farmers (*dhaner upore*) and tied trade credit (*dadon*) should dissipate. In a rare confluence of thinking, both the radical and neoclassical students of rice markets agree: improving rural infrastructure and access to HYV technology will benefit the often vulnerable marginal farmers.

Performance

The marketing margin, one common indicator of competitiveness and economic efficiency, was estimated to be 21 percent of the retail price of coarse rice in 1989/90 (Chowdhury 1992). Farruk (1972) found the margin to be 26 percent in 1969/70. For 1983/84 Islam et al. (1985) report a margin ranging from 23 to 26 percent. These historical findings have to be compared carefully before one can draw conclusions about the trend of the marketing margin. Comparison of margins must be based on comparable marketing channels in terms of distance and the nature of routes to be used as an indicator of change in competitiveness. Farruk's estimate is basically a regional estimate (Barisal and Nymensingh) where average distance involved was roughly 50 kilometers. Islam et al. base their estimate on country-wide marketing activities with an average distance marketed of 90 kilometers. Chowdhury's estimate represents a country-wide sample with a focus on recently emerging markets. His market-

TABLE 4.5 Farm credit, 1989/90

Credit	Land Ownership Size				District	
	Marginal	Small	Medium	Large	Progressive	Nonprogressive
Source of credit (percent of farms borrowing)						
Dhaner upore	7	9	4	2	3	7
Banks	3	15	12	17	10	22
Informal	7	18	21	17	16	23
Average borrowing (thousand taka)						
Dhaner upore	22	5	10	6	5	9
Banks	2	4	5	10	5	9
Informal	3	4	4	8	6	4
Total	27	14	19	24	16	22
Share of borrowed volume (percent)[a]						
Dhaner upore	84	27	22	4	9	18
Banks	4	31	34	53	32	53
Informal	11	42	44	44	59	29
Total	100	100	100	100	100	100
Duration (weeks)						
Dhaner upore	6	7	7	5	5	8
Banks	4	4	4	5	4	5
Informal	na	na	na	na	na	na
Average	5	5	6	5	4	7
Monthly interest rate (percent)						
Dhaner upore	33	20	28	46	29	33
Banks	16	16	18	16	18	16
Informal	120	19	15	19	11	29
Weighted average	43	18	19	19	15	23

SOURCE: Chowdhury (1992).

NOTES: Marginal farms have fewer than 0.5 acres. See Table 4.2 for definitions of other farm sizes and of progressive and nonprogressive districts. na indicates not available.

[a]Totals may not be precise owing to rounding.

ing margin estimate is based on an average distance of 140 kilometers. Making these historical estimates precisely comparable is a daunting task. Nevertheless, approximate standardization for distance marketed provides a sense that the marketing margin may have fallen over the past two decades.

Most studies of rice and paddy markets find profit margins per unit of capital high, undoubtedly one reason for rapid entry into the trade (Farruk 1972; Islam et al. 1985; Chowdhury 1992). Chowdhury's recent assessment concludes that on average profit margins are "high but not excessive" (Chowdhury 1992:87).

The spatial integration of markets has attracted much attention to studies on rice, perhaps because the availability of secondary price data makes such analysis relatively inexpensive to carry out. All such studies agree that some price transmission does occur between Dhaka and other major rice markets; that is, they conclude that markets are not totally segmented. Yet most find only partial integration, particularly in the rainy season. Early studies conclude that only about 20 percent of major markets are well integrated with Dhaka (Ravallion 1987; Ahmed and Bernard 1989). A more recent examination (Goletti 1993a) suggests that figure may have risen to between 35 and 50 percent. He also notes that improved infrastructure, particularly roads, improves integration.

How efficiently do traders process available market information? In an early landmark study, Ravallion (1987) concluded that incorrect trader expectations of future prices led to excessive stockholding (popularly known as hoarding) during the 1974 famine. He also found that such informational inefficiency continued through 1983/84. More recent evidence, however, suggests improvement. Using an extended data set, Goletti (1993a) concurs that markets processed information inefficiently during the 1974 famine but finds that since 1975 they have become more information-efficient.

The bottom line? The two most recent major studies of Bangladeshi rice markets both rate them as vigorously competitive. Evaluating the early 1980s, Islam et al. (1985:12) report "intense competition" among traders. And during the early 1990s Chowdhury (1992:89) concludes that "mostly, in the study year, rice agents behave like competitive profit-makers, not profiteers." Over time, low barriers to entry have contributed to growing competition in rice and paddy markets (Ravallion 1987; Chowdhury 1992). Even the most prominent skeptics, Crow and Murshid (1990, 1993), admit that growing access to HYVs and improved infrastructure lead to increased competition, less tied credit, and more favorable prices for farmers and consumers. Given rapid growth in all these parameters (HYV area has grown at a rate of 8.5 percent per year since the 1970s, irrigated area at 10 percent, telephones at 9 percent, rural roads at 14 percent, water transport at 5 percent), competitiveness can only have increased.

Although Bangladesh's rice markets have grown rapidly since the 1960s, some regions remain stagnant and geographically isolated, particularly in the rainy season. It is also likely that markets in these underdeveloped areas become more volatile during periods of scarcity and bad crop years. In addition, extractive, exploitative credit and trade practices do exist in these regions. But these examples appear to be quantitatively small and diminishing over time with the rapid growth in HYV adoption, rural infrastructure, and numbers of marketing agents. Overall, a picture of robust growth emerges, with increasingly competitive rice and paddy markets. This conclusion does not argue for complacency, of course, but for the aggressive continuation of the policies that have led to these favorable trends: access to HYVs, modern inputs, alternative credit, rural roads, telephones, and other rural infrastructure.

Wheat Markets

Consumption

Historically an inferior good in the rice-based Bengali diet, wheat consumption has taken root in Bangladesh, particularly in urban areas. Growing from next to nothing in the 1950s to about 2 million tons in the 1990s, wheat now accounts for nearly 15 percent of total foodgrain consumption (Table 4.6). Growth in consumption was driven in the 1950s, 1960s, and 1970s by food aid imports of wheat and its subsequent distribution in urban areas, often at subsidized prices (see Chapters 8 and 9).

The resulting change in consumer preferences has been reflected in gradually changing demand elasticities for wheat (see Chapter 5). While income elasticities of demand remained consistently negative throughout the 1970s in both urban and rural areas, estimates from the late 1980s indicate that demand

TABLE 4.6 Broad changes in wheat markets

Variable	1960s	1970s	1980s	1990s
Availability				
Total (thousand metric tons per year)	492	1,443	2,504	2,365
Per capita (kilograms per year)	8	19	26	20
Source (percent)				
Public imports	92	88	61	46
Private imports	0	0	0	7
Domestic production	8	12	39	47
Total	100	100	100	100
Structure of public wheat distribution (percent)				
Monetized sales channels[a]	93	86	59	34
In-kind distribution[b]	7	14	41	66
Total	100	100	100	100
Number of mills				
Compact	na	na	na	196
Major	na	na	411	53
Roller	na	na	na	445
Atta chakkis	na	na	7,733	11,287
Total			8,144	11,981

SOURCES: Computed from BBS production data and MOF statistics on government offtake through 1997/98. Number of mills reported in Chowdhury (1993a).

NOTE: na indicates not available.

[a]Monetized channels include the ration channels (not in existence after 1994), essential priorities (the military and police), other priorities, large employers, flour millers, and open market sales.

[b]In-kind distribution through nonmonetized channels (formerly called relief channels) include FFW, VGD, Test Relief, Gratuitous Relief, and FFE.

elasticities may have turned slightly positive in urban areas (Ahmed and Hossain 1990; BBS 1995; Goletti 1993b; Pitt 1983). For this reason urban demand has dominated the growth of wheat consumption. Today, urban areas account for half of wheat consumption even though they house only 20 percent of the country's population (Chowdhury 1993b).[12]

Currently, households consume wheat in one of two principal forms: as *atta* or in refined flour products. *Atta,* a coarsely ground, whole-wheat flour, is used to produce *ruti,* a flat, unleavened bread often consumed as a morning meal or snack. Domestic wheat, exclusively composed of soft varieties, is best suited for preparing *atta* and *ruti.* In contrast, refined flour products such as bread and biscuits depend on imported hard wheats from North America and Europe. Given increasing demand for refined flour products, large urban flour millers demand primarily imported hard wheat for their mills, although up to 20 percent of the mix may consist of domestic wheat (Chowdhury 1993b).

Wheat consumption is less seasonal than that of rice. Demand, particularly in urban areas, remains steady throughout the year, as do public imports and offtake through their monetized channels. Consequently, urban wheat mills and wholesalers operate at a relatively steady year-round pace, although trading and assembly increase in the dry season, when the wheat harvest and Food-for-Work (FFW) seasons converge, generating a dry-season bulge in assembly and distribution.

Marketing Channels

IMPORTS. To supply the growing demand for wheat products, a large network of marketing agents has grown up to channel wheat from the government import pipeline to millers and consumers (see Figure 4.4). Public wheat imports accounted for 90 percent of wheat availability during the 1960s and 1970s as a result of government's wheat import monopoly. But by the 1990s, with the rise of domestic production and newly permissible private imports, the public share in total supply had fallen to slightly under 50 percent, or about 1.1 million tons per year (Table 4.6).

Government-imported wheat, representing half of all domestic wheat supplies, is distributed by the Ministry of Food (MOF) through a variety of offtake channels (see Chapter 6 for greater detail). Initially, MOF sold all wheat through privately owned but publicly controlled ration shops (located mainly in urban areas) or directly to urban flour millers. Collectively, these ration shops, flour mills, and open market sales channels are referred to as monetized public food distribution channels. But in the 1970s changes in donor food-aid

---

12. Household consumption data since the early 1980s have chronically understated domestic wheat consumption (in some years by 40 to 70 percent) compared with figures on availability (see Chapter 6). In large part, this disparity arises from the difficulty in separating out and measuring consumption of wheat eaten in the form of wheat-based processed foods (Chowdhury 1993; Osmani 1990).

FIGURE 4.4 Wheat marketing subsector map, 1992/93

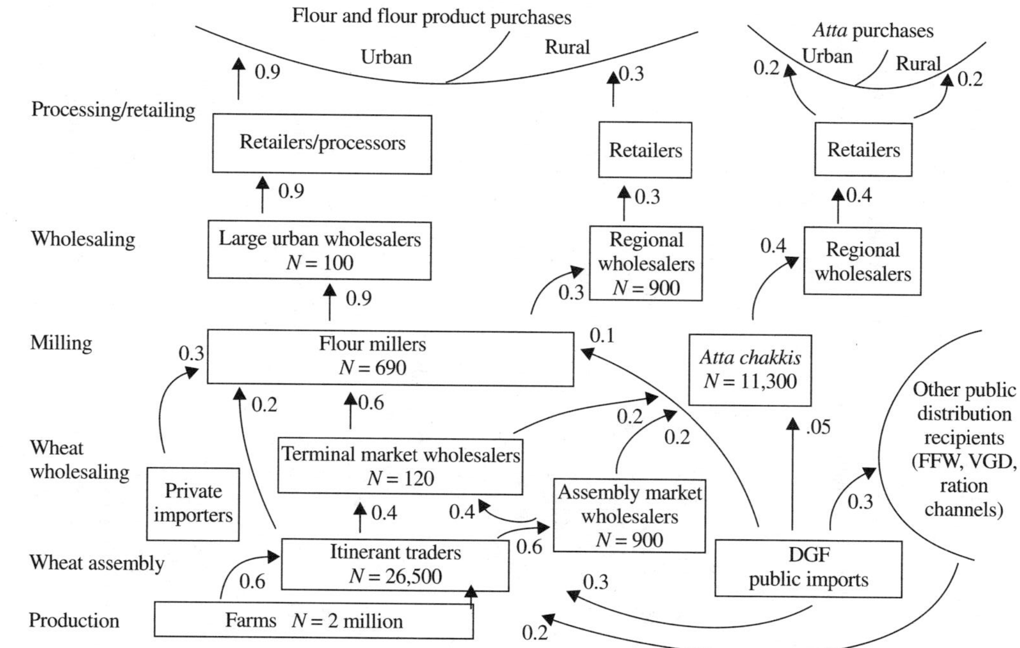

NOTE: Figures for volume of wheat are in million metric tons.

legislation led to the large-scale availability of humanitarian food aid for in-kind distribution to the poor through FFW and Vulnerable Group Feeding (VGF) programs. Originally referred to as relief channels, these direct, in-kind distributions to the poor have now supplanted the monetized "for sale" channels in importance. Relabeled as non-monetized channels in the evolving jargon of food-aid donors, in-kind distribution to the poor grew to about half of public wheat offtake by the early 1990s.[13] Since then, its share has continued to climb, reaching 90 percent by 1998, or about 1 million tons per year (WFP 1998).

PRODUCTION. Even though wheat became an established and low-cost part of the Bangladeshi diet during the 1960s and 1970s, domestic production remained insignificant. But after the 1974 famine, when wheat prices soared and new HYV seeds became available, local farmers suddenly found it to be a profitable dry-season crop (Chowdhury, Morris, and Meisner 1994). They expanded domestic wheat production steadily through the mid-1980s, when it plateaued at slightly more than 1 million tons in 1994. Production again jumped in the second half of the 1990s, rising to about 1.8 million tons by 1997/98 (Chapter 2).

WHEAT TRADE. From the public food-aid pipeline and from domestic farmers, a network of about 27,000 *bepari* and assembly market wholesalers funnels wheat to the urban flour mills in eastern Bangladesh. In the early 1990s the mills received about 300,000 tons of public wheat per year directly from the DGF through the flour millers' channel (WFP 1995).[14] Yet this has historically proven insufficient to meet their requirements, so they supplement their government allocation by actively purchasing stock or DGF delivery orders (DOs) from a variety of other intended recipients of government wheat—for example, *atta chakkis* (local term for small-scale wheat crushers); ration dealers; FFW managers; and households receiving direct distribution of wheat from FFW, VGD, and Food for Education (FFE) programs. For convenience much of this intermediation takes place through simple trade in DOs. Trade sources estimate that *atta chakkis* sell DOs representing between 40 and 75 percent of their public wheat allotment to representatives of major and compact millers (Chowdhury 1993b).

To channel imported public wheat from FFW and other nonmonetized public distribution channels, wheat *bepari* congregate in project areas during the dry season, when FFW reaches its height. According to most estimates,

13. During the second half of the 1980s food-aid donors shifted terminology to emphasize their intent of moving humanitarian food aid from its unabashed relief focus to one aimed at promoting development (for example, through improved rural infrastructure or women's business activities), albeit still via direct food distribution to the poor.

14. Since October 1992, with the advent of liberalized private wheat imports, government has reduced deliveries through the flour millers' channel to only about 30,000 tons per year. Millers are intended henceforth to rely on direct private import rather than public wheat imports.

scheme managers pilfer and sell about 30 percent of FFW wheat through a variety of well-honed practices, often by overreporting work completed (Chowdhury 1993a; Hossain and Akash 1993; WGTFI 1994). FFW workers, legitimate recipients of these in-kind rations, sell a further 40 to 60 percent of their wheat allotments immediately on receipt (Ahmed and Shams 1994). Overall, Chowdhury (1993b) estimates that in 1992/93 FFW scheme managers and recipients sold at least 50 percent—probably closer to 75 percent—of total FFW wheat to *bepari* and mill representatives, who promptly funneled it back from the rural FFW sites to the urban centers where demand for hard wheat remains concentrated (Chowdhury 1993b).[15]

Wheat wholesaling, like milling, remains tightly concentrated in Bangladesh's four large urban centers. Between 60 and 120 large-scale wheat wholesalers handle about 50 percent of all wheat marketed, leading to tight geographic and industrial concentration (Figure 4.4).

MILLING. Wheat millers, who produce refined flour and *atta,* likewise congregate in Bangladesh's four largest urban centers, where demand is concentrated and 75 percent of their milling capacity is located. The largest and most modern mills dominate urban wheat milling. Although they account for only 2 percent of all mills, the major and compact millers process 48 percent of all milled wheat (Chowdhury 1993b). In contrast, about 11,000 *atta chakkis,* with simple huller mills, produce *atta* in dispersed locations throughout Bangladesh.

Because of wheat's recent emergence as an important foodstuff and government's historic monopoly on both import and distribution, trends in private wheat marketing are not well cataloged. The fragmentary evidence available, however, suggests rapid growth after independence in 1971, particularly in the late 1980s and early 1990s, when growing domestic production and gradual liberalization of private imports accelerated the scale of private assembly, import, and distribution. In modern wheat milling one of the few available time series suggests rapid recent growth, with an increasing capacity of about 8 percent per year from 1985 to 1992 (Chowdhury 1993b).

Conduct

Given historically stringent public control of wheat import and distribution, private marketing of wheat began as a clandestine affair. Only with the rise in domestic production and the recent liberalization of private imports has large-scale private trading of wheat become legitimate. Yet even today, given continued large-scale reliance on the siphoning of wheat from nonmonetized public channels to supply private urban mills, wheat marketing retains an illicit aura. One need only visit an FFW site on distribution day to see the slinking,

15. Wheat traders consider even the 75 percent figure an underestimate (Chowdhury 1993b).

evasion, and over-the-shoulder looks of would-be market makers among the *bepari* and scheme managers. Always a shadowy business, wheat trading still thrives on payoffs and under-the-table premiums. Chowdhury (1993b) estimates that these "invisible" rent payments account for about 30 percent of the total official value of wheat.

The concentration of geography and scale have led to collaboration among large wheat wholesalers and millers. The early private wheat imports of 1992/93 primarily involved consortia of wheat millers rather than individuals acting alone. The group has proven to be a well organized and influential association, effectively lobbying for a reduction of wheat import tariffs in the fall of 1993.

Whether collaboration has given way to collusion remains an open question. Appearance certainly invites the suspicion that heavy industrial concentration, tight geographic proximity, and high marketing margins might be correlated. Basing his research on the only large-scale study of wheat markets to date, Chowdhury (1993b) has been unable to document the existence of collusive practices. Any conclusion, however, requires further research.

Performance

The operation and performance of wheat markets are less well documented than they are for rice. Even the popular analyses of spatial price integration remain unavailable for wheat markets. In general, private importers seem to respond to incentives; they nearly doubled private wheat imports during 1994/95 compared with the year before, raising them to 430,000 tons during that year's domestic production slump (WFP 1995). And market *bepari* busily respond to incentives for backhauling rural food-aid wheat distributions to urban wholesalers and mills. But do they do this efficiently?

Marketing margins offer the only available, although imperfect, quantitative measure of wheat market performance. Wheat marketing margins, at 41 percent of retail price, clearly exceed the 21 percent average for coarse rice. Does this difference represent collusion or legitimately higher marketing costs? Wheat marketing costs may truly be higher for two reasons: (1) high invisible costs of leaching wheat from the public offtake channels and (2) longer-than-necessary transport routes, from port to rural areas and back to urban centers when rerouting FFW wheat.

Contrasts and Overlap

Rice and wheat markets have both grown rapidly in Bangladesh since the 1960s. Yet in virtually every other way, the two markets differ (Table 4.7).

In terms of scale, rice markets overwhelm wheat. Their sources of supply, consumption, and distribution differ substantially as well. Rice remains domestically produced, privately marketed, and spatially dispersed. In con-

TABLE 4.7 Contrasting rice and wheat markets, 1990–98

Variable	Rice	Wheat
Availability (million metric tons)	16.6	2.4
Source (percent)[a]		
Domestic production	98	47
Private imports	2	7
Public imports	1	46
Total	100	100
Consumption location (percent)		
Urban	18	50
Rural	82	50
Milling capacity (percent)		
Share in four largest urban centers	na	75
Share in top 2% enterprises	na	48
Stocks, July 1 (percent)		
Farm	64	28
Trade	26	8
Public	10	64
Total	100	100
Marketing		
Average distance traveled (miles)	80	
Marketing margin (percent of retail price)	25	41

SOURCES: Chowdhury (1992, 1993).

NOTES: Time-series figures averaged from 1989/90 through 1997/98. na indicates not available.
[a]Totals may not be precise owing to rounding.

trast, wheat supply depends largely on imports (both public and private) and consequently on highly concentrated supply lines.

Spatial marketing flows and geographic concentration differ substantially as a result of dissimilar supply sources and consumption locations. Urban demand for wheat has led to the heavy concentration of marketing and milling facilities in a handful of populous eastern cities. Apart from import pipelines directed to these cities, the other principal artery connects these eastern hubs with supply lines from the northwest, where surplus production is concentrated and in-kind distribution of food-aid wheat leads to major reverse flows back to the east. Rice, in contrast, flows in many directions. The sequential and often patchy regional adoption of HYVs has stimulated a growing and evolving pattern of interregional trade, one in which urban centers no longer predominate as final destinations.

Seasonality differs as well. The rhythm of rice production and prices follows the two major rice crops: the aman crop, harvested in November and December, and the boro crop, harvested in May and June. But steady urban demand and import supply lines make wheat marketing and processing less seasonal. FFW distributions and the domestic wheat harvest, which coincide during the dry season, generate a seasonal marketing surge in March and April, although it does not coincide with the busy rice marketing during the early monsoon boro and aus harvests.

Not surprisingly (given their different supply sources, different seasonality, different geographic concentrations of production and demand, and the consequently different direction of commodity flows), rice and wheat marketing channels largely fail to intersect. Paddy *bepari* do not market wheat. Rice wholesalers do not handle wheat. Given the different milling technologies, rice millers do not as a rule mill wheat. Only about 9,000 of the very smallest rice husking mills double as *atta chakkis* during the wheat harvest season (Chowdhury 1993a). Even the historically largest intersection in rice and wheat markets, at the MOF, has diminished considerably. Although public distribution still dominates wheat supply channels, the government's role in rice markets has dwindled to insignificance since the decline in large-scale public procurement and rice stocks beginning in the mid-1990s. Today, for the most part, rice and wheat markets in Bangladesh remain physically separate.

Performance and the concentration of market power likewise contrast. Wheat marketing remains highly centralized. Focused on four major urban demand centers and feeding off the dominant supply pipeline of publicly imported wheat, the large urban mills and 60 to 120 wheat wholesalers control roughly 50 percent of all marketed wheat. In contrast, rice production, consumption, and processing remain more evenly dispersed. Although a small clutch of terminal market *aratdars* dominated the rice trade in the late 1960s and 1970s, competition and changing geographic flows have radically altered the market structure. On-farm paddy stocks, small rural rice mills, and itinerant paddy processors now dominate as symbols of Bangladesh's growing and newly decentralized rice markets.

As to measures of performance, the limited available evidence lends more confidence in the efficiency of rice markets than in wheat. Marketing margin, the sole common indicator available, stands at 21 percent of retail price for rice but jumps to 41 percent for wheat. This disparity arises, at least in part, because of substantial rents imposed on private agents who distribute public wheat outside of intended channels. Longer supply routes for wheat, including a considerable volume of back hauling, may contribute to the spread. Given heavy concentration of market power among wheat importers, wholesalers, and millers, subsequent collusion remains possible if unproven.

Policy Implications

Policymakers' interest in wheat markets focuses on two issues: concentration and monetization. As to the first, limited evidence on the performance of wheat markets fuels lingering concerns that heavy market concentration and high marketing margins might be related. Recent and probably continuing declines in food-aid wheat are likely to accelerate the privatization of wheat markets via growing private import. To the extent that this shift reduces the prospects for graft implicit in public-to-private wheat distribution costs, it will soften marketing costs and margins. For the remaining humanitarian food aid, the slowest of the aid-funded wheat flows to recede, monetization rather than in-kind distribution has attracted some support (Alam et al. 1991; Chowdhury 1993b; WGTFI 1994). In Bangladesh monetization involves the sale of imported food-aid grain at port followed by cash distribution to beneficiaries. Given pervasive evidence of large-scale de facto monetization by food-aid scheme managers and recipients, public monetization at port could reduce the double transport costs currently imposed as FFW and other nonmonetized public wheat supplies move to rural areas at public expense only to make a return trip on private marketing agents' account. Thus, monetization might also diminish the costs of supplying growing urban demand for wheat products.

In rice markets long-run trends make a case for lessening public intervention. Changing price seasonality—reduced time between price peaks and now-diminished seasonal price spreads—has followed naturally as a consequence of rapid growth in dry-season rice production and suggests less need for public efforts at seasonal price stabilization. The parallel rise in private paddy stocks, mostly geographically dispersed and on farms, suggests a diminished imperative for the holding of public rice stocks. Indeed, some studies suggest that increases in public rice stocks may simply squeeze out private stocks (Chowdhury 1993a). Similarly, recent experience with the private import of foodgrains suggests that in this way private traders can soften deficits in domestic production, thus reducing (although perhaps not eliminating) the need for public stockholding and emergency import. Given receding levels of international food aid and the growing experience of private sector importers, the Bangladeshi government's historically pervasive public role in foodgrain import and sale seems destined to decline, as indeed it has in recent years.

But in the short run, recent upheavals, both market-driven and political, warn against expectations of further rapid divestiture of public intervention in foodgrain markets. Although the 1994/95 foodgrain production shortfall and consequent price spike was aggravated by fertilizer shortages, transport disruptions, and political unrest and even though private rice imports totaling 930,000 tons cushioned availability after the falloff in rice production during 1997/98, these episodes of production volatility have left many observers cautious about further reducing public involvement in foodgrain markets. As both government and private traders continue to digest the major downsizing in direct public foodgrain marketing initiated during the early 1990s, recent events suggest that future change in public involvement may be evolutionary rather than revolutionary. Just where that road may lead is a question addressed in Chapters 10 and 11.

References

Ahmed, A. U. 1990. Equitable agricultural growth through irrigation-induced technological change: A case study of Bangladesh agriculture. Ph.D. diss., Colorado State University, Fort Collins, Colo., U.S.A.

Ahmed, A. U., and Y. Shams. 1994. Nutritional effects of cash versus commodity-based public works programs. Bangladesh Food Policy Project Manuscript 63. Washington, D.C.: International Food Policy Research Institute. Mimeo.

Ahmed, M. 1988. Assessment of rice processing technologies in Bangladesh with emphasis on milling technology. Dhaka: Bangladesh University of Engineering and Technology, Institute of Appropriate Technology. Mimeo.

Ahmed, R. 1979. *Foodgrain supply, distribution, and consumption policies within a dual pricing mechanism: A case study of Bangladesh.* IFPRI Research Report 8. Washington, D.C.: International Food Policy Research Institute.

Ahmed, R., and A. Bernard. 1989. *Rice price fluctuation and approach to price stabilization in Bangladesh.* IFPRI Research Report 72. Washington, D.C.: International Food Policy Research Institute.

Ahmed, R., and M. Hossain. 1990. *Developmental impact of rural infrastructure in Bangladesh.* Research Report 83. Washington, D.C.: International Food Policy Research Institute.

Ahsan, F., R. Amin, N. Chowdhury, and N. Farid. 1994. Report of the rapid rural appraisal on private foodgrain stocks in Bangladesh, 1993/94. Bangladesh Food Policy Project Manuscript 50. Dhaka: International Food Policy Research Institute/Bangladesh Ministry of Food, Food Planning and Monitoring Unit. Mimeo.

Alam, M., N. Chowdhury, and K. A. S. Murshid. 1991. Report of the task force on food policy. Dhaka: Bangladesh Ministry of Planning. Mimeo.

Bangladesh Bureau of Statistics (BBS). 1969. *Master survey of agriculture, 1967–68.* Dhaka: Bangladesh Bureau of Statistics.

———. 1995. *Summary report of household expenditure survey, 1991–92.* Dhaka: Bangladesh Bureau of Statistics.

Chowdhury, L. H., and A. W. N. Ahmed. 1994. *History of the Ministry of Food, Government of Bangladesh.* (4 vols.). Bangladesh Food Policy Project Manuscript 57. Washington, D.C.: International Food Policy Research Institute. Mimeo.

Chowdhury, N. 1992. Rice markets in Bangladesh: A study in structure, conduct and performance. Bangladesh Food Policy Project Manuscript 22. Washington, D.C.: International Food Policy Research Institute. Mimeo.

———. 1993a. Interactions between private rice stocks and public stock policy in Bangladesh: Evidence for a crowding out. Bangladesh Food Policy Project Manuscript 37. Washington, D.C.: International Food Policy Research Institute. Mimeo.

———. 1993b. The structure and conduct of Bangladesh's wheat markets: Some emerging insights. Bangladesh Food Policy Project Manuscript 40. Dhaka: International Food Policy Research Institute, Bangladesh Food Policy Project. Mimeo.

———. 1994. Credit and Bangladesh's foodgrain market: New evidence on commercialization, credit relations, and effect of credit access. Bangladesh Food Policy Project Manuscript 64. Dhaka: International Food Policy Research Institute, Bangladesh Food Policy Project. Mimeo.

Chowdhury, N., M. Morris, and C. Meisner. 1994. Comparative advantage of wheat in Bangladesh: Technological, economic and policy issues. Dhaka: Centro Internacional de Mejoramiento de Maiz y Trigo/International Food Policy Research Institute. Mimeo.

Crow, B. 1989. Plain tales from the rice trade. *Journal of Peasant Studies* 16 (January): 198–229.

Crow, B., and K. A. S. Murshid. 1990. The finance of forced and free markets: Merchants' capital in Bangladesh grain markets. Paper presented to a meeting of the American Economic Association and Union for Radical Political Economics, December 29, Washington, D.C.

———. 1993. The finance of trade and agriculture in a backward area of Bangladesh. In *Real markets: Social and political issues of food policy reform,* ed. C. de Alcántara. London: Frank Cass, for the United Nations Research Institute for Social Development.

Department of Agricultural Marketing (DAM). 1974. Survey on paddy sales in the aman season of 1973–74. Dhaka: Department of Agricultural Marketing. Mimeo.

———. Various. Monthly price data. Dhaka: Department of Agricultural Marketing. Mimeo.

Dey, M. M. 1988. Technological change in Bangladesh's rice economy. Ph.D. diss., University of the Philippines, Los Banos.

Fafchamps, M., and B. Minten. 1998. Return to social capital among traders. Markets and Structural Studies Division Discussion Paper 23. Washington, D.C.: International Food Policy Research Institute. Mimeo.

Farruk, M. O. 1972. *Structure and performance of the rice marketing system in East Pakistan.* New York: Cornell University Special Publication.

Food Planning and Monitoring Unit (FPMU)/International Food Policy Research Institute (IFPRI). 1992. Report of the rapid rural appraisal on wheat marketing. Bangladesh Food Policy Project. Dhaka: International Food Policy Research Institute. Mimeo.

Goletti, F. 1993a. The changing public role in a rice economy moving toward self-sufficiency: The case of Bangladesh. Bangladesh Food Policy Project Manuscript 44. Dhaka: International Food Policy Research Institute. Mimeo.

———. 1993b. Food consumption parameters in Bangladesh. Bangladesh Food Policy Project Manuscript 29. Dhaka: International Food Policy Research Institute. Mimeo.

Hossain, M., and M. M. Akash. 1993. Public rural works for relief and development: A review of the Bangladesh experience. Working Paper on Food Subsidies 7. Washington, D.C.: International Food Policy Research Institute. Mimeo.

Hossain, M., M. A. Quasem, M. M. Akash, M. Mokaddem, and M. A. Jabber. 1990. Differential impact of modern rice technology: The Bangladesh case. Dhaka: Bangladesh Institute of Development Studies. Mimeo.

International Fertilizer Development Center (IFDC). 1994. Farm-level fertilizer price and availability survey [Monthly]. Dhaka: International Fertilizer Development Center. Mimeo.

Islam, A., M. Hossain, N. Islam, S. Akhter, E. Harun, and J. N. Efferson. 1985. A benchmark study of rice marketing in Bangladesh. Dhaka: Bangladesh Rice Research Institute/Directorate of Agricultural Marketing. Mimeo.

Osmani, S. R. 1990. Notes on some recent estimates of rural poverty in Bangladesh. *Bangladesh Development Studies* 18 (September): 75–87.

Pitt, M. 1983. Food preferences and nutrition in rural Bangladesh. *Review of Economics and Statistics* 65 (February): 105–114.

Rahman, M. 1988. Problems and prospects of rice processing technology in Bangladesh: An entrepreneur-researcher's viewpoint. Dhaka: Bangladesh University of Engineering and Technology, Institute of Appropriate Technology. Mimeo.

Raquibuzzaman, M. 1968. Marketed surplus of selected agricultural commodities in Pakistan. *Pakistan Development Review* 7 (Spring): 23–49.

Ravallion, M. 1987. *Markets and famines.* Oxford: Oxford University Press.

Working Group on Targeted Food Interventions (WGTFI). 1994. Options for targeting food interventions in Bangladesh. Dhaka: International Food Policy Research Institute. Mimeo.

World Food Programme (WFP). 1995. Bangladesh foodgrain digest. Dhaka: World Food Programme, June. Mimeo.

———. 1998. Bangladesh foodgrain digest. Dhaka: World Food Programme, June. Mimeo.

5 Trends in Consumption, Nutrition, and Poverty

AKHTER U. AHMED

Changing Patterns of Foodgrain Demand

Foodgrain consumption dominates household spending in Bangladesh. On average, rice and wheat consumption accounts for 50 percent of total household expenditure, with this share rising to 64 percent for the poorest households (BBS 1995). As nutrition, foodgrains dominate to an even greater extent, accounting for nearly 80 percent of all calories consumed—73 percent from rice and about 6 percent from wheat. Thus, foodgrain consumption remains key not only to the evolution of domestic foodgrain prices and markets but also to trends in nutrition and poverty.

On the demand side of rice and wheat markets, changing tastes and consumption patterns have accompanied major changes in supply. Rice, historically the preferred staple, retains its position today in the land where "Have you eaten?" translates directly as "Have you taken rice?" Consequently, as incomes have edged upward, so has per capita intake of rice. Both microlevel consumption data and aggregate national availability computations indicate upward trends in rice consumption since the 1970s (Table 5.1).

Over time, however, falling income elasticities of demand suggest that rice consumption has begun to slacken. Differences in data sources, data collection methodology, and estimating methods make comparisons across studies difficult; yet estimated expenditure elasticities have generally tended downward. In rural areas, amid wide variation, estimated expenditure elasticities have declined from about 0.8 during the 1970s to about 0.5 in the late 1980s and still lower in the 1990s.[1] In the steadily growing urban areas, preference for rice has fallen off even more dramatically. According to the household expenditure surveys (HES) of 1981/82 and 1991/92 (the last two using comparable estimation methods), urban expenditure elasticities for rice have fallen from 0.28 to 0.08 over the 10-year interval (BBS 1995). In the aggregate,

1. See Alamgir and Berlage (1973), Mahmud (1979), Pitt (1983), Bouis (1989), Ahmed (1981), Chowdhury (1982), Ahmed and Hossain (1990), Goletti (1993), Ahmed and Shams (1994), and BBS (1995).

TABLE 5.1 Consumption of rice and wheat

Foodgrain	1973/74	1976/77	1981/82	1983/84	1985/86	1988/89	1991/92
Rice (kilograms per person per year)							
Consumption as measured by HES							
Rural	129.2	120.2	147.4	153.4	165.6	163.8	175.8
Urban	104.5	119.1	132.3	127.9	137.3	144.2	151.8
Total	127.0	120.1	145.3	150.2	162.0	161.2	172.6
Availability	141.0	134.9	139.0	140.5	137.7	137.7	144.7
Availability/consumption	1.11	1.12	0.96	0.94	0.85	0.85	0.84
Wheat (kilograms per person per year)							
Consumption as measured by HES							
Rural	30.9	17.8	19.9	22.9	18.7	21.5	12.6
Urban	56.6	28.3	31.1	27.0	19.8	19.4	17.2
Total	33.2	18.8	21.4	23.4	18.9	21.2	13.2
Availability	22.7	11.3	23.5	26.4	19.9	29.5	22.2
Availability/consumption	0.68	0.60	1.10	1.13	1.05	1.39	1.68
Cereal expenditure as percent of total household spending							
Rural	59.5	69.5	61.5	56.9	50.8	52.9	na
Urban	49.0	55.5	43.5	44.8	36.3	38.6	na
Total	58.8	68.1	58.1	55.3	48.5	50.6	na

SOURCES: Household consumption from HES data (BBS 1988a, 1988b, 1991, 1995). Availability computed from BBS (1992), Ahmed and Chowdhury (1994), FPMU, WFP (1996).

NOTE: na indicates not available.

recent estimates suggest that overall national expenditure elasticity of demand for rice now falls in the range of 0.35 to 0.45 (Table 5.2). In terms of quantity rather than expenditure elasticity, these estimates are likely to be even smaller. So as incomes continue to grow and urbanization increases from today's about 20 percent population share, growth in domestic demand for rice will continue to soften. Indeed, preliminary analysis of data collected through a 1997/98 IFPRI survey indicates that income elasticity of demand for rice has approached zero (IFPRI, BIDS, and INFS 1998).

Wheat, a nontraditional food item in Bengal, was first introduced in large quantities under the U.S. Public Law 480 food-aid programs during the 1950s and 1960s (see Chapters 6 and 8). In tandem with rising food-aid imports, wheat availability has risen from a negligible 2 kilograms per person per year in the 1950s to 8 kilograms in the 1960s and has stabilized at 20 to 25 kilograms per person in the 1990s. Even in recent decades wheat intake remains closely tied to food-aid inflows, as the surge in 1973/74 demonstrates (Table 5.1).

Three decades of subsidized wheat distribution through urban ration channels have left their mark on urban palates. In the early years after independence, urban wheat consumption per capita was nearly double the rate prevailing in rural areas. Even with the falloff in urban ration subsidies and the rerouting of subsidized wheat imports to targeted rural programs, urban wheat consumption remains generally higher than that in rural areas (Table 5.1). Note, too, that the HES classifies prepared wheat-based foods such as bread, cakes, *ruti* (a flat, unleavened bread), and sweets separately from wheat grain and wheat flour. This leads to an understatement of the magnitude of urban preference for wheat and explains the growing gap between apparent wheat consumption and its availability (Table 5.1). Taking into consideration prepared wheat-based food products, one can estimate that half of all wheat is now

TABLE 5.2 Estimated expenditure elasticities of demand for foodgrains

		Expenditure Elasticities		
Foodgrain	Year	Rural	Urban	National
Rice				
Goletti	1988/89	0.39	0.15	0.34
HES	1991/92	0.55	0.08	0.46
Ahmed and Shams	1991/92	0.68	na	na
Wheat				
HES	1991/92	–0.38	0.39	–0.17
Ahmed and Shams	1991/92	–0.22	na	na

SOURCES: BBS (1995), Ahmed and Shams (1994), Goletti (1993).

NOTE: na indicates not available.

TABLE 5.3 Foodgrain expenditure elasticities by quartile

	Rural		
	Goletti	Ahmed and Shams	Urban
Rice			
Bottom quartile	0.80*	1.05*	0.58*
Second quartile	0.71*	na	0.43*
Third quartile	0.64*	na	0.19
Top quartile	0.03	0.48*	–0.03
All	0.39*	0.68*	0.15*
Wheat			
Bottom quartile	–1.37*	–0.58*	–0.21
Second quartile	0.05	na	0.33*
Third quartile	–1.00	na	–0.02
Top quartile	–0.19	0.11	0.29*
All	–0.44*	–0.22	0.01

SOURCES: Goletti (1993), Ahmed and Shams (1994).

NOTE: na indicates not available.

*Significant at 90% level.

consumed in urban areas, which account for only 20 percent of the country's population (Chowdhury 1993).

In the early years after its introduction, wheat remained an inferior good among the rice-eating Bengalis. Virtually all studies before the 1990s estimate negative expenditure elasticities of demand for wheat (see Pitt 1983; Ahmed and Hossain 1990). Yet in recent years wheat has become a normal good in urban centers, where HES estimates suggest that its expenditure elasticity has risen from –0.01 in 1981/82 to 0.39 in 1991/92 (BBS 1995). Using the same set of data but conducting a more disaggregated analysis, Goletti (1993) confirms the BBS results except for the bottom quartile of the urban population, whose people still consider wheat an inferior good. Although it also remains inferior in rural areas, wheat seems to be on the brink of becoming a preferred (normal) good among high-income rural consumers (Tables 5.2 and 5.3).[2] So as incomes continue to rise in rural and urban areas, and as urbanization accelerates, market-based demand for wheat will continue to grow. Given that wheat production reached a plateau in the mid-1980s and increased competition for planting space with boro rice (see Chapter 12), growing demand for wheat will require greater imports, which will be increasingly privatized as food-aid shipments continue to decline.

2. While this conclusion is supported by Ahmed and Shams (1994), it is contradicted by Goletti (1993). Nevertheless, the relevant coefficients of both studies are not significantly different from zero.

Variations in Nutritional Status

Despite per capita growth in the availability and intake of rice and wheat, a skewed income distribution and low average income levels for the bulk of the population mean that many Bangladeshis remain at nutritional risk. Fully half of Bangladesh's population cannot afford an adequate diet (Rahman and Hossain 1992; WGTFI 1994). For the severely poor (the bottom 25 percent of the population), caloric intake hovers between 60 and 80 percent of nutritional requirements (Rahman and Hossain 1992; Ahmed 1993b). To identify those most at risk, the following discussion presents evidence from a three-round rural survey of consumption and nutrition conducted by the International Food Policy Research Institute (IFPRI) between October 1991 and November 1992 (Ahmed 1993b).

How Does Income Affect Food Consumption and Nutrition?

Table 5.4 shows the pattern of food and nutrient intake and the nutritional status of children across expenditure groups. Estimates of daily nutrient intake were determined by weighing food intake at household and individual levels. The recall method was used for recording food consumption outside the home.

For the entire sample, about 63 percent of total expenditures go to food. As household income rises, the share spent on food falls in accordance with Engel's Law. The patterns show that, while per capita intake of all four nutrients increases as income rises, calorie and protein intake is more responsive to changes in income (expenditures) than are the micronutrients iron and vitamin A. The results also reveal that the intake of all four nutrients by female household members in all expenditure groups is consistently lower than that of the male household members.

To determine calorie adequacy of a household member, one should compare the actual caloric intake of that individual with his or her caloric requirement. The principal components of calorie requirements are basal metabolic rate (BMR), weight, age, sex, and level of physical activity. Calorie requirements for each individual are calculated using the anthropometric and physical activity level data collected in the survey. As shown in Table 5.4, the average caloric intake is far below requirements for all household members for the poorest 25 percent of rural households. Female members are much worse off than males, indicating a gender-biased household behavior that discriminates against female members when food is allocated.

Table 5.4 also presents the cost of nutrients and income relations. Except for vitamin A, the unit costs of calories, protein, and iron increase as incomes rise. This pattern indicates that, with rising income, households tend to diversify food consumption to include higher-priced nutrients.

In general, nutritional studies in low-income countries suggest that preschool children and pregnant and lactating women face the most acute nutri-

TABLE 5.4 The effects of income on food consumption and nutrition

	Expenditure Quartile				
Indicators	First	Second	Third	Fourth	All
Per capita monthly expenditure (taka)	197	332	436	732	424
Expenditure share of food (percent)	74.8	68.4	62.1	47.8	63.3
Calorie intake (kcal per person per day)	1,601	1,970	2,156	2,305	2,008
Male	1,794	2,169	2,385	2,520	2,217
Female	1,427	1,768	1,909	2,054	1,789
Calorie adequacy (percent)	82.9	99.1	107.0	111.0	100.0
Male	87.8	103.2	113.6	114.2	104.7
Female	78.5	94.9	99.9	107.2	95.1
Protein intake (grams per person per day)	39	48	53	62	51
Male	43	53	58	68	56
Female	34	43	48	56	45
Iron intake (milligrams per person per day)	25	28	29	31	28
Male	28	30	32	34	31
Female	23	25	26	28	25
Vitamin A intake (micrograms per person per day)	429	455	514	656	513
Male	446	480	577	752	563
Female	414	429	446	544	458
Costs of nutrients					
Calorie (taka per thousand calories)	3.72	4.35	4.70	5.57	4.58
Protein (taka per 10 grams)	1.54	1.80	1.92	2.11	1.84
Iron (taka per 10 milligrams)	2.33	3.12	3.49	4.18	3.28
Vitamin A (taka per 100 micrograms)	0.04	0.06	0.06	0.07	0.06
Nutritional status of children under age five					
Height-for-age *Z* score	−2.52	−2.47	−2.58	−2.14	−2.43
Weight-for-age *Z* score	−2.43	−2.35	−2.38	−2.16	−2.33
Weight-for-height *Z* score	−1.17	−1.05	−1.09	−1.06	−1.09

SOURCE: Ahmed (1993b).

NOTE: Nutrient intake estimates are based on 24-hour food weighing data.

FIGURE 5.1 Intrahousehold calorie adequacy (intake per requirement)

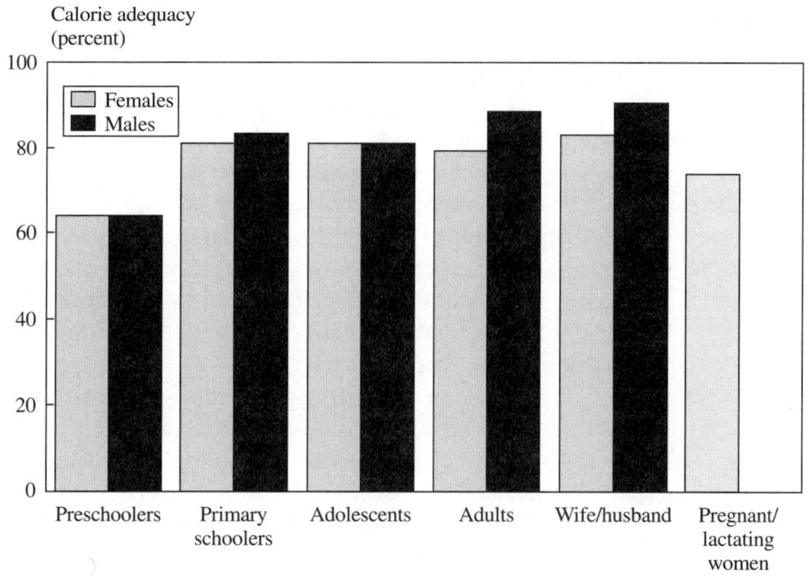

SOURCE: Ahmed (1993a).

tional risks. The present study provides corroborating evidence from Bangladesh. Figure 5.1 shows the intrahousehold calorie adequacies by age and sex groups of poor households. Preschool children are clearly at the greatest risk of undernutrition, followed by pregnant and lactating women.

Table 5.4 reports the nutritional status of preschool children (ages 0 to 59 months), which is determined on the basis of anthropometric data for all preschool children in the sample households relative to a particular growth standard. The standards devised by the U.S. National Center for Health Statistics (NCHS) are used in this study. The levels of nutritional status are expressed in *Z*-score values.[3] The results show that the children of the highest income group (fourth expenditure quartile) are nutritionally better off than those belonging to the lowest (first expenditure quartile) income group. The differences of *Z* scores between the lowest and highest income groups of children are statistically significant.

3. *Z* score = actual measurement – 50th percentile standard deviation. Levels of nutritional status in comparison with a reference population can be conveniently expressed in terms of *Z*-score values. A *Z*-score value of 0 indicates a child who is normal, and a negative value indicates an anthropometric measurement below the one in the reference population.

Regional Variation

IFPRI conducted its household consumption and nutrition survey in eight villages in eight *thanas* (administrative units consisting of a number of villages) located in the four divisions of the country. Four of the survey villages lie in distressed areas, the other four in nondistressed areas. The four distressed areas have been identified using the World Food Programme's distress map in which each of the country's 460 rural *thanas* has been categorized by its relative distress level. The distress level is determined by factors such as foodgrain surplus or deficit, agricultural wage rate, population density, number of landless households, employment opportunities, and susceptibility to natural disasters. Employment opportunities, the incidence of natural calamities, agricultural technology, infrastructural development, disease, sanitation, and food prices all vary substantially across the survey villages.

Table 5.5 presents the results of the analysis according to some major indicators of household welfare. The difference in per capita income (expenditure) between the lowest-income village (Puthimari) and the highest-income village (Ramnagar) is 87 percent. These two villages also represent extremes in per capita calorie intake. Puthimari belongs to Chilmari *thana,* which is one of the most distressed areas in Bangladesh due to landlessness caused by erosion from the Jamuna River. A high proportion of households have lost their land to the river. Cultivated land is mostly unirrigated, and subsistence farmers predominantly grow local aman rice. Rice accounts for 92 percent of all agricultural income, yet the average marketed surplus of rice is only 19 percent.

In contrast, Ramnagar, located in Harinakundu *thana,* is quite advanced in agricultural technology. The village is located in the Ganges-Kapotakh (GK) irrigation project area, and the entire cultivated land is irrigated during the dry season. Most farmers grow two crops of high-yielding rice, and the average marketed surplus of rice is 50 percent. Rice, however, accounts for only 41 percent of agricultural income. Betel leaf, an entirely commercial crop in the village, is widely grown and constitutes about 54 percent of agricultural income on average. Indeed, betel leaf is the principal source of cash income of the village households.

Table 5.5 also shows the variability in the nutritional status of preschool children and women of child-bearing age, the nutritionally most vulnerable groups. Although there is no noticeable association between village-level household income and the nutritional status of preschool children, the variation in the nutritional status of children and women is substantial between villages.

Seasonal Variation

IFPRI repeated the 1991/92 household consumption and nutrition survey three times over the one-year period to capture seasonal changes in consumption and nutritional patterns. The first survey round was conducted during the October–

TABLE 5.5 Regional variation in expenditures, food consumption, and nutritional status

						Preschool Children		Women of Child-Bearing Age	
Village	Thana	Total Expenditure	Food Expenditure	Calorie Intake	Calorie Adequacy	Calorie Deficients	Weight for Age below -3 Z score	Calorie Deficients	Body Mass Index Less Than 18.5
		(taka per person per month)		(kcal per person per day)	(percent)	(percent)		(percent)	
Puthimari	Chilmari*	224	145	1,697	86.7	73.5	26.6	85.6	68.6
Purba Kalyan	Kurigram*	252	165	1,737	86.9	82.0	29.9	83.5	59.1
Chak Haricharan	Daulatpur*	268	188	1,848	91.0	72.5	30.2	75.5	56.5
Nurpur	Hobiganj	304	212	1,744	90.5	66.7	30.7	79.2	76.4
Dolomba	Adamdighi	317	201	1,790	91.1	80.2	21.7	76.6	57.1
Char Shamail	Shibchar*	347	214	1,799	91.3	85.6	30.8	72.4	59.8
Jhapua	Barura	369	255	1,964	99.6	65.2	36.0	63.5	66.1
Ramnagar	Harinakundu	419	243	2,018	99.5	64.8	26.3	71.4	51.6
Coefficient of variation (percent)		19.4	17.0	6.3	5.0	10.2	13.5	8.7	12.0

SOURCE: Ahmed (1993b).

NOTE: Food consumption estimates are based on 24-hour food weighing data.

*Distressed *thana*.

November 1991 lean season, the second during the January–March 1992 peak season, and the third during the September–November 1992 lean season. The first survey round included only low-income households. Although higher-income households were included in the second and third rounds, seasonal comparisons are made only for low-income households to be analytically consistent.

Table 5.6 highlights the improvements in major welfare indicators from the lean to the peak seasons for low-income rural households. Fluctuations in both food prices and incomes drive these seasonal variations. Prices peak in March/April and September/October. Absence of employment before the aman harvest (September/October) makes the second lean season especially acute, particularly for the rural landless, who depend on wage labor for their income. During the 1970s employment opportunities diminished considerably in the dry-season months of January and February. But today, with the advent of widespread cultivation of irrigated, winter boro rice, employment and wage incomes remain high early in the year. Income seasonality, of course, varies by occupation, and fishermen are among the most vulnerable. Poor sanitation and increased incidence of disease aggravate the health status of the poor during both lean seasons. Poor water quality emerges as a problem in March through April, just before the monsoon rains begin, contributing to incidents of diarrhea. Prevalence of diarrhea resurges in September and October. These conditions coincide in the two lean seasons in Bangladesh, the first in March/April and the second, more severe, in September/October (Chen 1983; Chowdhury 1992). Nutritional stress reaches its peak in these months.

Poverty

Scale

Consumption shortfalls, compared to a nutritional norm, remain the most common means of defining numbers of people in poverty. Regardless of method, most estimates for Bangladesh suggest that about 50 percent of the overall population cannot afford an adequate diet (Ahmed, Kahn, and Sampath 1991; Hossain and Sen 1992; Rahman and Haque 1988; Ravallion and Sen 1996). They likewise agree that the great bulk of Bangladesh's poor live in rural areas, where slightly more than half of all people live below the poverty line, compared with about one-third of urban dwellers.

Trends

Changes over time in the poverty level have aroused considerable interest and passionate debates in Bangladesh. Although the Bangladesh Bureau of Statistics' HES remains the standard time-series microdata on which analysts base their estimates, changing data collection methodology (a switch from seven-

TABLE 5.6 Seasonal variations in consumption and nutrition of low-income household members

Indicator	Lean Season (1991)	Peak Season (1992)	Change from Lean to Peak Seasons
			(percent)
Income (taka per person per month)	190	267	40.5
Expenditure (taka per person per month)	257	266	3.5
Food expenditure (taka per person per day)	188	194	3.2
Calorie intake (calories per person per day)			
All family members	1,573	1,752	11.4
All male	1,757	1,921	9.3
All female	1,401	1,597	14.0
Calorie adequacy (percent)			
All family members	79.5	89.9	13.1
All male	81.7	94.8	16.0
All female	77.4	85.3	10.2
Calorie deficient population			
All family members	77.1	62.8	–18.5
All male	75.2	57.3	–23.8
All female	78.9	67.7	–14.2
Protein intake (grams per person per day)	41	43	4.9

SOURCE: Ahmed (1993b).

NOTE: Estimates of calorie and protein intakes are based on 24-hour food weighing data.

day recall to daily diaries in 1983/84) has compromised efforts to make comparable assessments over long periods of time. Further complicating intertemporal comparisons are intermittent famines, floods, and droughts, which lead to difficulties in finding appropriate beginning and ending years on which to base long-term comparisons.

To simplify a contentious subject, it is most convenient to consider the period between 1983/84 and 1991/92, when the HES has used a consistent data collection methodology. This also coincides with a rapid breakthrough in foodgrain technology and production. Virtually all analysts agree that during this period the incidence and depth of poverty declined slightly, although progress was uneven. There was, however, a slight increase in poverty in 1988/89 and 1991/92 (see Table 5.7). Although this increase is inconsistent with several non-HES–based field estimates that suggest improvement over this period (Ahmed and Shams 1994; Rahman and Hossain 1992; Rahman 1994b), it seems clear that any sustained and significant downward trend in poverty has yet to take root in Bangladesh. Because levels of poverty fluctuate yearly, any observed improvements fall within the measurement error of the trend line.

Regrettably, most studies also agree that these modest improvements in overall poverty mask a stagnation, if not a deterioration, in the welfare of the extreme poor, a group that straddles the outer limits of human survival (Rahman and Hossain 1992). Behind this stagnation lies acute land pressure, growing population, and a consequent steady increase in landlessness. The Gini coefficient of land distribution has increased from 0.49 in 1960 to 0.65 in 1991 (Sen et al. 1990; Rahman and Hossain 1992; BBS 1991). This tenuous claim on a key productive asset reduces not only earning power but also the ability of the poor to weather setbacks emanating from ill health, disease, or natural calamity. Increasing lack of access to land probably lies at the root of a worrisome skewing of income distribution over time (Table 5.7).

Impact of Evolving Foodgrain Markets

Time-series inferences are, of course, fraught with peril since many factors change all at once. Population growth, world prices, government policy, and weather all vary from year to year, making it difficult to separate the impact of each. What then, if any, is the connection between maturing foodgrain markets and the virtual stagnation observed in the level and incidence of poverty? Since foodgrain markets and the welfare of the poor intersect at two key junctures—rice price and labor demand—the following discussion briefly reviews the impact of increased foodgrain productivity and production on each.

Labor demand and wage rates have clearly increased after the recent adoption of Green Revolution foodgrain technology. The introduction of high-yielding varieties (HYVs) coupled with the expansion of dry-season irrigation

TABLE 5.7 Recent trends in poverty in Bangladesh

Measurement	1983/84	1985/86	1988/89	1991/92
Head-count index of poverty (percent)				
Urban	40.9	30.8	35.9	33.6
Rural	53.8	45.9	49.7	52.9
Total	52.3	43.9	47.8	49.7
Poverty gap index (percent)				
Urban	11.4	7.3	8.7	8.4
Rural	15.0	10.9	13.1	14.6
Total	14.5	10.4	12.5	13.6
Gini index of inequality (percent)				
Urban	29.8	31.4	32.6	31.9
Rural	24.6	24.6	26.5	25.5

SOURCE: Ravallion and Sen (1996).

have increased labor demand and wage rates in areas where the new technology has been adopted. Labor demand per hectare rises about 30 percent when farmers switch from traditional to high-yielding rice varieties. Therefore, wage rates rise by 35 to 40 percent in high-adopter villages (Hossain et al. 1990). Although population pressure may erode these gains over time, the net effect of the new foodgrain technology has been to increase both agricultural employment and wage rates to levels above what they would have been otherwise. Because of this, the poor have benefited from the new foodgrain technology that led the production surge of the late 1980s and early 1990s.

Productivity-induced production growth in excess of population increase has also led to a softening in real prices of rice and wheat (see Chapters 2 and 4). This, too, benefits net consumers of rice, principally the rural landless and urban dwellers. A poverty monitoring survey conducted by the Bangladesh Institute of Development Studies (BIDS) during the rice price fall of 1992 concluded that rural landless and wage laborers with fixed money incomes saw their real income rise appreciably as a result of the falling rice price (Rahman 1994a).

IFPRI field studies during the same period likewise concluded that the rural poor increased their real income and nutritional (calorie) intake between the lean season of 1991 and 1992, when the nominal rice price fell by 20 percent (Figure 5.2).[4] As in the BIDS study, IFPRI researchers found that welfare indicators other than consumption and nutrition, such as landholdings and employment, were similar in the lean seasons over the one-year period. Compared to 1991, however, the households paid about 20 percent less to purchase rice in 1992. This fall in rice price offered increased consumption opportunities to the poor families. They took advantage of these opportunities by consuming not only about 38 percent more rice but also about 77 percent more high-protein foods such as milk, meat, and eggs. Moreover, these families increased their purchases of nonfood commodities, such as clothing, by 17 percent.

The rural poor, however, drastically reduced their wheat consumption by 68 percent. Because rice is their preferred cereal, poor families responded to falling rice prices by shifting from wheat to rice. Nevertheless, this decrease in wheat consumption was more than offset by the large increase in rice consumption, and the net effect was a 23 percent increase in total foodgrain consumption.

The combined effect of the change in food consumption patterns resulted in about a 12 percent increase in calorie intake by low-income families. Among family members, children appear to have gained considerably more than the adults from low rice prices and higher calorie intake. Poverty, defined as access to a nutritionally adequate diet, therefore fell significantly from 1991 to 1992.

4. See Haggblade and Rahman (1993) for a review of why prices fell during this period.

FIGURE 5.2 Gaps in calorie intake

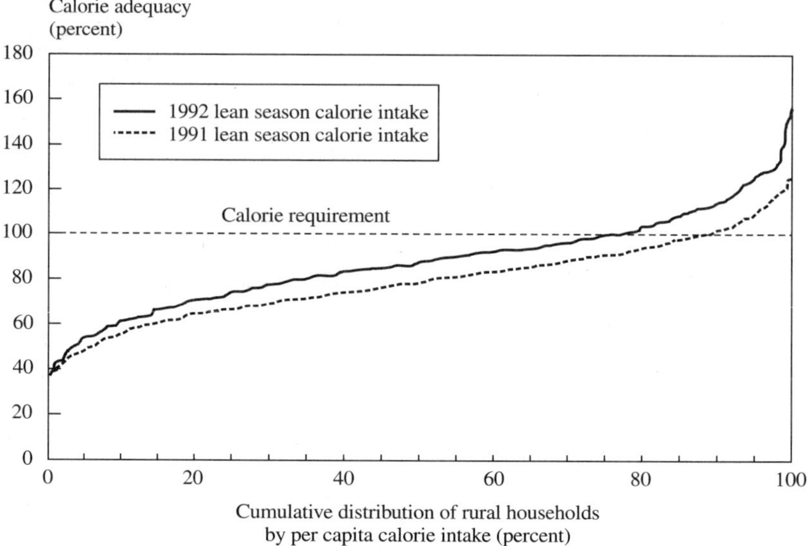

SOURCE: Ahmed (1993b).

About 15 percent of the low-income sample population moved above the poverty level.

Figure 5.2 shows, however, that the upward shift in the calorie intake curve from 1991 to 1992 was not a parallel shift; the richer low-income households benefited disproportionately. This shift has important policy implications for targeted interventions, suggesting that, from the large fall in rice price, the relatively better-off households gained more than did the extremely poor ones. As Figure 5.2 shows, the most undernourished gained very little, if any, improvement in their calorie adequacies. What could be the factors underlying this pattern? Although further in-depth inquiry is required to explain it, a number of hypotheses can be advanced. First, the share of other foods such as wheat, millet (China), barley (Satu), sweet potato, and so on relative to rice is larger in extremely poor households. When the rice price falls without simultaneous falls in prices of these other foods, as is likely in the short run, these households increase their rice consumption while reducing consumption of other foods. Thus, the calorie situation does not change much. Second, the income gain from the price fall is counterbalanced by a fall in money income. The type of activities these households are involved in is sensitive to the rice price even in the short run. Some rural wage rates have been found to move in the same direction as rice prices. Third, the Engel curve in the case of the extreme poor behaves differently from normal curves; in this case there is a short fall or flatness to the curve at the beginning before it starts rising with income. The logic is that among such poor, the basic minimum need for clothes and shelter is compelling so that any small increase in income is used for these purposes. Fourth, extremely poor households are constantly in debt, and any gain in income, including gain from a falling rice price, is used to repay debt. Osmani and Chowdhury (1983) observed similar phenomena in studying the short-run impact of the Food-for-Work (FFW) program in Bangladesh. It seems that the extremely poor deserve special treatment in government programs for poverty alleviation. The analysis of the 1992 price fall indicates that, to relieve nutritional stress among vulnerable households, targeted income transfers (without purchase requirements) would be more effective than either general or targeted food price subsidies.

In general, evidence suggests that the productivity-led increases in foodgrain production described in Chapters 2 and 3 have proven beneficial to Bangladesh's poor. On the supply side the new HYV technology has increased labor demand and rural wage rates. On the demand side modest production increases combined with overall sluggish demand have dampened real rice prices and further raised real incomes of the poor above the level that would otherwise have prevailed.

Although it has undoubtedly improved the welfare of the rural and urban poor over what it would otherwise have been, Green Revolution foodgrain technology has not alone been able to solve Bangladesh's deep-seated poverty. Over time, population growth and increasing landlessness have eroded the gains of the new technology, and additional efforts are required to confront Bangladesh's extreme poverty. Looking forward, economic and food policymakers in Bangladesh must find a way to stimulate rapid economic growth to support the extreme poor, to develop employment-creating sectors, and to craft carefully targeted interventions in critical periods, a subject to which we return in Chapter 11.

References

Ahmed, A. U. 1993a. Food consumption and nutritional effects of targeted food interventions in Bangladesh. Bangladesh Food Policy Project Manuscript 31. Washington, D.C.: International Food Policy Research Institute. Mimeo.

———. 1993b. *Patterns of food consumption and nutrition in rural Bangladesh.* Washington, D.C.: International Food Policy Research Institute.

Ahmed, A. U., H. A. Khan, and R. K. Sampath. 1991. Poverty in Bangladesh: Measurement, decomposition and intertemporal comparison. *Journal of Development Studies* 27 (July): 48–63.

Ahmed, A. U., and Y. Shams. 1994. Demand elasticities in rural Bangladesh: An application of the AIDS model. *Bangladesh Development Studies* 22 (March): 1–25.

Ahmed, A. W. N., and L. H. Chowdhury. 1994. History of the Ministry of Food, Government of Bangladesh (4 vols.). Bangladesh Food Policy Project Manuscript 57. Dhaka: International Food Policy Research Institute. Mimeo.

Ahmed, R. 1981. *Agricultural price policies under complex socioeconomic and natural constraints: The case of Bangladesh.* IFPRI Research Report 27. Washington, D.C.: International Food Policy Research Institute.

Ahmed, R., and M. Hossain. 1990. *Developmental impact of rural infrastructure in Bangladesh.* Research Report 83. Washington, D.C.: International Food Policy Research Institute.

Alamgir, M., and L. Berlage. 1973. Estimation of income elasticity of demand for foodgrain in Bangladesh from cross-section data: A skeptical view. *Bangladesh Economic Review* 1 (October): 387–408.

Bangladesh Bureau of Statistics (BBS). 1988a. *Report of household expenditure survey, 1983/84.* Dhaka: Bangladesh Bureau of Statistics.

———. 1988b. *Report of household expenditure survey, 1985/86.* Dhaka: Bangladesh Bureau of Statistics.

———. 1991. *Report of household expenditure survey, 1988/89.* Dhaka: Bangladesh Bureau of Statistics.

———. 1992. *Bangladesh statistical yearbook, 1992.* Dhaka: Bangladesh Bureau of Statistics.

———. 1995. *Summary report of household expenditure survey, 1991–92.* Dhaka: Bangladesh Bureau of Statistics.

Bouis, H. E. 1989. *Prospects for rice supply/demand balances in Asia.* Washington, D.C.: International Food Policy Research Institute.

Chen, L. C. 1983. Interactions of diarrhea and malnutrition: Mechanisms and interventions. In *Diarrhea and malnutrition: Interactions, mechanisms, and interventions,* ed. L. C. Chen and N. S. Scrimshaw. New York: Plenum Press.

Chowdhury, N. C. 1993. The structure and conduct of Bangladesh's wheat markets: Some emerging insights. Bangladesh Food Policy Project Manuscript 40. Dhaka: International Food Policy Research Institute.

Chowdhury, O. H. 1982. Complete consumer model: A preliminary estimate for Bangladesh. *Bangladesh Development Studies* 10 (March): 91–104.

———. 1992. Nutritional dimensions of poverty. Paper presented at the National Workshop on Rural Poverty, Bangladesh Institute of Development Studies, March 12–13, Dhaka.

Edirisinghe, N. 1987. *The food stamp scheme in Sri Lanka: Costs, benefits, and options for modification.* Research Report 58. Washington, D.C.: International Food Policy Research Institute.

Goletti, F. 1993. *Food consumption parameters in Bangladesh.* Washington, D.C.: International Food Policy Research Institute.

Haggblade, S., and M. Rahman. 1993. The laws of gravity: A review of rice price movements during the boro season of 1992. Manuscript 38. Dhaka: International Food Policy Research Institute. Mimeo.

Hossain, M., M. A. Quasem, M. M. Akash, M. Mokaddem, and M. A. Jabber. 1990. Differential impact of modern rice technology: The Bangladesh case. Dhaka: Bangladesh Institute of Development Studies. Mimeo.

Hossain, M., and B. Sen. (1992). Rural poverty in Bangladesh: Trends and determinants. *Asian Development Review* 10 (January): 1–34.

International Food Policy Research Institute (IFPRI), Bangladesh Institute of Development Studies (BIDS), and the Institute of Nutrition and Food Sciences (INFS). 1998. Commercial vegetable and polyculture fish production in Bangladesh: The impacts on income, household resource allocation, and nutrition. Draft report. Washington, D.C., and Dhaka. Mimeo.

Mahmud, W. 1979. Foodgrain demand elasticities of rural households in Bangladesh: An analysis of cross-pooled data. *Bangladesh Development Studies* 7 (Spring): 75–87.

Osmani, S. R., and O. H. Chowdhury. 1983. Short run impacts of Food for Work programs in Bangladesh. *Bangladesh Development Studies* 11, nos. 1 and 2 (March–June): 1–235.

Pitt, M. 1983. Food preferences and nutrition in rural Bangladesh. *Review of Economics and Statistics* 65 (February): 105–114.

Rahman, A., and T. Haque. 1988. *Poverty and inequality in Bangladesh in the eighties: An analysis of some recent evidence.* Bangladesh Institute of Development Studies Research Report Series 91. Dhaka: Bangladesh Institute of Development Studies, December, pp. 1–75.

Rahman, H. Z. 1994a. Low price of rice: Who loses, who gains? Findings from a recent survey of rural Bangladesh. Dhaka: Bangladesh Institute of Development Studies. Mimeo.

———. 1994b. Rural poverty update, 1992–93. Dhaka: Bangladesh Institute of Development Studies. Mimeo.

Rahman, H. Z., and M. Hossain, eds. 1992. *Re-thinking rural poverty: A case for Bangladesh.* Dhaka: Bangladesh Institute of Development Studies.

Ravallion, M., and B. Sen. 1996. When method matters: Monitoring poverty in Bangladesh. *Economic Development and Cultural Change* 44 (July): 761–792.

Sen, B., M. Hossain, O. H. Chowdhury, S. Hamid, and H. Z. Rahman. 1990. *The face of rural poverty in Bangladesh: Trends and insights.* Dhaka: Bangladesh Institute of Development Studies.

Working Group on Targeted Food Intervention (WGTFI). 1994. *Options for targeting food interventions in Bangladesh.* Washington, D.C.: International Food Policy Research Institute.

World Food Programme (WFP). 1996. Bangladesh foodgrain digest. Dhaka: World Food Programme, June. Mimeo.

PART II

Historical Perspective on Public Food Interventions

6 History of Public Food Interventions in Bangladesh

A. W. NURUDDIN AHMED,
LUTFUL HOQUE CHOWDHURY,
AND STEVEN HAGGBLADE

Since the 1940s, the Ministry of Food and its predecessor agencies have been the single largest purchaser, importer, stockholder, and distributor of foodgrains in Bangladesh. During World War II the government in British India laid the foundation for large-scale public marketing by arrogating large powers for itself: monopolies on foodgrain imports and tight control of procurement, movement, stockholding, and distribution. At the same time it adopted legislation severely restricting foodgrain movement and stockholding by private traders. This chapter outlines the evolving administrative structure, scope, and objectives of this direct buying and selling by public agents.

Origin and Evolution of the Food Administration

Wartime Emergency, 1939–1947

In March 1942 Japanese forces occupied Rangoon, unleashing a stream of refugees across the border to British India. At a single stroke Bengal Province found itself on the front lines of World War II (Slim 1956). The rapidly advancing hostile forces put foodgrain markets in Bengal into double jeopardy. Not only did the forces threaten communications, transportation, and physical security, but they also cut off rice supplies from Burma, a major traditional exporter to Bengal. Then in October a great cyclone struck the West Bengal coast near Midnapore, laying waste to a strip of land seven miles wide and triggering widespread flooding and extensive damage to the aman crop, then in flower. In December Japanese air raids struck Calcutta, spreading terror and halting the city's rice trade (Knight 1954). In the general panic rural prices doubled between mid-November and early December. They quadrupled by May 1943, creating massive failure of purchasing power and culminating in the Great Bengal Famine of 1943, in which 1.5 million rural Bengalis perished (Knight 1954; Sen 1981).

Spurred by the unfolding tragedy in Bengal, British India redoubled its efforts to control wartime foodgrain distribution. It established a central Food

Department in 1942 and issued a foodgrains control order in May, instructing provinces to prohibit the export of foodgrains except under permit. Provincial authorities in Bengal cordoned off the historically surplus Rajshahi Division in November and December to facilitate government procurement for rice-poor Calcutta. They likewise requisitioned available foodgrain stocks in Calcutta and began a controlled distribution to all of its residents, large employers, and the army. The newly constituted Bengal Civil Supplies Department (Table 6.1) issued formal rationing orders in October 1943 and began large-scale urban ration distribution, known as statutory rationing (SR), in January 1944.

By July 1943 district officers in rural areas received authority to set up gruel kitchens for emergency feeding. But provincial authorities routed all incoming food supplies through Calcutta rather than dispatching them directly to the most affected outlying areas. In fact, they distributed little food to rural areas until the viceroy's visit to Bengal in October, when he ordered that the army immediately begin assisting with emergency food distribution (Knight 1954). By November military and civilian authorities had established 6,600 gruel kitchens throughout Bengal, but the supplies came too late to prevent widespread starvation.

Under these extraordinary circumstances food officials in Bengal focused on two principal objectives (Table 6.2). First, they denied rice to the advancing Japanese troops by purchasing and removing stocks from border districts and by removing boats from coastal areas. Not surprisingly, this move seriously impeded internal foodgrain movements within the province. Second, authorities ensured food supplies to those prosecuting the war: the army, large factories, and all of urban Calcutta, the center of war industries and government administration. By the time price controls were introduced in June 1942, rice had disappeared from the market. The government responded by prohibiting exports but was ultimately forced in May 1943 to remove all price controls in favor of controlling supply to key constituencies.

Favorable harvests in 1944 and 1945 did little to exorcise the trauma of wartime famine and the distressing memory of a government too feeble to stem the panicky withdrawal of private stocks from the market. Bengal emerged from its wartime experience badly scarred, with a visceral fear of private speculators and a firm conviction that strong government control would remain necessary to prevent such calamities in the future. After the hostilities ended, the government extended emergency legislation that enabled continuation of strict government food controls (see Chapter 7). These controls, as well as the new public food administration, continued in force until independence from British rule in August 1947.

Postwar Controls, 1947–1955

After partition from India, East Pakistan inherited a system of tight urban food controls and an abiding fear of the private market. Consequently, Pakistani and

TABLE 6.1 Administrative history of Bangladesh's government food operations

Time Period	Food Administration	Number of Staff	
		Secretariat	Operational
Bengal Province, India, 1788–1947			
1942–47	Food Department, Government of India	na	na
	Secretariat	na	na
	Directorate General of Food	na	na
	Regional food controllers	na	na
1943–47	Provincial government, Bengal	na	na
	Civil Supplies Department	na	494
East Pakistan, 1947–70			
1947–55	Provincial government, East Pakistan		
	Civil Supplies Department	20	500
	Provincial secretariat		
	Regional directors and inspectors		
1955–56	None: Civil Supplies Department abolished, staff released, stocks sold, rationing system abolished	0	0
1956–70	Provincial government, East Pakistan		
	Food and Agriculture (Food) Department	64	na
	Secretariat		
	Directorate General of Food	124	na
Bangladesh, 1971–present			
1971–74	Food and Civil Supplies Ministry		
1975–present	Ministry of Food	167	10,595
	Secretariat	186	12,685
	Directorate General of Food	142	11,598
1983	Enam Commission reorganization	171	11,680
1993	Directorate General of Food reorganization	171	8,500

SOURCES: Ahmed and Chowdhury (1994), Knight (1954).

NOTE: na indicates not available.

TABLE 6.2 Evolving objectives of the Bangladesh food administration

Objectives and Instruments	Wartime Emergency, 1942–47	Postwar Controls, 1947–55	Aborted Abolition, 1955–56	Ration System Buildup, 1956–76	Reorienting Large-Scale PFDS, 1976–92	Downsizing and Adjusting, 1993–present
Rice denial	Anti-Japanese Boat denial Cordoning Export prohibition Movement controls	Prevent smuggling to India Compulsory border-belt procurement Cordoning Export prohibition Movement controls				
Ensure urban and priority-group food supply	Public import Compulsory procurement Urban cordoning Ration distribution			Food aid Public import Ration distribution	Food aid Public import Voluntary procurement Reduced rations	
Disaster preparedness	Public controls			Small public stocks Relief ministry established	Large public stocks	Moderate public stocks Private import permitted
Production self-sufficiency					Large-scale voluntary procurement	
Expand distribution to the poor					FFW, VGD, RR, AC	FFE
Price stabilization					OMS Large public stocks	Moderate public stocks Private imports

SOURCES: Knight (1954), Ahmed and Chowdhury (1994), Atwood et al. (1994), Haggblade (1994).

NOTES: AC = *atta chakkis;* FFE = Food-for-Education; FFW = Food-for-Work; OMS = open market sales; PFDS = public food distribution system; RR = rural rationing; VGD = Vulnerable Group Development.

East Pakistani authorities extended all of wartime India's enabling legislation and control orders (Chapter 7) and maintained the administrative machinery of the Civil Supplies Department (CSD) virtually intact.

Denying rice exports remained a pillar of government food policy, and the fear of smuggling to India replaced fear of the Japanese (Table 6.2). To staunch traditional export flows from the former East Bengal, the newly constituted East Pakistani authorities cordoned off surplus districts such as Rajshahi Division that were contiguous with India and had long-standing trade links to Calcutta and West Bengal. To enforce its rice export ban, the government instituted cordons, movement controls, and compulsory border belt procurement.

As a key part of its food policy, the government continued to guarantee a supply of food to important consumers in urban areas (Table 6.2). To supply them, the CSD distributed primarily imported rice and wheat. Supplies of locally procured rice remained highly variable, and even in years of relatively high procurement they accounted for far less than one-third of total offtake. Forced sale at low prices led to largely ineffective procurement drives; only in years of tension along the border did procurement exceed 30,000 metric tons (Berlage 1972).[1]

Government management of food stocks continued to grow, and urban-based SR remained the centerpiece of the public food distribution system. By statute SR's enabling legislation required a complete enumeration of the designated urban populations and mandated that the government supply allow ration quotas to every enumerated inhabitant. The CSD fulfilled this obligation through controlled ration dealers and the issuance of ration cards. In 1949 SR was extended from the 3 major towns of Dhaka, Narayanganj, and Chittagong to 11 smaller towns. In 1960 it receded back to the three big cities. In addition, the CSD continued to supply food rations to the army and police through what later became formalized as the essential priorities (EP) channel. Large employers also continued to receive government food rations intermittently during the 1940s and early 1950s but on a full-time basis from the late 1950s onward (Table 6.3).

In an attempt to direct some public food distribution to rural areas and the poor, East Pakistan introduced modified rationing (MR) in 1949. Through a need-based priority classification, embodied in the distribution priority (DP) list, MR aimed to distribute rations to the poorest elements of the rural population. But such rations were not guaranteed by statute, and allocations proved highly variable from year to year. In effect, MR served as the rationing system's safety valve, balancing inflows and offtake from one year to the next. As a result, coverage remained partial and variable throughout the 1950s and 1960s.

1. All further references to tons indicate metric tons.

TABLE 6.3 Overview of public food distribution channels

Duration	Intended Beneficiaries	Commodities Distributed	Peak	Size at Peak: Recipients	Size at Peak: Offtake
				(hundred thousand persons)	(thousand metric tons)
Ration channel sales					
Statutory rationing (SR), 1944–92	All residents of large urban cities	Rice, wheat, salt, sugar, oil	1975–79	3,200	420
Modified rationing, 1949–89	Low-income residents of rural areas and towns not covered by SR	Rice, wheat, salt, sugar, oil	1970–74	6,500	930
Large employers, 1958–present	Employees of firms with more than 50 workers	Rice, wheat	1975–79	2,400	90
Essential priorities, 1947–present	Armed forces, police	Rice, wheat, salt, sugar, oil	1995	1,400	180
Other priorities, 1958–present	Government employees in non-SR areas	Rice, wheat	1980–84	5,100	390
Flour mills, 1975–present	Flour mills	Wheat	1990–93	0.7	200
Atta chakkis, 1988–present	Small huller mills	Wheat	1990–92	10	100
Rural rationing, 1989–92	Low-income residents of rural areas and towns not covered by SR	Rice, salt	1990–92	6,600	350
Open market sales					
Open market sales, 1978–present	Untargeted price stabilization	Rice, wheat	1994–95	na	260
Free sale/auction	Stock disposal	Rice, wheat	1986	na	70
In-kind distribution					
Food-for-Work, 1974–present	Seasonal work for poor rural dwellers	Wheat	1985–89	2,300	530
Vulnerable Group Development, 1975–present	Poor mothers and children	Wheat	1985–89	750	280
Food-for-Education, 1993–present	Poor households for primary school enrollment of their children	Wheat	1995	400	150
Test relief, 1950–present	Temporary relief for needy households; food in exchange for work	Rice, wheat	1970–74	na	90
Gratuitous relief, 1950–present	Temporary relief for needy households	Rice, wheat	1970–74	na	90

SOURCES: Ahmed and Chowdhury (1994), Ahmed and Billah (1994), Chowdhury (1989), Berlage (1972), Knight (1954), WGTFI (1994).

NOTE: na indicates not available.

FIGURE 6.1 Public foodgrain procurement and distribution

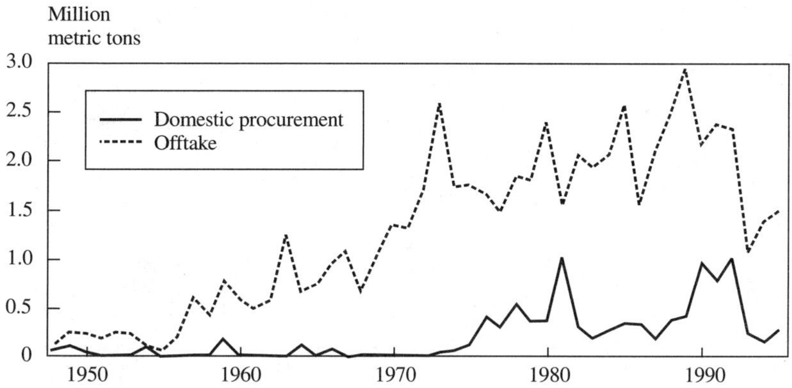

SOURCES: Ahmed and Chowdhury (1994), Berlage (1972), FPMU (1995), Hamid (1991).

Overall, public food distribution remained focused on tight government control in Dhaka, Narayanganj, and Chittagong, which the CSD carried out by cordoning and tightly monitoring private traders. In these early years urban controls extended well beyond foodgrains to include pulses, oil, salt, and sugar as well as many basic nonfood items. Yet outside these urban centers, the CSD's direct involvement in food markets remained marginal. Despite the strong language of written food regulations, the department's actual purchases and distribution of food remained limited in rural areas. Given its heavy concentration on only three urban centers, the rationing system remained small overall, averaging an offtake of slightly under 200,000 tons per year during the postwar period (Figure 6.1).

Aborted Abolition, 1955–1956

During the 1950s ongoing ration subsidies averaged about 25 percent of market price (Figure 6.2), and the provincial administration was generally perceived to be top-heavy. After the bumper rice harvest of 1953/54, the government of East Pakistan set up the Civil Supplies Reorganization Committee in August 1954 to review options for reducing food subsidies and the CSD budget. At the same time, as so often happens in Bangladesh, political expediency intersected with changing conditions in food markets. Following the Bengali language movement of 1952 and an opposition party victory in the 1954 provincial elections, the government decided to abolish the CSD in the province, effective March 31, 1955. It discontinued the rationing system in August 1955, sold off all public food stocks, and fired all employees.

Immediately thereafter, however, the aman harvest of 1955/56 proved to be one of the worst of the decade. As rice prices began rising rapidly in the

FIGURE 6.2 Ration prices as share of market prices for rice and wheat

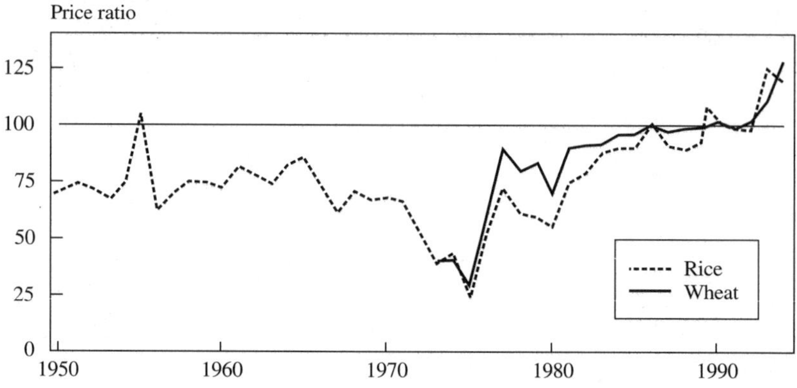

SOURCES: Ahmed (1979), Berlage (1972), Khalil (1991), WFP (1995).

early months of 1956 (Berlage 1972), the resentment of Bengali nationalists combined with the ferocious lobbying of disenfranchised departmental employees to create a general furor that quickly led the government to reverse its decision. East Pakistan reinstituted rationing in January 31, 1956, reconstituted the Civil Supplies Department, and rehired all former employees by April 1.

Ration System Buildup, 1956–1976

Restoration of the ration system in 1956 launched two decades of steady expansion of the public food system. Public foodgrain distribution soared from about 300,000 tons per year during the 1950s to more than 1.7 million tons annually during the 1970s (Figure 6.1). Wheat, mostly imported as food aid, fueled this steady rise in public distribution. U.S. food-aid shipments of wheat to Pakistan propelled growth, which began in 1953 and rose steadily thereafter, particularly during the early 1960s. As other donors joined in the early 1970s, food-aid shipments grew to account for about 75 percent of total public foodgrain supplies, dwarfing domestic procurement (at about 10 percent) and government commercial imports (the remaining 15 percent) (Table 6.4). Given large volumes and highly concessional terms—subsidies of 30 to 50 percent compared to commercial cash imports (Ahmed 1979)—food aid in its early years became a profitable source of revenue for both the Pakistan and the East Pakistan governments.

Even with expanding ration quotas (Figure 6.3), food-aid availability rapidly outpaced the needs of SR's urban constituents. As a result, the growing inflows of food aid permitted rapid expansion of the number of official public distribution channels. Government employees and primary school teachers

TABLE 6.4 Trends in direct public purchase and distribution of foodgrains

Trend	1950s	1960s	1970s	1980s	1990–92	1993–98
Public foodgrain distribution (thousand tons per year)						
Wheat	53	450	1,262	1,628	1,492	958
Rice	262	354	467	541	802	501
Total	315	804	1,729	2,169	2,294	1,460
Public distribution as a percent of total availability						
Wheat	51	90	87	64	64	40
Rice	4	4	4	4	5	3
Total (weighted)	4	8	14	14	13	8
Distribution outlets (percent of total offtake)						
Ration channels	na	92	87	59	57	20
Open market sales	na	1	1	8	6	12
In-kind distribution	na	7	12	33	37	68
Total	na	100	100	100	100	100
Sources of public foodgrains (percent)						
Domestic procurement	17	5	11	17	37	28
Government commercial imports	na	na	15	27	10	19
Food aid	83	95	74	56	53	54
Total	100	100	100	100	100	100
Domestic procurement (thousand tons per year)						
Wheat	0	0	7	99	58	73
Rice	51	33	183	281	862	311
Percent voluntary	na	42	88	100	100	100
Total	51	33	190	381	920	384
Procurement as a percent of domestic production						
Wheat	0	0	2	9	6	5
Rice	1	0	1	2	5	2

SOURCES: Ahmed and Chowdhury (1994), Berlage (1972), FPMU (1998), Hamid (1991).

NOTE: na indicates not available.

living outside the SR areas were added to the MR rolls in 1957, while offtake to large employers became a permanent feature of the ration system in 1958. Flour mills began receiving regular allotments from the CSD in 1971/72, and large employers (LE) and flour mills (FM) became separate offtake channels.

After independence in 1971, following a nine-month war of liberation, food aid inflows began to greatly expand after a short period, just as the new, democratic, pro-socialist government was inclined to enlarge the scope of the ration system. Thus, SR grew with the addition of two new cities, Khulna in 1972 and Rajshahi in 1975. MR likewise expanded significantly with the addition of parastatal employees, a population significantly swollen in the early independence years (Chowdhury 1989). Teachers and staff of secondary

FIGURE 6.3 Weekly statutory ration quotas for adults

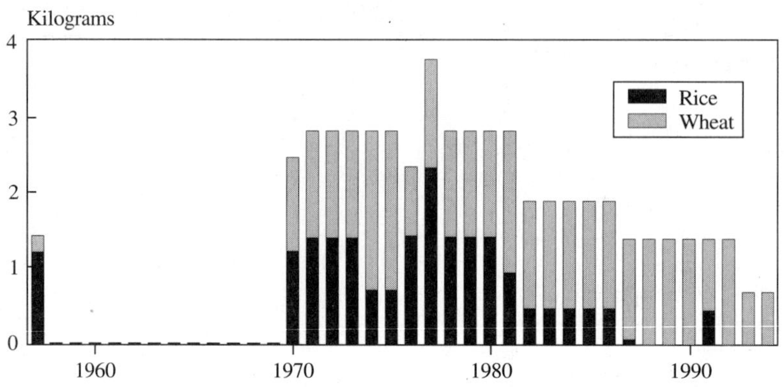

SOURCES: Ahmed (1979), Berlage (1972), Ahmed and Chowdhury (1994).

schools, colleges, and religious schools; retired primary school teachers; and residents of orphanages were added as well, leading to the creation of an additional channel known as other priorities (OP). The FM channel also saw offtake formally institutionalized during this period. By the mid-1970s the rapidly proliferating ration system was approaching its zenith (Table 6.4).

Reorienting Large-Scale Public Involvement, 1976–1992

Beginning in 1976, a second influx of food resources—15 years of large-scale domestic rice procurement—fueled an even larger build-up of public distribution. The cumulative effect of this flow, combined with continued high levels of food aid, produced an all-time high public offtake of 2.2 million tons during the 1980s and early 1990s (Table 6.4).

At the same time, to support growing calls for food self-sufficiency, the Ministry of Food stopped compulsory rice procurement in 1975 and began a 15-year campaign of voluntary procurement in an effort to stimulate local production by offering market prices at harvest season. For the first time, in the early 1990s, domestic procurement accounted for more than one-third of public food resources (Table 6.4).

Simultaneously, the stiff price inflation accompanying independence led to a ballooning of ration costs and placed a heavy drain on the public budget (Table 6.5). Coupled with the growing discomfort of food aid donors over the urban middle-class bias in the ration system, this led to a series of measures to reduce the heavy ration subsidy cost (see Chapter 9). Slowly but steadily, over the next 15 years, the government reduced ration quotas (Figure 6.3) as well as the price subsidy. By 1992 they had wrung the last price subsidy from the ration system (Figure 6.2).

TABLE 6.5 Food subsidies in the government budget

Fiscal Year	Net Food Account Subsidy[a]		
	(million taka)	(million dollars)	(percent of public development expenditure)
1973	783	101	20
1974	763	94	32
1975	916	76	17
1976	1,006	66	12
1977	na	na	na
1978	1,819	121	13
1979	1,839	118	17
1980	2,240	145	14
1981	3,810	212	24
1982	–520	–24	–3
1983	990	40	5
1984	580	23	3
1985	230	8	1
1986	1,970	65	10
1987	1,480	48	7
1988	2,540	80	13
1989	6,020	187	31
1990	11,430	328	62
1991	4,249	119	20
1996	11,803	262	10
1997	11,466	249	9

SOURCES: 1972/73 to 1975/76 from Ahmed (1979), 1977/78 to 1978/79 from Montgomery (1985), 1979/80 to 1990/91 from World Bank (1992).

NOTES: 1980–91 figures refer to revised budget totals. na indicates not available. Data from 1992–95 are not available.

[a]Cash costs of domestic procurement, government commercial imports, and government contribution to food aid imports (mainly freight) minus cash revenues from domestic food sales.

During the 1970s, food-aid donors pushed for a major reorientation of policy, reducing their contributions to the ration channels and introducing a new generation of poverty-oriented, in-kind distribution programs. In 1975 they began by introducing Food-for-Work (FFW) and Vulnerable Group Feeding (later Vulnerable Group Development, or VGD). In a parallel effort to reorient food subsidies to the rural poor, the Bangladesh government abolished the increasingly leaky MR system in 1989 and replaced it with a new channel called *pally* (rural) rationing.[2] They also likewise split off a new *atta chakkis* channel (for small processors of wheat) from the former MR system in an

2. A series of studies during the 1980s documented heavy pilferage from the MR system (in particular, Beacon Associates 1986, Eureka Ltd. 1986, and Chowdhury 1988b).

attempt to channel wheat price relief to rural areas where poor consumers would benefit (see Chowdhury 1989).

A final shift during the late 1970s and 1980s involved the introduction of price stabilization as an explicit policy objective in contrast with the largely quantitative targets that dominated earlier thinking. The Ministry of Food introduced an open market sales (OMS) channel in 1978 in an effort to stabilize the seasonal and interannual price fluctuations that had characterized the volatile 1970s (see Chapter 10).

Downsizing and Adjusting, 1993 to the Present

Both motors of the build-up—food aid and domestic procurement—stalled simultaneously beginning in 1993. As a result, total public foodgrain offtake fell precipitously by about 1 million tons per year—half of this due to a sudden falloff in food-aid inflows, the other half to an abrupt halt in large-scale domestic rice procurement (Figure 6.1). These changes in the public distribution system are discussed more fully in Chapter 9. Meanwhile, to link the past with the present, this chapter summarizes the major directions of change.

Adjusting to a world of shrinking resources, the Ministry of Food has begun to target its smaller resources more tightly toward the poor. Since 1993, the ministry has brought virtually all ration channel distribution to a standstill; only EP remains unscathed. Instead, it has focused on in-kind distribution to the poor through FFW and VGD allocations. The Government of Bangladesh has launched a new Food-for-Education (FFE) program in an effort to link food subsidies to the poor with expanded primary school enrollment of their children.

Meanwhile, the government's role in price stabilization, a key objective since the mid-1970s, has become less clear. Through the early 1990s diminished seasonal price swings due to the advent of the large boro rice crop began to allay concerns about wide seasonal swings. The liberalization of private foodgrain imports (in July 1992 for wheat and July 1993 for rice) has afforded an additional buffer against year-to-year swings in availability and prices. The price slump of 1992 followed by the big spikes of 1995, however, has forced politicians, consumers, and policymakers to reevaluate the government's public role in foodgrain price stabilization.

Disaster preparedness, a long-standing tenet of Bangladesh food policy, remains a concern. Clearly, the advent of large-scale private imports has reduced pressure on public stock requirements. In response to the 1994/95 aman and boro harvest shortfalls, private importers brought in 990,000 tons of foodgrains compared with 310,000 the year before (FPMU 1995). The production downturn of 1997/98 elicited a similar surge in private inflows as traders imported 930,000 tons of rice and a further 120,000 tons of wheat to cushion the reduction in aman production. Even so, 50 years after the Great Bengal Famine and 20 years after the famine of 1974/75, policymakers still suspect that some level of public foodgrain stocks (or options on forward foodgrain import deliveries) remains necessary. The level of such stocks remains a question for Chapter 10.

Evolving Instruments and Objectives

Distribution

Public food distribution has long been a key instrument of public food policy (Table 6.2). Through public distribution and tight marketing controls, the Ministry of Food and its predecessor agencies have ensured food supplies (primarily of foodgrains) to urban areas. Through public distribution, the government has delivered subsidies to key constituencies—the politically influential urban middle class and more recently the rural poor. Through open market sales of public grains, the ministry has attempted to influence prices at peak seasons.

Stockholding

During the 1940s and 1950s the government relied primarily on closely monitoring privately owned food stocks rather than on direct public ownership. But in the 1960s the public holding of foodstocks emerged as an important instrument of public food policy. Initially, public stocks aimed to provide physical insurance for disaster relief. For this purpose, procurement manuals in the 1960s suggested an emergency reserve of 600,000 tons of foodgrains. Then after following the emergencies of the early independence years, the newly constituted Government of Bangladesh made increased public warehousing and stock acquisition a high priority (Figure 6.4). In recent years, as price stabilization has become a more prominent objective of food policy, public food stocks have been used as a thinly veiled threat to private traders not to send prices too high.

Procurement

Food imports have long dominated as supply source for the public food distribution system (PFDS). Local procurement, almost exclusively of rice, has varied over time in scale and form in response to evolving policy objectives. For over three decades, from the mid-1940s to the mid-1970s, compulsory procurement, in conjunction with cordoning and movement controls, became an instrument in the battle to stanch smuggling. Given low procurement prices, these public drives amounted to little more than attempted confiscation. They met with widespread evasion and procured feeble quantities.

But from the mid-1970s through the early 1990s, procurement became an instrument of price support for farmers, the Ministry of Food's contribution to promoting food production and self-sufficiency. During the first big voluntary

FIGURE 6.4 Government foodgrain storage capacity

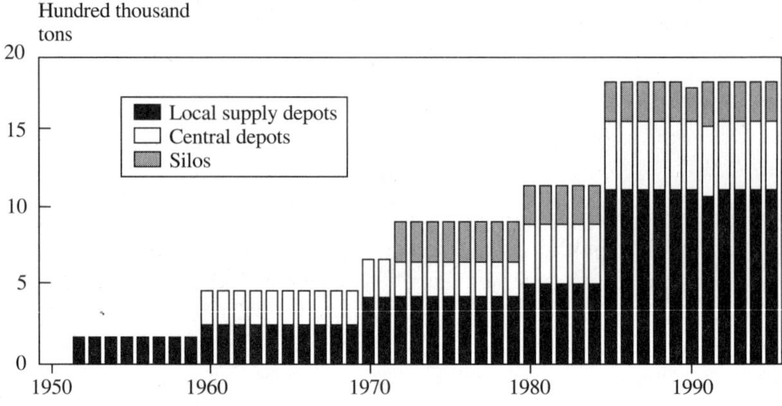

SOURCE: Ahmed and Chowdhury (1994).

procurement drive in the late 1970s, the Directorate General of Food (DGF) procured both directly through temporary purchase centers and indirectly through authorized grain dealers (AGDs). The AGDs were expected to buy at fixed procurement prices and deliver to government warehouses charging only a fixed commission markup. In reality, the AGDs belied the trust reposed in them and bought grain at market prices rather than at the higher procurement price, thus earning extra profits for themselves. In the second procurement surge, from the mid-1980s to the early 1990s, the DGF relied on millgate contractors to procure paddy and mill it into rice. In theory, like the AGDs, millers were to pay the government's preannounced procurement price to farmers and charge DGF only a fixed milling commission. Widespread suspicion that this resulted in price support for millers and food officials rather than for farmers (Chowdhury 1992; Rahman 1992c), coupled with the high cost of rice relative to wheat, led to suspension of large-scale rice procurement at millgate in 1992/93. Since then, the DGF has procured much smaller volumes through competitive tender (Rahman 1992a, 1992b, 1992c, 1993; IFPRI 1992). In 1996/97, however, the government began procurement at a price fixed close to the market price and to procure directly from traders and farmers.

Causes of Change, Past and Future

Recurrent emergencies in 1943, 1970, and 1974/75 have triggered direct public involvement in food distribution and sustained it over time. A fading but lingering distrust of private traders further sustains interest in ongoing public participation.

Once engaged in direct public marketing, the government's operational agencies have grown in scale and then shrunk again to match resource availability. In all but wartime, resource availability has governed the scale of government stockholding and food distribution. Because most resources in the form of food aid come from outside the country, external views have shaped the structure and focus of the PFDS. Domestic political philosophy has likewise played a strong role, particularly in the rapid ration build-up after independence in the early 1970s. In addition, strong lobbying by vested interest groups—the Food Department, ration recipients, dealers, and millers—has undoubtedly influenced the shape of public involvement, perhaps most clearly in the resurrection of the CSD in 1956. Recent large reductions in resource flows through the PFDS have greatly reduced the size and influence of key interest groups, particularly the ration recipients and the millers. Consequently, their interest and impact has waned markedly.

What can the past foretell of the future? Given a probable continued fall in food-aid inflows, it seems likely that domestic resource availability and the overall food situation will govern the size and shape of the PFDS in coming years.

References

Ahmed, A. U., and Billah, K. 1994. Food for Education Program in Bangladesh: An early assessment. Bangladesh Food Policy Project Manuscript 62. Washington, D.C.: International Food Policy Research Institute. Mimeo.

Ahmed, A. W. N., and L. H. Chowdhury. 1994. History of the Ministry of Food, Government of Bangladesh (4 vols.). Bangladesh Food Policy Project Manuscript 57. Washington, D.C.: International Food Policy Research Institute. Mimeo.

Ahmed, R. 1979. *Foodgrain supply, distribution, and consumption policies within a dual pricing mechanism: A case study of Bangladesh.* IFPRI Research Report 8. Washington, D.C.: International Food Policy Research Institute.

Atwood, D., A. S. M. Jahangir, H. Smith, and G. Kabir. 1994. A history of food aid in Bangladesh. Paper presented at the seminar "Evolving Food Markets and Food Policy in Bangladesh," held by the International Fertilizer Development Center, Dkaha, May 2–4.

Beacon Associates. 1986. The existing system of public foodgrain distribution in Bangladesh and proposals for restructuring. Report prepared for the Bangladesh Ministry of Food. Dhaka: Beacon Associates. Mimeo.

Berlage, L. 1972. Demand and supply policies for foodgrain in Bangladesh. Center for Population Studies Report 7. Cambridge, Mass.: Harvard University. Mimeo.

Chowdhury, N. 1988a. Accounting for subsidized food resources distributed in statutory rationing in Bangladesh. *Bangladesh Development Studies* 16 (December): 41–64.

———. 1988b. Where the poor come last: The case of modified rationing in Bangladesh. *Bangladesh Development Studies* 16 (March): 27–54.

———. 1989. The changing food system: Storage, marketing and distribution issues. In *Food strategies in Bangladesh: Medium and long term perspectives,* ed. Bangladesh Planning Commission. Dhaka: University Press.

———. 1992. Rice markets in Bangladesh: A study in structure, conduct, and performance. Bangladesh Food Policy Project Manuscript 22. Washington, D.C.: International Food Policy Research Institute. Mimeo.

Eureka (Bangladesh). 1986. *Study on subsidies in public foodgrain distribution system in Bangladesh.* Dhaka: Eureka.

Food Planning and Monitoring Unit (FPMU). 1995. Food situation report, June 1995. Dhaka: Bangladesh Ministry of Food. Mimeo.

———. 1998. Data base on food situation. Dhaka: Bangladesh Ministry of Food.

Haggblade, S. 1994. Evolving food markets and food policy in Bangladesh. Bangladesh Food Policy Project Manuscript 64. Washington, D.C.: International Food Policy Research Institute. Mimeo.

Hamid, M. A. 1991. A database on agriculture and foodgrains in Bangladesh, 1947/8–1989/90. Dhaka, Bangladesh.

International Food Policy Research Institute (IFPRI). 1992. Progress in tendering for rice. Bangladesh Food Policy Project Policy Brief 2. Dhaka: International Food Policy Research Institute. Mimeo.

Khalil, M. I. 1991. The agricultural sector in Bangladesh. Dhaka: U.S. Agency for International Development (USAID), September. Data base.

Knight, H. 1954. *Food administration in India, 1939–47.* Stanford, Calif., U.S.A.: Stanford University Press.

Montgomery, R. 1985. Statutory rationing and modified rationing: Causes and effects. *Bangladesh Development Studies* 13 (March): 109–116.

Rahman, M. 1992a. An operational review, public procurement of rice by open tender in Bangladesh (boro season of 1992). Bangladesh Food Policy Project Manuscript 21. Dhaka: International Food Policy Research Institute. Mimeo.

———. 1992b. Public procurement of paddy and rice in Bangladesh, millage and storage adjustment for efficiency. Bangladesh Food Policy Project Manuscript 13. Dhaka: International Food Policy Research Institute. Mimeo.

———. 1992c. A viable procedure of open tender for public procurement of rice in Bangladesh. Bangladesh Food Policy Project Manuscript 12. Dhaka: International Food Policy Research Institute. Mimeo.

———. 1993. Review of Ministry of Food's Tender No. 5, the first aman tender of 1992/93. Bangladesh Food Policy Project Manuscript 25. Dhaka: International Food Policy Research Institute. Mimeo.

Sen, A. K. 1981. *Poverty and famine: An essay on entitlement and deprivation.* Oxford, U.K.: Clarendon Press.

Slim, Field Marshall the Viscount. 1956. *Defeat into victory.* London: Cassel.

———. 1995. Bangladesh foodgrain digest, June. Dhaka: World Food Programme. Mimeo.

Working Group on Targeted Food Interventions (WGTFI). 1994. Options for targeting food interventions in Bangladesh. Bangladesh Food Policy Project Manuscript 28. Dhaka: International Food Policy Research Institute. Mimeo.

World Food Programme (WFP). 1995. Bangladesh foodgrain digest. Dhaka: World Food Programme, June. Mimeo.

7 Legal Environment Affecting the Foodgrain Trade

SHAMSUR RAHMAN

Historical Background of Emergency Food Legislation

The Government of India issued a wartime Proclamation of Emergency on September 3, 1939, empowering the federal government to enact legislation on any subject it deemed proper—even areas normally within the sole purview of the provincial legislatures, such as the production, trade, and distribution of foodstuffs. This legislation encompassed all of British India, including the present-day countries of Bangladesh, India, and Pakistan.

During World War II the government continued to regulate the production, treatment, storage, movement, transport, distribution, disposal, acquisition, use, and consumption of many essential commodities, including foodgrains. Provincial governments also instituted measures establishing controls on foodgrain supply, including direct government procurement and distribution.

When the war ended, the British parliament enacted new legislation extending the authority of the Indian federal government to regulate production, storage, and commerce in foodgrains. Under this authority the governor-general of India enacted the Essential Supplies (Temporary Powers) Act (1946), the key postwar act controlling foodgrains. It empowered the federal government to

1. regulate the production and manufacture of any essential commodity;
2. control the prices at which essential commodities could be bought or sold;
3. regulate the storage, transport, distribution, disposal, acquisition, use, and consumption of any essential commodity;
4. prohibit the withholding from sale of any essential commodity;
5. require any person holding stock of an essential commodity to sell the stock at the price and to the persons specified by government order;

This chapter summarizes Rahman (1993).

6. regulate or prohibit any commercial or financial transactions relating to foodstuffs if authorities deemed these transactions detrimental to the public interest; and
7. collect any information or statistics with a view to regulating or prohibiting any of the aforesaid matters.

After Indian independence all laws made during the British period, including the Essential Supplies Act, were continued by virtue of the provisions of the 1947 Indian Independence Act. In this way the Governments of Bangladesh, India, and Pakistan inherited a common legislative framework for controlling the supply and distribution of foodgrains.

Entrenching the Temporary Measures

During the war the government enacted various legislative acts as temporary measures. Yet even after the war, large portions of this legislation continued. Although provisions of the Essential Supplies Act allowed it to expire six years after the revocation of the Proclamation of Emergency (1939), both the act and its subordinate legislation continued year after year through a series of enactments: the India (Proclamation of Emergency) Act (1946), the India (Central Government and Legislature) Act (1946), the Emergency Provisions (Continuation) Ordinance (1946), and the Essential Supplies (Continuation of Temporary Powers) Ordinance (1955).

After partition and the creation of Pakistan, the new constitutions of 1956 and 1962 made specific provisions to continue the existing laws, even those in force under British rule. During 1958 and 1969 martial law was proclaimed in Pakistan, and several martial law instruments were issued that allowed existing laws to continue.

Likewise, during Bangladesh's war of independence from Pakistan, the Government of Bangladesh in exile at Mujibnagar issued the Laws Continuance Enforcement Order under which all existing laws enacted before March 25, 1971, were continued, remaining in force until they are repealed. Thus, all Indian federal orders in force under the Essential Supplies Act and all provincial legislation issued by the legislatures of Bengal, East Bengal, and East Pakistan continued in newly independent Bangladesh.

Evolution of Legislation Affecting Foodgrains

Acts Relating to Foodgrains

THE EAST PAKISTAN CONTROL OF ESSENTIAL COMMODITIES ACT (1956). Even in the 1990s all orders regulating foodgrains in Bangladesh emanate from a single legal authority, the East Pakistan Control of Essential Commodities Act of 1956—the legal bridge between the emergency legislation issued during World War II and the controlling orders in effect today. East Pakistan's earlier source of authority to legislate control of foodgrains, the Essential Supplies (Continuance of Temporary Powers) Ordinance (1955), was issued by the central government of Pakistan and due to expire in April 1956. As the law was about to lapse, East Pakistan entered into a period of near-famine conditions. Anxious to continue their control of foodstuffs, the provincial legislature enacted the Control of Essential Commodities Act. According to the member in charge of the draft bill, "[because] these commodities are in short supply and their equitable distribution necessary, it is considered expedient in the public interest to have some control over these commodities for some time more." Since the act did not specify any time limit, it continues in force today.

The Control of Essential Commodities Act was designed to control the production, treatment, keeping, storage, movement, transport, supply, distribution, acquisition, trade, use, and consumption of essential commodities within East Pakistan. *Essential commodity* was defined to mean, among many other commodities, foodgrains, edible oilseeds, and oils. The most important provision of this act is Section 3, which allows the government to issue orders it feels necessary for ensuring supplies of any essential commodity or for securing its equitable distribution and availability at a fair price.

According to this enactment, orders made under this and prior legislation remain in effect until rescinded. Thus, the act continues wartime legislation on hoarding, cordoning, price control, rationing, and all forms of foodgrain control in independent Bangladesh. Furthermore, the orders made under this act were designated to prevail over the provisions of other acts. Today this act continues to sustain a wide array of subordinate orders issued under its auspices.

THE HOARDING AND BLACK MARKET ACT (1948). Enacted by the central legislature of Pakistan, this law aimed to prevent hoarding and black market dealings in essential commodities, including foodgrains. *Black market* was defined as selling, distributing, acquiring, or disposing of foodstuffs at a price greater than the maximum one fixed by law. *Hoarding* was defined as stocking or storing anything in excess of the maximum quantity allowed under any law. As recently as December 1989, for example, it was illegal for any ordinary private citizen in Bangladesh to hold more than 750 kilograms of rice. Although still in effect, this act is not generally enforced.

Orders Relating to Foodgrains

Under enabling emergency legislation the Government of India issued a spate of foodgrain control orders during World War II. As exigencies arose, the provincial governments also issued regulatory orders controlling foodgrains under authority delegated to them by the Defense of India Act (1939). At first many orders were issued pertaining to foodstuffs, but as time passed the number of orders diminished. Many orders were made and later rescinded, while some were reissued and modified over time. Others remain in effect through a series of saving clauses in postwar legislation but are not enforced because the food supply in Bangladesh has improved (Table 7.1).

THE EAST BENGAL (COMPULSORY LEVY OF FOODGRAINS) ORDER (1948), THE EAST PAKISTAN (PROCUREMENT OF FOODGRAINS IN BORDER BELT) ORDER (1965), AND THE EAST PAKISTAN (PROCUREMENT OF FOODGRAINS) ORDER (1965). Of these three procurement orders only the Procurement of Foodgrains Order remains in force. It was issued by the provincial government of East Pakistan under the Control of Essential Commodities Act (1956). Like its predecessors, this order enables the government to procure excess aman rice and paddy from producers, specifying compulsory, fixed-price sale at a rate of 112 kilograms of paddy per acre (0.41 hectare) for cultivable area in excess of five acres (2.02 hectares) of land. This order, however, is no longer enforced; and the government procures rice and paddy voluntarily from the market as does any other trader during the aman and boro seasons.

THE BENGAL RICE MILLS CONTROL ORDER (1943). The provincial Government of Bengal issued the Bengal Rice Mills Control Order as one of its measures to combat the Bengal Famine. The government took stock of the number of rice mills in the province and the total capacity available for milling rice by introducing a licensing requirement for every operator of a mechanical rice mill. The licensee is required to submit a report on its stocks of rice and storage warehouses. Every mill manager is required to follow orders governing the purchase, sale, and distribution of rice or paddy. Further, the manager must give priority to supplying government requirements before filling other contracts. The order also requires that a rice mill receive paddy only from persons specifically listed in its license application. Moreover, the millers are restricted to purchasing paddy only from the area mentioned in their license. A miller may only deliver rice to a person holding a government permit and may not move the rice from the mill premises to any other place without a government permit.

This order remains on the statute books, but it is only partially enforced. Some provisions, particularly those requiring the abrogation of contracts with private parties in favor of government, may violate provisions of the other existing contract acts. This complex web of legal provisions has inhibited the development of competitive markets. Although the provisions are not fully enforced, their presence in the statute books is a powerful obstacle to long-term investments, bank loans, and business contracts.

THE EAST BENGAL FOODSTUFFS PRICE CONTROL AND ANTI-HOARDING ORDER (1953). Under the Essential Supplies Act (1946) the provincial government issued this order and gave itself the power to fix maximum prices at which any foodstuff may be sold by a retailer, a wholesaler, or any other

TABLE 7.1 Current status of acts and orders relating to foodgrains in Bangladesh

Regulation	Purpose	Status	
		Legally in Force?	Enforced?
1. East Pakistan Control of Essential Commodities Act, 1956	Regulates production	Yes	Yes
	Controls prices		
	Regulates storage, transport disposal, acquisition		
	Prohibit hoarding		
2. Hoarding and Black Market Act, 1948	Prevents black market sales	Yes	No
	Prevents hoarding		
3. Food (Special Courts) Act, 1956	Provides enforcement of foodgrain contraventions	Yes	No
4. East Pakistan (Procurement of Foodgrains) Order, 1965	Requires compulsory sale of paddy to government	Yes	No
5. Bengal Rice Mills Control Order, 1943	Licenses mills	Yes	Partly
	Requires report of stocks		
	Gives priority to government requirement		
6. East Bengal Flour and *Dal* Mills and *Chakkis* Control Order, 1948	Restricts sale without a permit	Yes	Partly
7. East Bengal Foodstuffs Price Control and Anti-Hoarding Order, 1953	Specifies maximum allowable private stocks	Yes	No
	Restricts duration for holding stocks		
8. Further notification on East Bengal Foodstuffs Price Control and Anti-Hoarding Order, 1953	Restricts quantities held	Yes	No
	Restricts movement		
	Fixes maximum sale price		
9. East Bengal Essential Foodstuffs Anti-Hoarding Order, 1956	Prohibits holding large stocks	Yes	No
	Restricts movement		
10. East Bengal Foodgrains (Disposal and Acquisition) Order, 1948	Requires sale of excess stock	Yes	No
	Requires delivery of foodgrains at specified place		
11. East Bengal Foodgrains (Movement and Control) Order, 1949	Prohibits export without permit	Yes	Yes
12. Guest Control Order, 1984	Limits extravagant consumption on social occasions	Yes	No
13. Bengal Rationing Order, 1943	Introduces government rationing system	Yes	No
14. East Bengal Urban Area Rationing Regulations, 1956	Extends rationing to some urban areas	Yes	No
15. East Bengal Rationing (Establishment) Enquiry Order, 1949	Ascertains ration requirements for institutions	Yes	No
16. East Bengal Rationing Preparatory Enquiry Order, 1949	Ascertains ration requirements for individuals	Yes	No

SOURCE: Rahman (1993).

person. Here, the word *foodstuff* means rice, paddy, wheat, and wheat products. The order provides that no businessperson shall trade in foodstuffs except under a license granted by the government. Private holding of large foodgrain stocks is prohibited; and the government may direct that no family, retailer, or wholesaler keep or control any foodstuff above a specified quantity and time period. If it finds such excess stocks, the government may dispose of them as it sees fit.

Many notifications have been issued under this order. The most recent, on October 4, 1987, provided the following stipulations:

1. No trader may, without a license, keep in his or her control foodstuffs in excess of 750 kilograms.
2. No wholesaler or retailer may keep in his or her control more than 187 and 19 metric tons of rice or paddy, respectively.
3. Except for an importer, no trader of foodstuffs shall keep in his or her control any foodstuff for longer than 20 days from the date of purchase and shall not keep it in one place for more than 7 days.
4. No importer of rice may, from the date of import, keep in his or her control the imported rice for a period longer than
   a. 30 days for 100 percent of the imported rice,
   b. 50 days for 50 percent of the imported rice,
   c. 65 days for 25 percent of the imported rice, or
   d. 75 days for less than 25 percent of the imported rice.
5. Every importer of rice must report to the district controller of food about the stock and sale of the imported rice.

In December 1989 the government rescinded this notification. Accordingly, since 1990, there has been no impediment for traders or businesspeople to control any quantity of foodstuffs for any period. Nevertheless, the order enabling further notifications to be issued is still in force.

THE EAST BENGAL CORDONING ORDER (1947), THE EAST PAKISTAN CORDONING ORDER (1958), AND THE BANGLADESH CORDONING ORDER (1974). These orders, made under the Essential Supplies Act of 1946, restricted all persons from moving essential commodities, particularly rice and paddy, from one region to another. A government-issued permit was required to move foodgrains from the area specified in the order to any other. These orders were made during times of foodgrain shortages and famines. With the improvement in the food situation, however, all the orders have been rescinded; thus, there is no longer any control of internal foodgrain movement. Traders can now, without any hindrance, purchase any quantity of rice or paddy and move it to any place within the country.

THE EMERGENCY (REGULATION OF RATIONED ARTICLES AND INTERNAL PROCUREMENT OF RICE AND PADDY) ORDER (1975). In the face of yet another famine, the president of Bangladesh issued a Proclamation of Emergency on December 28, 1974. Under ensuing emergency powers the government also issued the Regulation of Rationed Articles and Internal Procurement of Rice and Paddy Order, which prohibited the taking of any rationed article (rice, paddy, wheat, and so on) out of any rationed area by any person other than the government or an appointed wholesaler or retailer.

The Proclamation of Emergency was revoked on November 27, 1979, and both the emergency powers and the order died natural deaths.

THE EAST BENGAL FOODGRAINS (MOVEMENT CONTROL) ORDER (1949). Created by the provincial government under Section 3 of the Essential Supplies Act of 1946, this order restricts the export of foodgrains from the province of East Bengal. In 1949 the province had a large deficit in food production and had to import large quantities of foodgrains. Although the order does not absolutely bar the export of foodgrains, it requires exporters to obtain a permit from the director of food, who for many years routinely denied such requests. Only in the 1990s has the government allowed private businesspeople to export rice. This order is still in effect and enforced.

THE GUEST CONTROL ORDER (1984). The Government of Bangladesh issued this order under the East Pakistan Control of Essential Commodities Act of 1956. Similar orders had been issued in 1959, 1965, and 1978, although all were rescinded. The 1984 order, however, remains in force. Like its predecessors, it aims to restrain people from great extravagance on social and religious occasions.

THE BENGAL RATIONING ORDER (1943) AND THE EAST BENGAL URBAN AREA RATIONING REGULATIONS (1956) MADE THEREUNDER, THE MODIFIED RATIONING ORDER (1956), AND THE VILLAGE AND MUNICIPAL AREAS RATION ORDER (1988). One of the most important steps taken to combat the Great Bengal Famine of 1943 was the introduction of a rationing system through the Bengal Rationing Order. To fight starvation and ameliorate urban conditions, the provincial Government of Bengal issued this order in exercise of the powers delegated to it under the Defense of India Act (1939). Simultaneously, the government created a Civil Supplies Department to administer foodgrain orders in general and the rationing system in particular.

When first issued, the Bengal Rationing Order was enforced in Calcutta but not in any part of East Pakistan, now Bangladesh. Later, in 1956, when the food shortage in East Pakistan became acute, the order was extended to East Bengal. The Urban Area Rationing Regulations were created under the Bengal Rationing Order to introduce the rationing system to the cities of Dhaka, Chittagong, and Narayanganj and then later to Rajshahi, Khulna, and Rangamati. Once operational, the system supplied the six urban areas with a range of essential commodities, dominated by foodgrains, at subsidized prices (see Chapters 6 and 11 for details). Now that the food supply has improved, market traders sell grain at or below ration prices (see Chapter 6). With strong markets the urban rationing system has fallen into disuse, making these regulations largely moribund.

The Modified Rationing Order was issued to expand the rationing system to rural villagers who had been deprived of the benefits of the urban rationing system. The government rescinded the order in 1988, abandoning the flawed system in favor of a successor program known as rural (*pally*) rationing. To establish the new system, the government issued the Village and Municipal Areas Ration Order. After a series of studies documenting leakages of more than 70 percent in rural rationing (BRAC 1991; Ahmed 1993), this order was rescinded in April 1992, terminating the system.

In general, the rationing system in Bangladesh has collapsed under the weight of corruption and competition. The one ration law remaining on the statute books—the Bengal Rationing Order and its accompanying Urban Area Rationing Regulations—is essentially inoperative. Today, private sector traders and businesspeople control the trade in foodgrains.

Impact on the Private Foodgrain Trade

The descriptions of acts and orders regulating foodgrain markets are bewildering. Every food crisis generated either a legal enactment or an order designed to control the foodgrain market. The impact of this web of legal strangulations on market development has not been evaluated, but it is not difficult to guess. Various marketing studies, of course, demonstrate that foodgrain markets are efficient and that marketing costs are not unduly high. But no study that uses traditional methods to assess costs would necessarily be able to gauge the hidden transaction costs involved in hedging against legal acts and orders enacted to control foodgrain markets. Of course, most acts and orders have been kept in the statute book but are not enforced. But non-enforcement does not guarantee that in remote villages a police officer will not use their existence as a pretext to collect undue charges from traders. How an order remaining in the statute book but not enforced can still adversely affect business is demonstrated by the case of trade credit and, to a lesser extent, of milling.

Credit for Foodgrains Trade

Historically, the government has banned the private stockholding of foodgrains above modest amounts. Given this long-standing restriction, the Bangladesh Bank issued a series of circulars severely curtailing bank credit to grain traders and millers because contraband activity in which collateral was susceptible to confiscation was a risky proposition for lending. But in December 1989, after more than 40 years of stringent anti-hoarding legislation, the government rescinded its last notification, and in February 1990 and October

1992 the bank subsequently withdrew its circulars limiting bank lending to foodgrain traders (IFPRI 1992; Slouver 1994).

Nevertheless, the weight of tradition hangs heavy. Two generations of bank managers have been schooled to avoid lending to the foodgrain trade. As a result, only large rice millers today enjoy appreciable access to formal bank credit (Chowdhury 1993; Slouver 1994), and given historically tight government control of the banking system, the quality of the mill-lending portfolio is low. As late as November 1993, delinquency rates stood in excess of 80 percent (Slouver 1994). Meanwhile, bank credit to paddy and rice traders also remains limited (Chowdhury 1993; Slouver 1994). It is desirable, of course, that foodgrain traders, like other sectors of the economy, have full access to the services of the formal banking system, and the legal prerequisites facilitating that access are now in place. In time the foodgrain sector will benefit.

Milling

The government has not lifted the legal impediments imposed under the Bengal Rice Mills Control Order of 1943. Although only the licensing provisions are enforced, the potential for forced purchase hangs over the millers. To liberalize and encourage private trade in foodgrains, the government probably should rescind this order because the millers fear that the government may ask them at any time to sell their stocks of rice at a fixed price. The Bengal Flour and *Dal* Mills and *Chakkis* Control Order (1948) still governs wheat milling, although it no longer applies to *dal* mills.[1] The government, however, does not rigorously enforce it. Many roller flour mills and *chakkis* have been established without being licensed. Because the government, through other actions, is encouraging private trade in wheat and wheat products, the order could create legal impediments to the open sale of wheat and wheat products and should be rescinded to allow private sector activity to thrive.

Summary

Many remnants of the World War II legislation controlling foodgrains have been rescinded, and many still remain in the statute books but are unenforced. Only a handful of acts and orders are both in effect and actively implemented (see Table 7.1). Thus, the remaining dozen or so legal instruments do not dramatically impede private trade in foodgrains, yet their continued existence hang over the heads of traders and bankers. As recently as December 1989, the government severely restricted traders' allowable stockholdings. The legal instruments in effect make reinstitution of controls simple: a routine cabinet decision would suffice to reintroduce stringent limits on procurement, stocks,

1. *Dal* is a lentil popular in Bangladesh. *Chakkis* are small milling enterprises that grind wheat without refining it first, producing a whole-grain flour called *atta*.

movement, and pricing. Although reintroduction appears unlikely in the present political environment, the potential remains.

As a consequence, foodgrain controls have left two principal legacies: (1) withered formal bank lending for foodgrain trade and (2) a buoyant but wary private sector, heavily controlled in the past and uncertain now about the government's commitment to free-trade principles for foodgrains. To address the first issue, the government has removed restrictions on foodgrain lending, and credit reform is under way. As for lingering doubts about the remaining legislation, further legal reform may be the best way to bury the uncertainties inherited from the famine of 1943.

Prospects for Further Legal Reform

To expunge the remaining remnants of the wartime emergency foodgrain controls, the government has two courses of action open. The first involves removal of the remaining, largely unenforced, orders that give form to foodgrain controls (items 4 through 16 in Table 7.1). Alternatively, the government could simply repeal the Control of Essential Commodities Act of 1956. Since all existing foodgrain control orders depend on this act for legislative authority, its removal would automatically sever all subordinate orders. The first option offers the path of least resistance since recission of orders requires a cabinet decision, while the second option requires action by parliament. Sequential removal of the subordinate orders and then the act itself would best sever links with the wartime emergency legislation. Such reform would not in any way constrain government action in the event of a future disaster. Under provisions in the present constitution, the government enjoys complete latitude to make any law on any subject it deems proper, including control of essential commodities. The chosen path of legal reform will reveal how confident Bangladeshi policymakers are that conditions leading to the famines of 1943 and 1974 are now behind them. Either option would be a powerful symbol of Bangladesh's confidence in its rapidly growing private foodgrain markets.

References

Ahmed, A. U. 1993. *Operational performance of the rural rationing program in Bangladesh.* IFPRI Bangladesh Food Policy Project Working Paper 5. Washington, D.C.: International Food Policy Research Institute.

Bangladesh Rural Advancement Committee (BRAC). 1991. Grain for the poor: A look at the pally rationing system in Bangladesh. Dhaka: Bangladesh Rural Advancement Committee. Mimeo.

Chowdhury, N. 1993. Credit and Bangladesh's foodgrain market: Is more targeting of credit necessary? Bangladesh Food Policy Project Manuscript 47. Dhaka: International Food Policy Research Institute. Mimeo.

International Food Policy Research Institute (IFPRI). 1992. *Progress in tendering for rice.* IFPRI Policy Brief 2. Dhaka: International Food Policy Research Institute.

Rahman, S. 1993. A review of legal restrictions affecting the foodgrain trade in Bangladesh. Dhaka: International Fertilizer Development Center/International Food Policy Research Institute. Mimeo.

Slouver, C. 1994. Preliminary foodgrain credit assessment. Paper presented at the seminar "Evolving Food Markets and Food Policy in Bangladesh," held by the International Food Policy Research Institute and the Bangladesh Ministry of Food, Dhaka, May 2–4.

8 Food Aid in Bangladesh: From Relief to Development

DAVID A. ATWOOD, A. S. M. JAHANGIR, HERBIE SMITH, AND GOLAM KABIR

This chapter examines food-aid trends and motivations and their impact in Bangladesh. As the world's second largest food-aid recipient (after Egypt) between 1975 and 1992, Bangladesh has operated a number of innovative and well-documented food-aid programs. Historically, donors have provided more than half of all the government's food supplies, often stipulating the distribution prices and offtake channels for their donations. Consequently, they have been key actors influencing the size, shape, and evolution of Bangladesh's public food distribution system (see Table 8.1).

Government and donor motivations, goals, and actions have often overlapped, but they have not been identical. Government concerns emanate from long experience with erratic food production in the fertile but unpredictable, flood-prone river delta that makes up most of the country. Interventions in the food sector originated in the famine codes of the nineteenth century, the ration channels set up after the Great Bengal Famine of 1943, and more recently in the lessons learned from the 1974 famine (see Chapter 6). Government motivations and actions have also been conditioned by public perceptions, fiscal and foreign exchange constraints, and the need to maintain the support of the middle class and the military in a fragile political environment.

Donor motivations have evolved over time. Between 1955 and 1971 (before independence), the original surplus disposal and trade promotion goals of U.S. Public Law (P.L.) 480 provided much of the rationale for food aid (Epstein 1985; ITDEF n.d.). Amendments to that law in the 1960s encouraged developmental and humanitarian uses of U.S. food aid and served as the basis for more developmental uses of food aid in Bangladesh. During the 1970s development and humanitarian motivations became increasingly important for all food-aid donors in Bangladesh. Criteria for evaluating food aid include shortfalls in food production below national consumption requirements as well as balance of payments and budget deficits. From the days of East Pakistan until the early 1990s, Bangladesh has met all of these criteria.

TABLE 8.1 Average concessional and commercial import of foodgrain by source (thousand metric tons)

Source	1975–79	1980–84	1985–89	1989–94	1975–94
Concessional imports					
United States	510	478	439	355	446
World Food Programme	142	149	268	262	205
Canada	154	217	254	187	203
European Community	148	125	169	107	137
Australia	77	81	55	47	65
Japan	33	112	74	48	67
Others	114	58	133	52	89
Total concessional	1,178	1,120	1,392	1,058	1,212
Total commercial	292	581	731	304	477
Total imports	1,470	1,801	2,123	1,362	1,689

SOURCE: DGF.

Although clearly partners, food-aid donors and the government have an asymmetrical relationship: donors have budget power, while the government has in-country commodity control. The donors can decide, in any given year, whether or not to provide food aid and the conditions (political, management, sales, accountability, reporting, or policy) the government must accept to continue receiving aid. Often these conditions go well beyond the disposition of donors' food, concerning overall government food management and policy. Nonetheless, donors rarely postpone or eliminate shipments for nonfulfillment of conditions. Moreover, the Bangladeshi government has some leeway in controlling the disposition of stocks, despite specific donor conditions, because all food-aid shipments come under its control and are mingled with other stocks in the government system.

The history of food aid and Bangladesh's overall public food distribution system (PFDS) are inextricably intertwined. Since the 1950s, food-aid donors have become significant stakeholders, lobbying to reshape the PFDS according to their own visions. Because of the enormous scale of food aid, donors have had a major influence in the evolution of the public food system in Bangladesh (see Table 8.1). To begin with, donor food permitted the expansion of the original East Pakistan government rationing system. Then in the 1970s donors began shifting food resources away from the ration system and into targeted programs for the poor. Eventually, in 1992 and 1993 donor conditions on government sales and distribution reduced government food sales (see Chapter 6). Food-aid sales have generated a significant budgetary resource for the Government of Bangladesh in the form of local currency proceeds, which have served since the early 1960s to support both overall government budget needs as well as specific projects, especially in infrastructure and agriculture.

Food Aid in East Pakistan, 1955–1971

During Bangladesh's years as East Pakistan, the United States was the world's principal supplier of food aid. Under P.L. 480, with its twin mandates of surplus disposal and market development, the United States shipped its first food aid to Pakistan in 1955.

In an era when stringent legislative controls forbade private import and even large-scale stockholding or movement of foodgrains, the market development mandate of food aid had to be fulfilled by sales through the only existing important marketing channel available, the government ration system. By subsidizing imported wheat, selling it at 25 to 50 percent below market price for at least two decades (see Chapter 6), the food-aid sales via ration channels swelled wheat imports and consumption appreciably, ultimately changing tastes and enlarging the acceptability of wheat in the overwhelmingly rice-based Bengali culture. After 40 years of food-aid wheat imports, trends in consumption, production, and import reveal the success of this market development effort (see Chapters 2 and 5).

Amendments to P.L. 480 in 1959 and again during the 1960s affected U.S. food aid to Pakistan in two major ways. First, humanitarian and developmental goals became increasingly important in food-aid programming. Second, recipient countries' local currency payments to the United States for P.L. 480 commodities became a specific concern, in part because of growing local currency accounts in countries such as Pakistan, whose payments were made in rupees. The law encouraged the use of these local currencies within the recipient country for humanitarian and developmental purposes. This broadening of objectives permitted the initiation of the East Pakistan Rural Works Program (RWP) in 1961, a turning point in food-aid programming funded from P.L. 480's local currencies (Sobhan 1968).

Conceived by the Harvard Advisory Group attached to the Pakistan Planning Commission, RWP attempted to redress the imbalance of resources that existed between East and West Pakistan by putting underused human resources to work on nation-building projects. The program used P.L. 480 counterpart funds generated from a four-year Title I agreement with Pakistan to build infrastructure in partnership with local community councils (Sobhan 1968). Because past efforts to mobilize volunteer labor for public works had failed, the new program used cash to pay laborers for their work.

In 1962 the government asked the Academy for Rural Development in Comilla (now known as the Bangladesh Academy for Rural Development, BARD) to undertake pilot projects to assist in the design of the Rural Works Program.[1] While this experiment with design was progressing, the program

1. In the words of the academy's director Akhter Hameed Khan, "The Academy's research helped in designing a Rural Works Program to build essential infrastructure. It laid the foundation for rural progress. It brought gainful employment to large numbers of landless laborers during the

was implemented throughout East Pakistan and continued until 1968. During that period rural infrastructure projects (rural roads, bridges, culverts, canals, and embankments) valued at nearly 872 million rupees (US $182 million) were constructed.[2] Between 1961 and 1968 RWP generated 208 million person-days of employment. Until 1969 the program was funded entirely from P.L. 480 monies. Despite attempts to continue the program after independence, the government's own resources were inadequate, and it slowly ended at the same time that FFW programs were growing, fueled by donated food aid (Brundin and Hjalmar 1978).

Independence and the 1974 Famine, 1971–1974

Humanitarian concerns became the overwhelming motivator of food-aid shipments to Bangladesh in the two years after independence in 1971. In the first few months India was the chief food-aid supplier (Sobhan 1982). Soon, however, a number of countries responded with shipments, and the new government began significant commercial imports. Despite war-related disruptions in food production, infrastructure, and marketing, the new nation was able to avoid famine in the early postwar years, in part because of large food-aid contributions and government commercial imports.

Nevertheless, serious food problems developed in late 1973 and into 1974. During several critical months in 1974, food imports fell to a trickle. The government's ability to import foodgrains commercially was exhausted due to the near depletion of foreign exchange reserves and the rising price of foodgrains on world markets. At the same time donor food aid fell precipitously, and U.S. food aid abruptly halted.[3] This reduction in food imports and aid was followed by flood and famine, events that would affect donor food aid and government food policy for the next 20 years. Those who remember this period

---

dry winter months, the slack season for farming. It resolved the tragic paradox of thousands of sturdy men sitting idle. There was on the one hand in our overcrowded villages an army of unemployed and on the other a crying need for earthwork. Here was a program to put them together as a key is put in a lock. It grappled simultaneously with two great problems" (Khan 1983:12).

2. All further references to dollars indicate U.S. dollars.

3. Three factors accounted for reduced food-aid levels. First, the United States–Soviet grain deal and broader international market developments (through effects on prices and availability) reduced worldwide food availabilities. Second, donor fatigue with what was increasingly perceived as a compromised post-independence relief effort involving unacceptable levels of graft and corruption (McHenry and Bird 1977; Gerin-Lajoie 1975) accounted for some of the reduction. Third, U.S. food aid stopped abruptly just as Bangladeshi needs were increasing. This halt was a result of a U.S. policy dispute with the government regarding export of jute sacks to Cuba—a cold war decision at a time when certain U.S. observers and policymakers saw food aid (and the threat of withholding it) as a worthy instrument of foreign policy (Rothschild 1976). Further details on how delayed food aid affected the famine are provided in Crow (n.d., 1990), Sobhan (1979, 1982), McHenry and Bird (1977), Parkinson (1981), and Sen (1981).

recall the difficulties Bangladesh faced in obtaining donor food aid when it was needed most.

The consequences of the 1974 famine are well documented. Prices tripled while rural wages fell, making it impossible for the very poor to purchase adequate amounts of food. Estimates of famine-related deaths range between 26,000 and 1.5 million (Sen 1981; Quddus and Becker 1988). Both the price rise and the fall in wages were triggered by severe flooding of the monsoon rice crop. The price hike is widely attributed to traders' overreaction to news of the upcoming bad crop, inadequate government stocks, and the failure of public stock distribution to effectively moderate prices (Sen 1981; Ravallion 1990; Quddus and Becker 1988; Crow n.d., 1990).

In this critical period government food ration channels continued to serve primarily the politically important urban middle class rather than the populations in greatest need—the low-income urban and rural dwellers. In the supply crunch resulting from reduced food aid and domestic production, the priority ration channels for politically important groups maintained normal distribution levels at the expense of those channels directed at the poor (Clay 1978; Eureka Ltd. 1986; Ravallion 1990; Sobhan 1982).

Donors, government, and outside observers drew a number of lessons from the famine, three of which affected future food-aid programs. First, it became clear that the famine occurred when poor people were faced with high food prices. Second, inadequate public stock levels (and the role of inadequate donor food aid in contributing to those levels) were viewed as critical elements contributing to the famine. Third, government ration channels were seen as being at best ineffective and at worst as contributing factors to mortality.

As a result of the 1974 famine, donors veered for the next two decades on the side of higher rather than lower food-aid levels when faced with uncertain food needs in Bangladesh. They pushed for improvements in targeting food aid and in policies affecting the PFDS, food pricing, and markets. Rarely, however, did they push so hard as to slow down or jeopardize continuing food-aid shipments necessary to keep PFDS stocks at adequate levels. Avoiding a repeat of the famine remained uppermost in the minds of donor programmers and government policymakers for the next 20 years.

The aftermath of the 1974 famine influenced donor and government thinking in other ways too. The monsoon harvest in 1975 was a good one. In addition, monetary changes and substantial food-aid imports that had arrived too late for the 1974 famine led the price of rice to decline substantially. Government-maintained PFDS offtake in the ration channels kept prices at low levels (Stepanek 1979; Clay 1978, 1981). The reduction and stagnation of grain prices led to growing donor concern that increasing foodgrain production would be difficult in a climate of low prices. Donor and government concerns about security stocks and ration channels as well as getting food to the poor were thus complemented by a growing concern that government food supply decisions needed to be implemented in ways that did not undermine production incentives.[4]

A dialogue on these issues began through USAID, later including the World Bank and ultimately most of the food-aid donors. Throughout this exchange, each side has operated within its own institutional, political, and resource constraints. The government has been constrained by the political requirement of meeting the food needs of the uniformed services and the urban middle class and, until the mid-1980s, of not increasing rice producer prices so much as to undercut incentives for jute production. Donors have been constrained by the availability of suitable commodities and the difficulties of getting food aid to arrive in time to respond to a crisis. Both sets of actors, however, have tried to change the system to prevent a recurrence of the 1974 famine while creating a favorable environment for greater foodgrain production. Changes to promote a more conducive agricultural environment, whether through rural infrastructure or better pricing policies, have been slow, however, because of concerns dating from 1974 about stocks and supply.

As a result of the famine, donors embarked on three long-term food-aid activities. First, new relief programs targeting poor rural people were initiated and expanded. Second, some donors used food-aid commodities and conditions to initiate policy discussions with the government regarding food prices and marketing. Third, donors and the government agreed to use local currency from food-aid sales for a variety of activities intended to increase food production. This agenda marked a turning point in the evolution of Bangladesh's public food system, leading to the gradual downsizing of the government ration system and the growth of private markets and in-kind targeted food distribution programs.

The Rise of Donor-Funded Targeted Food Programs, 1975–1992

Historically, Food-for-Work (FFW), the Rural Maintenance Program (RMP), and Vulnerable Group Development (VGD) have been the largest of the donor-funded targeted food-aid programs. Although initially instituted as primarily relief efforts, these targeted programs have evolved steadily toward a focus on development objectives. While Chapter 11 examines the rationale and effectiveness of these programs as targeted transfer programs for the poor, discussion in this chapter focuses on their developmental aims and impact.

Food-for-Work

In 1974 the government launched the national Food-for-Work (FFW) program with 32,000 metric tons of wheat from its own resources. The program pro-

4. Indeed, the U.S. statute requiring the U.S. Agency for International Development (USAID) to certify annually that its food aid is not creating disincentives to local production (known as the Bellmon Determination) was added to P.L. 480 after Congressman Henry L. Bellmon visited Bangladesh at this time, when food aid exceeded the ability of the government to distribute it without creating such local disincentives.

vided a food wage to workers engaged in construction and rehabilitation of rural infrastructure. Using labor-intensive technologies, FFW aimed to provide direct food relief and employment to rural landless and near landless people while constructing rural earthwork projects such as irrigation canals, flood control and land reclamation embankments, roads, and water reservoirs that could ultimately lead to increased economic opportunity.[5]

At first FFW principally served a relief function and was targeted at certain categories of people whose need for relief was urgent. The program operates primarily during the dry season from mid-December to mid-March in what until the mid- to late 1980s was the slack agricultural work season after the aman harvest, before aus cultivation had begun, when rural unemployment was most acute. Through at least the mid-1980s, the primary goal of FFW remained relief by providing direct employment, and the potential development impact of the constructed works remained secondary.

Since the earliest days of the program, a series of studies has documented FFW's effectiveness in relieving the dry-season unemployment and income problems of the poor and the landless.[6] Despite strong documentation of good targeting to low-income laborers, FFW nevertheless posed several problems. Substantial leakage rates, due in part to mismanagement and graft, were documented (BIDS/IFPRI 1986). Most important and most often, donors questioned the FFW roads' development impact and became increasingly concerned about environmental damage caused by the roads (Abt Associates 1989).

Ultimately, the Bangladesh FFW experience offers a challenge to the growing viewpoint that rural public infrastructure employment is an effective way to reduce poverty while creating sustainable development. Explicitly or implicitly, this viewpoint assumes that rural public employment programs that effectively target the poor can simultaneously be well managed in the siting and construction of infrastructure. Bangladesh's history of technical, programming, and administrative difficulties in successfully siting and building FFW infrastructure for sustainable development impact counsels caution in making this assumption.

Vulnerable Group Feeding and Development

In 1975 WFP initiated the Vulnerable Group Feeding program under which a monthly wheat ration (of 31.25 kilograms) was provided to destitute, landless, or otherwise vulnerable women. With growing support from Australia, the European Economic Community, Canada, Germany, France, and others, the program grew to provide food assistance to nearly a half million destitute women and their households each year.

5. In many respects the FFW program has followed the RWP model of the East Pakistan era.
6. See Alwang (1991) and Osmani and Chowdhury (1983).

As with the FFW program, the objective of Vulnerable Group Feeding was redefined in the early 1980s. The program was renamed Vulnerable Group Development (VGD)—Self-Reliance for Poor Women—to reflect the change in orientation from relief to development. The development focus came in the form of training in skills needed for poor women to become self-reliant, encouragement of monthly cash saving, and integrating VGD food distributions and training with support and management from nongovernmental organizations.

The April/May 1992 review and appraisal mission pointed out that the program has been successful in supplying food to those who do not have enough to eat but not in providing participants with the full package of development services. Since that time, the availability of the full development package has expanded to cover more than two-thirds of all participants.

Rural Maintenance Program

The Rural Maintenance Program (RMP), like VGD, targeted destitute rural women. The Canadian International Development Agency (CIDA) initiated RMP in 1983 through CARE in response to two major problems: (1) the lack of routine maintenance systems for earthen farm-to-market roads and (2) the inability to reach a significant number of destitute women who are outside the existing relief and employment programs (CIDA 1990). Today the program employs more than 60,000 destitute women in the year-round maintenance of approximately 60,000 miles of farm-to-market earthen roads in about 80 percent of the country's 4,451 unions. The program is similar to the East Pakistan RWP in the sense that women are paid in cash largely from local currencies generated from the sale of Canadian food aid rather than in kind. A 1992 CIDA-commissioned evaluation concluded that RMP has, in general operational and administrative terms, been effectively and efficiently managed by CARE over the years. The deficiencies in program management appear related largely to the absence of experimentation, innovation, and long-term strategic vision related to program sustainability and increasing its development impact.

Increasing the Development Impact of Targeted Relief Programs

In 1985 and 1986 World Food Programme (WFP) evaluations found significant progress in the development of rural infrastructure and a change in the government's attitude that Food-for-Work (FFW) and Vulnerable Group Development (VGD) were dole programs. The WFP evaluations identified the main constraint to further improvement as the absence of government complementary resources commensurate with the input of donor food aid (WFP 1988, 1991). While many of the donors with important food contributions to targeted programs also provided program food aid sold through monetized channels to support the government's investment budget, these resources were not available to expand the developmental objectives of the targeted programs. In January 1988 a joint WFP and Bangladeshi government seminar "Food for

Human and Infrastructure Development in Bangladesh" was convened to explore ways of overcoming the deficiencies in planning, administrating, and implementing food assistance programs (Bangladesh and WFP 1988). The practical outcome of the seminar was the commissioning of the joint Bangladesh government/donor task force known as Strengthening the Institutions for Food Assisted Development (SIFAD). A number of donors, including the United States, WFP, Canada, the European Community, Australia, and Britain, provided financial support (WFP 1988, 1991).

With a goal of incorporating food resources more closely into the mainstream of national development planning, SIFAD completed its recommendations to the Bangladeshi government in July 1989 (WFP 1991). The most important recommendation envisioned an expanded role for the Planning Commission in planning and programming projects funded by food aid.[7] The intent was to ensure that food-aid–funded programs were institutionalized as part of the formal development process and that complementary resources were provided to improve implementation and impacts. The task force also recommended that FFW, VGD, and RMP be implemented by the appropriate Bangladeshi government technical ministries rather than by the Ministry of Relief and Rehabilitation to maximize the programs' developmental impact.

By the mid-1990s, after 20 years of slow evolution, both the WFP and CARE FFW programs, as well as VGD and RMP, seemed poised to institutionalize their developmental objectives. The WFP and CARE activities have developmental goals, plan to concentrate resources on properly designed and implemented activities, and, as recommended by SIFAD, are implemented by developmentally mandated ministries. Nevertheless, neither the WFP nor the CARE program has been incorporated into government development planning to create a formal process of marrying food with the cash resources needed to make the programs productive and efficient. With the exception of FFW water projects and a new European Union food-aid and development program, the cash resources to pay the developmental costs of FFW and VGD (that is, to pay for bridges and culverts in FFW and for the costs of complementary nongovernmental organization training of VGD participants) come from sales of modest amounts of donor FFW and VGD food that would otherwise go directly

7. Both the government and some donors have had second thoughts about the SIFAD recommendations. Initial government resistance focused on shifting these programs out of the Ministry of Relief and Rehabilitation, but most of that change has by now been accomplished. Donor concern has focused on the time and programming constraints implied by putting food aid under the authority of the Planning Commission. Some donors and government policymakers have quietly moved most of the programs out of relief to a more developmental orientation before the programs are covered by the commission. For example, WFP has moved its FFW programs so that they are now implemented by the Line Ministries (the Bangladesh Water Development Board, the Ministry of Local Government, and others). CARE has requested and received permission to negotiate its new five-year agreement for its Integrated Food for Development program with the Ministry for Local Government's Engineering Department.

as food transfers to program beneficiaries. With declining food-aid levels and increased sales to pay these developmental costs, the result is a decline in the number of direct beneficiaries.

While the targeted programs make do with modest monetization of program commodities to pay the costs of expanding their developmental impact, larger-scale program food aid has provided local currency resources to the government for many years, primarily in support of government investment budget projects. During the 1970s and 1980s the local currencies generated resources in support of government investment, primarily in agriculture, rural development, irrigation, and road construction. This contribution to support development programs, however, has substantially declined in recent years.

Food Aid to Support Food Policy Reforms, 1978–1990

The first serious donor attempt to analyze Bangladesh food policy issues was a USAID assessment made in 1975 and 1976 (Crow 1990). This analysis focused on the integration of domestic procurement, imports, and open market sales—three crucial ingredients for stabilizing the domestic food market (World Bank 1985). It was followed by a food policy review carried out by the World Bank in 1977 and by a January 1978 Aid Group food policy meeting.

Beginning in 1978 and 1979, USAID and the World Bank programs included explicit food policy conditions based on the analyses and policy dialogue in 1976–78. USAID/Bangladesh initiated food policy conditions through its 1978 multiyear Title III food-aid program. The food policy agenda was further reviewed by the World Bank in 1979, which included food policy conditions in that year's import program credit (IPC). This was followed by a joint World Bank/Planning Commission review in 1980 and an Aid Group meeting in the same year. Canada included food policy reforms in its 1983 food-aid agreement. Other donor agreements have either referred to the food policy issues pursued by USAID, Canada, and the World Bank or have provided informal support in occasional donor-government policy review meetings without including specific food policy conditions in their programs. Other donor support for general food policy reforms has been manifested through the growing shift of food aid from the ration channels to the targeted programs.

The donor-government policy agenda pursued since the late 1970s includes (1) reduction and redirection of food subsidies away from the middle class and reduction of ration channels, (2) liberalization of the foodgrain trade, (3) containment of abnormal price increases through an open market sales program, (4) incentive prices to farmers, and (5) liberalization of imports. In addition, food-aid policy dialogue has paid continued attention to maintaining adequate public foodstock levels while eliminating policy constraints on private sector grain storage.

Reduction and Redirection of Food Subsidies

The Bangladesh government and donors have agreed for two decades on the need to provide subsidized food to poor people with inadequate incomes. Differences have arisen, however, over the relative role of ration channels versus other programs in effectively targeting subsidized food. The goal of donors, and of many in the government as well, was to rationalize subsidies by redirecting them from the ration channels (which benefited privileged groups) to channels benefiting the neediest recipients, who mostly live in rural areas.

USAID's first Title III agreement in 1978 supported this general approach by excluding sales through the ration channels targeted toward the middle class; Title III food would be sold only through the open market sales (OMS) channel or to modified rationing (MR) Category A beneficiaries (rural poor who pay no tax). In the 1981 USAID Title III sales agreement, the Bangladesh government agreed to implement a series of steps to reduce the ration subsidy system as outlined in the government's 1980 Food Security Plan.

Subsequent USAID Title III sales agreements and amendments vigorously pursued the elimination of subsidies from the key urban ration channels serving the middle class. Subsidy was defined as the difference between ration channel prices and the prevailing OMS price. A specific timetable was stipulated in the 1987 USAID Title III sales agreement for removal of the remaining subsidy from these two channels in phases. Canada's 1983 food-aid agreement also included conditions related to government reductions in foodgrain subsidies in the ration channels (Ehrhardt and Spearman 1983). Beginning in 1987, donor policy discussions and conditions—through the vehicle of food-aid agreements—regarding reduction and elimination of subsidies were supported by the International Monetary Fund's Structural Adjustment and Extended Structural Adjustment Facilities for Bangladesh, in which capping revenue expenditures by reducing subsidies, including food subsidies, figured prominently.

By the early 1990s the elimination of these subsidies made rationing channels unattractive to the beneficiaries (see Chapters 6 and 9). This drove a large proportion of these beneficiaries to the market to meet their foodgrain requirements, thereby strengthening market forces, private sector distribution, and production incentives.

Liberalizing Foodgrain Marketing

Since the 1943 famine, all administrations—British, Pakistani, and Bangladeshi—have looked on foodgrain traders with suspicion, tending to believe that their speculation and hoarding lies at the root of famines. Accordingly, since 1943, various laws have been promulgated to control foodgrain traders, specifically by restricting trader stocks, the interdistrict movement of foodgrains, and foodgrain trading credit (see Chapter 7).

These laws increased the costs of foodgrain trade, encouraged illicit activity, subjected traders to harassment or blackmail, and, more generally, increased costs and risks while decreasing the incentives for private storage and trading of foodgrains. The negative impact of these laws was first pointed out by the World Bank (1979). Subsequently, reduction in foodgrain trade restrictions became a condition in World Bank IPCs. USAID also initiated dialogues with the Bangladesh government in the early 1980s on the need to relax and eventually abolish these inhibiting laws. These conversations, however, did not find a place in the USAID Title III food-aid sales agreements until 1987. Broader donor-government discussion of this sensitive topic was difficult, although the Asian Development Bank has included it among policy conditions for a credit to strengthen food policy.

Containment of Abnormal Price Increases

As an alternative to ration channel subsidies, the World Bank (1977) has recommended a generalized price intervention tool known as open market sales (OMS).[8] The government launched OMS shortly thereafter with wheat supplied under USAID's 1978 multiyear Title III food-aid program. The purpose was to supplant ration sales by OMS to contain rising market prices more effectively. The first sale occurred in September 1978. Initially, sales were limited to only licensed dealers and flour millers. World Bank calculations have suggested that 100,000 metric tons in the open market has the same impact on market prices as 167,000 metric tons in the ration distribution.

OMS was put to a real test for the first time in the fall of 1981 and the spring of 1982, but it did not fully succeed in holding the prices to a desired level because the government failed to inject sufficient foodgrain through the channel. Finally, OMS succeeded in moving a sizable quantity of grain to the rural markets between July and October 1982. Although the quantity disbursed was much lower than the estimated deficit (approximately 50 percent lower), the program was able to hold back a potentially disastrous price increase (Montgomery et al. 1983).

OMS gradually became a regular tool for containing foodgrain price increases in the lean seasons and any other period of short supply. In the 1984/85 fiscal year OMS was initiated early in July in response to price increases caused by poor aus and boro production. Its success in containing prices, however, was limited because sufficient grain was not initially made available through the program (Beacon Associates 1986). The government better appreciated the role OMS can potentially play in moderating price increases during the periods of short supply in 1986/87, 1987/88, and 1988/89 following the devastating floods of 1987 and 1988. Substantial quantities of

8. The earlier open market operations (OMO) program, while similar in name, was quite different in concept and operation. OMO consisted of sales to preselected dealers. OMS was more open with much fewer restrictions on buyers and therefore significantly more market-oriented.

grain were channeled to the rural and urban markets, which helped contain abnormal price increases and thereby prevent famines.

Because of the late 1980s breakthrough in foodgrain production (and with a second crop moderating dry-season price rises), there was rarely a need in the early 1990s to initiate large quantities of OMS sales to stabilize foodgrain prices. But that situation changed quickly during the middle of the decade.

Incentive Prices to Farmers

Until 1974/75 government procurement of foodgrains, often compulsory, took place at price levels well below the free market. Domestic procurement had been considered a means of feeding the rationing system rather than a way of increasing foodgrain production. The USAID and World Bank food policy agenda was aimed at reorienting the procurement program toward increasing productivity. USAID's 1978 Title III agreement and the World Bank's 1979 IPC both included conditions related to improving the performance of the procurement program as a means of increasing production incentives.

Procurement-related food-aid policy conditions did not always succeed in maintaining floor prices during good harvests. Nonetheless, they improved the government's overall procurement capability, encouraged it to increase the level of procurement (boro, in particular), and changed its outlook about the procurement program. The government began regarding the procurement drive largely as a tool to support postharvest prices, and these improvements did help halt steep falls in such prices.

But setting a relatively high target procurement price had unintended consequences. First, in years of good harvest and low market price, it caused a stock management problem because the government was unable to sell sufficient rice without violating food-aid agreement conditions and avoiding a loss. Second, significant differences between official procurement and market price promoted rent seeking among government officials. Third, by 1990 it had raised the deficit on the food account to a staggering taka 8.2 billion, equivalent to about $200 million (World Bank 1992). This last development led the government in the early 1990s to limit the costs of food management and policy, even at a time when donor conditions were ending.

Liberalizing Foodgrain Imports

Although donors have generally pursued the issue of prudent import planning and private sector import of foodgrains through informal dialogues with the government, the World Bank's 1992 food policy report formally recommended opening up foodgrain imports to the private sector (World Bank 1992). The bank, however, has never included private foodgrain import as a policy condition in any of its programs. Only in the 1987 Title III agreement did USAID include private wheat import for the flour millers as a policy condition. The IMF's Structural Adjustment and Extended Structural Adjustment Facilities and the Asian Development Bank's food crop sector loans also included such conditions during the late 1980s.

Despite the keen interest of both the government and the donors, delays in negotiations, donors' predicaments, and handling constraints at the ports have made prudent import planning difficult. Restrictions on private sector wheat imports were eventually withdrawn in 1992. Within a few months, private imports had reached nearly 350,000 metric tons of wheat and have continued on a significant scale since. Initially, no import duty was imposed on wheat imports.

Shrinking and Rethinking Food Aid, 1992–Present

Since 1992, food aid and food policy have entered uncharted waters characterized by complexity, confusion, and declining food-aid levels. Initiative in food policy management and reform has clearly shifted from donors to the government. As a result of the food account's massive deficits during the late 1980s and 1990, fiscal discipline has become the government's key consideration in food policy and management decisions. Even though donor food policy conditions have been phased out or ended, the government has imposed strict limits on the fiscal costs that food policy management can incur.

Three separate developments have combined to build uncertainty, undermine the standard operating procedures for managing monetized food aid through the PFDS, and create the need for both donors and government to forge a new food-aid strategy for the 1990s and beyond: macroeconomic stabilization, increased domestic foodgrain production in Bangladesh, and a growing need for emergency food worldwide. These developments have worked together in various ways to reduce food-aid levels to Bangladesh. Recent growth rates in foodgrain production exceed the population growth rate, and it is clear that Bangladesh now has the capacity to produce additional foodgrain if effective demand (primarily dependent on incomes of the poor) were to grow. At the same time, the success of the government's macroeconomic stabilization program has led to an unprecedented increase in public revenue and foreign exchange reserves. While success in promoting investment and economic growth would reduce or eliminate these surpluses, and possibly take up the existing foodgrain productive capacity as well, the three basic rationales for food aid have been seriously eroded in Bangladesh: budget support, foreign exchange support, and filling the food gap. Bangladesh's success in stabilization and agriculture has also come during a time of growing emergency food need and declining food-aid budgets worldwide.

Given these changes in the international and domestic environments, donors and government face serious choices regarding food aid in the years ahead. Despite both the reduced availability of food aid worldwide and the continued capacity of Bangladeshi agriculture to produce enough rice for all who can buy it, tens of millions of people below the poverty line remain hungry in Bangladesh. Additionally, the patterns of food production and poverty have changed considerably, with dry-season wage employment, food availability, and wheat harvesting posing challenges to the traditional FFW pattern established when the dry season was a slack time of major food stress.

Donors must also shift the pattern of food-aid distribution to match recent changes in available public food outlets. Major monetized food aid will have to sell commodities through OMS or be discontinued and possibly replaced with targeted programs. At the same time, a focus on better targeting, reduced leakage, and better management as well as increasing the development impact of such programs will need to be strengthened.

The ultimate food-aid question is not for donors but for government: in a poor society in which long-term development and short-term targeted food relief are both required to help poor people, what is the appropriate resource mix? Is the government willing to use some of its own resources to continue targeted food programs if donor food-aid levels continue to decline? Are these resources better spent in the long-term development activities that will help the poor in a sustainable way? Or can targeted food-aid programs such as FFW, VGD, and the most recent Food-for-Education (FFE) program be effective long-term development programs while also serving the immediate needs of the poor?

References

Abt Associates. 1989. The impact of CARE's Rural Roads and Bridges Program in Bangladesh. Dhaka: Abt Associates. Mimeo.

Alwang, J. 1991. A literature review of public food distribution in Bangladesh. Working Paper 1. Washington, D.C.: International Food Policy Research Institute. Mimeo.

Bangladesh and World Food Programme (WFP). 1988. Report of the Seminar on Food Aid for Infrastructure Development in Bangladesh. January 18–19, Dhaka. Mimeo.

Bangladesh Institute of Development Studies and International Food Policy Research Institute (BIDS/IFPRI). 1986. Development impact of the Food-for-Work Program in Bangladesh. Dhaka and Washington, D.C.: Bangladesh Institute of Development Studies and International Food Policy Research Institute. Mimeo.

Beacon Associates. 1986. Report on the existing system of public foodgrain distribution in Bangladesh and proposals for restructuring. Dhaka: Beacon Associates. Mimeo.

Brundin and Hjalmar. 1978. Food for Work saturation level and constraints to expansion study. Dhaka: U.S. Agency for International Development (USAID), October. Mimeo.

Canadian International Development Agency (CIDA). 1990. Evaluation of food aid program to Bangladesh. Dhaka: Canadian International Development Agency. Mimeo.

Clay, E. 1978. Food aid and policy in Bangladesh. *Bangladesh Journal of Agricultural Economics* 1 (December): 112–113.

———. 1981. Poverty, food insecurity, and public policy in Bangladesh. In *Food policy issues in low income countries,* ed. E. J. Clay, R. Chambers, H. Singer, and M. Lipton. World Bank Staff Working Paper 473. Washington, D.C.: World Bank.

Crow, B. n.d. U.S. politics in Bangladesh: The making and the breaking of famine. In *Development policy and practice,* ed. Open University Development Policy and Practice Research Group. Working Paper 4. Milton Keynes, England: Open University Technology Faculty.

———. 1990. Moving the lever: A new food aid imperialism. In *The food question: Profits versus people,* ed. Henry Bernstein, B. Crow, M. Mackintosh, and C. Martin. London: Earthscan.

Ehrhardt, R., and D. Spearman. 1983. Food aid and food policy in Bangladesh: Report of a food policy review mission. Dhaka, October. Mimeo.

Epstein S. 1985. U.S. bilateral and multilateral food assistance programs. Report 85-114 ENR. Washington, D.C.: Library of Congress, Congressional Research Service, March.

Eureka (Bangladesh) Ltd. 1986. Study on subsidies in public foodgrain distribution system in Bangladesh. Dhaka, October. Mimeo.

Gerin-Lajoie, R. 1975. On the mission to Bangladesh: Report to the secretary of state for external affairs. Ottawa: Canadian International Development Agency, March. Mimeo.

International Trade and Development Education Foundation (ITDEF). n.d. *A compilation of informational materials on United States Public Law 480: The United States food for peace program, 1954–1984.* Washington, D.C.: U.S. Agency for International Development (USAID).

Khan, A. H. 1983. Rural development approaches and the Comilla model. Dhaka. Mimeo.

McHenry, D., and K. Bird. 1977. Food bungle in Bangladesh. *Foreign Policy* 27 (Summer): 72–88.

Montgomery, R., et al. 1983. Open market grain sales as a public policy instrument for moderating food price fluctuations in Bangladesh. Dhaka: U.S. Agency for International Development (USAID)/Bangladesh, July. Mimeo.

Osmani, S. R., and O. H. Chowdhury. 1983. Short-run impacts of Food for Work programs in Bangladesh. *Bangladesh Development Studies* 11, nos. 1 and 2 (March–June).

Parkinson, J. 1981. Food aid. In *Aid and influence: A case of Bangladesh,* ed. J. Faaland. New York: St. Martin's Press.

Quddus, M., and C. Becker. 1988. Food price bubbles and the 1974 Bangladesh famine. Boulder, Colo., U.S.A.: Economic Institute, November. Mimeo.

Ravallion, M. 1990. Markets and famines. Dhaka: Oxford University Press.

Rothschild, E. 1976. Food politics. *Foreign Affairs* 54 (January): 285–307.

Sen, A. 1981. *Poverty and famines.* Oxford: Oxford University Press.

Sobhan, R. 1968. Basis democracies, works programs, and rural development in East Pakistan. Dhaka: Oxford University Press.

———. 1979. Politics of food and famine in Bangladesh. *Economic and Political Weekly,* December 1, pp. 24–28.

———. 1982. *The crisis of external dependence: The political economy of foreign aid to Bangladesh.* London: Zed Press.

Stepanek, J. 1979. *Bangladesh: Equitable growth?* New York: Pergamon Press.

World Bank. 1977. *Bangladesh: Food policy review.* Report 1764a-BD. Washington, D.C.: World Bank, December 12.

———. 1979. *Bangladesh: Food policy issues.* South Asia Department Report 2761-BD. Washington, D.C.: World Bank, December 19.

———. 1985. *Bangladesh: Economic and social development prospects.* Report 5409. Washington, D.C.: World Bank.

———. 1992. *Bangladesh food policy review: Adjusting to the Green Revolution.* Report 9641-BD (vols. 1 and 2). Washington, D.C.: World Bank, February 28.

World Food Programme (WFP). 1988. Vulnerable Groups Development Program: Assisted by WFP/Canada/ Sweden/European Economic Community/ Government of Bangladesh/Australia. Final Monitoring Report for 1987/88. Dhaka, December. Mimeo.

———. 1991. Vulnerable Groups Development Program: Assisted by Australia/ Canada/European Economic Community/Federal Republic of Germany/WFP/ Government of Bangladesh/Australia. Final Monitoring Report for 1989/90. Dhaka, January. Mimeo.

9 Dynamics and Politics of Policy Change

TAWFIQ-E-ELAHI CHOWDHURY AND
STEVEN HAGGBLADE

The Stakes

For drama and intrigue, the story of food policy reform in Bangladesh is difficult to match. Played out over two decades, since the 1970s, this fascinating and complex tale has involved powerful interest groups, including at least three different governments of Bangladesh, half a dozen key food-aid donors, millions of ration recipients, 10,000 ration shop dealers, an equal number of officials managing government food programs, and more than 1,700 millers who supply government rice (Table 9.1). Motives and tactics have changed over time, with the principals exhibiting a wide range of behavior—from idealism to opportunism; from gentle persuasion, to explicit conditionality, to the application of military force—and, not least, patience and guile.

The stakes have been high. During the late 1980s more than 2.5 million metric tons of foodgrains passed annually through the public food distribution system (PFDS), an amount equal to 14 percent of total national consumption.[1] This massive volume of grain, with its accompanying procurement awards, carrying contracts, and distribution outlets, afforded ample opportunity for creativity in graft. At its peak in the late 1980s and early 1990s, the PFDS handled more than $200 million annually in government-procured rice and $250 million in food-aid wheat.[2] In the process, the system delivered more than $250 million per year in direct food subsidies.[3]

Like most good drama, Bangladesh's food policy reforms built up suspense slowly, to a peak in 1992. Tension rose gradually as two long waves of

1. Further references to tons indicate metric tons.

2. All references to dollars indicate U.S. dollars.

3. In normal years food-aid donors financed about $150 million of the roughly $250 million in gross cost, while the Government of Bangladesh financed the remaining $100 million. At its high-water mark in 1989/90, the cost of government-financed food gross cost rose from $100 million to $300 million when an unusually large volume of public rice imports coincided with major domestic procurement. Amounting to 15 percent of government revenues in that year, the huge cost provoked a storm of protest and accelerated cries to reduce government involvement and exposure in food markets.

TABLE 9.1 Key stakeholders in Bangladesh's food policy reform

Participant	Policy Role	Numbers	Stake circa 1990
Reformers			
Government of Bangladesh	Make policy		
Mujibur Rahman (1972–75)	Expanding urban ration channels	1	Government-financed food subsidies estimated at $100 million per year
Zia Rahman (1975–81)		1	
Mohammad Ershad (1982–90)	Ration subsidy erosion	1	
Begum Zia (1991–95)	Major downsizing of public food system	1	
Shaik Hasina (1996–)			
Civil service	Policy implementation and advocacy		
Ministry of Food	Ration system reform	1	Welfare of beneficiaries
Ministry of Agriculture	Higher procurement price	1	Farm price support
Ministry of Finance	Subsidy withdrawal	1	$100 million in subsidies
Planning Commission	Subsidy withdrawal, compliance with food-aid conditionality	1	Reprogramming of savings
Food aid donors			
USAID	Analysis and conditionality	1	415,000 metric tons of food aid
Canada	Analysis and conditionality	1	220,000 metric tons of food aid
World Food Programme	None	1	300,000 metric tons of food aid
European Economic Community	None	1	180,000 metric tons of food aid
Australia	None	1	50,000 metric tons of food aid
Others	None	8	120,000 metric tons of food aid
World Bank	Analysis and conditionality	1	Economic efficiency and fiscal health

Resistors of Change			
Millers	Vigorous protest of procurement reforms	1,700	$225 million in procurement contracts ($130,000 per miller)
Ration dealers	Weak protest of ration withdrawal		A share of $100 million in ration subsidies
Rural rationing	Weak protest of ration withdrawal	9,100	$1,200 per dealer
Statutory rationing		1,700	$900 per dealer
Directorate General of Food employees	Covertly resist reforms	11,500	A share of the $250 million in total (food aid plus government-financed) food subsidies
Ration cardholders			
Modified/Rural Rationing	No response to reforms	6.1 mil	10–30% share of $60 million subsidy ($3 per recipient)
Statutory rationing	No response to reforms	3.2 mil	No remaining foodgrain subsidy; large subsidy on oil ($0.50 per recipient)
Essential priorities	No response to reforms	0.5 mil	$25 million in food subsidies ($50 per recipient)
Other priorities	No response to reforms	5.1 mil	No remaining subsidy

SOURCES: Ahmed (1991), Ahmed (1993), Ahmed and Chowdhury (1994), Chowdhury (1989), Haggblade et al. (1994).

adjustment increased pressure in the public food system. The first wave, between 1972 and 1989, aimed to expand and reform the ration channels, while the second, from 1981 onward, plotted their demise.

Tension climaxed in 1992 and 1993, when ration channel loyalists lost the upper hand and the second group, out to dismantle the system, held sway. In what proved to be a crucial move, government abolished the largest remaining ration channel, rural rationing, in 1992. At the same moment falling market prices completely eroded incentives to draw from its principal urban counterpart, statutory rationing (see Chapter 6). As offtake from both major ration channels dried up, more than a million tons of rapidly molding stocks piled up in public warehouses with no obvious outlet in sight. The resulting imbalance sent reformers and protesters, grappling furiously, head over heels down a slippery slope, struggling to re-equilibrate the now seriously imbalanced public food system. A flurry of blows from government reformers provoked counterattacks by vested interest groups and further government adjustments. When the dust cleared, the reformers emerged victorious, having presided over a major downsizing of the PFDS.

The Actors

Reformers

Initiating action in this drama was the series of post-independence governments of Bangladesh, with their widely different political philosophies: from the socialist and heavily interventionist policies advocated just after independence to the market-oriented, less interventionist stance adopted by subsequent governments (Table 9.1). Yet even within each government, coalitions of politicians and bureaucrats have adopted conflicting positions. In cabinet debates on pricing for government rice procurement, the Ministries of Agriculture and Food have consistently disagreed: the Agriculture Ministry favors high prices for farmers, while the Food Ministry generally advocates lower prices that benefit consumers. The Planning Commission and the Ministry of Finance have also played roles in the food policy debates by virtue of their responsibility for donor relations and the government budget. Since the early 1980s, the Finance Ministry in particular has emerged as a strong supporter of reductions in food subsidies, pointing to heavy leakage and high cost. Even individual members of parliament became directly involved in executing food policy when the Ershad regime (1982–90) gave members (rather than district food committees) direct authority to appoint rural rationing dealers. As a longtime recipient of subsidized foodgrain rations, the military has also remained implicitly involved in food policy. Even the most reform-minded governments have circumspectly declined to advocate abolition of the military's essential priority ration channel, presumably for fear of antagonizing the armed forces, which have twice seized power since independence.

Half a dozen food-aid donors, by virtue of their large programming volumes, have retained a major interest in the smooth functioning of Bangladesh's public food system. Most prominent have been the U.S. Agency for International Development (USAID), the World Food Programme, Canada, the European Economic Community, and Australia (see Chapter 8). As the largest donor, USAID has played a particularly active role in Bangladesh food policy, commissioning a stream of analytical work (Montgomery 1983; Shahadat Ullah 1988; IFPRI 1993) and placing explicit policy conditions in a succession of Title III food-aid agreements (1978–89).

The World Bank, although not a food-aid donor, has also influenced the evolution of Bangladesh food policy. Because food is such a large part of the Bangladesh economy and its government budget, the bank became involved in food policy as part of its general economic lending and import credit programs. It has also contributed to legal, commercial, and financial reforms, all of which have affected policies governing foodgrain production and distribution. Like USAID, the World Bank (1977, 1979, 1992) has commissioned a sequence of important analytical food policy reviews.

Resisters of Change

Ration recipients, particularly the 3 million cardholders in urban areas and their 5 million counterparts in priority channels, enjoyed large subsidies in the early days of the rationing system. Although numerically comparable, their rural counterparts (recipients of modified and subsequently rural rationing allocations) are geographically dispersed and have been unable to organize an effective lobby for continued support (Table 9.1).

The thousands of ration dealers have proved better organized, however, through their dealers' associations. Still more effective as a lobbying force, despite their relatively smaller numbers, are the rice millers who supply domestic rice for government procurement. Of course, officials in the Directorate General of Food and other line ministries that operate the government's food distribution machinery have a large stake in retaining a substantial PFDS. Although the government's anticorruption squad routinely files charges against food officials, many others successfully collaborate with ration dealers, millers, and food-aid workers to obtain a share of this enticing government-financed food subsidy.

Interaction and Intrigue: The Sequencing of Policy Reforms

Long Waves in Food Policy Reform

Reform in food policy has come in long waves and short bursts (Table 9.2). The long waves have focused on the ration system, the centerpiece of government food interventions since World War II. Beginning at independence, the government devoted its energies to expansion and reform of the ration channels. In this effort, which lasted through 1989, an unusual alliance of idealists and rent seekers patched up the system in a series of extensions and operational facelifts through as late as 1989. In contrast, a second contingent, centered primarily in the Ministry of Finance and allied with a group of food-aid donors, became convinced that the ration system had grown corrupted, co-opted, and far too expensive to maintain. Starting in 1981, this group patiently implemented a long-term plan to erode the system by gradually reducing the ration subsidy. Both groups agreed that the ration system required serious attention. Yet while one worked to reform the system and plug its many leaks, the other strove to kill it by gradually reducing the subsidy in ration allocations.

TABLE 9.2 Chronology of food policy reforms

Date	Policy Decision
Creation of the public food system	
1939	Defense of India Act enacted to control foodgrains.
1943	Civil Supplies Department created to manage wartime ration system.
1956	New legislation extended rationing system at the end of emergency wartime laws.
Long waves in food policy reform	
Ration system expansion and reform	
1972–74	Urban ration channels expanded significantly.
1974	House-to-house military search for illicit ration cards took place.
1980–86	There were major evaluations of ration channels.
1988	*Atta chakkis* distribution targeted rural areas.
1989	Rural Rationing replaces Modified Rationing
Plotting its demise	
1978	Planning Commission advocated phasing out ration subsidies.
1981	Subsidy reduction began with Public Law 480 agreement linking ration price to procurement price.
1991	Rural rationing was suspended in December.
Short bursts in food policy reform	
1992	Rural rationing was abolished in May.
1992	Private wheat import was allowed in July.
1992	Restrictions on foodgrain lending were rescinded in October.
1992	Procurement was stalled in November.
1992	Millgate contract was abandoned in November.
1993	Staff reduction was proposed in the Directorate General of Food.
1993	Private rice import was allowed in July.

SOURCES: Knight (1954), Ahmed and Chowdhury (1994), Atwood et al. (1994), Haggblade (1994).

RATION SYSTEM EXPANSION AND REFORM. The first long wave of reform aimed to expand coverage and improve performance of the ration system. It began in the turbulent post-independence years, when the large-scale destruction of infrastructure and foodstocks, which compromised food security for many, coincided with the arrival of a socialist government inclined to expand the government's direct role in all sectors of the economy, including food distribution. In this environment, the newly elected government eagerly increased both the volume and the number of ration channels beyond the two inherited at independence: statutory rationing (established in 1944), a large urban rationing system; and modified rationing (established in 1949), its smaller, rural counterpart. Through irregular, residual public food supplies, modified rationing intermittently supplied a large constituency including low-income rural dwellers, large employers, and government employees working outside the handful of urban centers served by statutory rationing (see Chapter 6).[4]

After independence in 1972, the newly elected Awami League government roughly doubled ration allocations through urban statutory rationing and expanded the overall ration system offtake by 50 percent (Table 9.3). At the same time it carved out a bevy of new channels to guarantee rations to key groups formerly served (irregularly) under modified rationing: the flour millers channel and the so-called other priority channel, which served teachers (including retired primary school instructors), parastatal employees, and orphanages. As Chowdhury (1989) explains, "by 1978, virtually all groups with defined employment or social characteristics which conferred on them a measurable degree of populousness and political clout had worked their way out of MR [modified rationing] and into the security of priority status" in one of the new ration channels. Meanwhile, the rural poor lingered on in the still-variable modified rationing enrollment lists.

Observing widespread abuses in the rationing system, the Awami League government of Sheik Mujibur Rahman deployed army troops in April and May 1974 to help police and Food Department ration officers conduct house-to-house searches for fraudulent ration cards (*Bangladesh Observer,* April 25 and May 18, 1974; Ravallion 1990). Then in late 1974 and early 1975, the government launched another major campaign to weed out counterfeit cards. At the end of this exercise, police, Food Department, and military investigators had recovered more than 1 million fraudulent ration cards (*Bangladesh Observer,* January 4, January 30, and March 18, 1975). Yet despite this show of force, heavy leakage persisted. As history would later reveal, the pen proved mightier than the sword in taming the ravenous rationing system.

4. Essentially, modified rationing provided the mechanism for balancing inflows and outflows of public foodgrains. Since public procurement varied substantially from year to year while offtake through statutory rationing remained stable, the residual available for distribution through modified rationing fluctuated considerably from one year to the next.

TABLE 9.3 Ration channel distribution over time

Ration Channel	1970	1975	1980	1985	1990	1995
	(thousand metric tons of rice plus wheat)					
Statutory rationing	225	445	424	245	203	0
Modified rationing	769	574	296	323	0	0
Rural rationing	0	0	0	0	404	0
Atta chakkis[a]	0	0	0	0	66	15
Flour millers	41	149	165	127	192	27
Large employers	29	94	72	53	39	16
Other priorities[b]	43	235	440	314	308	14
Essential priorities[c]	23	96	90	113	139	174
Others	0	0	0	0	0	11
Total ration channels	1,130	1,593	1,488	1,175	1,325	257

SOURCE: DGF.

NOTE: All entries are three-year averages centered around the indicated year.

[a]Rural mills producing whole-grain wheat (*atta*).

[b]Parastatal employees, government employees, teachers, student hostels, and orphanages.

[c]Recipients are primarily the military and the police.

A series of major evaluations during the early and mid-1980s documented continued leakage from the system, especially from the original statutory and modified rationing channels. These studies also highlighted the irregularity and nutritional insignificance of rations supplied through modified rationing, the one remaining channel serving the rural poor (Ahmed 1979; INFS 1978; Beacon Associates 1986; FPMU 1986; Chowdhury and Rushdi 1988). In response the government expanded rural distribution outlets by rechanneling a portion of modified rationing wheat through small rural mills (called *chakkis*) that produced whole-grain wheat (called *atta*) for the low-income population. Established in November 1988, the *atta chakki* distribution targeted poor regions through small millers rather than ration shops (Beacon Associates 1986; Chowdhury 1989).

Shortly thereafter, in 1989, the ration channel reformers in the Ministry of Food decided to clean house. Abolishing modified rationing outright (although retaining the rural *chakki* distribution as a separate channel), they immediately replaced the modified rationing shops with a successor program known as rural (*pally*) rationing. This new incarnation differed from its predecessor in several ways. First, offtake was to be guaranteed rather than variable. In addition, to target low-income groups more carefully, the government declared that only the poorest from the distribution priority list (the Class A recipients) would be entitled to draw rations, and they were to receive rice rather than the wheat distributed through modified rationing. In a still greater departure from convention, under rural rationing the dealers would be selected by local members of parliament instead of district food committees (Beacon Associates 1986; Ahmed 1993).

Billed as a major reform, this facelift did little to improve performance of the system. Leakage of rations to unintended beneficiaries, already more than 50 percent in modified rationing (Beacon Associates 1986), worsened under rural rationing (Ahmed 1993; BRAC 1991). Moreover, the overtly political selection of ration dealers was read as an explicit intention to use the ration system for patronage and graft.

The fall of the Ershad government and the ensuing election of Begum Zia in 1991 paved the way for yet another attempt at ration system reform. Combining political opportunism with astute food policy, the newly elected government suspended rural rationing in December 1991 as its first major move in food policy. As later events would prove, this was also its most important move. The government permanently abolished rural rationing in May 1992, a step that closely followed two evaluations documenting leakage in excess of 70 percent (BRAC 1991; Ahmed 1993). On fiscal grounds alone, the abolition of rural rationing saved roughly $60 million in annual subsidy costs that had gone primarily to rent-seeking ration dealers, food officials, and members of parliament (Ahmed 1993). Sweeter still, the government cut off a major fund-raising source for opposition members by denying them the kickbacks demanded for awarding rural rationing dealerships. Given the well-documented siphoning of subsidies, the new government could expose corruption while at the same time laying it at the feet of the old regime.

The abolition of rural rationing was accomplished quickly, smoothly, and early in the new regime. At the same time a host of other reforms—introduction of a value-added tax, currency liberalization, and financial sector reform—saturated the media. Consequently, this minor adjustment in what was widely known as a leaky and expensive ration channel attracted little attention.

Yet even after the fall of rural rationing, a coalition of idealists and vested interest groups held out hopes of resuscitating the venerable system in yet another round of ration system reform. In part to deflect potential political heat, the government in the summer of 1992 commissioned the Working Group on Targeted Food Interventions to review alternatives to rural rationing. Had anyone cared to object (and a few donors did inquire), the government could demonstrate its careful approach to reform in the wake of the previous unsuccessful attempt. The working group review, however, gave no solace to advocates of further reform—the optimistic, the naïve, and the nefarious. It concluded categorically that the ration system was leaky and expensive and beyond repair. The report's first recommendation read: "No new ration channels. Resources available for poor households can be far more effectively delivered through other (non-ration channel) programs" (WGTFI 1994:56). Thus, the working group wrote the epitaph for Bangladesh's rural rationing channel. At roughly the same time, its urban counterparts and progenitors died of natural causes as the result of the second long wave of food policy reforms.

PLOTTING THE SYSTEM'S DEMISE. The second long wave of food policy reform aimed to squeeze the subsidies gradually out of the ration system. Slowly and almost imperceptibly, over more than a decade, deliberate subsidy reduction extinguished incentives for cardholders to draw rations and for rent seekers to misappropriate grain. Ultimately, the bulk of the ration system died from lack of interest by both its exploiters and its intended beneficiaries.

The Bangladesh government first advanced the subsidy reduction scheme in 1978 after an interministerial committee recommended that subsidies be gradually eliminated. Committee members envisioned a reduced role for government, an expanded role for private trade, and a redeployment of the considerable fiscal savings for development investments (Bangladesh Planning Commission 1978). USAID, the major food-aid donor, quickly allied itself with this group of reformers as did the Canadian government.[5] Since 1981, as stipulated in a succession of Public Law 480 food agreements with the U.S. government, the Ministry of Food has regularly raised its ration price by tying offtake price to procurement price. In support of this move the 1983 Canadian food-aid agreement specified similar conditions. After a series of sobering ration channel evaluations, particularly those by Beacon Associates (1986) and FPMU (1986), the 1987 U.S. agreement solidified the reform agenda by stipulating a 1989 deadline for complete subsidy elimination from the major urban channels: statutory rationing and other priorities.

To squeeze subsidies out of the ration system, this alliance of donors and government reformers adopted a simple but clever strategy: they linked the ration offtake price to a fixed markup over government's procurement price. Given the high priority accorded to enhanced foodgrain production in the post-independence years and the Ministry of Agriculture's strong insistence on incentive prices for farmers, the steady rise in government procurement price ensured a parallel climb in ration prices with a consequent steady erosion of the ration subsidy (Chapter 6). By linking procurement and offtake prices, USAID and its allies forced the government to choose between a policy favoring producers and one favoring consumers. The fixed markup did not permit them to subsidize both. Through this link, which was enforced by explicit food-aid conditions, the subsidy reduction allies enlisted the support of the powerful Ministry of Agriculture and the Planning Commission, whose top priorities in Bangladesh's first three development plans included increased foodgrain production.

---

5. The World Bank also allied itself strongly with the food policy reforms through policy conditions attached to their import credit programs. These conditions, however, dealt with procurement, anti-hoarding legislation, import liberalization, and open market price stabilization rather with ration system subsidy reductions. See Chapter 11 for details.

Simultaneous efforts to boost foodgrain production contributed to the subsidy erosion in another important way—by bringing down real foodgrain prices on the open market. Major investments in agricultural research and rural infrastructure during the late 1960s and early 1970s laid the foundation for greatly expanded agricultural productivity. A series of subsequent reforms in agricultural input markets (in irrigation, fertilizer, and pesticides) realized this potential by enabling a large jump in dry-season irrigated foodgrain production (Chapter 3). One consequence of these gains was falling real foodgrain prices (Chapter 2). Like a pair of giant scissors, a steadily rising ration price coupled with the fall in real market price cut out the ration subsidies from two directions, making most ration outlets unenticing to cardholders (Chapter 6). By the early 1990s, after more than a decade of shrinking ration price subsidies and enormous leakage from the ration channels, cardholders had little at stake in the system.

Consequently, in striking contrast with food policy reforms elsewhere, the demise of Bangladesh's major ration channels aroused little passion or protest from ration cardholders. Although many millers protested the resulting falloff in lucrative government procurement contracts, no politicians or violent mobs stormed the streets on behalf of the intended beneficiaries. For the cardholders had lost nothing.

CONVERGENCE. The two long waves of food policy reform converged in mid-1992. From July 1992 through November 1993, an abrupt 20 percent fall in nominal rice prices punctuated a two-decade trend of downward real foodgrain prices, just after the government had abandoned rural rationing (Haggblade and Rahman 1993; Rahman 1994). With this further fall in rice prices, statutory rationing and other priorities ground to a standstill by eroding cardholder incentives to draw grain. At the same time, liberalization of private foodgrain imports (from July 1992 for wheat and July 1993 for rice) made the large employers' and flour millers' channels redundant. Now able to import directly by themselves, these large institutions no longer needed to purchase government imported grain at a controlled price. Thus, the demise of rural rationing in May 1992 sounded the death knell of the venerable rationing system, which had been erected and expanded over the prior 50 years. After mid-1992, only the small but highly subsidized military and police rations continued on any significant scale (Tables 9.3 and 9.4).

Short Bursts in Food Policy Reform

The suspension of rural rationing knocked the PFDS severely out of balance, necessitating a series of rapid adjustments to restore the system to a new, lower-level equilibrium. The largest ration channel before its demise, rural rationing had distributed more than half a million tons of rice per year—more than half of all public offtake of rice. With its principal outlet plugged, govern-

TABLE 9.4 The demise of the ration channels

	Share of Public Foodgrain Offtake			
Period[a]	Ration Channels	Open Market Sales	Relief Channels[b]	Total Annual Public Foodgrain Distribution
		(percent)		(thousand metric tons)
1947–49	na	na	na	199
1950–59	na	na	na	315
1960–69[c]	95	1	4	805
1970–79	87	1	12	1,730
1980–89	60	7	33	2,169
1990–92	57	6	37	2,294
1993–98	20	12	68	1,460

SOURCES: DGF, Ahmed and Chowdhury (1994), WFP (1994).

NOTE: na indicates not available.

[a]Year refers to end of fiscal year; i.e., 1993–98 refers to 1992/93–1997/98.

[b]Non-monetized, in-kind distribution through Food-for-Work, Vulnerable Group Feeding and Development, Test Relief, Gratuitous Relief, and Food-for-Education.

[c]Estimated percentages for 1960s based on distribution during 1968/69 and 1969/70.

ment warehouses soon overflowed with rice. The result, according to the beleaguered director of supply and distribution, was "a Himalayan mountain of rice" with no obvious channel for release. Given the poor keeping quality of boro rice (about six months for government-grade grain), the large public stocks appeared to be rapidly deteriorating by late 1992.

Therefore, in late 1992 and early 1993 the government was forced to unload its huge stockpile (1 million tons) of rapidly deteriorating rice. To do so, government turned to food-aid donors for assistance, requesting a one-time rice-for-wheat swap in the Food-for-Work (FFW) program. In other words, the government proposed to distribute surplus rice in FFW projects rather than the customary food-aid wheat. Most of the large FFW donors agreed to the swap, allowing the program to digest the initial stock surplus inherited from the demise of rural rationing (Table 9.5).[6] Nevertheless, although the rice-for-wheat swap solved the surplus problem temporarily, long-term resolution required a reduction in procurement.

Rice procurement came to a screeching halt in November 1992 as the government worked to restore balance between procurement and lower rice

6. The swap led to a wheat surplus later in 1993 when the undistributed food-aid wheat piled high. The government ultimately auctioned some wheat and sold the remaining through its open market sales outlet in late 1993, thus fully purging the initial stock excess created by the demise of rural rationing (see Chapter 10).

TABLE 9.5 Rebalancing stocks in the public food distribution system

Stocks	1989/90	1990/91	1991/92	1992/93	1993/94	1994/95	1996/97
Rice				(thousand tons)			
Offtake	675	971	759	475	350	329	739
Procurement	918	727	940	233	144	246	513
Opening stocks	314	818	528	723	443	236	427
Months of offtake in opening stock	5.6	10.1	8.3	18.3	15.2	8.6	9.2
Wheat							
Offtake	1,489	1,401	1,586	598	1,026	1,224	653
Opening stocks	648	330	512	504	663	305	489
Months of offtake in opening stock	5.2	2.8	3.9	10.1	7.8	3.0	5.0

SOURCES: DGF as cited in FPMU (1993), WFP (1996).

offtake. In a deft move the Ministry of Food took the occasion to suspend millgate contracting under which it had previously purchased rice at fixed and generally above-market prices from selected millers (Rahman 1992b; Haggblade and Rahman 1993). Because many millers vied for the privilege of supplying grain at above-market prices, the contracting system was riddled with corruption and kickbacks.[7] Simultaneously, the government introduced a series of procedural reforms in which it experimented with raising quality requirements in procurement grades and purchasing at market price through open tenders (Rahman 1992a, 1992b, 1993).

Other cost-saving management reforms followed at the Ministry of Food. Both lower procurement and lower offtake through ration channels suggested that worker reductions were possible at the ministry. Largely through golden handshakes and early retirement, the reformers proposed a scheme for reducing authorized staffing from 13,600 to 8,500.[8] The ministry introduced a new invoicing system and new management accounting and thoroughly reviewed transport contracting, procedures, and rates (FAO 1993).

During the same period, in keeping with Bangladesh's general policy of economic liberalization, the government not only reduced its own role in foodgrain markets but also facilitated expansion of private trade to fill the gap. Beginning in July 1992 the government allowed private import of foodgrains, initially without any import duty. Private traders responded by bringing in more than 300,000 tons of wheat by December. Since the government incurs handling costs of roughly $50 per ton (WGTFI 1994), this transfer of wheat imports from public to private agents saved the Government of Bangladesh about $15 million annually. In a parallel liberalizing move, the government in December 1989 had rescinded the last notification limiting private stockholding of foodgrains in response to policy conditions imposed by USAID. This permitted the Bangladesh Bank, as part of general financial sector reform, to withdraw limits on bank credit for foodgrain traders beginning in February 1990 and October 1992. Overall, these reforms have significantly reduced the scale of government involvement in foodgrain markets, generating about $75 million in cost savings annually since 1992.

To redeploy some of those savings into new, more effective targeted programs, the government launched a new Food-for-Education (FFE) program in August 1993, attempting to combine improved food targeting for the poor with promotion of primary school enrollment, then the top national priority. Initially financed entirely from Bangladesh government resources, FFE later attracted support from major food-aid donors. The FFE initiative represents the first major government food initiative in the post-ration era (see Chapter 11 for details).

7. See Ahmed (1993) and Rahman (1992b) for examples.

8. Because of vacancies in about 2,000 posts, the envisioned reduction in actual payroll was from 11,500 to 8,500 workers.

Counterattacks

The largest overt opposition to the general reformist movement in food policy has come from the millers who formerly supplied government millgate contracts. In November 1992, when the government curtailed both procurement and the fixed-price millgate contracting system, the millers fought back furiously with a widespread, well-orchestrated campaign to reinstitute large-scale government rice procurement at fixed prices. The North Bengal Rice Millers Association, 8,000 strong, emerged virtually overnight to spearhead this campaign. Members blockaded the streets of Dinajpur, a principal procurement market. They protested in Bogra, Netrokona, and Pirgonj as well as throughout northwestern Bengal. They threatened to shut down 25,000 rice mills in northern Bengal and ran a blistering newspaper campaign advocating increased procurement.[9] Save the Farmer committees sprang up simultaneously in most districts, inspired by political opportunism (*Daily Ittefaq,* September 9, 1993). Everything in this media blitz highlighted the welfare of farmers, which the millers purported to advance by insisting on high procurement prices that they could then pass on to farmers.[10] Unfortunately, all research agrees that individual farmers rarely, if ever, receive the government procurement price from millers. Instead, they receive the market price, while the millers retain the intervening rents (Chowdhury 1992; IFPRI 1992).

The role of the government's own food managers in combating reform is difficult to gauge since it is never overt. That they are involved in sharing rents in the system is clear. Millers, food officials, and (in the old days) ration dealers carved up the PFDS spoils through a complex system of kickbacks and bribes. With this web of payoffs threatened, extraordinary tension developed behind the scenes in late 1992. Although many honest and competent officials operate in the Directorate General of Food, a significant minority involved in corrupt practices has contributed to backsliding in key elements of reform, particularly in the downsizing of ration channels and the reduction and reform of government procurement.

Most striking in this roster of counterinsurgents are the absentees—the 15 million ration cardholders. Their lack of response contrasts starkly with subsidy removal in other countries, such as Egypt, Liberia, and Tunisia, where

9. Press reports in the following editions give a flavor of the millers' response: *Bhorer Kagoj,* October 15, 1992; *Morning Sun,* November 1 and November 4, 1992; and *Daily Ittefaq,* November 17, 1992.

10. Typical of the genre is the following short article from the November 17, 1992, issue of the *Daily Ittefaq,* the largest Bangla daily newspaper in Bangladesh: "Demonstration at Netrokona: Reporter from Netrokona informed that a procession was brought out by Rice Millers Association, rice mills laborers, and concerned people protesting against government decision on procurement of rice through tender instead of purchase directly or from millers. The processionists demanded withdrawal of government decision and submitted memorandum to deputy commissioner and district controller of food. The Rice Millers Association in a press conference organized later declared that due to the government decision *farmers will be deprived of fair price*" (my translation; emphasis added).

ration recipients protested violently and effectively. Such protests often derail food reforms and sometimes governments as well. But in Bangladesh gradually falling subsidies and the parallel fall in market price have gradually and completely eroded cardholders' stake in the system. Since cheap grain is now readily available on the market, ration recipients have found little cause to complain.

Outcome

Government emerged from this series of reforms with its role in food markets reduced. It exited in the early 1980s from the multipurpose ration shop offering everything from edible oil to sugar candy (Table 9.6). Even in foodgrains, the focus of the public food system from its inception, the PFDS shrunk from 2.5 million tons of offtake in the late 1980s to 1.6 million tons in 1998. Simultaneously, private trade has expanded in import, marketing, and distribution.

The structure of government's smaller distribution program has altered as well. With the demise of most ration channels, open market sales (along with essential priorities) remains the only significant monetized offtake channel (Tables 9.3 and 9.4). Given greatly dampened seasonal price movements resulting from nearly year-round rice harvest, even the open market sales have been modest except as a channel for surplus stock disposal, as with the deteriorating wheat stocks in late 1993. For targeting the poor the government has abandoned the nonfunctional ration channels in favor of the non-monetized, in-kind distribution programs long operated by food-aid donors.

Although the government has substantially reduced its presence in foodgrain markets, no one yet knows how low it can go. Are open market sales

TABLE 9.6 The decline of noncereals in the public food distribution system (annual public distribution)

	Noncereals			Cereals	
Year	Sugar	Salt	Oil	Rice	Wheat
	(thousand tons)		(thousand liters)	(thousand tons)	
1970	na	na	na	344	875
1975	74	26	21	275	1,470
1980	79	85	31	597	1,345
1985	61	na	18	428	1,631
1990	35	23	14	745	1,713
1995	0	0	10	412	1,176

SOURCE: Personal contact with DGF.

NOTES: Three-year averages are centered on the indicated year.

na indicates not available.

still required, even with the greatly dampened price seasonality? How large must public security stocks be? What is an optimal size for relief programs targeted at the poor? (Chapter 10 addresses these questions directly.) Consequently, a clear enunciation of the government's role is yet to emerge. Political uncertainty and attempted backpedaling, led primarily by millers, have compounded the government's difficulty in defining its position. Despite several attempts, the government has not yet been able to produce a new national food policy or clearly define its role in a liberalized and growing foodgrain economy, although the existing 1988 policy is inconsistent with present practice (Bangladesh MOF 1988).

Implications for Managing Reform

Preconditions

Two fundamental changes paved the way for the downsizing of Bangladesh's food programs. First was a productivity-led surge in foodgrain production. Government invested early and heavily in agricultural research and rural infrastructure. Then as improved foodgrain varieties came from the research stations, input market reforms unleashed a wave of expanded productivity founded on high-input, irrigated agriculture. The fall in real foodgrain prices was instrumental in weaning ration recipients from subsidized government grain onto the free market, where inexpensive grain can be had without the long lines and bureaucracy of the rationing system.

Second and equally important was the defusing of major potential opposition groups: the ration cardholders and the ration dealers. By gradually lifting the offtake price and hence reducing the food subsidy in ration channels, the government steadily eroded incentives for cardholders to draw rations and for ration dealers and food officials to reroute them. In this way the government and its donor allies effectively averted opposition from the large number of urban ration recipients.

Speed of Reform

In the present case gradual reform worked better than a quick shock treatment would have. In the early 1980s, when the food reforms began, the government faced too many large vested interest groups to bulldoze with impunity. The ration cardholders, the ration dealers, the military, the food officials, and the millers all had substantial stakes in the system. The key to Bangladesh's reform lay in defusing opposition from the largest potential opposition group, the 15 million cardholders. These legitimate beneficiaries are typically able to press their case forcefully and effectively. When they are neutralized by gradually eroding subsidies to zero, only the rent seekers remain (the ration dealers, the food officials, and the millers), and they have a difficult time pressing overtly for continued subsidies to siphon. Slow erosion of ration subsidies was key to the Bangladesh reforms.

The government did move quickly, however, at the end when the abolition of rural rationing necessitated rapid subsequent adjustments in procurement and food management. Whether intentional or not, the truncation of rural rationing proved to be a savvy move for launching the end game. The imbalance it created, between heavy inflows and reduced outflows, led to a politically embarrassing buildup of deteriorating public foodstocks that demanded further action. This suggests that, in general, selection of a strategically positioned first domino may facilitate further reforms and forestall efforts to derail momentum.

Enlisting Allies

External allies, particularly USAID, the World Bank, and Canada, helped to execute food policy reform by placing conditions on food and lending programs that helped stiffen the resolve of government reformers. The donors' explicit conditions enlisted the strong support of the Planning Commission and the Ministry of Finance, which were loathe to jeopardize the massive and largely additional flow of food aid. The donors also redirected political heat from government reformers to themselves, thus providing cover for internal advocates of change. Interministerial allies proved crucial as well. In particular, the Ministry of Agriculture became a forceful lobbyist for reductions in food subsidies, although it might not have known it at the time. By linking ration price to procurement price, donor food-aid conditions effectively channeled the ministry's eagerness for high procurement prices into indirect advocacy of higher ration prices. In fact, the ministry's zeal in elevating procurement price may have contributed to reform in another way as well. By leading to periodically large spreads between procurement and market price (Haggblade 1994), the steady escalation of procurement price surely accelerated the explicit rent seeking in millgate contracting. This in turn strengthened government's hand when it initiated steep reductions in procurement and reform of the millgate contract.

Cementing Reforms

The principle of a modest role for government in foodgrain markets is generally accepted within the Bangladesh government. But the exact parameters governing public involvement are not yet set in stone. Several attempts to preserve these changes in the form of a revised national food policy have foundered due to political uncertainty and heavy personnel turnover at the Ministry of Food. Meanwhile, an unusual alliance—of millers, rent seekers within the Directorate General of Food, and idealists who genuinely distrust private markets—continues to lobby for a return to large-scale government control in foodgrain markets. Bangladesh's current national food policy, written in 1988, is dated and out of step with current, lighter government involvement in markets (MOF 1988). Ongoing lobbying suggests one final lesson: clear, written policy statements may serve as an important aid in cementing a reform.

In the future Bangladesh's food policy will continue to evolve as domestic markets develop, as international markets adjust to changes in world trade flows and the provisions of the new General Agreement on Tariffs and Trade (GATT), and as budget problems and crises elsewhere put pressure on scarce international food-aid resources. But change in Bangladesh's public food programs will move forward from a much smaller base, unencumbered by the bulky ration system created during the Great Bengal Famine and frayed but patched up over the ensuing five decades. Along with its foodgrain markets, Bangladesh's food policy has also matured.

References

Ahmed, A. U. 1993. *Operational performance of the rural rationing program in Bangladesh.* Bangladesh Food Policy Project Working Paper 5. Washington, D.C.: International Food Policy Research Institute.

Ahmed, A. W. N., and L. H. Chowdhury. 1994. History of the Ministry of Food, Government of Bangladesh. Washington, D.C.: International Food Policy Research Institute. Mimeo.

Ahmed, R. 1979. *Foodgrain supply, distribution and consumption policies within a dual pricing mechanism: A case study of Bangladesh.* Research Report 8. Washington, D.C.: International Food Policy Research Institute.

———. 1991. *Cost of public food distribution in Bangladesh.* Bangladesh Food Policy Project Manuscript 5. Washington, D.C.: International Food Policy Research Institute.

Atwood, D., A. S. M. Jahangir, H. Smith, and G. Kabir. 1994. A history of food aid in Bangladesh. Paper presented at the seminar "Evolving food markets and food policy in Bangladesh," held by the International Fertilizer Development Center, Dhaka, May 2–4.

Bangladesh Ministry of Food (MOF). 1988. *National food policy.* Dhaka: Bangladesh Ministry of Food.

Bangladesh Planning Commission. 1978. Report of the Committee on Gradual Reduction of Food Subsidy. Dhaka: Bangladesh Planning Commission and Ministry of Finance.

Bangladesh Rural Advancement Committee (BRAC). 1991. Grain for the poor: A look at the pally rationing system in Bangladesh. Dhaka: Bangladesh Rural Advancement Committee. Mimeo.

Beacon Associates. 1986. The existing system of public foodgrain distribution in Bangladesh and proposal for restructuring. Dhaka: Beacon Associates. Mimeo.

———. 1988. Modified rationing in Bangladesh: An exercise in reform to increase its effectiveness. Dhaka: Beacon Associates. Mimeo.

Chowdhury, N. 1989. The changing food system: Storage, transport, marketing and distribution issues. In *Food strategies in Bangladesh: Medium and long term perspectives,* ed. Bangladesh Planning Commission. Dhaka: University Press.

———. 1992. Rice markets in Bangladesh: A study in structure, conduct and performance. Washington, D.C.: International Food Policy Research Institute. Mimeo.

Chowdhury, N., and A. A. Rushdi. 1988. Modified rationing in Bangladesh: An exercise in reform to increase its effectiveness. Dhaka: Beacon Associates. Mimeo.

Chowdhury, N., Q. Shahabuddin, and O. H. Chowdhury. 1986. Report on the existing system of public foodgrain distribution in Bangladesh and proposal for restructuring. Dhaka: Bangladesh Ministry of Food/Beacon Associates. Mimeo.

Food and Agriculture Organization (FAO). 1993. Reorganization of the Directorate General of Food: Terminal report. Dhaka: Food and Agriculture Organization. Mimeo.

Food Planning and Monitoring Unit (FPMU). 1986. Study on subsidies in the public foodgrain distribution in Bangladesh. Dhaka: Bangladesh Ministry of Food. Mimeo.

———. 1993. *Food situation report, 1992/93.* Dhaka: Bangladesh Ministry of Food.

Haggblade, S. 1994. Evolving foodgrain markets and food policy in Bangladesh. Bangladesh Food Policy Project Manuscript 64. Washington, D.C.: International Food Policy Research Institute. Mimeo.

Haggblade, S., and M. Rahman. 1993. The laws of gravity: A study of rice price behavior in the 1992 boro season. Bangladesh Food Policy Project Manuscript 38. Washington, D.C.: International Food Policy Research Institute. Mimeo.

Haggblade, S., S. A. Rahman, and S. Rashid. 1994. Statutory rationing: Performance and prospects. Draft report. Dhaka: International Food Policy Research Institute, Bangladesh Food Policy Project, Mimeo.

Institute of Nutrition and Food Science (INFS). 1978. Economic and nutritional effects of Food for Relief work projects. Dhaka: University of Dhaka.

International Food Policy Research Institute (IFPRI). 1992. *Open tendering for rice.* Bangladesh Food Policy Project Policy Brief 1. Dhaka: International Food Policy Research Institute.

———. 1993. Summary of research output: Working papers and manuscripts. Washington, D.C.: International Food Policy Research Institute. Mimeo.

Knight, H. 1954. *Food administration in India, 1939–47.* Stanford, Calif., U.S.A.: Stanford University Press.

Montgomery, R. 1983. Open market grain sales as a public policy instrument for moderating food price fluctuations in Bangladesh. Dhaka: U.S. Agency for International Development (USAID). Mimeo.

Rahman, H. Z. 1994. Low price of rice: Who loses, who gains? Dhaka: Bangladesh Institute of Development Studies. Mimeo.

Rahman, M. 1992a. An operational review: Public procurement of rice by open tender in Bangladesh (boro season of 1992). Washington, D.C.: International Food Policy Research Institute. Mimeo.

———. 1992b. A viable procedure of open tender for public procurement of rice in Bangladesh. Washington, D.C.: International Food Policy Research Institute. Mimeo.

———. 1993. Review of Ministry of Food's Tender No. 5: The first aman tender of 1992/93. Washington, D.C.: International Food Policy Research Institute. Mimeo.

Ravallion, M. 1990. *Markets and famines.* Dhaka: University Press.

Shahadat Ullah, A. H. 1988. Open market sales policy in Bangladesh: Its performance and prospect in price stabilization. A report prepared for the Bangladesh Ministry of Food, USAID, and International Food Policy Research Institute. Dhaka: U.S. Agency for International Development (USAID). Mimeo.

Working Group on Targeted Food Interventions (WGTFI). 1994. Options for targeting food interventions in Bangladesh. Washington, D.C.: International Food Policy Research Institute. Mimeo.

World Bank. 1977. *Bangladesh: Food policy review.* Report 1764a-BD. Washington, D.C.: World Bank.

———. 1979. Bangladesh: Food policy issues. South Asia Department Report 2761-BD. Washington, D.C.: World Bank. Mimeo.

———. 1992. *Bangladesh food policy review: Adjusting to the Green Revolution.* Report 9641-BD (vols. 1 and 2). Washington, D.C.: World Bank.

World Food Programme (WFP). 1994. Bangladesh foodgrain digest. Dhaka: World Food Programme, June. Mimeo.

———. 1996. Bangladesh foodgrain digest. Dhaka: World Food Programme, June. Mimeo.

PART III

The Changing Case for Government Intervention

10 Price Stabilization and the Management of Public Foodgrain Stocks in Bangladesh

FRANCESCO GOLETTI

Historically, price stabilization of rice has been one of the main objectives of Bangladesh food policy; and since the 1970s, through technological change and increasing market integration, the country has considerably reduced price variability both within and between years. Given these changes, to what extent should price stabilization continue to be pursued? Should the objective of stabilization be abandoned in view of the changes in market structure and technology? Or is it enough to reduce the emphasis? What level of public stocks are required to achieve this aim?

This chapter reviews the case for price stabilization and the continued maintenance of large public foodgrain stocks in Bangladesh. It begins with an assessment of the relative importance of private markets and public interventions as forces in declining price volatility. Discussion then turns to rationales for continued price stabilization, which center around new, lower levels of price variation. Finally, the chapter evaluates the level of public stocks required to meet two main objectives: price stabilization and emergency response to natural disasters.

Causes of Declining Price Variability

Variability in the price of rice, the main food staple of Bangladesh, has declined considerably over the years. Variability within years, measured by the coefficient of variation of monthly prices, decreased from about 14 percent in the 1970s to about 7 percent in the 1980s (Table 10.1). Variability between years, measured by the coefficient of variations of annual prices around trend, has declined considerably—from 28 to 7.5 percent since the 1970s. Relative to border prices, variability within years has declined, whereas variability between years has shown only a modest difference. For the 1990s data exist through 1996/97, and analysis of variability for those seven years indicates that price variability has slightly increased (Table 10.1).

Even though the government did not follow clear guidelines to reduce price variability, its numerous interventions in the foodgrain sector have con-

TABLE 10.1 Rice price variability

Period	Inter-Year Variation Coefficient	Intra-Year Variation Coefficient	Average Foodgrain Stock
	(percent)		(kilograms per capita)
1970s–80s	14.8	10.4	3.48
1970s	28.1	13.9	2.97
1980s	7.5	7.3	4.00
1991–97	8.7	8.4	6.40

SOURCE: Author's calculations based on wholesale coarse rice price from the Bangladesh Department of Agricultural Marketing.

tributed to price stability (Shahabuddin 1991; Chowdhury 1987). By procuring foodgrains in the months immediately after harvest, the government supports prices; by releasing foodgrains in the lean season through public distribution programs, it puts downward pressure on prices. Although these interventions have no major effects (Goletti 1994), the actions influence expectations and support the perception that the government can smooth seasonal fluctuations and, in the case of severe production shocks, intervene to moderate price fluctuations within years. After all, Bangladesh has not experienced a famine even slightly comparable to the one in 1974, although the country has endured more severe production shocks since then.

To isolate the contribution of stock policy to price stability from other factors such as seasonality and supply and demand shocks, the government's first task is to find an appropriate measure of price variability. This is done by taking the variance of price changes, which is conditional on the information available for each time period. The conditional variance can be computed by modeling price changes as an Autoregressive Conditional Heteroscedasticity (ARCH) process (Engle 1982). This variance changes over time and can be taken as a measure of variability (Goletti 1994).

Figures 10.1 and 10.2 show the relationship over time between the conditional variance of prices and rice stocks. The tremendous shocks of 1974 are clearly detectable as is the progressive decline of price variability over time. Nevertheless, periods such as 1977, 1980, and 1983 show considerable variability.

Identifying the autoregressive process relating price variability and government stocks allows one to test the hypothesis of stabilizing stock policy. The long-run elasticity of public stock on price variability is equal to −1.14 and statistically significant at the 95 percent level. That implies that a 10 percent increase in the level of public stock would in the long run reduce the variability of prices by about 11 percent.[1] Between the 1970s and the 1980s the average

1. This empirical relation is based on conditions prevailing during the 1970s and 1980s; changes in conditions that have occurred in the 1990s may imply a weakening trend. The evidence

FIGURE 10.1 Conditional variance of prices (percent)

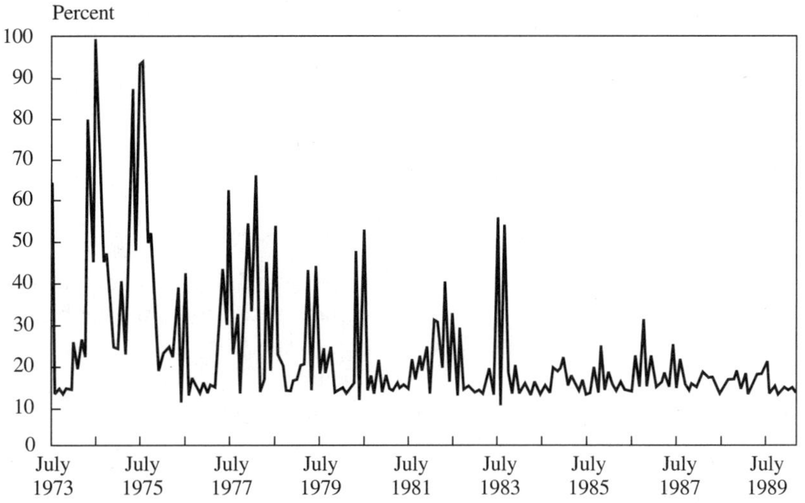

SOURCE: Author's calculations from price data from BBS.

FIGURE 10.2 Total public foodgrain stock

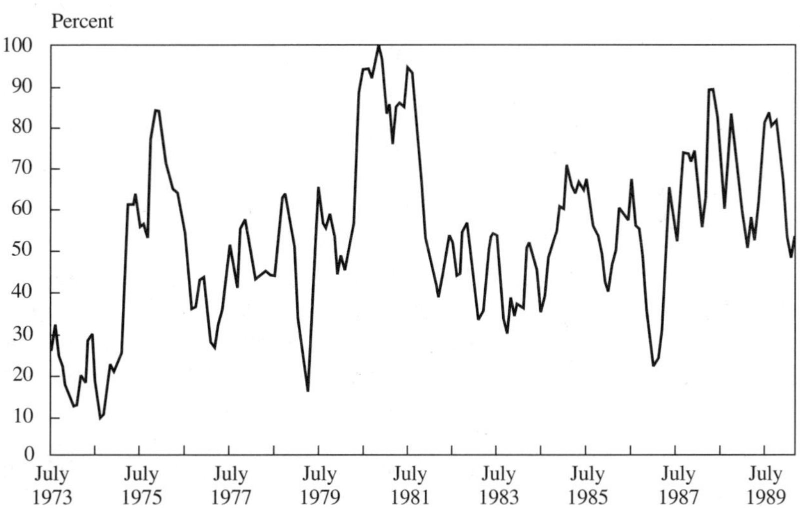

SOURCE: BBS (various).

---

reported in Chapter 4 on the crowding out of private stock by public stock is relevant here. The consistency between the results reported in that chapter and the relation between public stock and price variability discussed here is examined further in this chapter.

level of public stock per capita increased by 35 percent and price variability decreased by 73 percent (Table 10.1), suggesting that about 55 percent of the decrease in price variability can be explained by stock policy, with the remaining 45 percent attributable to changes in factors such as production variability, market integration, and infrastructure.

Benefits of Price Stabilization

Microeconomic Benefits: Consumer and Producer Surplus

Most of the micro-based literature on food price stabilization points to its negligible role in improving the economic welfare of society. The total benefit of stabilization lies in transfers of economic surplus from gainers (typically producers) to losers (usually consumers). When risk is incorporated into the analysis, the benefits from price stabilization are larger. Nevertheless, even when stabilization has positive effects on economic surplus, these benefits are usually limited in the case of food prices (Newbery and Stiglitz 1981).

From the point of view of the consumer, price stabilization improves welfare if the expected utility derived from consumption of all goods is lower than the utility computed at the stabilized price. Stabilization does improve expected utility if the following condition is satisfied (Turnovsky, Shalit, and Schmitz 1980):

$$[s_r \cdot (\eta_{ry} + R^C) - \eta_{rr}] < 0, \tag{10.1}$$

where

s_r = the budget share of rice consumption,
η_{ry} = its income elasticity of demand,
η_{rr} = the own price demand elasticity, and
R^C = the coefficient of relative risk aversion for consumers.

This result suggests that the desirability of price stabilization increases with the absolute size of the coefficient of relative risk aversion and decreases with the magnitude of the income and price elasticities. Poor households with a high budget share of food and high risk aversion are most likely to benefit from price stabilization.

Newbery and Stiglitz (1981) show that the benefits B of price stabilization to producers, as a proportion of the income y_0 before price stabilization, can be approximated by

$$\frac{B}{\bar{y}_0} = \frac{\Delta\bar{y}}{\bar{y}_0} - \frac{1}{2}R(\bar{y}_1)\left\{\sigma^2_{y_1}\left(\frac{\bar{y}_1}{\bar{y}_0}\right)^2 - \sigma^2_{y_0}\right\} \tag{10.2}$$

where $\bar{y}_i$ is the mean of y_i, $\sigma^2_{y_i}$ is the squared coefficient of variation of y_i, and $\Delta\bar{y} = \bar{y}_1 - \bar{y}_0$, and $R(\bar{y}_0)$ is the producer coefficient of relative risk aversion, computed as the mean of the income before price stabilization.

The Turnovsky, Shalit, and Schmitz (1980) condition (10.1) for price stabilization to improve the consumer's surplus is not satisfied in most of the cases considered for Bangladesh, where the range of the coefficient of risk aversion for consumers varies between –1 and –3 (Table 10.2). Only when the coefficient of relative risk aversion is very high, about –3, is the consumer's surplus for most of the population increased by stabilization. That value of risk aversion is high relative to other studies (see de Janvry, Bieri, and Nuñez 1972; Pinstrup-Andersen, Ruiz de Londoño, and Hoover 1976).

The Newbery and Stiglitz (1981) approximation (10.2) to compute producer surplus also shows that, unless risk aversion is high, the benefit to producers is small (Table 10.3). On average such benefits are about 0.9 percent when the coefficient of relative risk aversion is –1 and 1.4 percent when the coefficient of relative risk aversion is –3.

Only when risk aversion is high does price stabilization benefit producers and consumers to any extent. For values of risk parameters not greater than 2, the effects are small—less than 2 percent of total income for producers and negative for most consumers.

Poverty and Price Stabilization

Even though static efficiency gains may be small in the aggregate, a distribution of these gains in favor of low-income groups might strengthen the case for price stabilization. To explore the impact of stabilization on poverty, consider a standard food-based definition of poverty that defines a household to be poor if it consumes a total number of calories per capita less than a specified minimum level. The popularity of a food-based poverty line lies in its focus on physical survival and low calorie intake, which constitute the main manifestation of poverty (Hossain and Sen 1992; Ravallion 1995).

To apply this definition, one must express total caloric intake in terms of food consumption, which is in turn related to prices and income. When rice price changes, the consumption of all food commodities changes as well, due partly to a substitution effect, partly to an income effect.

The poverty measure can be expressed as a function of prices p_r, a parameter α measuring the depth of poverty, and the variability σ_r of prices (Goletti 1994):

$$W = W(p_r, \alpha, \sigma_r), \tag{10.3}$$

where the parameter α measures the concern for the poorest. As α becomes larger, this measure gives more emphasis to the position of the poorest households (Foster, Greer, and Thorbecke 1984).

By simulation one can determine the expected value of this function and compare it to the value of the poverty measure computed at the mean price. Complete price stabilization at the mean μ_r will be successful at reducing poverty if

TABLE 10.2 Price stabilization and expected utility

Quartile	Coefficient of Relative Risk Aversion R^C	Budget Share s_r	Income Elasticity η_{ry}	$s_r(R^C + \eta_{ry})$	Price Elasticity η_{rr}
Rural first	–1	45	0.8	–0.09	–0.89
Rural second	–1	41	0.71	–0.12	–0.71
Rural third	–1	37.3	0.64	–0.13	–0.55
Rural fourth	–1	26.2	0.03	–0.25	–0.39
Urban first	–1	37.3	0.58	–0.16	–1.02
Urban second	–1	31.3	0.43	–0.18	–0.76
Urban third	–1	24.7	0.19	–0.2	–0.38
Urban fourth	–1	12.7	–0.03	–0.13	–0.5*
Rural first	–2	45	0.8	–0.54	–0.89
Rural second	–2	41	0.71	–0.53	–0.71
Rural third	–2	37.3	0.64	–0.51	–0.55
Rural fourth	–2	26.2	0.03	–0.52	–0.39*
Urban first	–2	37.3	0.58	–0.53	–1.02
Urban second	–2	31.3	0.43	–0.49	–0.76
Urban third	–2	24.7	0.19	–0.45	–0.38*
Urban fourth	–2	12.7	–0.03	–0.26	–0.5
Rural first	–3	45	0.8	–0.99	–0.89*
Rural second	–3	41	0.71	–0.94	–0.71*
Rural third	–3	37.3	0.64	–0.88	–0.55*
Rural fourth	–3	26.2	0.03	–0.78	–0.39*
Urban first	–3	37.3	0.58	–0.9	–1.02
Urban second	–3	31.3	0.43	–0.8	–0.76*
Urban third	–3	24.7	0.19	–0.69	–0.38*
Urban fourth	–3	12.7	–0.03	–0.38	–0.5

SOURCE: Author's calculations based on demand parameters from Goletti (1993).

NOTE: Price stabilization improves expected utility if $s_r(R^C + \eta_{ry}) < \eta_{rr}$.

* indicates cases when price stabilization improves expected utility.

TABLE 10.3 Benefit to producers

Coefficient of Relative Risk Aversion	Elasticity of Supply	Elasticity of Demand	Coefficient of Variation of Total Rice Production	Total Benefit as Percent of Initial Income
−1	0.2	−0.6	5	0.3
−1	0.4	−0.6	5	0.4
−1	0.2	−0.6	10	1.6
−1	0.4	−0.6	10	1.4
−1	0.2	−0.8	5	0.3
−1	0.4	−0.8	5	0.3
−1	0.2	−0.8	10	1.5
−1	0.4	−0.8	10	1.3
Average	0.3	−0.7	8	0.9
−2	0.2	−0.6	5	0.4
−2	0.4	−0.6	5	0.4
−2	0.2	−0.6	10	2
−2	0.4	−0.6	10	1.8
−2	0.2	−0.8	5	0.4
−2	0.4	−0.8	5	0.4
−2	0.2	−0.8	10	1.9
−2	0.4	−0.8	10	1.9
Average	0.3	−0.7	8	1.2
−3	0.2	−0.6	5	0.4
−3	0.4	−0.6	5	0.5
−3	0.2	−0.6	10	2.4
−3	0.4	−0.6	10	2.5
−3	0.2	−0.8	5	0.5
−3	0.4	−0.8	5	0.6
−3	0.2	−0.8	10	2.2
−3	0.4	−0.8	10	2.2
Average	0.3	−0.7	8	1.4

SOURCE: Author's calculations based on BBS (various) production data and linear supply and demand discussed in Braverman et al. (1990).

$$W(\mu_r, \alpha, \sigma_r) < E_{pr} W(p_r, \alpha, \sigma_r), \tag{10.4}$$

where $E_{pr} W(p_r, \alpha, \sigma_r)$ is the expected value with respect to the variable p_r.

A case for partial price stabilization is given when the expected poverty associated with a variable price with coefficient of variation σ_{1r} is lower than the expected poverty in the presence of higher variability, as measured by a coefficient of variation σ_{2r}, where $\sigma_{1r} < \sigma_{2r}$:

$$E_{p1r} W(p_{1r}, \alpha, \sigma_{1r}) < E_{p2r} W(p_{2r}, \alpha, \sigma_{2r}). \tag{10.5}$$

The validity of this comparison rests on the assumption that the two distributions have the same mean. When the mean changes, the comparison becomes blurred by the overlapping of effects derived from the changing mean of the distribution and the variability of the distribution.

The results of the simulation of the poverty measure suggest that for $\alpha \geq 2$ poverty is a convex function of prices, implying that price stabilization will reduce poverty (Newbery and Stiglitz 1981). This intuition is confirmed by showing that the expected poverty is an increasing function of the coefficient of variation σ_r of prices, whereas $\alpha \leq 1$ is basically stationary (Figure 10.3).

For moderate price variability, when the coefficient of variation of price is less than 8 percent, none of the measures of poverty changes significantly. Only when price variability is high (when the coefficient of price variation is above 8 percent) does the behavior of expected poverty differ depending on the emphasis on the poorest, as summarized by the value of the parameter α.

When $\alpha = 0$, the poverty measure is interpreted as the number of people below the poverty level. In this case poverty does not change to any appreciable degree when the variability of prices increases. This casts some doubt on the validity of using price stabilization to reduce poverty. The same result applies when $\alpha = 1$ and the poverty measure is interpreted as the average gap of calorie consumption below the poverty line. When prices fluctuate, households cross the poverty line in both directions. On average, simulation shows that the number of crossings above and below the poverty line compensate each other. Only when $\alpha \geq 2$, implying that deviations below the poverty line are weighed

FIGURE 10.3 Expected poverty

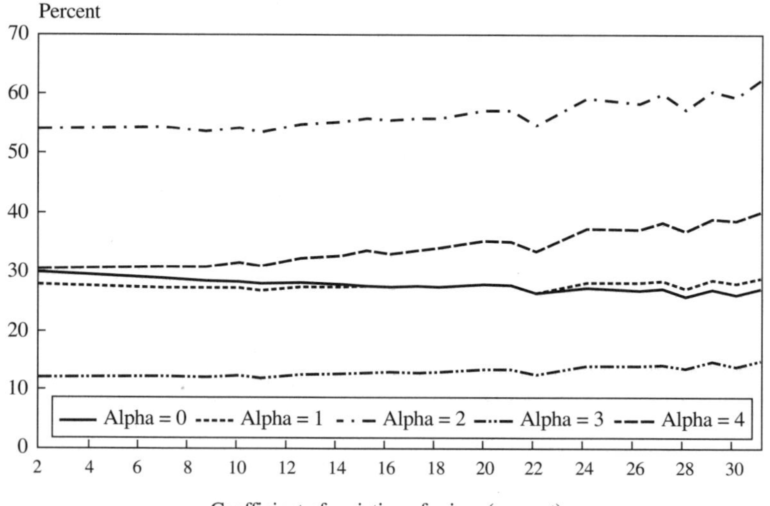

SOURCE: Author's calculations.

heavily, does the rate of expected poverty increase to an appreciable degree when prices become more variable. In this case price stabilization reduces poverty; however, even here the contribution is low.

Macroeconomic Benefits of Price Stabilization

Some observers of food policy in Asia suggest that rice price stabilization may offer significant macroeconomic benefits not captured by static micro-based models. In particular, more stable rice prices may provoke accelerated rates of economic growth (Timmer 1989, 1996, 1997). According to this argument, by reducing risks to rice production and marketing, stable rice prices can affect both the quantity and the quality of agricultural investments, inducing higher levels of private investment in irrigation equipment, soil fertility, marketing, and processing facilities. Because rice price fluctuations destabilize other prices as well, reducing price risk in rice markets will translate into reduced risk throughout the economy. In turn, risk reduction in other sectors will induce more productive and efficient investment allocations throughout the economy and hence higher rates of aggregate economic growth. In the early stages of economic growth, when rice forms a large share of gross domestic product (GDP), the resulting acceleration in real output can significantly boost aggregate economic growth.

An interesting but controversial test of this hypothesis has concluded that government rice price stabilization in Indonesia added a 1 percent increase to the rate of overall GDP growth during the first half of the 1970s (Timmer 1996, 1997). This estimated addition to aggregate economic growth dropped to 0.6 percent of GDP in the second half of the 1970s and from 0.3 to 0.2 percent in the 1980s. Yet even these lower figures generated aggregate economic gains far higher than the costs incurred in price stabilization efforts through the state marketing agency known as Badan Urusan Logistik (BULOG) (Timmer 1996).[2]

In Bangladesh, unfortunately, this hypothesis remains untestable; for during the years when government intervened most heavily to stabilize rice prices, it likewise controlled import, installation, and distribution of irrigation equipment, fertilizer, high-yielding varieties of seeds, and fertilizers. Thus, any latent desire to boost private farm investment will be effectively muffled by overwhelming state control of agricultural inputs and investments. What the rate of agricultural investment and output growth would have been without these direct controls remains unknown.

2. A comprehensive survey of literature on price stabilization (Islam and Thomas 1996) shows that research on the macroeconomic impact of price stabilization is not only extremely thin but also weak in terms of analytical rigor and detail when compared to microeconomic analysis. In addition to the Indonesian case studies, Islam and Thomas find only a few multimarket approaches that fall far short of macro dimensions. A recent study on Indonesia by Robinson, El-Said, and San (1998), which employs Computable General Equilibrium modeling, found no or negative impact of BULOG operations on the growth of the Indonesian economy.

Optimal Stocks for Price Stabilization

Why Stabilize Prices?

Although the economic rationale for price stabilization may be in doubt, the political imperative is not. Despite wide differences in political philosophy, the successive governments of post-liberation Bangladesh have been alive to the need for publicly held foodgrain stocks. In a fragile democracy such as Bangladesh, these stocks are sound political insurance. Regardless of who is in power, opportunistic opposition parties are guaranteed to score political points if rice prices fall too low or spike too high or if cyclones and flooding catch an unwary government flat-footed and unable to respond. Thus, emergency stocks and price stabilization remain stout pillars on which political leaders in Bangladesh lean, despite the heavy financial costs of large-scale public rice and wheat stocks. In such circumstances, it becomes useful to estimate the costs and benefits of various policy options; for if the government decides to hold foodgrain stocks to stabilize prices, it should do so in the least expensive manner.

Old Benchmarks Outdated

In the past, food security in Bangladesh has often been identified with high levels of public foodgrain stocks that moderate price fluctuations. In 1979, for example, the World Bank recommended a stock level of 1.5 million metric tons as of July 1 of every year and 1.2 million tons as of November 1.[3] Although the government agreed that such high levels were necessary, in the years after 1981 stocks have rarely exceeded 1.2 million tons. Taking into account the population growth, the per capita figures of stock levels have been much smaller than those the World Bank recommended in 1979. Yet rice and wheat prices have become more stable (Table 10.1).

Moreover, since the World Bank's 1979 recommendations, the foodgrain sector of Bangladesh has witnessed remarkable changes in the seasonality and intra-year responsiveness of rice production, both of which have contributed to built-in price stabilizers (Ahmed and Bernard 1989; Chowdhury 1987; also see Chapters 2 and 4). At the same time, declining food aid and the demise of leaky government ration channels have led to steadily declining targeted offtake programs (Chapter 9). Together, these changes suggest that stock policy guidelines need to be revised downward.

A General Framework for the Design of Optimal Stock Policy

Analysis of public foodgrain policy requires a framework that accounts for the cost implications of different stock levels. For example, consider the cost of

3. Further references to tons indicate metric tons.

100,000 tons of foodgrains (35 percent rice and 65 percent wheat) evaluated at average 1988/89 world prices. This cost, equal to $20.8 million, or taka 671.2 million, represents approximately 5.4 percent of the agricultural Annual Development Programme (ADP) budget and 1.4 percent of the total ADP budget.[4] In 1988/89 alone the average public stock of foodgrains was 1.2 million tons.

Both Bangladeshi policymakers and external donors have long searched for an effective stock policy, but arriving at a precise figure that represents the optimal level of public stocks requires the correct framework. In this chapter the optimal level of public foodgrain stock is defined as the level of stock that helps attain certain objectives (such as price stabilization, targeted public distribution, and security stocks) at minimal cost. This definition is limited since the benefits of these public interventions are not precisely evaluated and incorporated into the analysis. Important questions related to the targeting, effectiveness, and leaks associated with public distribution programs must be examined within and between households (Ahmed 1992). Moreover, the policy process itself—which is sometimes weighted by different interest groups—is not modeled. Without entering into political economy the framework presented here responds to different objectives of the political process that influences foodgrain policy in Bangladesh. It produces a range of estimates of optimal stocks and the corresponding degree of public intervention, providing room for gradual reform in public stock management and reduced interventions.

Estimation of the optimal public stock requires a comprehensive model that integrates a dynamic foodgrain sector with chosen policy regimes and well-defined objectives and cost functions. Three stages are involved in the design of the optimal stock policy problem. The first stage specifies the objectives, constraints, instruments, and options for policy. The second specifies, identifies, and estimates characteristics of a dynamic model of the foodgrain sector based on policy considerations from stage 1. The third compares and evaluates policy options derived from the first two stages.

Policy Objectives

Setting policy objectives for the public foodgrain system depends on the policy process and the interrelations among various interest groups. The formalization of a measure of achievement is often difficult because the objectives are expressed in general terms. Nevertheless, such formalization is critical in the effort to operationalize the policy design.

Here, three specific objectives are considered: price stabilization, price support, and cost minimization. The more general goal of poverty reduction is incorporated into the analysis by considering various degrees of targeted distribution to the poor.

---

4. All references to dollars indicate U.S. dollars.

1. Price stabilization minimizes the variance of prices around a target. For this objective to be precise, a target price must be specified for the period of the policy exercise, and therein lies the difficulty. Three elements must be taken into account in this specification: (a) the long-term trend of domestic prices, (b) seasonal fluctuations, and (c) the behavior of world prices. The target becomes a weighted average of these elements in which the weights reflect the relative importance attributed to them by policy-makers.
2. Price support refers to a specific support-price level, which is often implicit in the larger objective that prices should be within a certain band around a target price.
3. Cost minimization can be specified for any level of offtake desired in targeted distribution programs by providing an expression for the cost—in this case the operating balance of the food accounts. Basically, this cost refers to the difference between expenditures and revenues associated with the desired level of operation of the public foodgrain system. Expenditures arise from the domestic and international procurement of foodgrains and from storage costs. Revenues arise from sales of foodgrains through either subsidized channels or open market operations.

Policy Constraints

There are different types of policy constraints that express various degrees of policy concern and feasibility of limits. Some constraints simply state the non-negativity of endogenous variables such as prices and stocks. Capacity constraints take into account the physical storage facilities. For example, as of June 30, 1990, the storage capacity of the government food godown and silos was 1.761 million tons (BBS 1991).

Constraints on stock variables also take into account minimum stock requirements related to both deadstocks (the amount of stock needed for the system to be operational) and minimum stock levels needed for food security. For the latter constraint, the public food distribution system must hold sufficient stocks to meet three months of average offtake requests (505,000 tons), to cover the time period necessary for importing foodgrains to replenish the stock. This security stock serves as a cushion against calamities such as severe cyclones, droughts, and flooding. Finally, a constraint is also related to foreign exchange reserves, incorporating the consideration that food imports compete with other imports in the allocation of scarce foreign reserves.

Policy Instruments

In the past, instruments for price stabilization policy have often taken the form of fixed prices in procurement, ration distribution, and even open market sales. Influenced by the movement toward a more liberalized system, the gap has closed between fixed prices and market prices. The liberalizing trend has also oriented the choice of instruments toward open market operations, both in sales to reduce prices and in purchases to support prices. Moreover, the possibility of using international trade through the more efficient phasing of imports and exports opens the way to a new set of instruments. Therefore, the policy options presented in the following discussions are paired with the instruments of market operations (both sales and purchases) and exports and imports of foodgrains.

Packages of Policy Options

A policy option can be considered a package of objectives, constraints, and instruments. Here, four such options are considered: the small-change policy characterized by price stabilization cum cost minimization; the pure cost minimization policy that uses both open market operations and imports but is not concerned with price stabilization; the trade policy, in which both imports and exports are allowed; and a price band mechanism.

SMALL CHANGES. According to this option, the objective is to minimize the cost of operations, maintaining prices within a band of 4 percent around the target. The policy instruments are open market operations and imports. Constraints on capacity and food security stock requirements are specified as are constraints on maximum procurement and foreign exchange reserves. The foreign exchange constraint imposes a ceiling on foreign exchange that can be spent on imports: the foreign exchange equivalent of foodgrain imports in the baseline.

TARGETED DISTRIBUTION AT MINIMUM COST. In this case the objective of the policy is to minimize the present value of cost. The basic issue here is to see how the public food distribution assumed in the baseline can be carried out at minimum cost without concern for price stability. The instruments chosen are open market operations and imports. The constraints are the same as those in the previous policy. By comparing this policy with the benchmark policy, one can highlight the cost of price stabilization.

TRADE POLICY. This policy is a generalization of the benchmark policy. Instead of limiting trade transactions only to imports, it allows exports as well. This policy is particularly timely in view of Bangladesh's recent movement toward rice self-sufficiency and comparative advantage.

PRICE BAND POLICY. Whereas all previous policy options try to optimize a prespecified objective function, the price band policy operates by setting a target price, a price band, and a rule of intervention.

Generally, the chosen target price is a weighted average that takes into account the long-term trend of domestic and world prices as well as seasonality (Ahmed 1990). The price band is defined with reference to the target price and specifies an upper and a lower intervention price that should trigger open market operations. Usually, the upper and lower trigger prices are symmetrical in relation to the target price. Under this rule of intervention the government undertakes market sales until either prices drop to the ceiling of the band or public stocks reach the minimum operational level. Similarly, when prices go below the lower price of the band, the government undertakes open market purchases until either the maximum stock capacity is reached or prices rise to the lower level of the band. Finally, when prices are within the band, no open market operations are undertaken unless stock constraints are binding.

A price band rule can be simply stated, is relatively easy to implement, and is readily understandable. Nevertheless, the outcome is not optimal because this rule does not use all the available information. As a fixed rule, it can be computed as a solution of an optimization problem (Buiter 1981). The most limiting factors about price band rules are their vulnerability to speculative attacks (Salant 1983), their inability to accommodate several constraints, and (when they are otherwise feasible) their cost.

The Link between Public and Private Foodgrain Systems

The design of foodgrain stock policy requires knowledge of how the foodgrain system functions. Otherwise, it is difficult to propose and evaluate different policy options to improve upon the current situation.

The government affects the availability of foodgrains through imports, domestic procurement, and public distribution. Each of these activities is reflected in the public stock balance equation:

$$g\_s_t = \delta \cdot g\_s_{t-1} + g\_m_t - g\_x_t + \mathrm{proc}_t - \mathrm{offt}_t, \qquad (10.6)$$

where

g_s_t = government stock at a time t,
g_m_t = government imports,
g_x_t = government exports,
proc_t = procurement of domestic production, and
offt_t = offtakes at time t (that is, public distribution).

The coefficient δ accounts for losses of grains in public storage facilities. Both procurement and offtakes are domestic operations that can be conducted in a variety of ways and affect the level and variability of prices. The foodgrain sector in Bangladesh is represented mainly by rice and wheat. Whereas rice is predominant in production, representing more than 95 percent of total foodgrains, wheat is dominant in public distribution. Given the substitutability of rice and wheat, the demand for these two grains must be determined simultaneously. Both commodities are storable, and private stocks play an important role in moving commodities over both time and space.

The interrelationship between private sector decisions concerning production, consumption, storage, and marketing, and government decisions related to public distribution, procurement of domestic production, imports, and stock management is the basis for determining prices within the foodgrain system. The private sector decisions must be consistent with public sector decisions:

$$c_t + p\_s_t = \lambda\_q_t - \text{proc}_t + \text{offt}_t + p\_m_t - p\_x_t + p\_s_{t-1}, \qquad (10.7)$$

where c_t, p_s_t, p_m_t, and p_x_t refer to consumption, private stocks, private imports, and private exports at time *t*, respectively. The coefficient λ refers to utilization of production for consumption.

The link between the private and public sectors lies in the two elements that appear in both equations (10.6) and (10.7)—namely, procurement and offtakes. By affecting the balance between demand and supply, they affect prices and therefore private stocks. Unless the reactions of the private sector are taken into account, the effectiveness of policy cannot be improved. In an extreme case, if private stocks change in a direction opposite from the direction of public stocks, stock policy could be completely ineffective.

Nevertheless, this conclusion based on static relations has dynamic dimensions as well. If the government procures in the harvest season to increase its stock but private traders respond by releasing their stocks at the same time and in the same amount, there will be no impact on market prices. All else being equal, the same result would ensue, even if private traders do not release their stocks but simply refrain from purchasing in the harvest season and if changes in stocks and prices are measured in reference to the previous harvest season. If private traders release their stocks after the harvest in response to public procurement, the harvest season prices will increase but post-harvest prices will become depressed, thus affecting price variability.[5] The effect will be different if the government increases its stock by import rather than procurement. Stock increase by import will not have a direct impact on prices as procurement will. But indirect impact through traders' response will be similar in cases of both import and procurement. Moreover, information on government stock buildup is more widely, easily, and quickly known to traders in the case of procurement. Without considering these dynamic factors, a conclusion drawn from static logic may appear inconsistent but is not necessarily so.[6]

5. Obviously, price elasticity of demand would be an important factor determining the extent of price changes. As various cross-section data and time-series estimates of price elasticities will show, there are considerable variations in these estimates. With the gradual decline of income elasticities of demand, it is only logical to expect price elasticities to also decline.

6. Here, Chowdhury's (1994) report that a 1-unit increase in public stock leads to a 0.83-unit reduction in private traders' stock and Goletti's finding that a 1 percent increase in public stock reduces price variability by 1.14 percent require explanation. First, however, note that Chowdhury focuses on traders' short-run behavior using data from 1990/91, whereas Goletti attempts to measure the long-run impact of public stock on price variability using a more complex model and data from the 1970s and 1980s. Goletti's formulation includes a mechanism of supply response, while Chowdhury's does not. Nevertheless, the consistency of short-run price response to changes in public stock can be examined through a numerical calculation—a heroic attempt indeed. Let us assume that the government increases its stock (base level of 600,000 tons) by 10 percent through

Policy Evaluation

Each policy option consists of a set of specified policy objectives, a set of constraints, the dynamic model of the foodgrain system, and a set of policy instruments needed to achieve those objectives. The evaluation of different policy options is based on a series of criteria such as price stability, fiscal cost, foreign exchange reserves needed to import foodgrains, and the level of public stocks. The comparison of different outcomes helps improve policy by allowing policymakers to gain better understanding of the tradeoffs involved.

For policy evaluation to be meaningful, a relevant baseline must be considered. The baseline here refers to the three-year period between 1990/91 and 1992/93, a total of 12 seasons (each year comprises 4 seasons). The choice of baseline reflects the trend of the foodgrain sector toward sustained production growth. Total cost for the baseline is more than taka 14 billion, the coefficient of variation of rice prices is 6.2 percent, and the average foodgrain stock level is more than 1.1 million tons. The behavior of variables and costs in the baseline are reported in Table 10.4. This exercise facilitates comparison of potential policy options with the baseline that is already in place by focusing on ensuing price stability, cost efficiency, and food security.

SMALL CHANGES POLICY. The baseline scenario gives the behavior of prices and stock when the exogenous variables are kept at their historical level. This option is called the benchmark option because it resembles recent policies and practices. The objective of the policy is to minimize cost and guarantee price stability and public distribution through imports and open market operations, which include sales and purchases. Unlike the dual system of the past, open market operations are undertaken at market prices, not fixed prices; and purchases are made in the open market, not through a system of licensed dealers. The policy's design should account for the behavior of the private

internal procurement. This leads to a reduction in traders' stock in the same season through release to market. Using Chowdhury's coefficient, this reduction is equal to about 50,000 tons (600,000 × 0.83). The net reduction in total market supply is 10,000 tons (60,000 – 50,000). As a percent of harvest season total market supply (9 million tons), this reduction is only 0.11 percent. Assuming a price elasticity of demand of –0.6, the market price increases by 0.18 percent in the same season. It is assumed that the government uses its procured grain to depress the lean season price by 0.18 percent (anything higher or lower than this extent of influence on price will change the price level as well as variability). With this assumption, the variability of price will be reduced by 2.4 percent (0.18/7.5), where 7.5 is the initial percent of variability. Elasticity of variability with respect to public stock is thus –0.24 compared to –1.14 percent estimated by Goletti. In an alternate scenario, if we assume that traders adjust their stock downward during postharvest months instead of harvest seasons, offtake from government stock in the lean season is zero, government increases stock by procurement, and the size of the lean season market is 7 million tons (a more realistic assumption), then the estimate of the elasticity of price variability with respect to changes in public stock is –1.58 compared to –1.14 found in Goletti's model. Because the two models were estimated with regression analysis of different data sets, it would be difficult to precisely disentangle the timing and manner of private stock adjustments in response to public stock change under the two models. But the direction of relations appears to be consistent.

TABLE 10.4 Summary of various policy options

Variable	Baseline	Small Change Policy	Cost Minimization	Trade	Price Band
Rice price (taka per maund)	398	399	432	401	379
Wheat price (taka per maund)	266	266	275	259	263
Rice stock (thousand metric tons)	622	519	231	454	803
Wheat stock (thousand metric tons)	506	284	284	348	934
Rice open market operations (thousand metric tons)	−129.2	32	97.3	−133.9	−142.9
Wheat open market operations (thousand metric tons)	−4.4	75.3	13.7	605	−57.9
Rice open market sales (thousand metric tons)	29.8	204.7	242	377.3	0
Wheat open market sales (thousand metric tons)	6.6	154.7	93	698.4	15.3
Rice open market purchases (thousand metric tons)	159	172.7	144.7	511.2	142.9
Wheat open market purchases (thousand metric tons)	11	79.4	79.4	93.3	73.2
Rice imports (thousand metric tons)	5.7	127.3	188.2	−39.6	5.7
Wheat imports (thousand metric tons)	325.9	360.7	299	891.2	325.9
Coefficient of variation of rice prices (percent)	6.18	4.46	6.6	3.69	4.78
Total cost (million taka)	14,572	275	−4677	−18,305	20,456
Procurement cost (million taka)	19,513	28,015	25,481	72,767	22,363
Foreign exchange cost (million U.S. dollars)	638	974	966	1,006	638

SOURCE: Author's calculations.

sector—in particular, for the effect of consumption and storage decisions on prices. Finally, the policy should consider a series of constraints: capacity of foodgrain storage, minimum stock requirements for food security and normal operations, and foreign exchange availability.

What outcome does the policy produce? With a total cost of only taka 275 million, it is possible to achieve price stabilization within a 4 percent band around the target. The resulting deflated rice price variability is given by a coefficient of variation of 4.4 percent versus a 6.2 percent in the baseline. The flexibility of this policy derives from imports and open market operations that take advantage of both the domestic and the international grain markets. This implies a more effective import policy and more active open market operations. The average foodgrain stock is 801,000 tons.

Some interesting patterns emerge from comparing the small changes with the baseline. The role of open market operations is highlighted. Rice purchases are extensively used during postharvest periods, and rice sales control price hikes in the lean season. High levels of open market purchasing raise the cost of procurement, but most of this cost is offset by frequent open market sales, which lower total costs and reduce price volatility. Import costs are slightly lower than those in the baseline because there are no rice imports, even though wheat imports are slightly higher.

TARGETED DISTRIBUTION AT MINIMUM COST. In this case the only objective of the policy is to minimize the total cost of public distribution. Both open market operations and imports are used to achieve this objective. The outcome is a policy path that results in a total nominal revenue of taka 4.6 billion. According to this scenario, the government allows prices to rise to a relatively high level, saving considerable resources in domestic procurement and profiting from open market sales. The rice price variability is 6.6 percent, and the average foodgrain stock level in this case is 513,000 tons. The effect of cost minimization is to reduce the amount of public stocks as much as possible. The cost difference between the benchmark and the cost minimization policy can be regarded as a measure of the cost of price stabilization since the two policies differ only in this respect.

TRADE POLICY. The trade policy differs from the benchmark insofar as it allows both import and export of foodgrains as well as open market operations. Since a new policy instrument (export) is allowed, the policy gives a much better outcome, with a total revenue of taka 18.3 billion. What is noteworthy is the incentive to export rice in international markets, where the quantity of export is limited to half a million tons in any season. Massive amounts of wheat are imported, giving more credibility to the swap of rice exports for wheat imports (see Chapter 13).

PRICE BAND POLICY. The apparent simplicity of price band rules is deceiving. These rules are usually difficult to implement because they either are not feasible, give rise to speculative attacks when public stock is low, or allow an overaccumulation of stock with associated high costs. For example, simulation of a rigid price band policy demonstrates that it is unfeasible to support the baseline level of public distribution without further imports. Because of the predetermined rules of the policy, new information does not get any consideration, and traders' expectations about market forces may be distorted. The government accumulates stocks, which tend to dampen market expectation and drive down prices. As public stocks reach 1.7 million tons, approaching capacity limits (2 million tons is the level used in the simulation), price variability cannot be contained within the band if the government is to reduce high public stocks. Attempts to stabilize prices above the floor of the band are frustrated by the intervention rules governing policy operations. Consequently, the cost of the program is also higher than it is in the baseline, reaching a level of taka 20.4 billion.

Some of these undesirable outcomes may be avoided by planning a more adequate price band width and a different target price. The rigidity of a price band, however, reduces the government's flexibility in reacting efficiently to new information in the foodgrain market. This unresponsiveness makes price bands complex to plan. Further, unless the band is changed periodically, the buffer stock tends to deplete or accumulate, at times to an unmanageably high level.

Emergency Stocks

Government stocks serve multiple purposes. They may be an instrument of price stabilization, becoming a by-product of the government's foodgrain purchases and sales. At the same time, stocks held for price stabilization purposes or for targeted distribution programs may cushion temporary supply shortages created by recurring natural disasters. Floods, drought, cyclones, and tidal bores are common in Bangladesh. Floods of various sizes and duration cause extensive damage not only to sources of current income (such as crops) but also to assets for future income (such as infrastructure, housing, and means of production). Permanent solutions to control the severity or reduce the extent of devastation from these calamities have so far remained beyond the nation's means; extending food and shelter to the affected population remains the government's only response. Yet without a rapid, adequate response, the government may create a political crisis for itself.

Within the first three to four days after a disaster, victims need special packages of prepared food because they may have lost all safe drinking water and cooking implements. Once people can cook rice and wheat, distribution of free foodgrain supply must occur. If the market supply of foodgrains can quickly resume normal functioning, relief operations can be conducted through cash grants cash-based construction programs. Nevertheless, numerous procedural difficulties complicate cash-based relief operations immediately after a natural disaster.

With a standing Food Department in possession of foodgrains, the government can turn to this agency for help in affected areas. Thus, the concept of a security stock has evolved and is deeply embedded in the thinking of food distribution managers. But Bangladesh has never established a physically separate security stock for emergency relief. As long as the total stock within the food distribution system contains a minimum level that ensures availability of foodgrains in an emergency, the purpose of the security stock is sustained within the total stock. Therefore, the estimate of optimal stock presented previously in this chapter includes some security consideration. Nevertheless, the extent and the basis of the security stock must be made clear so that security-conscious food policy managers are confident that the estimates of optimal stocks include an adequate provision for emergency relief.

Table 10.5 offers a perspective on recent disaster years, listing statistics on food prices and offtake from public stock in terms of deviation from the trend. Five disaster years—1979, 1984, 1987, 1988, and 1991—are included. Rice crop losses were estimated at 772,000 tons in 1979, 306,000 tons in 1984, 652,000 tons in 1987, and 1.280 million tons in 1988. They were reputedly close to 2 million tons in 1998. There was no loss of rice crop in 1991. Of these disaster years, 1979 was a year of drought as well as of minor flooding. In 1991 a tidal bore struck, accompanied by a cyclone that claimed about 130,000 human lives in the coastal belt of the country. The other four years had excessive floods, with 1988 and 1998 ravaged by the worst floods in four decades.

Comparing these emergency years reveals several contrasts and important changes over time:

1. In disaster months, the offtake from the public stock generally increases beyond normal offtake, with a possible sobering impact on market prices.
2. Even though 1988 was a year of extraordinary flooding, the rice price increase due to flooding in September was surprisingly low—only 3 percent. Yet in 1979 prices spiked upward between 14 and 20 percent when the boro crops failed.
3. The peak monthly offtakes during the generally high demand months of September and October were lower in the flood years of 1987 and 1988 than for 1979.
4. Following the liberalization of private foodgrain imports in 1993, private importers have proven highly responsive to domestic supply shortages. In 1995 and 1998, years of domestic production shortfall and rising prices, private importers responded strongly (see Chapter 2).

In light of these observations, Chowdhury (1994) argues that the root cause for such differences is that rice markets were larger and more integrated in 1988 than they were in 1979. Therefore, after a calamity prices return quickly to their normal path due to releases of public stock as well as the sale of

TABLE 10.5 Market price of rice and offtake from the public food delivery system in five disaster years (percent deviation from trend)

	1979		1984		1987		1988		1991	
Month	Price	Offtake	Price	Offtake	Price	Offtake	Price	Offtake	Price	Offtake
February	–14.22	7.0	–3.07	30.4	–0.49	30.6	7.13	26.8	1.27	38.2
March	–9.26	19.7	1.09	42.5	7.95	44.3	8.51	37.0	5.71	37.5
April	–2.59	8.4	2.23	21.5	12.33	23.1	3.73	–73.4	2.14	1.8
May	–1.28	9.6	–0.64	17.5	0.80	–10.6	–7.48	–29.2	–2.24	21.1
June	14.23	25.7	–1.04	–17.3	2.43	–26.1	–6.66	–56.5	–1.16	–6.4
July	19.72	31.7	3.45	17.6	–5.77	–15.6	–4.31	–39.4	0.42	–3.6
August	13.15	36.2	0.42	43.0	1.35	–1.0	–3.98	–21.1	–0.14	4.8
September	9.18	51.7	5.51	59.9	1.36	34.9	3.56	22.0	3.5	30.3
October	–0.08	69.7	2.32	55.4	0.27	38.4	–0.68	53.3	4.18	67.7
November	–5.38	39.5	–2.38	68.9	–1.82	27.3	–1.90	43.7	–7.46	22.6

SOURCE: Computed from data in Chowdhury (1994).

NOTE: Estimation of trend is based on a 12-month moving average of monthly data.

private stock. The additional supply cushion of private imports has been a significant buffer since foodgrain trade liberalization in 1993. With market development, private imports and private stocks are playing a greater role than public stock in moderating prices. Thus, Chowdhury (1994) argues that demand for public emergency stocks has fallen over time.

Assuming 10 million affected people, a relief operation of 60 days, and an energy requirement of 1,800 calories per capita per day, Chowdhury (1994) has estimated a security stock requirement of about 287,000 tons. To this he adds consideration for transportation and other leakages to arrive at a figure of 300,000 to 350,000 tons. If one adds another 150,000 tons to this estimate as deadstock, the total quantity of security stock ranges from 450,000 to 500,000 tons and may be held in either rice or wheat.

If emergency reserves set the level below which public foodgrain stocks should not fall, the foregoing analysis suggests that minimum stocks levels are now far lower than the 1.5 million tons recommended by the World Bank (1979) two decades ago. The reasons are two. First, the bank estimates reflect a policy environment in which public foodgrain distribution was at its highest historical peak. Between the late 1970s and the late 1990s, external funding for targeted programs fell by about 1 million tons per year; therefore, stocks required to meet these lower offtake levels also fell. Second, as discussed in other chapters, there has been a fundamental change in policy and private market development in recent years, making private imports and privately held domestic stocks available to buffer foodgrain supply shortages. This contributes also to a decline in the required size of publicly held foodgrain stocks.

Conclusions

At the outset this chapter asked if the objective of price stabilization should be given up or if the emphasis on stabilization as an objective of foodgrain policy should be reduced. Moreover, what level of public foodstocks now seems necessary to meet price stabilization and emergency stock requirements? Analysis has shown that the microeconomic benefits of price stabilization in Bangladesh are small, the effects on poverty negligible, and the possible macroeconomic benefits of price stability unknowable. At the same time, the need for government price stabilization has diminished. The dramatic growth of the boro crop, which makes rice more regularly available during the year, has significantly dampened seasonal and inter-year price fluctuations. The corollary process of commercialization of rice and agriculture has increased tremendously, accompanied by growing market integration. Since 1993, private traders have repeatedly demonstrated their willingness to exercise newfound authority to import foodgrains during times of domestic shortfalls, thus providing another built-in supply and price stabilizer. Together these factors suggest that it is now possible to reduce emphasis on price stabilization as a main objective of foodgrain policy in Bangladesh.

How low can public foodgrain stocks go in this new commercial and production environment? In the coming years emergency stock requirements will set a floor of about 500,000 tons on public foodgrain requirements. The case for price stabilization and scale of public intervention, however, will remain a political question rather than an economic one.

This chapter demonstrates a range of the levels of optimal stock, running from 500,000 to 1.7 million tons, including a minimum or security stock of 500,000 tons, depending on the types of policies and instruments that the government is willing to pursue and employ. In the late 1980s optimal stock levels stood at the high end of this range, primarily because of high levels of Food-for-Work and government ration channel offtake. But in the austere 1990s, when both Bangladesh and donor governments have become more frugal, targeted distribution programs have fallen and so have optimal stock levels.

Assuming that the government is likely to adopt a gradual approach toward improvement of its current practices, one might estimate that a stock of 700,000 to 800,000 tons should be the level of optimal stock associated with the small change policy scenario. This option implies a reduction in stock from the current level of 1.1 million to 1.2 million tons, with a savings of about $130 million per year in the cost of the public food program.

References

Ahmed, A. 1992. *Operational performance of the rural rationing program in Bangladesh.* Food Policy in Bangladesh Working Paper 5. Washington, D.C.: International Food Policy Research Institute.

Ahmed, R. 1990. An outline for determining procurement price of foodgrains in Bangladesh. Washington, D.C.: International Food Policy Research Institute. Mimeo.

Ahmed, R., and A. Bernard. 1989. *Rice price fluctuation and an approach to price stabilization in Bangladesh.* Research Report 72. Washington, D.C.: International Food Policy Research Institute.

Bangladesh Bureau of Statistics (BBS). Various. *Statistical yearbook of Bangladesh.* Dhaka: Bangladesh Bureau of Statistics.

Braverman, A., et al. 1990. *Costs and benefits of agricultural price stabilization in Brazil.* Working Paper 564. Washington, D.C.: World Bank.

Buiter, W. H. 1981. The superiority of contingent rules over fixed rules in models with rational expectations. *Economic Journal* 91 (September): 647–670.

Chowdhury, N. 1987. Seasonality of foodgrain price and procurement program in Bangladesh since liberalization: An explanatory study. *Bangladesh Development Studies* 15 (March): 105–128.

———. 1994. National security stocks for Bangladesh. Washington, D.C.: International Food Policy Research Institute. Mimeo.

de Janvry, A., J. Bieri, and A. Nuñez. 1972. Estimation of demand parameters under consumer budgeting: An application to Argentina. *American Journal of Agricultural Economics* 54 (August): 422–430.

Engle, R. F. 1982. Autoregressive conditional heteroscedasticity with estimates of the variance of United Kingdom inflation. *Econometrica* 50 (July): 987–1007.

Foster, J., J. Greer, and E. Thorbecke. 1984. A class of decomposable poverty measures. *Econometrica* 52 (May): 761–766.

Goletti, F. 1993. Food consumption parameters in Bangladesh. Bangladesh Food Policy Project Manuscript 29. Dhaka: International Food Policy Research Institute. Mimeo.

———. 1994. *The changing public role in a rice economy approaching self-sufficiency: The case of Bangladesh.* Research Report 98. Washington, D.C.: International Food Policy Research Institute.

Hossain, M., and B. Sen. 1992. Rural poverty in Bangladesh. In *Food strategies in Bangladesh: Medium and long-term perspectives.* Dhaka: University Press.

Islam, N., and S. Thomas. 1996. *Foodgrain price stabilization in developing countries.* Food Policy Review 3. Washington, D.C.: International Food Policy Research Institute.

Newbery, D. M. G., and J. Stiglitz. 1981. *The theory of commodity price stabilization: A study in the economics of risk.* Oxford, England: Oxford University Press.

Pinstrup-Andersen, P., N. Ruiz de Londoño, and E. Hoover. 1976. The impact of increasing food supply on human nutrition: Implications for commodity priorities in agricultural research and policy. *American Journal of Agricultural Economics* 58 (May): 131–142.

Ravallion, M. 1995. Growth and poverty: Evidence for developing countries in the 1990s. *Economics Letters* 48 (June): 411–417.

Robinson, S., M. El-Said, and N. N. San. 1998. Rice policy, trade, and exchange rate changes in Indonesia: A general equilibrium analysis. Trade and Macroeconomics Discussion Paper 27. Washington, D.C.: International Food Policy Research Institute. Mimeo.

Salant, S. W. 1983. The vulnerability of price stabilization schemes to speculative attack. *Journal of Political Economy* 91 (February): 1–38.

Shahabuddin, Q. 1991. *A disaggregated model for stabilization of rice prices in Bangladesh.* Food Policy in Bangladesh Working Paper 3. Washington, D.C.: International Food Policy Research Institute.

Timmer, C. P. 1989. Indonesia: Transition from food importer to exporter. In *Food price policy in Asia: A comparative study,* ed. T. Sicular. Ithaca: Cornell University Press.

———. 1996. Does BULOG stabilize rice prices in Indonesia? Should it try? *Bulletin of Indonesian Economic Studies* 32 (August): 45–74.

———. 1997. Building efficiency in agricultural marketing: The long-run role of BULOG in the Indonesian food economy. *Journal of International Development* 9 (January–February): 133–145.

Turnovsky, S. J., J. Shalit, and A. Schmitz. 1980. Consumer's surplus, price instability, and consumer welfare. *Econometrica* 48 (January).

World Bank. 1979. *Bangladesh: Food policy issues.* South Asia Department Report 2761-BD. Washington, D.C.: World Bank.

11 Targeted Distribution

AKHTER U. AHMED

Defining the Problem

Scale

Despite recent economic growth, pervasive poverty and undernutrition persist in Bangladesh. According to the latest estimates, about half the population cannot afford an adequate diet (WGTFI 1994; Sen 1992; Ravallion and Sen 1996). Although long-term trends in the overall incidence of poverty show modest signs of improvement, the standard of living for those in extreme poverty has stagnated (Rahman 1994; Sen 1992). One-quarter of the population maintains a precarious existence. Chronically underfed and highly vulnerable, these people remain largely without assets (other than their own labor power) to cushion lean-season hunger or the crushing blows of illness, flooding, and other calamities. As a result, two-thirds of deaths among children under five years old are related to malnutrition (Hassan and Ahmed 1990).

The need for a targeted safety net remains strong. But with declining donor and government resources, targeting and program effectiveness must improve. Bangladesh possesses a wealth of institutional diversity and broad experience with alternate forms of assistance programs. The government has also shown a remarkable willingness to evaluate program effectiveness, confront shortcomings, and cancel or modify programs as a result. This chapter examines recent evaluations of alternative program designs in hopes of distilling lessons that will assist in targeting scarce resources more effectively in the future.

The Target

A series of recent studies suggests that the households most vulnerable to inadequate food intake are female-headed and those headed by day laborers, fishermen, and boat pullers.[1] Overall, about 87 percent of the undernourished

1. See Ahmed (1993a, 1993b), Chowdhury (1992), WGTFI (1994), Hossain and Sen (1992), and the discussion of variations in nutritional status in Chapter 5.

population lives in rural areas, while the rural population itself is about 75 percent of the total population. Although located throughout the country, the most undernourished are concentrated in flood-prone rural areas, particularly along major riverbanks and in urban slums. For these people hunger is particularly acute during the September/October lean season, when food prices peak. The absence of employment before the aman rice harvest in November makes this season especially difficult, particularly for the rural landless, who constitute about 50 percent of the rural population and depend on wage labor for their income (see Box 11.1). Within these poor households, pregnant and lactating women and preschool children face the most acute nutritional risk (Hassan and Ahmed 1990; Ahmed 1993a; WGTFI 1994; Chowdhury 1992).

BOX 11.1 The agony and privation of a poor family

Abdul Karim, about 35, is the head of a landless household. He lives with his wife, Ayesha, and their three children in Puthimari village of Chilmari Thana, one of the most distressed areas of Bangladesh. Abdul's household is among the many severely poor households in the village that were not covered by any government intervention program. The household was included in the control group of IFPRI's consumption and nutrition survey.

Abdul's one-room house, with walls made of *kash* (a tall, wild grass) and bamboo and a roof of straw is too small for his family. It is clear that the household is in extreme poverty. The severity of the family's malnutrition is evident from their skeleton-like features.

IFPRI field investigators Zobair and Farzana interviewed Abdul and Ayesha. "You can see our miserable condition. Yet we are not included in any of the government programs," Abdul said bitterly. "It is true that most of them who are getting ration are also poor, but none of them are as needy as we are."

"Two days ago, I worked on an neighbor's land, weeding his radish field. He gave me 5 taka, and a meal of rice and dal for the whole day's work," Abdul continued. "Yesterday, I went to him again, but he offered me only 3 taka and a meal. I accepted and worked from morning till evening."

The day we visited them, nobody in the family could find any work. Abdul spent his 8 taka to buy about a kilogram of wheat. Ayesha was frying the wheat in an earthen pot. "I soaked the wheat in salt-mixed water before frying. The wheat becomes hard and brittle after frying. This fried wheat is all we have for today's meal. From this, I have to save some for tomorrow also," Ayesha said. Farzana asked her why they didn't crush the wheat to make *atta* (whole-wheat flour). "With *atta* from this wheat I could make only a few *rooti,* which the children would ➤

eat in no time because they are so hungry. Instead, we can chew the fried wheat for a long time," Ayesha explained. "I know that I am cheating my own children," she sobbed, "But what can I do? We don't have money to buy more wheat or rice. Nobody wants to hire me or my husband for work because we are so weak. But if we can't find work, then we can't eat, and without eating we will become weaker."

Abdul nodded. "She is right. Aswin and Kartik [the lean season] are the most difficult months. Many children in this area die during this time. They are so weak that even simple diseases kill them," he said, looking at his own children. "But things will improve after a month during aman rice harvest. Everybody will get work. Ayesha will parboil paddy and husk rice in farmers' houses."

"But what will happen to us next? The river will probably take away our house next year." Ayesha expressed her anxiety and then maintained, "We were not this poor when we got married. We had some land, and we produced enough rice for our small family during that time. But one night, there was a big land erosion and the *rakkushi* [a legendary animal, like a dragon] river swallowed our land. Except this house, we have nothing left now. Last month, I sold my gold nose pin to a neighbor for one-fourth the price my husband paid for it. With that money we bought some rice and wheat."

Abdul sold a mango tree early that month for only 100 taka. "The tree could easily fetch 500 taka. Big and sweet mangoes used to grow on that tree. But the man who bought the tree cut it for firewood because it could go into the river during the next flood. You see, the river is the cause of all our misery," Abdul concluded.

The interview was over, and we were about to leave Abdul's house. At that time, Biplab, Abdul's eight-year-old son, came running with a large and beautiful water hyacinth flower in his hand. He gave the flower to Farzana and said shyly, "Please come again." Farzana had managed to hold her tears during the interview. She could not hold them any longer.

SOURCE: Ahmed (1992).

Rationale for Targeted Intervention

Because of the severity and magnitude of undernutrition in Bangladesh, food policy must aim at improving the nutritional status of the poor. Freedom from hunger and malnutrition is a basic human need; therefore, food security and improved nutritional status are beneficial outcomes in themselves. Moreover, a malnourished population contributes less effectively to economic development than does a properly fed, physically strong, and active one. As a result, Bangladesh is paying a high price for its widespread malnutrition and the resulting low productivity of its labor force. Efforts to ensure food security and eradicate malnutrition are good investments in human capital that will contribute to a healthy, growing economy.

In the long run poor families require increased employment and incomes to ensure adequate food intake. Consequently, any long-term solution to malnutrition requires widespread, labor-intensive economic growth. Such growth, however, is a slow process for improving food security of vulnerable people.

As an interim solution, targeted intervention programs may provide needed income and thereby improve food consumption and nutrition. But the need overwhelms available resources. Recent estimates suggest that income transfers on the order of $2.6 billion per year would be required to raise the underfed population to minimum nutritional standards (WGTFI 1994).[2] Yet resources for targeted interventions stand at less than one-tenth that amount, and the aid-financed portion of those funds may shrink further in the future. Therefore, for maximum impact the government must carefully target its scarce resources to particular people, locations, and seasons.

Strategies of Existing Targeted Programs

What Do the Poor Need?

Improvement in nutritional status requires not only family and individual access to food but also effective biological use of the food consumed. While income transfers may improve access at the household level, intra-household allocation and biological use depend on a number of other factors, including health and sanitation, internal decision making, and caring behavior. Thus, while adequate income and access to food are necessary in ensuring adequate nutrition, they are not always sufficient.

What Do Existing Targeted Programs Deliver?

The following discussion reviews the complete spectrum of food-assisted targeted programs in Bangladesh and is based on a series of International Food Policy Research Institute (IFPRI) studies carried out in Bangladesh between 1991 and 1994 (Ahmed 1992, 1993a; Ahmed and Billah 1994; Ahmed and Shams 1994; Ahmed et al. 1995; WGTFI 1994). These programs include the now defunct statutory rationing and rural rationing programs, Vulnerable Group Development (VGD), Food-for-Work (FFW), the Rural Maintenance Program (RMP), and the Food-for-Education (FFE) pilot program. Table 11.1 summarizes their salient features.

STATUTORY RATIONING. The grandfather of the Bangladeshi rationing system, statutory rationing began in the major towns of East Bengal in

2. Here and elsewhere, references to dollars indicate U.S. dollars.

TABLE 11.1 Profile of targeted intervention programs, 1994

Program	Coverage	Description	Donors	Commodity Delivered	Delivery Agent	Number of Beneficiaries	Target Identification
						(thousands)	
Food-for-Work	Seasonal, national	Labor-intensive public works	U.S. Agency for International Development, World Food Programme, Canada, Australia, European Union, Germany, Netherlands, Belgium, France, Sweden, United Kingdom	Wheat	Government (PIC)[a]	4,000	Self-selection, willingness to work
Vulnerable Group Development	Year-round, national, concentrated in distressed regions	Monthly ration in return for training	World Food Programme, Canada, European Union, Australia, Germany	Wheat	Government (PIO)[b]	450	Local committee
Rural Maintenance	Year-round, national	Cash for work by destitute women for rural road maintenance	Canadian International Development Agency	Cash	Banks	55	Local committee and willingness to work
Food-for-Education	Year-round, national	Monthly ration to vulnerable households in return for regular school attendance by their children	U.S. Agency for International Development	Wheat	Schoolteachers	na	School management committee

SOURCES: Ahmed and Billah (1994), WGTFI (1994).

NOTE: na indicates not available.

[a]PIC = project implementation committee, a union-level committee set up to manage FFW implementation.

[b]PIO = project implementation officer, Ministry of Relief, posted at *thana* level.

1956. Under this classic model all urban residents, regardless of income level, received a ration card allowing them to purchase a weekly allotment of basic foods at a steep subsidy, which decreased through the 1980s (see Chapter 9). The scheme discontinued in 1994. An IFPRI study (Haggblade, Rahman, and Rashid 1993) reports that in the early 1990s the statutory ration cardholders were middle- to upper-income groups, not recent migrants or the urban poor. Dealers leaked more than 95 percent of all foodgrains distributed under the scheme onto the open market at market price. The IFPRI study concludes that the scheme had outlived its usefulness. It did not aim to benefit the needy; and even its intended target, the urban middle class, did not benefit. Only dealers gained from the system by reselling the wheat and oil at market prices when price spreads permitted.

PALLY (RURAL) RATIONING. The rural counterpart of urban rationing, *pally* (rural) rationing offered rice for sale at a 25 percent subsidy to administratively selected, low-income rural residents. During its brief lifespan (1990–92) the program was the largest ration channel in the public food distribution system. Its performance, however, was far from satisfactory, operating with about 70 percent leakage (see Box 11.2). Despite the program's negligible impact on the rural poor, the government paid out subsidies of $60 million per year (Ahmed 1992). For these reasons the government abolished it.

BOX 11.2 A shrewd way of beating the system

During our survey, the owner of a rice mill in Bogra District revealed an ingenious method of abusing the Rural Rationing (RR) program through the government rice procurement system. Bogra is one of the largest rice procurement areas in the country. The rice miller, an apparently wealthy and educated man, confessed that he was involved in the deal, and described the method as follows:

1. In the procurement program, the government buys rice through a system known as the millgate purchase contract. The contract rice miller purchases paddy, and after milling the paddy, supplies rice to the government at a fixed price that includes the milling charge (10,544 taka per metric ton during the survey). The officer in charge of the local storage depot and the *thana* food controller sign and issue a weight quality stock certificate (WQSC) to the contract miller to supply rice. The miller produces the WQSC at a designated bank and receives cash payment for the supplied rice.
2. In this rent-seeking process, however, a portion of the millgate purchased rice is not supplied by the miller. Instead, this quantity ➤

is shown in the allotment of rice in the RR program. A delivery order is issued by the food officials to the RR dealer for his full allotment of rice. The RR dealer pays the subsidized price for the full allotment but receives a lesser quantity of rice. Later, the RR dealer gets back the money he paid for the quantity he did not receive.

3. In this process, the government pays a price of 10,544 taka per metric ton for a quantity of rice that is not received. In the official record the same quantity is shown as delivered to the RR program at a subsidized price of 7,340 taka per metric ton. The difference between the millgate purchase price and the RR issue price (that is, 3,204 taka per ton) is shared by the parties involved in the deal.

   An example will show the magnitude of profit that can be made through this process: the monthly officially recorded RR rice offtake from a typical LSD in Bogra is about 98 metric tons of rice. If one-half of this quantity disappears in the process described, then about 157,000 taka can be earned in a month in one local storage depot during procurement seasons.
4. The government also pays for other bills arising from this fictitious transaction. These bills are:

   - Carrying charge of rice from the mill to the local storage depot (about 3 taka per ton per kilometer) paid to the carrying contractor (for the rice that was not carried);
   - Handling charges at the local storage depot (about 2 taka per bag of rice) paid to the handling contractor to receive the millgate purchased rice and deliver the RR rice (for the rice that was not handled);
   - Payment for shortages allowed for storage loss (for the rice that was not stored). These bills, arising from the nonexistent transaction, must be charged to the government to keep the accounting in order.

SOURCE: Ahmed (1992).

FOOD-FOR-WORK PROGRAM. Initiated in 1975 after the famine, this program has played an important dual role in generating wage employment and developing rural infrastructure. FFW provides wages in kind (usually in wheat) to rural laborers for earth-moving construction work. It targets intended low-income beneficiaries by imposing an arduous work requirement. In recent years FFW has generated more than 100 million workdays of employment each year, directly benefiting about 4 million people. Indirect beneficiaries of the rural infrastructure thus developed are the people living in areas in which the schemes are undertaken. Nevertheless, a high degree of resource leakage (30 to 35 percent) means that many potential benefits are not fully realized. About 85 percent of program resources are used during the January–May dry season.

When FFW first began, January through March was one of two slack seasons; but with the advancement of irrigation-induced technology in agriculture, this is no longer true in many areas of the country. Thus, the program competes increasingly with the crop sector labor demand in many areas and may be having an adverse effect on crop productivity. Thus, incremental income gains attributable to FFW per se may have fallen over time. Although food insecurity continues to be most pronounced during September and October, the program largely fails to address this problem because of difficulties in undertaking earthwork immediately after the monsoon season.

VULNERABLE GROUP DEVELOPMENT. VGD originated in 1975 as a relief program and currently provides in-kind wheat payments as a development input to enable destitute rural women to improve their economic and social condition. In 1994, 450,000 women received VGD rations. Selected by administrative screening, recipients receive a monthly free ration of 31.25 kilograms of wheat for two years, transfers that substantially improve the food security of the beneficiary households. A complementary package of development services (incorporating functional skills in literacy, market-oriented income earning skills, legal awareness, savings, and access to credit) was introduced in 1988. The program operates at a relatively low level of leakage (about 14 percent).

RURAL MAINTENANCE PROGRAM. Introduced in 1983, RMP employs destitute women to maintain earthen roads. Currently, the program employs 55,000 women to maintain approximately 88,000 kilometers of essential farm-to-market rural roads in 3,700 Bangladeshi unions (out of a total of 4,451 unions).[3] RMP disburses cash through direct transfers to the women's group bank account. Funds for cash wage payments are generated from the sales of Canadian food aid through the food delivery system's monetized channels. By avoiding the physical handling of cereals, RMP substantially reduces project costs as well as system leakage, which is virtually zero in this program.

FOOD-FOR-EDUCATION. The innovative FFE program was started by the government in 1993 on a large-scale pilot basis. Most children from the poorest families in Bangladesh do not attend school because they cannot be spared from contributing to their family livelihood. The FFE food ration (given in wheat) becomes the income entitlement that enables a poor family to release

3. A union is a local administrative unit consisting of several villages. On average there are about 10 villages per union in Bangladesh.

children from household obligations so they can go to school. An early IFPRI assessment of the program suggests that FFE has been highly successful in increasing primary school enrollment, promoting attendance, and reducing dropout rates (Ahmed and Billah 1994). Nevertheless, although the program has generally reached low-income households, so far it has failed to entice children of the ultra poor to attend school. Due to effective administrative targeting, FFE operates at a low level of leakage (7 percent). There have been concerns, however, about the quality of education provided in FFE-supported schools as a result of increased enrollment rates and teachers' involvement with food distribution. Another thorough evaluation of the program is due.

The Impact of Existing Programs

The Cost-Effectiveness of Income Transfers

IFPRI studies have analyzed the cost-effectiveness of income transfers for each of the targeted food programs, the results of which are summarized here (Table 11.2). Cost-effectiveness is measured by the cost of supplying 1 taka of income to a target household. The costs in this calculation include the income transfer itself and the administrative cost of delivering food or cash to the beneficiaries. The benefits include only the income actually received by targeted households. Consequently, any pilferage or leakage to noneligible households represents a system loss, which is deducted from the income benefit. It is important to recognize that these calculations evaluate RMP, VGD, FFW, and FFE purely as vehicles for targeting income relief. Any development impact beyond the direct income transfer benefits and any costs clearly associated with the development objectives (for example, the cost of materials for construction of culverts for FFW) are excluded.

Among existing programs, RMP, FFE, and VGD transfer income to poor households at least cost. A cash-for-work scheme, RMP delivers 1 taka of income to target households at a cost of 1.3 taka, the lowest cost of all. FFE and VGD transfer 1 taka of income at a cost of 1.6 taka. RMP lowers cost by operating at close to zero leakage and avoiding the cost of commodity handling. FFE and VGD operate with low leakages by offering recipients standard, well-publicized entitlements; establishing group solidarity through regular monthly meetings; and physically gathering beneficiaries during distribution, which enables them to take collective action if necessary to ensure delivery of rations.

In contrast, rural rationing proved to be the least effective at directing income to vulnerable households. It operated with enormous leakage and bore the high costs associated with handling commodities. As a result, the system required 6.6 taka to transfer 1 taka to a target household.

TABLE 11.2 Cost-effectiveness of targeted income transfer programs (per ton of grain)

Costs	Rural Rationing		Vulnerable Group Development			Rural Maintenance Program		Food for Work (CARE)		Food for Work (World Food Programme)		Food-for-Education	
		(rice)			(wheat)		(cash)		(wheat)		(wheat)		(wheat)
Costs (U.S. dollars)					129		129		129		129		129
Grain purchase cost		272											
Sales receipts		207											
Net cost per ton		65											
Government contribution							16						
Administration													
Directorate General of Food		60			54		27		54		54		54
CARE/World Food Programme					1		13		42		1		
Ministries					2		1		8		8		8
Total cost per ton		125			186		170		223		192		191
	Ideal	Actual[a]	Ideal	Actual[b]	Actual[c]	Ideal	Actual[d]	Ideal	Actual[e]	Ideal	Actual[f]	Ideal	Actual[g]
Income transfer to vulnerable households													
Leakage (percent)	0	70	0	14	8	0	0	0	36	0	28	0	7
Income transfer per ton for grain monetized at world price (U.S. dollars)	73	19	129	111	119	129	129	129	83	129	93	129	120
Cost/income transferred	1.73	6.55	1.44	1.68	1.56	1.32	1.32	1.64	2.81	1.49	2.06	1.48	1.59

SOURCES: Rural rationing: Ahmed (1992); VGD, RMP, FFW: WGTFI (1994); FFE: Ahmed and Billah (1994).

NOTES: RMP pays cash wages for its work on rural roads. Cash is generated by monetizing wheat at the official ration price. Thus, the purchase price of wheat, handling, and monetization costs are included in the RMP calculations.

[a]International Food Policy Research Institute (IFPRI) figures. [b]IFPRI figures. [c]World Food Programme figures. [d]IFPRI figures.
[e]CARE figures. [f]Bangladesh Institute for Development Studies/IFPRI figures. [g]IFPRI figures.

FFW is the intermediate performer. Because of moderate system leakages and because it bears the cost of commodity handling, FFW transfers 1 taka to a poor household at a cost of 2.6 taka.

Income, Food Consumption, and Nutrition Effects

Table 11.3 characterizes rural rationing, VGD, FFW, RMP, and FFE beneficiary households. These characteristics are compared with those of the nonbeneficiary rural poor (first quartile) and average rural households. One of the most noticeable characteristics is that many RMP households are headed by females, as is a sizable proportion of VGD households. The data show that, among all targeted programs, income transfer from RMP is the highest, both in absolute terms as well as relative to household expenditures (62 percent). In contrast, the effect of rural rationing in increasing incomes was minimal, accounting for only about 4 percent of per capita household expenditures.

Table 11.4 shows beneficiaries' pattern of food consumption compared to the nonbeneficiary poor (first quartile) and average rural households. These findings are from IFPRI household surveys conducted to assess food consumption and nutritional effects of rural rationing, VGD, FFW, RMP, and FFE (Ahmed 1993a; Ahmed and Shams 1994; Ahmed and Billah 1994). These surveys included samples from both target and control households of the respective programs. The findings demonstrate that FFW, RMP, VGD, and FFE programs have significantly increased food consumption and calorie intake at the household level. Rural rationing, however, did not have any significant effect on food consumption. Foodgrains (rice and wheat) account for about 80 percent of total calorie intake, implying little diversity in diet among all beneficiary groups.

The results, however, reveal that none of the targeted programs has made any noticeable improvement in nutritional status (as determined by anthropometric measurements) of the preschool children who are nutritionally the most vulnerable (Table 11.5). These findings indicate that a household's access to food, although necessary, is not sufficient to eradicate malnutrition confronted by vulnerable individuals within the household. Community-level interventions, such as disease prevention, improved sanitation, safe water supply, and improved caring practices through the provision of proper education and training, will increase the effectiveness of targeted programs in improving the nutritional status of vulnerable groups.

Food Consumption from Increased Income: Cash versus In-Kind Transfer

A household will usually spend only a portion of its additional income on food purchases. Economists refer to this proportion as the marginal propensity to consume food (MPC). If, for example, 75 paisa (100 paisa = 1 taka) out of 1 taka in additional income is spent on food, then the value of the MPC is 0.75.

Do the beneficiaries of targeted programs have a higher MPC from income received in wheat than the MPC from cash income? If they do, then a

TABLE 11.3 Characteristics of program beneficiary and nonbeneficiary households

Characteristics	Rural Rationing	VGD	FFW	RMP	FFE	Rural Nonbeneficiaries	
						First Quartile	Average
Number of sample households	200	117	218	182	120	155	620
Household size (persons)	6.2	5.6	5.0	4.2	6.0	5.9	6.0
No schooling, adult male (percent)	62.6	65.3	74.7	71.7	70.3	68.7	54.9
No schooling, adult female (percent)	88.1	88.6	89.4	91.7	90.4	89.9	77.4
Female-headed household (percent)	6.0	27.5	4.6	93.4	5.7	7.1	4.2
Own cultivable land (decimal)[a]	21.0	17.0	15.4	2.2	na	na	na
Per capita monthly expenditures (taka)[b]	194	199	286	298	388	197	424
Per capita monthly income transfer (taka)	7	41	171	186	22	na	na

SOURCE: Ahmed (1993b).

NOTE: na indicates not available.

[a]A decimal = 1/100 acre.

[b]Expenditures exclude income transfer from programs.

TABLE 11.4 Comparison of food consumption patterns of program beneficiaries and nonbeneficiaries, 1992–94

	Beneficiaries of					Rural nonbeneficiaries	
Characteristics	Rural Rationing	VGD	FFW	RMP	FFE	First Quartile	Average
Budget share of food (percent)	75.2	75.6	75.6	70.2	68.2	74.8	63.3
Food intake (grams per person per day)							
Rice	337	313	394	409	330	377	463
Wheat	39	116	166	60	132	38	23
Pulses	7	8	7	9	na	5	10
Potatoes	13	8	58	54	na	24	48
Vegetables	199	140	187	220	na	156	188
Fish	32	21	15	14	na	18	35
Meat and eggs	1	0	9	10	na	3	6
Edible oil	3	3	6	6	na	3	6
Milk	1	1	21	15	na	2	12
Fruits	2	1	38	36	na	2	6
Sugar	1	1	21	15	na	1	5
Other	14	13	94	96	na	20	49
Calorie intake (kilocalories per person per day)	1,535	1,624	2,488	2,183	1,994	1,601	2,008
Rice (percent)	76	66	58	68	57	79	77
Wheat (percent)	9	25	22	10	23	8	4

SOURCE: Ahmed (1993b).

NOTE: na indicates not available.

TABLE 11.5 Prevalence of malnutrition among preschool children aged 6 to 60 months: Program versus control groups, 1992–94

Group	Height for Age		Weight for Age		Weight for Height	
	Average *Z* Score	Below 90 Percent of Standard Median (percent)	Average *Z* Score	Below 80 Percent of Standard Median (percent)	Average *Z* Score	Below 90 Percent of Standard Median (percent)
Rural rationing	–2.44	48.0	–2.39	69.8	–1.18	58.0
Rural rationing control	–2.59	51.2	–2.46	72.3	–1.20	56.0
VGD	–2.48	48.7	–2.40	73.0	–1.15	50.4
VGD control	–2.44	47.1	–2.42	72.5	–1.24	57.1
RMP	–2.55	50.8	–2.71	80.3	–1.48	68.9
RMP control	–2.43	37.1	–2.54	77.1	–1.42	62.9
FFW	–2.55	50.7	–2.58	76.8	–1.33	57.2
FFW control	–2.83	56.5	–2.74	86.4	–1.34	64.6

SOURCE: Author's calculations using data from IFPRI household surveys conducted during 1992–94 in Bangladesh.

NOTE: Differences between programs versus control groups are not statistically significant at the 0.05 level. Levels of significance are based on *t* test.

food-based program should be more effective in providing nutrition support than would an equivalent payment in cash. Using regression models, this chapter tests that proposition.

In the estimated models the total incomes of VGD, FFW, and RMP beneficiary households have been decomposed into cash income and income transfer in wheat (Table 11.6). The hypothesis tested is that there is no difference in MPCs for different sources of income. The *F* statistic is used to test whether the hypothesis is to be accepted or rejected, running the regressions under the model and the hypothesis. A test is also performed to examine whether the coefficients of income sources are significantly different in the model.

The test results suggest that the source of income does make a significant difference in the MPCs. The marginal propensities to consume food out of one's own cash income are 0.58 for VGD and 0.53 for FFW and RMP households, while the MPC from cash income transfer is 0.48 for RMP households. In contrast, the MPCs from income transfer in wheat are 0.92 for VGD and 0.61 for FFW households. The results of the Wald test (a specific statistical test for difference) suggest that the differences between cash income and income transfer in wheat are statistically significant.

These results conform with those of a number of studies of consumption effects of targeted food interventions in both developed and developing countries, which indicate that the MPC for in-kind subsidy transfer is substantially higher than that for cash income.[4] These studies include the U.S. food stamps program (Devaney and Moffitt 1991; Senauer and Young 1986; Benus, Kmenta, and Shapiro 1976); the rice and cooking oil subsidy program in the Philippines (Garcia and Pinstrup-Andersen 1987); the rice subsidy program in Sri Lanka (Edirisinghe 1987); and the rice subsidy program in Kerala, India (Kumar 1979).

Conclusion

The findings of IFPRI studies in Bangladesh suggest that households respond to changes in income and rice price by adjusting their food consumption patterns. Interventions through market prices, however, are unlikely to noticeably

4. Income in kind versus cash has implications for household effort to maximize utility from a given level of income and price constellation. The portion of the wheat income that a household may find to be larger than the normal taste-dictated level can be sold in the market and converted to cash if there are no transaction costs in doing so. But there may be transaction costs in the resale of income received in kind. The shadow price of commodities received as income in kind is thus presumably lower than the market price. This transaction cost may arise from labor costs in sale, search costs for finding a buyer for the commodity given by the government, and other unknown factors. Because of these costs and the consequent lower shadow price, the MPC of in-kind income could be higher than that of cash income. These lines of inquiry were not pursued in the study conducted in Bangladesh.

TABLE 11.6 Influences of forms of income on food consumption of program beneficiaries

	Estimated Parameters			
	VGD		FFW and RMP	
Explanatory variables	Model	Hypothesis	Model	Hypothesis
Constant	−0.36 (−0.22)	1.16 (0.73)	10.60 (4.21)[a]	10.81 (4.47)[a]
Own income	na	na	0.53 (28.45)[a]	na
Own cash income	0.58 (22.00)[a]	na	na	na
Borrowed cash income	0.61 (16.01)[a]	na	na	na
Other in-kind income	0.82 (13.93)[a]	na	na	na
Cash income transfer (RMP)	na	na	0.48 (11.92)[a]	na
Income transfer in wheat (VGD, FFW)	0.92 (5.82)[a]	na	0.61 (12.68)[a]	na
Rice price	−0.51 (−1.40)	−0.33 (−0.89)	−0.70 (−3.98)[a]	−0.60 (−3.46)[a]
Wheat price	0.78 (2.23)[b]	0.52 (1.47)	0.07 (0.44)	−0.13 (−0.93)
Household size	0.07 (0.94)	−0.06 (−1.31)	0.17 (1.22)	0.19 (1.56)
Number of guests	−0.183 (0.74)	−0.24 (−0.91)	na	na
Total income	na	0.62 (23.79)[a]	na	0.53 (30.77)[a]
F statistic	131.24[a]	199.31[a]	175.77[a]	257.11[a]
Adjusted R^2	0.89	0.87	0.73	0.73

SOURCE: Author's estimations using data from IFPRI household surveys conducted during 1992–94 in Bangladesh.

NOTE: Dependent variables are daily household food expenditures per adult equivalent unit. Figures in parentheses show *t* values. na indicates not available.

[a]Significant at the 0.01 level.

[b]Significant at the 0.05 level.

improve food consumption and the nutritional status of the extreme poor because this population lacks needed purchasing power and other factors hypothesized in Chapter 5. To relieve nutritional stress among the poorest, targeted income transfers are far more effective than are general or targeted food price subsidies.

If food is distributed in targeted interventions, wheat should be distributed rather than rice. Because wheat remains a less desirable grain in rural Bangladesh (see Chapter 5), it retains its self-targeting characteristic, making it a preferred commodity for targeted food interventions in rural areas, where it has the potential to increase the cost-effectiveness of such programs. In contrast, rice consumption increases steadily with income. This suggests that distributing rice in food-assisted intervention programs is not an efficient mechanism for targeting the poor.

Where cash is available, cash-based programs offer the most cost-effective income transfer mechanisms. Food is a cumbersome resource, while cash is more flexible and less costly to manage. Food transfers immediately raise program costs by 25 percent because of the internal transport and handling costs of these bulky commodities.

Nevertheless, evidence in Bangladesh as well as in a number of other countries indicates that programs that distribute food have a larger impact on increasing food consumption than do cash transfer programs. Thus, food distribution programs partly offset their higher operating costs and leakages when evaluated as nutrition support programs.

There are high degrees of regional and seasonal variations in food consumption and nutritional status. Thus, limiting interventions to specific distressed locations of the country and concentrating program resources during the lean season will considerably improve the cost-effectiveness of such interventions. Currently, no existing program has managed to target the acute lean season of September and October. Although year-round schemes such as VGD, RMP, and FFE do deliver transfers during this period, no scheme has successfully targeted the season exclusively. Because of difficulties in earthmoving during these monsoon months, efforts will require experimentation with new models of delivery and targeting. Given the acute stress of vulnerable groups (Chapter 5), seasonal targeting during September/October remains a high but challenging priority for the future.

Although VGD, RMP, and FFW programs have been successful in significantly improving household food security, they have had little impact on the nutritional status of children within recipient households. This points to the need to better incorporate nonfood components into targeted programs. An optimal programming mix should combine income targeting, disease prevention, improved sanitation, safe water, and attention to caring behavior.

To realize greater benefits from targeted programs, it is necessary to ensure accountability and reduce leakage. Participation of local bodies (or representatives of beneficiaries) at the stage of scheme selection and implementation should be strengthened. Moreover, if beneficiary communities share costs of public works programs, they are more likely to take an active part, be more accountable, and help reduce leakage.

In the past Bangladesh has been willing to modify or close down nonfunctional or underperforming targeted programs. In the future resources available for these programs will probably decline. As they do, implementers will need to monitor performance more rigorously than ever, evaluate programs closely, and insist on tighter targeting and management of its remaining programs.

References

Ahmed, A. U. 1992. *Operational performance of the rural rationing program in Bangladesh.* Working Paper on Bangladesh 5. Washington, D.C.: International Food Policy Research Institute.

———. 1993a. Food consumption and nutritional effects of targeted food interventions in Bangladesh. Bangladesh Food Policy Project Manuscript 31. Washington, D.C.: International Food Policy Research Institute. Mimeo.

———. 1993b. *Patterns of food consumption and nutrition in rural Bangladesh.* Washington, D.C.: International Food Policy Research Institute.

Ahmed, A. U., and K. Billah. 1994. Food for Education program in Bangladesh: An early assessment. Bangladesh Food Policy Project Manuscript 62. Washington, D.C.: International Food Policy Research Institute. Mimeo.

Ahmed, A. U., and Y. Shams. 1994. Nutritional effects of cash versus commodity based public works programs. Bangladesh Food Policy Project Manuscript 63. Washington, D.C.: International Food Policy Research Institute. Mimeo.

Ahmed, A. U., S. Zohir, S. K. Kumar, and O. H. Chowdhury. 1995. Bangladesh's Food-for-Work program and alternatives to improve food security. In *Employment for poverty reduction and food security,* ed. J. von Braun. Washington, D.C.: International Food Policy Research Institute.

Benus, J., J. Kmenta, and H. Shapiro. 1976. The dynamics of household and budget allocation to food expenditure. *Review of Economics and Statistics* 58 (May): 129–138.

Chowdhury, O. H. 1992. Nutritional dimensions of poverty. Paper presented at the National Workshop of Rural Poverty, March 12–13, Bangladesh Institute of Development Studies, Dhaka.

Devaney, B., and R. Moffitt. 1991. Food stamp program. *American Journal of Agricultural Economics* 73 (February): 202–211.

Edirisinghe, N. 1987. *The food stamp scheme in Sri Lanka: Costs, benefits, and options for modification.* Research Report 58. Washington, D.C.: International Food Policy Research Institute.

Garcia, M., and P. Pinstrup-Andersen. 1987. *The pilot food price subsidy scheme in the Philippines: Its impact on income, food consumption, and nutritional status.* Research Report 61. Washington, D.C.: International Food Policy Research Institute.

Haggblade, S., S. A. Rahman, and S. Rashid. 1993. Statutory rationing: Performance and prospects. Draft Report. Dhaka: International Food Policy Research Institute, Bangladesh Food Policy Project. Mimeo.

Hassan, N., and K. Ahmed. 1990. Regional variations in the intake of food and nutrients in rural Bangladesh: Its impact on nutritional status. *Bangladesh Journal of Nutrition* 3 (January): 51–76.

Hossain, M., and B. Sen. 1992. Rural poverty in Bangladesh: Trends and determinants. *Asian Development Review* 10 (January): 1–34.

Kumar, S. K. 1979. *Impact of subsidized rice on food consumption and nutrition in Kerala.* Research Report 5. Washington, D.C.: International Food Policy Research Institute.

Rahman, H. Z. 1994. Rural poverty update, 1992–93. Dhaka: Bangladesh Institute of Development Studies. Mimeo.

Ravallion, M., and B. Sen. 1996. When method matters: Monitoring poverty in Bangladesh. *Economic Development and Cultural Change* 44 (July): 761–792.

Sen, B. 1992. Rural poverty trends, 1983/64 to 1989/90. In *Re-thinking rural poverty,* ed. H. Z. Rahman and M. Hossain. Dhaka: Bangladesh Institute of Development Studies.

Senauer, B., and N. Young. 1986. The impact of food stamps on food expenditures: Rejection of the traditional model. *American Journal of Agricultural Economics* 68 (February): 37–43.

Working Group on Targeted Food Interventions (WGTFI). 1994. *Options for targeting food interventions in Bangladesh.* Washington, D.C.: International Food Policy Research Institute.

12 Agricultural Diversification: A Strategic Factor for Growth

WAHIDUDDIN MAHMUD, SULTAN HAFEEZ RAHMAN, AND SAJJAD ZOHIR

Seed-fertilizer technology has had a dramatic influence on cereal production in many developing economies, including Bangladesh. Agricultural diversification is the next stage in transforming traditional agriculture to a dynamic, commercial sector. Diversification in the product mix of agriculture, through a shift toward high-value products, has great potential for accelerating growth rates in production. To exploit this potential, forces within both the supply and the demand sides of the shift are important; but demand forces (the scope of market opportunities for high-value products) play a more important role in the initial stage of the process. Robust diversification cannot take place without exploitation of foreign demand. In low-income economies, domestic demand for high-value products such as fish, livestock products, horticultural products, and vegetables is generally low and does not have a significant impact on agricultural growth rate through diversification. Thus, an export-based strategy is generally the most productive route to follow. In Bangladesh rice contributes about 50 percent of the gross domestic product (GDP) in agriculture and 70 percent of the value of crop production. On the other hand, income elasticity of the demand for rice is low and declining over time (see Chapter 5). Therefore, agricultural diversification is a serious issue in the context of agricultural growth.

The prospect of agricultural growth through crop diversification raises a great many issues concerning agronomic sustainability, farm-level incentives, changing technologies, marketing efficiency and opportunities, comparative advantage, and macrolevel supply-demand balances. This chapter focuses on only a few of these issues, emphasizing analysis of growth sources and performance of the crop sector, which then leads to an assessment of agricultural supply response behavior and an evaluation of the structure of farmer incentives in relation to comparative advantage in crop agriculture. This chapter was developed from a comprehensive study conducted by the International Food Policy Research Institute (Mahmud, Rahman, and Zohir 1994), and many of its findings are based on 1990–91 field surveys on various aspects of production and marketing as well as from a data base of other studies.

Growth Performance in Crop Agriculture

Growth and Its Sources

For the overlapping periods 1973/74–1983/84 and 1979/80–1989/90, the annual growth of production for the crop sector as a whole is estimated at 2.08 and 1.62 percent, respectively. This growth barely kept pace with population growth, which increased at about 2.3 percent annually in the 1970s and 2 percent in the 1980s.[1] Between 1990/91 and 1997/98, production in the crop sector did not improve much (the growth rate averaged 1.7 percent), but population growth declined to about 1.6 percent in 1997/98. Growth in gross farm revenue (at constant prices) was due mainly to increased foodgrain production, which grew at a higher rate than did population through both periods (see Chapter 2 for details on the growth of foodgrains). Among non-foodgrain crops and crop groups, only vegetable production grew close to the rate of population growth. Perhaps the only other noteworthy instances of growth performance appear in the production trends of tea and tubers in 1973/74–1983/84, although in both cases production stagnated in the 1980s. On the other hand, the production of pulses declined, especially in the 1980s, while minor cereals exhibited the most dramatic rates of output decline. Area under oilseeds declined in both periods; however, production declined only marginally during the 1980s.

One may separate growth in crop agriculture into two potential sources: expansion of the cropped land and improvements in productivity per unit of cropped land. For the crop sector as a whole, the contribution of area expansion to growth has declined over time. Thus, most of the production growth in the 1980s came from the increase in revenue yield per hectare of gross cropped land.

Of the non-foodgrain crops, potato production increased at a high rate (4 percent annually) in 1973/74–1983/84, made possible by increases in both area and yields; but the momentum seems to have been lost. Sweet potatoes, a famine crop, is much favored under official policies for diversification, although its production has rapidly declined (4 percent annually) in the 1980s. For jute, tea, and mustard (the major oilseed crop), there were some yield improvements in 1973/74–1983/84 that could not be sustained in the 1980s. Area under pulses has declined significantly in the 1980s, but in the case of *masur* (lentils) yield improvements have compensated for the decline in area. This seems also to have been the case for chilies, the major spice crop. Among fruits the yield rate of mangos has been falling sharply, but there has been some

---

1. Compared to our estimates, considerably higher rates of growth of the crop sector are implied by the official national income series. The official statistics, however, fail to capture adequately the fact that the growth in foodgrain production has often been at the expense of noncereal crops (see Mahmud, Rahman, and Zohir 1994).

area expansion. Banana production has stagnated in the 1980s after experiencing some growth in the earlier period. Among vegetables the growth of production has occurred mainly through area expansion without much improvement in yields.

For all noncereal crops the increases in revenue productivity per hectare have kept the total value of production from falling since the area devoted to them has declined significantly, particularly in the 1980s. It is important to note, however, that these improvements appear to have resulted from reallocation of area in favor of higher-value crops rather than from any sustained yield improvements for individual crops or crop groups.[2] High-value crops such as vegetables, potatoes, fruits, and sugarcane have all gained in area (spices being the only exception), while area under low-value crops such as jute, pulses, oilseeds, and minor cereals has declined, particularly in the 1980s (see Mahmud, Rahman, and Zohir 1994).

Agricultural Supply Response: Market and Nonmarket Constraints

The efficacy of price policies in promoting crop diversification depends on the responsiveness of supply to variations in relative prices; for illustration we provide estimates on supply response. Nevertheless, many market and nonmarket factors underlie observed supply response that may hinder efforts toward crop diversification.

Supply Response

National-level time-series data for 1972/73–1989/90 were used to estimate area response equations for a number of crops and crop groups.[3] In view of the small number of observations, the study used a simple Nerlovian-type supply (area) response model that included lagged area, prices, yield, and irrigated area as explanatory variables. The findings suggest that total rice area as well as aus area barely respond to prices but that both boro and aman rice show some degree of responsiveness (Table 12.1). The short-run price elasticity for boro varies from 0.24 to 0.50, depending on whether or not the price effect is controlled for irrigation. These results suggest that the rice crops may respond to seasonal rice prices and that such a response may involve substitution among rice crops (thus reducing the effect at the aggregate level). The estimated short-run price response for wheat, jute, tobacco, and melons is modest and of high statistical significance. Sugarcane and oilseeds also show statistically significant price elasticities, although of relatively low magnitudes. For most

2. Note that all trends are measured at constant prices.

3. In the literature on the estimation of agricultural supply response, crop area is often taken as a proxy for production since the latter is more likely to be influenced by random natural factors. Area allocation decisions are, however, of direct interest here.

TABLE 12.1 Results of an estimation of the area response equation for crops and crop groups

Crop	Price Elasticity	Yield Elasticity	Lagged Area Coefficient	R^2	*D-W* statistic
Rice	0.06[a]	0.15[c]	na	0.88	1.72
Aus	0.4[a]	na	na	0.94	2.20
Aman	0.36[b] (0.55)	na	0.35[b]	0.97	2.18
Boro (1)	0.24[b]	na	na	0.98	1.62
Boro (2)	0.50[b] (2.86)	na	0.83[b]	0.97	2.50
Wheat	0.61[c] (5.24)	na	0.88[c]	0.98	2.21
Jute	0.49[c] (0.68)	0.15[c]	na	0.88	1.72
Sugarcane	0.15[c] (0.73)	na	0.79[c]	0.96	1.89[d]
Oilseeds	0.16[b]	na	0.14[c]	0.923	1.85
Mustard	0.13[c] (0.27)	na	0.52[c]	0.93	2.05
Linseed	0.11[b] (0.32)	na	0.66[c]	0.88	2.73
Sesame	0.25[b] (0.98)	na	0.75[c]	0.95	2.41
Pulses	0.11[a]	na	0.81[c]	0.92	na
Masur (lentils)	0.07[a] (1.09)	na	0.93[c]	0.91	2.03[d]
Katar	0.05[a] (1.20)	0.21[a] (4.86)	0.96[c]	0.99	1.94
Khesari	(0.04[b]) (0.25)	na	0.84[c]	0.94	2.54
Mashkalai	(0.11[a]) (0.91)	0.85[c] (7.27)	0.88[c]	0.99	2.22
Spices					
Chilies	0.05[c] (0.17)	na	0.68[c]	0.88	2.12
Onions	0.05[b] (0.09)	na	0.45[b]	0.70	1.89
Garlic	0.001[a] (0.01)	na	0.38[b]	0.82	1.73
Tumeric	0.03[c] (0.05)	0.34[c] (0.59)	0.42[b]	0.97	2.36
Ginger	0.04[b] (0.45)	na	0.90[c]	0.94	1.96[d]
Vegetables					
Brinjal	0.03[b] (0.08)	0.32[c] (1.04)	0.69[c]	0.94	1.72
Arum	0.30[a]	na	na	0.90	1.49[d]
Cauliflower	0.07[c] (0.51)	na	0.86[c]	0.99	1.69[d]
Cabbage	0.08[c] (0.28)	0.48[c] (1.83)	0.74[c]	0.99	1.95
Tomatoes	0.08[b] (0.29)	na	0.72[c]	0.96	2.40
Radishes	0.16[b]	2.83[c]	na	0.85	2.20
Beans	0.10[b] (0.51)	na	na	0.95	1.82[d]
Potato	0.01[b] (0.21)	na	0.94[c]	0.99	1.66[d]
Sweet potatoes	0.08[a]	2.27[c]	na	0.82	1.94[d]
Melons	0.23[c] (0.45)	na	0.49[b]	0.84	2.23
Tobacco	0.23[c]	1.87[c]	na	0.93	2.02
Cotton	0.16[a]	0.34[b]	na	0.69	1.61
Maize	0.09[b] (1.58)	na	0.94[c]	0.99	2.13
Barley	0.19[b] (2.79)	na	0.93[c]	0.99	1.89

SOURCE: Mahmud, Rahman, and Zohir (1994).

NOTES: Estimates are based on 17 observations. The coefficient of lagged area refers to a Nerlovian equation. The absence of an entry in this column indicates that the estimates are based on a cobweb equation. The main entries for price elasticity and yield elasticity show the estimated short-run area elasticities, while the long-run elasticities are shown within parentheses. Boro (1) and (2) represent estimates obtained with and without the irrigation variable, respectively.

na indicates not available.

[a]Estimates of the corresponding coefficient are significant at the 10 percent level.

[b]Significant at the 5 percent level.

[c]Significant at the 1 percent level.

[d]Estimates are adjusted for first- or higher-order serial correlation.

other crops the price responses are weak in terms of the magnitudes of short-run price elasticities or the statistical significance of the estimated price parameters.

The weak supply response in the case of low-value crops such as pulses, oilseeds, and minor cereals may be explained by the fact that their choice within the rice-based cropping patterns is mostly residual. Nevertheless, this is not a plausible explanation for high-value crops such as spices, potatoes, and vegetables. The problem may lie instead in the extremely high price fluctuations that often characterize the markets for these products, thus inhibiting any rational price expectations.

For a number of crops the response of area to yield changes is strong and statistically significant. In nearly all of these cases the estimated yield elasticities are several times higher than are the price elasticities. This suggests that farmers respond much more strongly to yield improvements (or declines) than to price changes, giving added importance to policy measures supporting technological improvements in high-value crops such as vegetables and spices. Such improvements would contribute to the growth of the crop sector through not only increased yields but also the induced shift of land toward these high-value crops.

Finally, the irrigation variable has a strong effect on area allocation for some crops and crop groups. (In each of these cases the estimated irrigation coefficient is statistically significant at less than 1 percent.) The irrigation coefficient, which is a measure of the change in area under the crop as a proportion of the change in total irrigation, is estimated at –0.35 for aus, 0.79 for boro, –0.08 for pulses, and –0.04 for oilseeds. In the latter two cases the estimates refer to the respective crop groups. These estimates, in numerical terms, are plausible and consistent with our previous findings that the expansion of modern irrigation strongly favors high-yielding varieties (HYV) in boro cultivation, which tends to replace almost entirely local aus, pulses, and oilseeds.[4]

Market and Marketing Risk

Agricultural marketing and its associated storage and processing functions are crucial to agricultural supply responses and prospects for crop diversification. There are likely to be considerable variations across agricultural commodities concerning the degree of market integration, reliability of price formation, and the extent of farmers' market participation. While rice marketing has been studied frequently in Bangladesh, there is far less information available about the marketing of other crops.[5]

4. Since the increases in irrigated area are entirely due to the expansion of modern irrigation, estimates mainly reflect the effect of modern irrigation.

5. See Maziruddin (1989) for a discussion of the agricultural marketing system in Bangladesh.

Analysis of primary data from the 1988/89 round of the Bangladesh Bureau of Statistics' household expenditure survey shows that, compared to rice, the proportions of output marketed are generally much higher for other crops. Moreover, poorer farm households account for a much larger share of marketed surplus of nonrice crops. For items such as vegetables and spices small farms have, in fact, a larger quantity of marketed surplus in absolute terms when compared to large farms. Therefore, the impact of improved marketing and price incentives on the supply response behavior of smaller farms and on their incomes deserves particular consideration in the context of policies for crop diversification.

Prospects for diversification also depend on the extent of year-to-year price fluctuations and associated risks to farm incomes. Average variability in annual prices, defined as the average of percent deviations (positive and negative signs ignored) of the observed prices from the estimated trend level for 1977–87, were estimated. Results show that, compared to foodgrains, price variability is higher for all non-foodgrain crops (with the exception of sugarcane) and is strikingly high for many crops. Most estimates fall between 5 and 6 percent for foodgrains, 10 and 12 percent for oilseeds and pulses, 15 and 25 percent for fruits and vegetables (including potatoes), and 20 to 40 percent for spices. Evidently, for many of these items the price variability is too high to allow any rational price expectations. Variability of harvest prices is generally higher than that of annual wholesale prices, suggesting that the price shocks are more severe at the level of primary markets during the harvest seasons. The integration of markets for vegetables and spices is much weaker than that of cereals.

Nonmarket Factors: Limits on Choice of Cropping Patterns

Cropping patterns in Bangladesh are delicately balanced within the annual cycle of rains and floods. Thus, farmers' production options and their perceptions of risk are often determined by the physical environment of crop production: the degree of seasonal flooding, the timing and quantity of rainfall, and soil characteristics.[6] Investments in irrigation and flood control as well as improvements in crop production technology can induce changes in cropping patterns by influencing physical constraints. There are large variations in the cropping patterns throughout the country, and many can be related to agro-climatic factors.[7]

Econometric analysis of cross-section data by regions suggests that flood-depth levels are important in determining cropping pattern.[8] More important,

6. See, for example, Bangladesh Master Plan Organization (1987) and Islam (1989).

7. These regional variations in cropping patterns are analyzed in Zohir (1993a) and Rashid (1989).

8. Data are from the 1983/84 *Census of Agriculture* and correspond to the 64 administrative districts of the country. For details see Mahmud, Rahman, and Zohir (1994).

irrigation has a positive impact on the adoption of HYV rice in all seasons, displacing local aus and broadcast aman during the moonsoon (kharif) and reducing the area under pulses, oilseeds, and spices in the winter (*rabi*) season.[9] The analysis also shows that rainfall and farm sizes are important determinants of area allocation decisions. Large farms were found to cultivate their land less intensively. Moreover, the proportion of rice land allocated to HYVs is higher on small farms than on large farms. Among nonrice crops there is little variation among farm-size groups in respect to area allocation for oilseeds and pulses; but the proportion of land under spices, vegetables, and potatoes is nearly twice as much for small farms as for large farms.

The cropping patterns in the country can be broadly classified into rainfed and irrigated patterns, which vary individually according to the degree of seasonal flooding. A fairly representative nationwide farm survey indicates that irrigation has a favorable impact on the annual cropping intensity on high and medium-high land but a negative impact on lower lands.[10] The higher the land, the larger the share devoted to noncereal crops within any of the irrigation categories. On the other hand, among all flood-depth levels the proportion of land allocated to noncereal crops is markedly lower under irrigated conditions than under rainfed ones. There is also a sharp contrast in the cropping patterns between modern and traditional irrigation, the latter being more conducive to diversified cropping patterns.

Traditional irrigation on highlands appears to strengthen the cultivation of not only wheat but also high-value noncereal crops such as potatoes, vegetables, and spices. The production conditions here may not be suitable for HYV boro cultivation, which needs continuous irrigation and flooding and is therefore much more water-dependent than are most other crops. But why do high-value noncereal crops not compete with HYV boro under modern irrigation? The answer may lie in a combination of technical and economic factors. As we shall discuss, there are risks associated with marketing these high-value crops. At the same time existing irrigation and on-farm water management systems do not allow rice and nonrice crops to be planted in the same service units. Therefore, growing nonrice crops under modern irrigation often requires farmers to allocate their entire land (or the major part of it) to these crops—hardly a preferred option for a risk-averse farmer. Because it is divisible, traditional irrigation allows farmers to grow these high-value but risk-prone crops on small parcels of land. Generally, there are large economies of scale in marketing. Thus, when markets are large or assured (as in the case of vegetable

9. Irrigated area in the 1983/84 census data could not be distinguished in terms of modern and traditional irrigation.

10. The farm survey was conducted in 1987 by the Bangladesh Institute of Development Studies in connection with a study on the adoption of HYV rice in Bangladeshi agriculture (Hossain et al. 1990). We are grateful to the authors of this study for allowing us access to the primary survey data.

belts near urban centers), noncereal crops are grown under modern irrigation on a significant scale. Export-led expansion of markets can induce farmers to use modern irrigation in producing such crops and reduce marketing costs.

Trade Policies and Structure of Agricultural Incentives

With structural adjustment measures available since the early 1980s, Bangladesh has moved toward a liberalized trade regime with flexible exchange rate management. Policy reforms have generally aimed at lowering tariff rates and freeing imports from quantitative restrictions. Nevertheless, trade in agricultural commodities continues to be restricted, and policy reforms did not affect them until the 1990/91 fiscal year. Nevertheless, the liberalization of the rice trade in 1994 and new promotional facilities for noncereal exports have had profound effects on agricultural trade.

The policy regime regarding foreign trade and exchange rate management can affect the structure of incentives within agriculture (as well as between agriculture and other sectors) through direct and indirect effects on domestic price formation. The direct effect on prices arises from commodity-specific policies such as taxes, subsidies, or quantitative restrictions on export and import. This effect is measured by the proportional difference between the domestic price and the border price (the so-called import or export parity price) at the prevailing official exchange rate. The indirect effect of the trade policy regime arises from its impact on exchange rate determination. High import tariffs, for example, would discriminate against exportables compared to importables by appreciating the exchange rate in relation to the equilibrium exchange rate that would have prevailed under a free-trade regime.[11] Therefore, to assess the combined effect of trade policies, one must estimate the border price at the equilibrium exchange rate in making the domestic-to-border price comparisons. Such a comparison could be taken as a measure of how, as a result of trade policies, the domestic price of a tradable commodity diverges from its true opportunity cost (that is, the border price that would have prevailed under an intervention-free regime).[12]

The way in which trade policies affect producer incentives in agriculture depends, of course, on the actual and potential trading status of agricultural and agriculture-based commodities. Foodgrains, primarily wheat, have constituted the major agricultural import item, and most has come as food aid. The import of rice has widely varied from year to year, with recent trends in import and

11. Such a policy is also likely to discriminate against exportables vis-à-vis nontradable domestic goods by lowering the relative price of the former.

12. Here, the free-trade equilibrium exchange rate is taken to represent the shadow price of foreign exchange. In this case one must also assume that the country is a price taker in the international market. See Timmer, Falcon, and Pearson (1983), Valdés and Siamwalla (1988), and Scandizzo and Bruce (1980).

domestic production suggesting that the country is nearing self-sufficiency in rice. Other important imports as a share of domestic supply are mustard seeds, edible oils, sugar, and cotton. Onions, chilies, lentils, and other pulses are also imported, especially in deficit years and lean seasons.[13] Tobacco is both imported and exported because of the differentiated product quality. There is virtually no foreign trade in potatoes, although there have been recent exports of vegetables and fruits, mainly to Bangladeshi communities in the United Kingdom and the Arab Middle East. There is some potential for exporting spices in the future, provided that domestic production increases.

Trends in Domestic-to-Border Price Ratio

To assess the effect of trade and exchange rate policies on agricultural incentives, we have made domestic-to-border price comparisons for a selected number of commodities both at the official and estimated equilibrium exchange rates. The time-series estimates of these ratios can help pinpoint how the trade policy environment has changed over time with respect to these commodities (Tables 12.2 and 12.3). The estimates of import parity prices are based on the assumption that imports compete with domestic production at the wholesale level.[14] For wheat and rapeseed, however, price comparisons are made at the farmgate level since reliable time-series estimates of domestic wholesale prices are not available.

RICE. Given the predominance of rice in crop agriculture, the impact of trade policy on agricultural incentives is largely determined by what happens to rice. The border price comparison for rice is for coarse-quality rice, which accounts for most of the rice produced in the country.[15] At the official exchange rate domestic rice price has mostly remained within the band of import and export parity prices, implying that in most years there has not been any positive or negative protection for rice through import or export taxation or trade restrictions. The trade policy, nevertheless, can be held responsible for lowering the domestic rice price through public import of foodgrains, mostly under food aid. The effect of such imports on domestic rice price is equivalent to an import subsidy as measured by the nominal rate of protection (NRP) at the import parity price.[16] The estimates presented here suggest that there might

13. Bangladesh also imports citrus fruits every year and bananas occasionally.

14. In the case of rapeseed, imports compete at the millgate level.

15. The average prices of 5 percent broken and 25 percent broken Thai rice are used to represent the price of coarse-quality rice in Bangladesh. Discussion with traders has suggested that the coarse rice produced in the country is markedly superior to the internationally traded 25 percent broken Thai variety. A recent market survey has also shown that domestic coarse rice consists of about 15 percent broke rice (see Chowdhury 1992); however, there is no internationally quoted price available for 15 percent broken Thai rice.

16. Note, however, that the extent of the price effect can be lower than that indicated by the NRP estimate based on the import parity price. Such an estimate still indicates the upper bound of negative protection resulting from direct trade policies.

TABLE 12.2 Domestic-to-border price ratios of selected commodities at the official exchange rate

Year	Rice[a]		Wheat Import Parity	Lentils Import Parity	Potatoes		Rapeseed Import Parity	Sugar Import Parity
	Import Parity	Export Parity			Import Parity	Export Parity		
1974/75	1.04	1.50	1.42	na	1.30	9.02	2.16	1.06
1975/76	1.02	1.48	1.33	na	1.13	4.97	1.91	1.46
1976/77	0.71	0.95	0.92	na	0.90	3.25	1.40	1.77
1977/78	0.70	0.92	0.92	0.77	0.82	3.16	1.30	1.82
1978/79	0.75	0.99	0.87	0.82	0.81	3.78	1.32	1.25
1979/80	0.71	0.96	0.83	0.79	0.77	3.23	1.37	1.49
1980/81	0.76	1.07	0.88	0.88	0.68	2.79	1.34	1.80
1981/82	0.80	1.14	0.90	0.99	0.56	1.75	1.16	2.53
1982/83	0.95	1.41	0.92	1.06	0.57	1.63	1.13	2.86
1983/84	1.04	1.65	0.99	0.82	0.65	2.07	1.45	3.60
1984/85	1.04	1.65	0.99	0.82	0.65	2.07	1.45	3.60
1985/86	1.08	1.76	1.12	0.88	0.77	2.79	1.76	3.43
1986/87	0.98	1.51	1.11	1.14	0.73	2.17	1.85	2.85
1987/88	0.94	1.40	1.04	1.19	0.81	2.19	1.96	2.34
1988/89	0.88	1.30	1.02	1.12	0.81	2.09	1.85	2.22
1989/90	0.84	1.27	1.07	0.87	0.80	2.27	1.98	2.40
1996/97[b]	0.94	1.23	1.01	na	na	na	2.01	2.60

SOURCE: Mahmud, Rahman, and Zohir (1994).

NOTES: Data are based on a three-year moving average of respective prices. For wheat and rapeseed, the price parity is at the farmgate level, for all other commodities at the wholesale level.

na indicates not available.

[a]Coarse-quality rice.

[b]Import parity price with import from India in 1996/97. This was not worked out in the source publication because the study was conducted before 1996/97.

TABLE 12.3 Trends in domestic-to-border price ratios of selected commodities at the equilibrium exchange rate

Year	Rice[a]		Wheat Import Parity	Lentils Import Parity	Potatoes		Rapeseed Import Parity	Sugar Import Parity
	Import Parity	Export Parity			Import Parity	Export Parity		
1974/75	0.762	1.028	1.005	na	0.997	4.840	1.467	0.760
1975/76	0.799	1.094	1.001	na	0.911	3.199	1.403	1.122
1976/77	0.566	0.726	0.721	na	0.746	2.259	1.073	1.433
1977/78	0.570	0.726	0.740	0.629	0.684	2.222	1.018	1.503
1978/79	0.617	0.792	0.713	0.680	0.689	2.693	1.052	1.038
1979/80	0.595	0.785	0.690	0.660	0.660	2.439	1.115	1.249
1980/81	0.635	0.871	0.721	0.735	0.579	2.118	1.088	1.506
1981/82	0.673	0.935	0.744	0.837	0.478	1.376	0.948	2.142
1982/83	0.793	1.127	0.746	0.881	0.477	1.250	0.905	2.416
1983/84	0.847	1.203	0.747	0.687	0.488	1.272	0.932	2.585
1984/85	0.853	1.277	0.788	0.669	0.543	1.537	1.131	3.021
1985/86	0.927	1.440	0.931	0.746	0.672	2.174	1.425	2.995
1986/87	0.868	1.297	0.963	1.010	0.653	1.787	1.572	2.541
1987/88	0.847	1.219	0.915	1.070	0.735	1.853	1.700	2.103
1988/89	0.787	1.128	0.897	0.999	0.731	1.773	1.594	1.991
1989/90	0.763	1.114	0.952	0.781	0.732	1.942	1.728	2.167

SOURCE: Mahmud, Rahman, and Zohir (1994).

NOTES: Data are based on a three-year moving average of respective prices. For wheat and rapeseed, the price parity is at the farmgate level; for all other commodities at the wholesale level.

na indicates not available

[a]Coarse-quality rice.

have been substantial negative protection for rice only in the late 1970s, which was eliminated in later years. In particular, recent policy changes that allow private sector imports of rice and import of rice from India have eliminated most trade-related protections for rice.

According to the equilibrium exchange rate, however, there appears to have been negative protection for rice in relation to the import parity price throughout the entire period under review. Even at the export parity price, there was substantial negative protection (25 to 30 percent) during the late 1970s. The domestic price of rice has therefore remained lower, at times substantially, compared to its opportunity cost in border price terms (which in a rice-import regime is represented by the import parity price at the shadow or equilibrium exchange rate). All this is changing, however, as the country approaches self-sufficiency in rice, while the implicit subsidy on wheat import has also been virtually eliminated. In the evolving scenario, the trade policies have become neutral to domestic rice price determination.

NONRICE CROPS. Trends in the domestic-to-border price ratio for wheat are similar to those for rice. In most years, however, the extent of divergence between the domestic price and the import parity price has been less for wheat. In fact, the domestic wheat market appears recently to have been somewhat protected at the official exchange rate, although not at the equilibrium rate.

The nominal rate of protection for sugar and mustard seed (represented by rapeseed) has been consistently positive and at times high.[17] Even at the equilibrium exchange rate, these items appear to have been heavily protected (with the exception of rapeseed in the early 1980s). Among crops and crop-based products these two enjoy substantial protection, if one takes into account the direct and indirect effects of trade policies. As will be discussed, much of the protection for sugar is absorbed by the inefficient public refineries that procure sugarcane at administered prices. But protection of sugarcane at the farm level is also provided through higher prices of *gur* (raw sugar), which is an inferior substitute for imported white sugar.[18] Lentils have been somewhat protected in recent years but only at the official exchange rate. During this period the country has become an importer of pulses after being self-sufficient for a long time. As regards potatoes, there is virtually no foreign trade; imports are limited to seed potatoes.[19] The domestic price of potatoes has remained mostly within the band of import and export parity prices both at the official

17. Mustard is also protected at the farm level through high protection provided to the edible oil industry.

18. The major share of the sugarcane produced in the country is used for traditional *gur* making.

19. At one time small quantities of potatoes were imported by the government, and a tiny quantity has recently been exported under government initiative.

and equilibrium exchange rates, implying that the effect of trade policy has been neutral.

Adjusting to Changing World Prices

Movements in the domestic-to-border price ratio, estimated at the equilibrium exchange rate, can be expected to depict the relative movements of prices in real terms in the domestic and world markets.[20] An analysis of these underlying price trends will help us understand how far domestic price movements have conformed with the changing comparative advantage as signaled by changes in world prices. Table 12.4 shows the trends in the border prices in real terms (that is, deflated by the world price index). While international agricultural commodity prices generally declined in the 1970s and 1980s, this decline was uneven across commodities. Deflated wholesale prices exhibit great similarity with harvest prices in domestic markets (Mahmud, Rahman, and Zohir 1994).

Note that the international price of rice fell dramatically in real terms in the mid-1970s and again during the first half of the 1980s. The domestic rice market (as well as the market for wheat) has been largely insulated from the international market because of trade controls and because domestic prices have remained mostly within the band of export and import parity prices.[21] Although the domestic foodgrain price fell dramatically after the food-crisis years of the early 1970s, this was due mainly to the large infusion of food aid. Thereafter, the steady increase in the domestic-to-border price ratio of rice through the mid-1980s was almost entirely due to the sharp fall in world prices, which brought the domestic price to the level of the world price. Since the mid-1980s, there has been a moderate decline in the domestic price of rice in real terms, while the world rice price has recovered to some extent (Table 12.4). This has again caused the domestic rice price to move downward within the band of the import and export parity prices. While there is some concern among policymakers about the resulting effect on the profitability of rice production, these movements in fact reflect a changing comparative advantage in Bangladeshi agriculture.[22] The country is approaching self-sufficiency in rice, while the domestic wheat price remains near its import parity level. Thus, the decline in the real rice price cannot be blamed on a cheap government food policy. The decline in real rice prices seems to be consistent with technological progress, particularly during the second half of the 1980s and the early 1990s.

20. The estimated equilibrium exchange rate can be taken to roughly depict the relative rates of domestic and international inflation.

21. Similarly, the exchange rate policy has had no effect on domestic foodgrain prices. Indirectly, however, the exchange rate and world prices do matter since they affect the size of food subsidy and the cost of food stocks.

22. Much will depend, however, on whether the momentum in the growth of rice production can be maintained.

TABLE 12.4 Trends in estimated border prices of selected commodities in constant 1985 dollars (U.S. dollars per metric ton)

Year	Rice	Wheat	Lentils	Potatoes	Rapeseed	Sugar	Jute
			c.i.f. Import Price[a]				f.o.b. Export Price[b]
1974/75	552	283	na	193	523	778	496
1975/76	402	226	639	166	442	476	479
1976/77	384	191	543	138	402	305	425
1977/78	377	188	564	125	387	251	435
1978/79	389	193	567	125	348	376	406
1979/80	394	206	658	150	333	434	352
1980/81	374	206	637	166	322	424	292
1981/82	332	201	539	169	328	280	273
1982/83	273	190	446	155	339	194	304
1983/84	256	179	483	143	337	160	456
1984/85	224	158	509	131	297	135	467
1985/86	194	133	493	110	228	131	416
1986/87	192	118	371	109	187	151	259
1987/88	210	126	361	114	172	180	247
1988/89	217	129	380	120	175	206	265
1989/90	213	121	444	118	158	195	267

SOURCE: Mahmud, Rahman, and Zohir (1994).

NOTES: na indicates not available. Estimated by deflating import (export) prices by world inflation index in U.S. dollar terms (1985 = 100). Based on a three-year moving average of respective prices.

[a] c.i.f. = cost, insurance, freight.

[b] f.o.b. = freight on board.

The high protection rates that have emerged in the case of oilseeds and sugar reflect the inability of domestic prices to adjust to changing world prices. As we shall see, this situation has important implications for the structure of comparative advantage vis-à-vis private profitability in crop agriculture. The world price of oilseeds (represented by rapeseed) has shown a secular trend of decline, which was most dramatic in the 1980s, when prices were nearly halved. The domestic price, on the other hand, fell sharply in the 1970s but only modestly in the 1980s. As a result, the nominal protection rate has been rapidly increasing since the early 1980s. The world price of sugar has been extremely volatile, with a sharp declining trend since the early 1970s and some recovery only in the late 1980s. During this time the country has moved from a regime of relatively modest protection and near self-sufficiency in sugar to one of high protection with large imports.

The decline in the world prices of both pulses (lentils) and potatoes in real terms has been more modest than that of other agricultural commodities. As discussed, the domestic prices of pulses have increased considerably over the years due to declining domestic production, and this is reflected in the increasing trends in the domestic-to-border price ratio. As Bangladesh moves from self-sufficiency to the importation of pulses, the world price has become relevant in deciding the country's comparative advantage in producing pulses. The domestic price of potatoes declined rapidly through the early 1980s due to high production growth, which caused the domestic price to move away from the import parity to the export parity level. But with a decline in production growth, the trends have been reversed. Note that due to high freight costs the estimated band between import parity and export parity prices is relatively wide for potatoes.

The world price of jute, Bangladesh's main export crop, has nearly halved since the early 1970s. There have been, however, large cyclical fluctuations in the world price that are reflected in the domestic harvest price. It is worth noting that, unlike the world price, the domestic price of jute in real terms has not shown a secular trend of decline to any significant extent. This is largely explained by the withdrawal of the export tax on jute in the late 1970s and the depreciation of the exchange rate in the 1980s. Thus, the reduced policy discriminations against jute have helped to maintain producer incentives over the long run even in the face of jute's deteriorating competitiveness in the world market.

Comparative Advantage in Crop Agriculture

Private profitability, the basis of farmers' decisionmaking, is based on a calculation of the prices that farmers actually receive or pay. These prices may diverge from the society's opportunity costs of inputs and outputs because of many distortions in the product and factor markets, such as those arising from trade restrictions, government taxes or subsidies, monopoly elements in marketing, surplus labor conditions, and segmentation in the capital market. Here we report the results of a profitability exercise designed to assess the pattern of comparative advantage vis-à-vis private profitability in crop production.[23]

To derive the economic price of agricultural output at the farmgate, the border prices must be appropriately adjusted by the economic costs of marketing and processing. These economic costs, in turn, are derived from the estimated financial costs by applying the economic prices of factor inputs in marketing and processing activities. The adjustment of border prices for marketing margins depends on assumptions about the location of producing areas and (in the case of import substitutes) the marketing stage at which domestic production competes with imports.[24] Here the wholesale market in Dhaka is taken as the appropriate marketing stage for this purpose.

The marketing and processing costs, in financial terms, are estimated from Rahman (1994). In the economic valuation of marketing costs, the pure profits are replaced by an imputed cost that in principle covers the social opportunity cost of working capital (as well as a premium for entrepreneurship and social risks).[25] Note that actual marketing profits are often quite high, presumably because of high private risks or market imperfections. Therefore, the estimated economic costs of marketing may be substantially lower than those in financial terms.[26]

The economic prices used for output valuation correspond to the marketing channels and producing locations covered by our marketing survey. On the other hand, the farmgate prices used in the financial profitability estimates for 1990/91 represent the normalized price for that year as well as the average for the country as a whole.[27] The two sets of estimates are thus not exactly comparable in terms of the location of the producing areas (although both correspond to normalized domestic and border prices, respectively, for 1990/91). There are large variations in harvest prices among regions and from one year to another. Therefore, estimated configurations of the harvest and wholesale prices (along with the associated marketing margins) in financial

23. On these issues see Timmer, Falcon, and Pearson (1983:139–147). Also see Little and Mirrlees (1974:145) for a definition of economic profitability.

24. For a discussion see Timmer, Falcon, and Pearson (1983:164–173).

25. To estimate the cost of working capital, an accounting rate of interest is applied to the economic valuation of the product in the pipeline along with the assumption about the average length of the turnover period.

26. Part of the discrepancy also arises from the economic pricing of labor and other inputs in the marketing and processing activities.

27. These estimates of harvest prices are based on the trend projections of official harvest price series as well as information gathered by our two surveys—one on agricultural costs and returns, the other on agricultural marketing (see Zohir 1993a; Rahman 1994).

terms for 1990/91 should be used only as a rough guide to how financial and economic prices compare in that time period.[28]

The estimates of crop yields and production input coefficients used in the profitability exercise are based on the findings from a survey on costs and returns of crop production that were reconciled with estimates from various other studies (Zohir 1993b). These estimates are taken as the average for the respective crop activities that may be distinguished by irrigation technology or seed variety.

Private profitability is estimated on the basis of the full cost of inputs; that is, both cash-purchased and family-owned inputs are valued at market prices. In particular, the prevailing market wage rates are used for valuing both family and hired labor.[29] For an economic profitability estimation, the inputs are, in principle, valued in terms of the output forgone in their alternative uses, which is converted into border price terms. The social opportunity costs of both family and hired labor are assumed to be the same, but labor used in slack-season activities is taken to have an opportunity cost significantly lower than market wages.[30] As regards chemical fertilizers, the export parity price at the farmgate is used for urea, while the import parity price is used for other types of fertilizers.[31] The economic costs of irrigation are estimated by imputing the rental value of machinery and adding to it the current operating costs, all converted into border price terms. The estimate of irrigation cost per hectare represents a weighted average of costs in respect to various modes of mechanized irrigation (such as pumps and tubewells). The estimate varies among different irrigated crops to reflect their varying water intensities.[32]

Estimates of Profitability

Tables 12.5 and 12.6 present estimates of economic and private returns per hectare for rice and nonrice crops. For some crops the economic profitability estimates correspond to alternative assumptions regarding their tradability status. Private profitability, however, is estimated using only a single set of normalized farmgate prices for 1990/91.

PROFITABILITY OF RICE CROPS. For rice, crop activities are distinguished by season, variety, planting method, and irrigation technique. Prof-

---

28. The wholesale prices reflect the Dhaka wholesale market and are also normalized to abstract from the effect of annual fluctuations.

29. Private profitability estimates based only on cash costs are reported in Zohir (1993b). These are appropriate only if the opportunity costs of family-owned inputs, including family labor, can be assumed to be near zero.

30. The estimates of labor inputs in work days are available by activity types from the survey data.

31. This reflects the actual trading status of chemical fertilizers in Bangladesh.

32. The standard estimate of irrigation cost per hectare is used for HYV boro; the estimates for other crops are obtained by applying the proportionate variations in financial costs of irrigation among crops as estimated from the survey.

TABLE 12.5 Private and economic profitability of rice crops (farm level), 1990/91

			Net Economic Returns		
Rice Crop[a]	Irrigation Technique[b]	Net Private Returns	Export Parity	Nontraded	Import Parity
			(taka per hectare)		
Boro					
HYV	Modern	8,335	5,442	11,132	16,485
Local T	All	4,643	3,763	6,554	9,170
Aman					
HYV	Modern	5,805	3,626	8,563	13,202
HYV	Rainfed	10,238	8,071	13,106	17,699
HYV	All	9,550	7,429	12,262	16,804
Pajam	All	6,401	4,924	8,997	12,824
Local T	Rainfed	3,786	3,019	5,856	8,515
Local B	Rainfed	2,772	2,274	4,470	6,525
Aus					
HYV	Rainfed	7,048	5,430	9,395	13,119
HYV	Modern	5,908	3,574	8,382	12,899
HYV	All	6,418	4,738	8,833	12,681
Local B	Rainfed/traditional	–165	–306	–1,605	3,383

SOURCE: Mahmud, Rahman, and Zohir (1994).

NOTE: Profitability is estimated as net of all costs except land rent and is therefore a measure of return to land (and management). Estimates are based on normalized domestic and world prices of rice for 1990/91.

[a]B, broadcast; T, transplant; Pajam, a locally improved variety.

[b]Modern irrigation includes mechanized irrigation by pumps and tubewells. "All" includes different irrigation techniques and represents the entire sample of the respective crop in the farm survey underlying this study.

itability estimates hinge on the implied incentives for shifting from local to modern varieties, the main source of growth in rice production. As discussed in Chapter 2, important likely shifts are from local transplant aman to HYV aman and from local broadcast aman and aus to HYV boro.[33] The economic profitability of such a shift (resulting gain in net economic returns per hectare) decreases with the economic price used for the valuation of rice output. The gains from the shift are large in the import and nontraded situations and in terms of private returns at the existing level of domestic rice price. These results also imply that the irrigation investments that induce the shift to HYVs are economically profitable. If we move to the export parity price, however, the

33. In addition, there may be a shift from the local variety to HYV within both aus and boro seasons, although further scope for changes within the boro season may be limited.

TABLE 12.6 Private land and economic profitability of nonrice crops (farm level), 1990/91

Crop	Irrigation Technique	Price Parity Basis	Net Economic Returns[a]		Net Private Returns
				(taka per hectare)	
Wheat	Modern	Import	747	(446)	184
	Nonirrigated	Import	2,701	(2,445)	2,046
	All	Import	1,757	(1,469)	1,149
Jute					
White	Rainfed	Export	5,809	(1,918)	–1,437
Tossa	All	Export	10,822	(5,693)	2,115
Cotton	Rainfed	Import	16,625	(13,135)	10,130
Tobacco (heat-cured)	Modern	Export	90,383	na	10,896
	All	Export	83,537	na	11,276
Sugarcane (for *gur*-making)	Modern	Import (sugar)	3,106	(8,812)	44,534
	Nonirrigated	Import (sugar)	–839	(3,525)	28,973
Oilseeds					
Mustard	Traditional/nonirrigated	Import (oilseeds)	–726	na	2,730
	Traditional/nonirrigated	Import (oil)	–2,907	na	2,730
Sesame	Traditional/nonirrigated	Import (oil)	–6,692	na	–2,197
Linseed	Traditional/nonirrigated	Import (oil)	–719	na	2,256
Pulses					
Masur (lentils)	Traditional/nonirrigated	Import	10,131	(6,971)	5,816
	Traditional/nonirrigated	Export	6,320	na	na
Gram	Traditional/nonirrigated	Import	7,698	(5,263)	4,376
Khesari	Traditional/nonirrigated	Import	7,979	(5,807)	5,286
Spices					
Chilies (dry)	Modern	Import	8,522	na	19,694
	Traditional/nonirrigated	Import	868	na	7,398
Onion	All	Import	36,697	na	41,538

MV (fresh)	Modern	Nontraded	29,247	na	16,043
	Traditional	Nontraded	32,342	na	19,289
	Traditional	Export	9,206	na	19,289
	All	Nontraded	26,402	na	16,698
MV (chilled)	All	Import	45,947	na	16,698
	All	Nontraded	34,960	na	16,698
Local (fresh)	All	Import	18,699	na	–2,412
	All	Nontraded	3,229	na	–2,412
Vegetables					
Brinjal	Traditional	Export	274,623	na	23,721
	Traditional	Nontraded	39,417	na	23,721
	Modern	Nontraded	48,246	na	47,398
Radishes	Modern/traditional	Export	241,102	na	11,620
	Modern/traditional	Nontraded	21,608	na	11,620
Cucumbers	Modern/traditional	Export	191,219	na	25,946
	Modern/traditional	Nontraded	37,858	na	25,946
Barbati (long-yard bean)	Traditional/nonirrigated	Export	167,244	na	29,731
	Traditional/nonirrigated	Nontraded	46,245	na	29,731
Arum	Traditional/nonirrigated	Nontraded	51,305	na	33,139
Tomatoes	Modern/traditional	Nontraded	88,775	na	63,462
Cabbage	Modern/traditional	Nontraded	50,657	na	33,770

SOURCE: Mahmud, Rahman, and Zohir (1994).

NOTE: na indicates not available. Private and economic profitability estimates based on normalized domestic and world prices for 1990/91.

[a]Figures in parentheses correspond to the projected world price for 1995 deflated to the 1990/91 base. For pulses, however, this figure corresponds to the alternative lower world price of lentils.

economic gains from the adoption of HYVs are greatly reduced (and almost eliminated in the case of irrigated HYV aman). Note also that the economic profitability of production of local aus for export is negative, indicating that the land should be shifted to nonagricultural use (if a shift to more remunerative crops is not possible).

Among the HYV rice crops boro HYV has the highest yield, but rainfed HYV aman is most profitable, evidently because there are no irrigation costs. Nevertheless, the expansion of HYV aman may increasingly depend on provision of supplementary irrigation during the wet season. There is scope for economizing on the cost of such irrigation by using the same installed irrigation facilities as are available for winter irrigation. This scope for economy is not, however, reflected in the present estimate of profitability for irrigated HYV aman since the irrigation costs for this crop are high.

There is a wide range of variations between the estimates of economic profitability of rice production for export and import substitution. In the nontraded situation the comparative advantage of rice in relation to other crops largely depends on evolving trends in the supply-demand balance and price determination in the domestic rice market. An analysis of this long-term trend and future prospects in rice, particularly the prospect of export of rice from Bangladesh, is presented in Chapter 13.

Profitability of Nonrice Crops

WHEAT. Wheat shows weak profitability, both private and economic. Although domestically grown wheat is now almost entirely modern variety, yields are low even under irrigatation. In fact, profitability seems to be lower under modern irrigation than when wheat is grown as a nonirrigated crop. Official crop statistics and other farm survey data show a decline in wheat yields. Although the reasons are not clear, agricultural scientists agree that there may be little scope for profitably expanding wheat production because of agro-climatic constraints (barring unanticipated breakthroughs in the development of heat-resistant and better-adapted varieties). With world prices expected to drop, there does not seem to be a significant advantage for Bangladesh's continued pace of expansion in wheat.[34]

JUTE. Jute, which is Bangladesh's main cash crop, appears to have higher economic profitability compared to local rice, its competitor. But at the lower projected price only the superior Tossa variety can clearly maintain this competitive edge. Because of relatively low farmgate prices, the private profitability of jute is much lower and can even be negative. Remember, however, that Bangladesh, as the world's largest exporter of jute, faces a down-sloping foreign demand curve for the export of jute and jute products, especially raw

---

34. See also World Bank (1991, 1:24). Morris, Chowdhury, and Meisner (1997) demonstrate the comparative advantage of wheat in certain areas of Bangladesh but show that there are limitations to the expansion of areas beyond those specific locations.

jute. As such, the marginal revenue earned from the export of raw jute will fall short of the f.o.b. export price, which is used here as the basis for estimating economic profitability. Therefore, the profitability estimates for jute indicate only average profitability at the present level of raw jute export (or at a different level of export resulting from an autonomous shift in demand in the world jute market).[35]

SUGARCANE. Of the sugarcane produced, 25 to 30 percent is processed into white sugar by state-owned refineries; the rest is mostly used for traditional *gur* making. About half of the country's need for white sugar is currently met from imports, while there is no foreign trade in either *gur* or sugarcane. Because of excessive milling costs incurred by the inefficient refineries, the economic (import parity) price of sugarcane at the farmgate is likely to be low or even negative.[36] There is evidently no comparative advantage in producing sugarcane for sugar milling, given the existing level of efficiency and the current world price of sugar. Instead, the economic profitability estimates presented here correspond to the use of sugarcane for producing *gur* as a substitute for imported sugar. But even for *gur* making, sugarcane production generates negative economic returns under its predominantly nonirrigated mode of cultivation; and the returns are low even with higher yields under modern irrigation. Although the world price of sugar is expected to increase, the economic returns still appear to be low for a year-round crop such as sugarcane. On the other hand, sugarcane shows strong private profitability made possible by the high protection provided to the domestic sugar industry.

OILSEEDS. Mustard seed, which makes up the largest share of oilseed production in Bangladesh, shows negative economic returns; but private profitability is positive (although modest) because of heavy protection provided to both oilseeds and edible oils. Bangladesh imports both rapeseed and rapeseed oil (which are close substitutes of mustard seed and oil), so local oil mills can use either imported or domestically produced oilseeds. The economic returns are lower (that is, the economic loss is larger) when we consider the import substitution of edible oil rather than that of oilseeds, which presumably stems from the inefficiency of the local oil-milling industry.[37] The economic returns from the production of other oilseeds are also negative.

---

35. While world demand for jute export from Bangladesh is inelastic in the short run, the long-term elasticity is likely to be high because of the competition between jute products and its synthetic substitutes and because of higher longer-run supply elasticities of other jute-exporting countries. Increasing concern for the environment may imply a reversing trend in the competitive strength of jute vis-à-vis synthetic products, but that realization has yet to emerge in the jute market.

36. This is apparent from the large processing margins for sugar, although we have not attempted to convert these into economic costs. Even these large margins, obtained indirectly by price comparisons, underestimate the actual financial costs of processing since they do not reflect the large financial losses incurred by the state-owned mills.

37. An implication is that the country would be better off by directly importing edible oil rather than processing imported oilseeds. We have considered here the costs of oil processing by

PULSES. Unlike oilseeds, pulses are strongly competitive as a nonirrigated dry-season crop in terms of both private and economic profitability. Although domestic prices are still generally lower than the import parity price, the country is on the verge of switching from self-sufficiency to an import regime, with substantial imports taking place in deficit years and slack seasons. The economic profitability of pulses is also estimated, corresponding to a lower border price for lentils, which may be more relevant with less trade restrictions (such as those regarding the source of supply). These lower profitability estimates, shown in parentheses in Table 12.6, are also reasonably high for a nonirrigated crop.

SPICES. Among spices, chilies have a low economic profitability measure except when grown under modern irrigation, which is uncommon. But because of high domestic prices, it remains strongly competitive with other dry-season crops. On the other hand, onions not only show high private returns but also a strong comparative advantage for import substitution. Note that the border prices used for chilies and onions refer to imports from India through land routes. Because India is one of the leading exporters of dried onions among developing countries, researchers may find it worth exploring if such prospects also exist for Bangladesh.[38]

POTATOES. Potatoes are appropriately treated as a nontraded product for economic valuation, although we have also estimated potential profitability under alternative import and export regimes. Of the total area under potatoes, about two-thirds is now under modern varieties, with yields that can be twice as much as those of local varieties. The production of modern-variety potatoes for domestic consumption appears to be highly profitable in terms of both private and economic returns, and there seems to be some export potential as well. The high profitability of chilled potatoes at the import parity price indicates that imports are desirable even during lean seasons, taking into account the economic costs of storage and chilling. In the nontraded situation, on the other hand, the economic profitability of chilled potatoes is even higher than that of fresh potatoes, showing that consumers' preference for lean-season potatoes, as depicted by the seasonal price spread, outweighs the economic costs of storage and chilling.[39] In other words, it would be desirable to encourage the storage and chilling of potatoes, which would also expand the size of the domestic market. Local potatoes, in contrast, have poor standing except in the unlikely situation of competing with imports—in this case, also, fresh in the post-harvest season.

VEGETABLES. Vegetables may show the most promising profitability estimates. At the current level of domestic prices vegetables appear to be

---

large-scale rotary mills rather than by traditional methods. The former is the dominant method used for supplying edible oil to urban centers.

38. Islam (1990: tab. 46).

39. The high seasonal price spread for potato was discussed previously in this chapter.

highly competitive in terms of both private and economic returns. In fact, the economic profitability of vegetable production for export seems to be fabulously high by the standard of most other crops. These exports, however, currently account for less than 1 percent of domestic production of vegetables. The marketing spreads between farmgate and f.o.b. prices are excessively large, partly due to inefficiencies in export marketing but mainly reflecting the extra profits earned by exporters in a segmented export market.

COTTON. The profitability estimate for cotton, which is grown in the aman season, suggests that it has a comparative advantage for import substitution. Even with a projected decline in the world price, its economic profitability would remain as high as that of rainfed HYV aman. The low domestic procurement price offered by the government-owned spinning mills in a monopsonistic market depresses the profitability of cotton production, which is still higher than any aman rice crop. Nevertheless, cotton is a minor crop; domestic production meets only about 10 percent of the country's total demand.

TOBACCO. In terms of private returns tobacco is only modestly profitable as a dry-season irrigated crop, but it shows high profitability when exported. The discrepancy between private and economic returns is due to high profits earned by exporters with limited access to foreign markets.[40] Most of the tobacco produced goes to the domestic market; but since tobacco consumption is socially discouraged, this raises the problem of economically valuing such consumption. Currently, government policy is to provide no support to tobacco production at the grower's level and to discourage the consumption of tobacco products through high taxes.

DID CROP PROFITABILITY CHANGE OVER TIME? The analysis of the economic profitability of the crops presented so far is based on 1990/91 production conditions and prices. Would it still hold true given current conditions? To explore this question, the 1990/91 results were updated using average prices for 1995/96, 1996/97, and 1997/98 and keeping the coefficient of production constant, implying no technological change. The results indicate that the relative economic profitability among crops has not changed between 1990/91 and 1997/98. Nevertheless, there are a few significant differences in absolute economic profitability.

First, in the case of rice, profitability falls significantly when the Indian (inland trade) price is used as the world price instead of the Thai (Bangkok) price, which was used in the 1990/91 study. With the rice trade with India emerging in recent years, the attractiveness of import substitution policy diminishes dramatically but nonetheless persists. The difference between import parity and export parity prices is also significantly reduced. Second, the economic profitability of potatoes (fresh) seems much larger in real terms in 1997/98 than in 1990/91 mainly because world prices are higher now.

40. Tobacco leaf is exported mainly to Holland, Sri Lanka, the United Kingdom, and the United States; and exports account for less than 10 percent of domestic production.

Shahabuddin (1999) estimated the economic profitability and domestic resource cost of various crops in Bangladesh using 1990/91 input-output relations but 1995/96 and 1996/97 prices. His results roughly mirror these findings. Vegetables, potatoes, cotton, pulses, jute, and HYV rice remain highly profitable, while sugarcane (sugar) and oilseeds remain products whose profitability is negative. The ranking of crops in terms of profitability remains almost the same in both studies.

EXPECTED PROFITABILITY WITH TECHNOLOGICAL INNOVATIONS. These profitability estimates are intended to reflect actual rather than potential farm practice. The relative profitability of crops can, however, change with technological improvements. Basing our calculations on fertilizer recommendation data and expected yields for particular improved crop varieties as reported by the Bangladesh Agricultural Research Council (BARC 1989), we constructed synthetic crop activities. The labor input requirements were estimated by applying an elasticity of 0.3 with respect to the envisaged increase in yield rates. These estimates indicate that there is only a small increase in the profitability of HYV boro compared to previous estimates. But for most other crops there are substantial improvements in both economic and private profitability, reflecting the higher productivity of the crop varieties as well as the effects of better farm practice (as implicit in the BARC recommendations).

Wheat and sugarcane, however, do not appear promising even in light of improved profitability. Under certain cropping patterns, wheat may still barely compete with HYV boro if we take into account the higher irrigation coverage made possible by growing wheat instead of rice. Remarkably, the economic profitability of mustard seed remains negative even though a substantial increase in yield (by about 40 percent) is envisaged.[41] This relates to the low world price of oilseeds and the nature of the improved production technology that is currently available.

On the other hand, the expected private and economic returns from the improved variety of lentils are as high as those of HYV boro, clearly making it a preferable crop because of its lower irrigation intensity. Both cotton and jute (even of the inferior white variety) show the potential to become more competitive in the aus and aman seasons, respectively. Modern-variety potatoes, which have a competitive edge even with existing farm practice, could attain much higher profitability and a comparative advantage for export. Nevertheless, the most spectacular gains in profitability would come from the adoption of certain high-yielding varieties of potato and vegetables such as brinjal, radishes, cucumbers, long beans, tomatoes, and cabbage.

Policy Perspectives

The profitability analysis gives rise to a number of conclusions regarding incentives for crop diversification that appear robust despite underlying con-

41. Cf. Mahmud, Rahman, and Zohir (1994: tabs A5.2 and A5.3).

ceptual and data problems. A striking feature is that several crops, including potatoes, vegetables, onions, and cotton, show economic and private returns that are as high or higher than those of HYV rice. While this result suggests considerable potential for crop diversification, it also demonstrates the need to investigate why these crops have performed so poorly (compared to HYV rice) in terms of land allocation and output growth. The answer may lie in a combination of economic and physical factors, some of which we have already alluded to.

There are high price risks associated with the marketing of crops such as potatoes, vegetables, and spices. On the other hand, the existing on-farm water management systems do not allow rice and nonrice crops to be planted in the same service units. As discussed, this discourages the use of modern irrigation for growing high-value but risky nonrice crops and may explain why land under modern irrigation is almost exclusively devoted to rice cultivation while high-value nonrice crops are widely grown under traditional irrigation (which, being divisible, allows such crops to be grown on small parcels of land). The situation poses a serious problem for crop diversification since the prospect for increasing the area under traditional irrigation is limited.[42] The problem needs to be solved by (1) reducing price risks through improved marketing, (2) making nonrice crops more profitable through technological improvements to compensate for high price risks, and (3) introducing water management systems that would allow rice and nonrice crops to be grown within the same service units.[43]

The prospects for agricultural growth through crop diversification depend on how far noncereal crops can compete with HYV boro rice under dry-season irrigated conditions. The estimates of potential profitability with technological improvements suggest that there is more unexploited technological potential in dry-season nonrice crops compared to boro rice, even with the existing available technologies. Nevertheless, the technical and socioeconomic constraints related to technology adoption for nonrice crops are still poorly understood. Because the cultivation of high-value crops through improved technologies is resource-intensive, improved marketing facilities for reducing price risks and providing credit are likely to be important determining factors in the diffusion of these technologies.

The profitability estimates pinpoint the critical role of marketing, storage, and processing functions in determining both economic and private returns of crop production. While there is evidence of a relatively efficient rice marketing system that has evolved over time, most noncereal crops are relatively disadvantaged in this respect. Marketing costs are high because of inadequate infrastructural facilities, high price risks, and private traders' lack of access to institutional credit. These high costs of marketing, in turn, have a depressing

42. Bangladesh Master Plan Organization (1987).

43. This may require special preparation of plots, as is practiced in some Southeast Asian countries.

effect on both the size of the market (by raising the consumer price) and on producer incentives (by lowering the farmgate price). The relatively high marketing costs in financial terms compared to those in economic terms can also be an important source of the divergence between private and economic profitability of crops.

It is important to examine how far the structure of incentives created by trade policies conforms with the country's comparative advantage. As regards rice, trade policy has become increasingly neutral as the country approaches self-sufficiency. Wheat appears to be slightly protected, although there can be little justification for such protection on the basis of comparative advantage.[44] The major anomaly in the incentive structure relates to sugarcane and oilseeds (and chilies), which show no comparative advantage but enjoy high rates of protection. Estimates of expected profitability with technological innovations suggest that for these crops there is no ground for applying the infant industry argument, if such an argument is at all relevant for crop production. The low economic profitability of sugarcane and oilseeds as well as high rates of protection for these crops have arisen from the sharp decline in the international prices of sugar and oilseeds. As discussed, this decline has not been adequately reflected in domestic price movements, particularly in the case of sugarcane, thus distorting the incentive structure.[45]

On the other hand, the trend decline in the world price of pulses has been much smaller than that of other agricultural commodities. This, along with the fact that the country has become an importer of pulses, explains why the crop now appears to have a relatively high economic value. At prevailing domestic prices, however, hardly any protection is provided for pulses. The price of potatoes has also increased modestly in the world market, so there is some potential for potato export to become economically profitable. As regards vegetables, although domestic prices are too far below export prices, this cannot be blamed on trade policies. Rather, it reflects limited access to the world market and a lack of infrastructural facilities for export. Nevertheless, estimates of the high economic profitability of vegetable export point to the need for government support to promote such exports. There is some negative protection in the case of jute and cotton, although these crops are found to be economically competitive. In both cases, prices are kept low to the advantage of public sector industries (although for raw jute there is also a case for export taxation because of the inelastic world demand). Onions may be the only example among the crops under study of a positive (and moder-

44. With grain imports being recently liberalized, there is an ongoing policy debate about whether duty-free wheat import by private traders should be allowed.

45. Admittedly, the world price of sugar is volatile, and subsidized oilseed export by western Europe has been the subject of intense controversy in recent debates on international trade reforms. These do not, however, seem to be sufficient grounds for revising our assessment of comparative advantage.

ately high) rate of protection being associated with high economic profitability.

Another way of looking at the profitability estimates for nonrice crops is that the country does not seem to have a comparative advantage in those items that currently compete with major imports: wheat, sugar, oilseeds, and edible oils.[46] On the other hand, crops that show high economic profitability, such as potatoes and vegetables, are currently produced either entirely for the domestic market or have only limited access to the world market. While import substitution, by its very nature, does not encounter a market problem, the profitability of nontraded crops would depend on the growth of domestic demand in relation to output growth. (Another related aspect is that, while import liberalization of sugar and edible oils would create pressures on the balance of payments, shifting to nontraded crops would not have a compensating favorable impact.) The domestic markets for noncereal crops, especially high-value ones, are limited in size because of generally low living standards in the economy. This underscores the need for exploring the possibility of exporting crops for which there is a potential comparative advantage.[47] Note, however, that in the past the production of vegetables, potatoes, spices, and fruits did not grow rapidly enough to satisfy even the growth in domestic demand, much less to create an exportable surplus. Therefore, efforts at export promotion must be part of an integrated strategy of technological improvement and the development of marketing and processing facilities that could elicit better supply responses.

References

Bangladesh, Master Plan Organization. 1987. Agricultural production systems. Technical Report. Dhaka: Bangladesh Ministry of Irrigation, Water, and Flood Control. Mimeo.

Bangladesh Agricultural Research Council (BARC). 1989. *Fertilizer recommendation guide*. Dhaka: Bangladesh Agricultural Research Council.

Chowdhury, N. 1992. *Rice markets in Bangladesh: A study in structure, conduct, and performance*. Washington, D.C.: International Food Policy Research Institute.

Hossain, M., M. A. Quasem, M. M. Akash, and M. A. Jabbar. 1990. Differential impact of modern rice technology: The Bangladesh case. Dhaka: Bangladesh Institute of Development Studies. Mimeo.

Islam, N. 1990. *Horticultural exports of developing countries: Past performances, future prospects, and policy issues*. Research Report 80. Washington, D.C.: International Food Policy Research Institute.

Islam, T. M. T. 1989. A review of farm production technology in Bangladesh. In *Bangladesh agriculture sector review: Sub-sectors of agriculture* (vol. 2). Dhaka: Bangladesh Ministry of Agriculture.

---

46. Cotton and onion are exceptions; but cotton is a minor crop, and onion is not an important import item.

47. A list of such crops may include many horticultural products and spices that have not been included in the present exercise.

Little, I. M. D., and J. A. Mirrlees. 1974. *Project appraisal and planning for developing countries.* London: Heinemann.

Mahmud, W., S. H. Rahman, and S. Zohir. 1994. *Agricultural growth through crop diversification in Bangladesh.* Working Paper 7. Washington, D.C.: International Food Policy Research Institute.

Maziruddin, K. 1989. Markets and marketing policies in accelerating growth. In *Bangladesh agriculture sector review: Markets and prices* (vol. 4). Dhaka: Bangladesh Ministry of Agriculture.

Morris, M., N. Chowdhury, and C. Meisner. 1997. *Wheat production in Bangladesh: Technological, economic, and policy issues.* Research Report 106. Washington, D.C.: International Food Policy Research Institute.

Rahman, S. H. 1993. *Analysis of agricultural commodity markets and prices in Bangladesh.* Bangladesh Institute for Development Studies/IFPRI Agricultural Diversification Project Working Paper 6. Dhaka: Bangladesh Institute for Development Studies.

———. 1994. *The impact of trade and exchange rate policies on economic incentives in Bangladesh agriculture.* Working Paper on Food Policy in Bangladesh 8. Washington, D.C.: International Food Policy Research Institute.

Rashid, H. E. 1989. Land use in Bangladesh: Selected topics. In *Bangladesh agriculture sector review: Land, water, and irrigation* (vol. 3). Dhaka: Bangladesh Ministry of Agriculture.

Scandizzo, P. L., and C. Bruce. 1980. Methodologies for measuring agricultural price intervention effects. World Bank Staff Working Paper 39. Washington, D.C.: World Bank.

Shahabuddin, Q. 1999. Report on comparative advantage in Bangladesh agriculture. Study conducted for the Food and Agriculture Organization. Dhaka: Bangladesh Institute of Development Studies. Mimeo.

Timmer, C. P. 1986. *Getting prices right.* Ithaca, N.Y., U.S.A.: Cornell University Press.

Timmer, C. P., W. P. Falcon, and S. R. Pearson. 1983. *Food policy analysis.* Baltimore: Johns Hopkins University Press.

Valdes, A., and A. Siamwalla. 1988. Foreign trade regime exchange rate policy and structure of incentives. In *Agriculture price policy for developing countries,* ed. J. W. Mellor and R. Ahmed. Baltimore: Johns Hopkins University Press for the International Food Policy Research Institute.

World Bank. 1991. *Bangladesh food policy review—Adjusting to the Green Revolution* (vols. 1 and 2). Report 9641-BD. Washington, D.C.: World Bank. Mimeo.

Zohir, S. 1993a. Zoning of Bangladesh: An exercise based on land allocation under various crops. Background Paper for the IFPRI-BIDS Agricultural Diversification Study. Dhaka: Bangladesh Institute of Development Studies.

———. 1993b. Problems and prospects of crop diversification in Bangladesh. *Bangladesh Development Studies* 21 (September): 73–90.

13 Prospects for Rice Exports in Bangladesh

FRANCESCO GOLETTI, A. S. M. JAHANGIR, AND SAJJAD ZOHIR

What is Bangladesh's potential for self-sufficiency in rice production? There have been both optimistic and pessimistic answers to that question. Observers expressed optimism in the early 1990s, when rice surpluses were publicized (World Bank 1992). Trends in production and prices supported that attitude: even with excessive flooding in 1988, farmers were able to cope, and aggregate rice production did not decline as anticipated. In subsequent years the country had good harvests, and increased adoption of modern rice varieties and expansion of boro plantings raised total rice productivity (see Chapter 2). With an enormous stock buildup in the public storage system, the government soon found it unfeasible to continue its procurement program. Even with declining imports, the real price of rice continued to drop, reaching a new low when, compared with the previous year, aman paddy prices declined by 25.4 percent in December 1992/January 1993 and boro prices declined by 33.6 percent in May/June 1993.

As rice prices fell, debates spread concerning export (*Daily Telegraph,* October 26, November 27, 1993; *Daily Ittefaq,* July 21, 31, September 4, 1993). The government began exploring the potential for rice export, signing an agreement with Sri Lanka for the export of 50,000 metric tons of rice (*Daily Observer,* October 27, 1993). But this euphoria subsided rapidly in the 1994/95 and 1995/96 seasons, when several natural factors depressed production and the country began to import rice—partly to fill the shortfall in production, partly as an election-year precautionary measure. The bumper harvest of 1996/97 again depressed the real price of rice significantly, and the parliament began to debate the export issue. But the flood of 1998 required large imports of rice (see Chapter 2). In short, optimism and pessimism about the prospect of self-sufficiency are as volatile as the weather-related fluctuations in rice production. And while the export of rice is an economic proposition, it is also an emotional issue for those who believe that it mocks poverty alleviation efforts.

Because current policies are based on presumptions about the future of the economy and carry implications for growth of the real economy as well, it is necessary to view the future realistically and to examine the level of projected surplus. The existence of a surplus, however, does not guarantee that it will be exported. The first step is to learn if there is a comparative advantage for Bangladesh in exporting rice to international markets, an advantage that could have positive effects on food security. Next, it is important to discover the conditions under which such a surplus could be generated, how it might provide a comparative advantage, and how the government could facilitate the actual exporting process. Remember, however, that the existence of a surplus and favorable price incentives are no guarantee that the private sector will seize the opportunity for international trade. Quality standards in production and appropriate marketing logistics are the final ingredients in the development of a successful export.

Background

Since the 1970s, three major changes have affected Bangladesh's foodgrain sector. First, rice production—the country's primary staple—has been sustained and stabilized through the adoption of high-yielding varieties and modern technology (Chapter 2). Second, while production grew at a rate of 2.7 percent in the 1980s, population growth was about 2 percent. As population growth has decreased moderately (from 2.32 in the 1970s to 2.03 in the 1980s), urbanization has increased rapidly. Along with sustained production growth, lower population growth and an accelerated process of urbanization have generated an excess supply of rice in good crop years. In the absence of any exports, this excess supply has depressed prices. Third, the policy environment has been characterized by an increasingly favorable attitude toward the development of a private market. Restrictions on domestic and international trade in foodgrains, irrigation equipment, and fertilizers have been lifted; public intervention in the foodgrain system has been reduced; and privately marketed surplus has grown from 15 percent of total production in 1972/73 to 50 percent in 1990/91 (see Chapter 4).

In view of these developments, the government has had to redefine its role in the foodgrain sector. An excess supply of rice could result in either the fall of domestic prices or an opening to international export markets. Although rice is the preferred staple food in developing Asian countries (where the majority of the world's population lives), the proportion of rice production traded internationally is small and has remained virtually unchanged since the mid-1970s. Thus, any export strategy should be weighed carefully in light of this thin international market and any domestic effects on production, consumption, and prices.

The Prospect of a Rice Surplus

The foodgrain projections presented here are based on an interactive model of demand and supply that captures various dimensions of the foodgrain system

(Goletti 1994). First, foodgrains are disaggregated into rice and wheat. Second, rural and urban disaggregations are brought into the picture. Third, demand is disaggregated by income quartiles. Fourth, the model incorporates differential assumptions for rural and urban income growth. Finally, the supply side takes into account the response of hectarage to prices and yield (see Mahmud, Rahman, and Zohir 1993).

Various scenarios are considered for the exogenous variables, such as yield, income, population growth, and distribution of growth between rural and urban areas. The results reported refer to three scenarios for the exogenous yield growth (see Goletti 1994):

1. In the high-growth scenario rice yield is assumed to grow at 2.4 percent per year.
2. In the low-growth scenario rice yield is assumed to grow at 2.0 percent per year.
3. In the middle case lies the expected value of all assumptions regarding the whole complex of exogenous variables.

In the medium case the rice surplus will be 224,000 tons by the end of the 1990s and will progressively grow until it reaches 1.3 million tons by the end of the second decade of the twenty-first century (Table 13.1). These figures are projected with prices constant (Figure 13.1). The following main conclusions have been derived from them:

1. Only under the high-growth scenario will Bangladesh, in about two decades, reach self-sufficiency in both rice and wheat. Under the medium-growth scenario rice growth will not be able to compensate for the wheat deficit.
2. Cereal self-sufficiency will probably be outside of production possibility for a long time. Nevertheless, the rice surplus could be swapped in international markets for wheat so that food security could still be achieved.

TABLE 13.1 Expected values of foodgrain surplus or deficit

	Rice			
Year	High Growth	Medium Growth	Low Growth	Wheat
		(thousand metric tons)		
1999/2000	655	224	–205	–1,535
2009/10	1,853	633	–568	–1,683
2019/20	3,226	1,301	–1,161	–1,846

SOURCE: Authors' calculations.

NOTE: A positive number indicates a surplus, a negative number a deficit.

FIGURE 13.1 Rice surplus scenarios

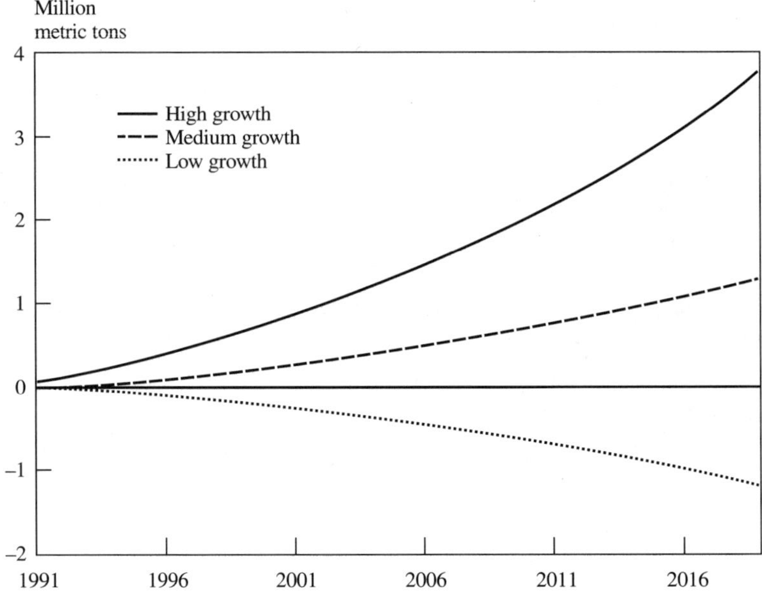

SOURCE: Authors' calculations.

FIGURE 13.2 Rice price scenarios

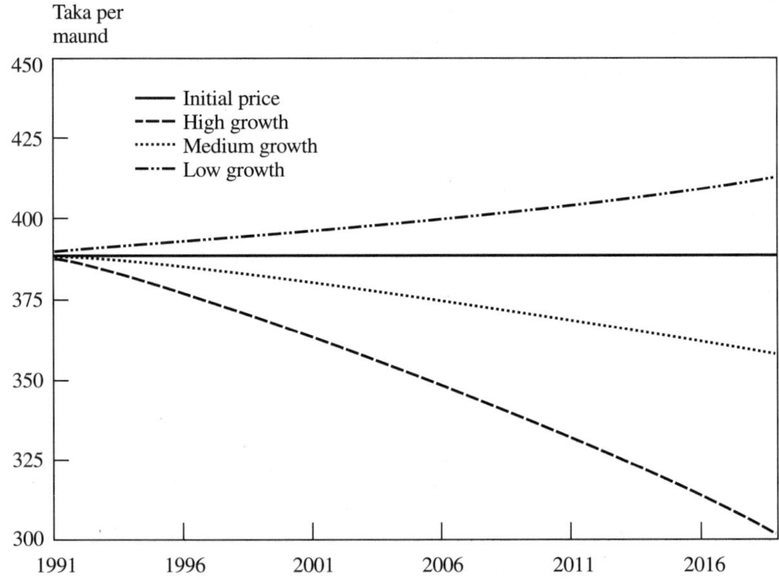

SOURCE: Authors' calculations.

NOTE: 1 maund = 37.32 kilograms.

TABLE 13.2 Expected values of foodgrain prices

Year	Rice			Wheat
	High Growth	Medium Growth	Low Growth	
		(taka per maund)		
1999/2000	369	382	395	261
2009/10	340	372	403	259
2019/20	303	358	412	249

SOURCE: Authors' calculations.

NOTE: 1 maund = 37.32 kilograms.

3. Given the limited amount of surplus or deficit as a percentage of total production, the expected effects are modest once prices are allowed to adjust (see Figure 13.2).

This last point is supported by Table 13.2, which reports the behavior of prices when demand and supply are in equilibrium and no international trade is occurring. When prices are allowed to respond, the excess demand is zero, and the real prices of rice and wheat will decrease by 8 and 16 percent, respectively, over three decades. The reason for the larger decrease in wheat prices is the negative income elasticities of demand for this commodity.

More interesting is the effect on per capita consumption of various groups. Total foodgrain consumption increases for all income groups except for the urban rich. But as a consequence of income growth that is likely to be biased toward urban dwellers, the urban poor benefit from growth more than the rural poor do (see Figure 13.3).

In summary, price changes in real terms will be modest in the case of rice and slightly more appreciable in the case of wheat. In any scenario, most groups will gain from growth of production, particularly those in the lower urban quartiles.

World Rice Exports and Domestic Prices

Between 1975 and 1990 world rice exports averaged only 4.1 percent of total production. During the same period world production grew at a rate of 2.67 percent compared to a 2.57 percent growth achieved in exports. Table 13.3 shows that together the five major exporting countries achieved an annual export growth of 4.75 percent in 1975–90. There was, however, a wide variation of growth among countries, from –7.08 percent for Myanmar to 39.46 percent for Vietnam. Thailand is the only other country whose export growth of 8.6 percent exceeded the average growth. Growth rate for the United States and

FIGURE 13.3 Consumption per capita of foodgrains

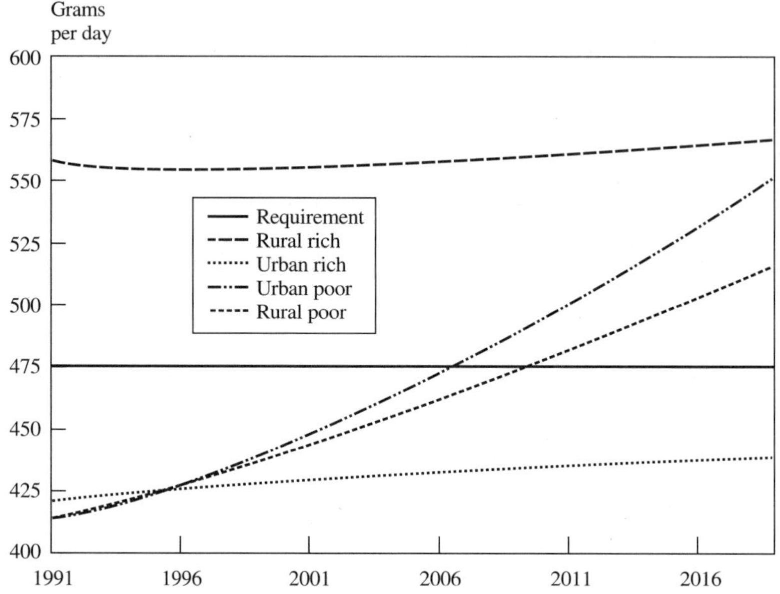

SOURCE: Authors' calculations.

Pakistan was below average—at 0.61 percent and 2.54 percent, respectively. Nevertheless, comparison shows that the export growth of the major exporting countries exceeded by far the overall growth of 2.57 percent in world export during the corresponding period.

The market share of the top five exporters increased from 57.3 percent in 1975–79 to 71.1 percent in 1985–90. Moreover, the proportion of export to milled production for these countries grew at the rate of 2.12 percent in 1975–90 compared to a negative growth of 0.1 percent for the world as a whole. This demonstrates that the major exporters are generally well equipped to tackle a sluggish world market, and they do better compared to other competitors when the world market experiences a boom.

The growth rate of rice production in Bangladesh was surpassed only by Vietnam and Myanmar among the major five exporters; the same held true for yield growth (see Table 13.4). In 1985–90, however, Bangladesh's growth of both rice production and yield was higher than the average for all the major exporters except Vietnam.

Rice Varieties

The rice prices of the various varieties traded in the domestic markets are key to export considerations. Analysis of these prices and of comparable interna-

TABLE 13.3 Rice export levels, market shares, and ratios to milled production of major exporters

Year	Myanmar	Pakistan	Thailand	United States	Vietnam	Total
			(percent)			
Annual growth rate of exports						
1975–90	−7.08	2.54	8.6	0.61	39.46	4.75
1975–79	8.29	14.85	19.56	2.24	23.15	10.42
1980–84	4.39	−0.14	11.4	−9.83	194.71	2.41
1985–90	−30.38	−0.57	2.86	5.04	65.45	5.36
Average market share						
1975–90	4.4	8.4	29.2	21.0	1.8	64.7
1975–79	5.1	8.2	20.5	23.2	0.3	57.3
1980–84	5.8	8.7	28.5	21.2	0.3	64.4
1985–90	2.6	8.2	37.1	18.9	4.2	71.1
Annual growth rate of market share						
1975–90	−9.7	−0.05	6.04	−1.96	63.67	2.18
1975–79	−0.76	5.83	10.67	−6.63	−87.4	1.51
1980–84	5.93	1.24	12.8	−8.52	142.86	3.85
1985–90	−32.61	−2.38	1.12	3.23	63.94	3.59
Average rice exports as a share of milled production						
1975–90	6.15	30.86	28.94	59.39	1.96	20.54
1975–79	7.76	27.04	20.16	61.16	0.46	18.32
1980–84	7.68	32.80	28.96	62.12	0.36	20.90
1985–90	3.53	32.43	36.23	55.63	4.55	22.10
Annual growth rate of rice exports as a share of milled production						
1975–90	−10.12	1.68	6.45	−0.87	45.63	2.12
1975–79	4.50	8.91	17.56	0.31	−79.29	8.17
1980–84	2.90	−1.06	7.73	−2.75	145.09	−0.22
1985–90	−29.87	−0.87	2.77	1.20	60.49	3.98

SOURCES: FAO Agrostat data base; USDA ERS (1991).

NOTE: Growth rates have been computed using a semi-logarithmic linear trend equation fitted to the time-series data based on the least square method.

tional grades will help determine competitiveness in the international market. Here, Thai prices for the ordinary varieties are compared with similar varieties of Bangladeshi rice because Thailand is the single largest exporter of such rice and is geographically close. Similarly, prices of Pakistani basmati rice are compared with Bangladeshi aromatic varieties.

Thai export standards classify rice into different grades based on physical properties such as length of grain, degree of milling, percentage of broken and damaged grain, colored grain, moisture level, and impurities. Such standards and specifications are practically nonexistent in Bangladesh, where rice is classified into three broad categories based on growing seasons: aus, aman, and

TABLE 13.4 Paddy rice production and yields of Bangladesh and major exporting countries

Year	Bangladesh	Myanmar	Pakistan	Thailand	United States	Vietnam
Annual growth rate of paddy rice production (percent)						
1975–90	2.5	2.91	0.85	2.16	1.47	4.15
1975–79	1.02	3.75	5.9	2.07	1.95	–0.38
1980–84	1.66	1.46	0.93	3.68	–7.09	7.45
1985–90	3.71	–0.65	0.34	0.06	3.83	3.91
Average paddy rice yields (metric ton per hectare)						
1975–90	2.12	2.69	2.41	1.95	5.58	2.50
1975–79	1.88	2.03	2.35	1.81	5.09	2.03
1980–84	2.07	3.01	2.53	1.97	5.27	2.43
1985–90	2.37	2.98	2.37	2.04	6.24	2.94
Annual growth rate of paddy rice yields (percent)						
1975–90	2.30	3.3	–0.06	1.07	1.83	3.41
1975–79	1.13	6.03	0.96	0.47	–0.22	–2.78
1980–84	2.54	2.63	0.14	2.23	1.84	7.24
1985–90	2.91	–1.21	–1.84	–0.68	0.38	3.07

SOURCES: FAO Agrostat data base. 1990 data from USDA ERS (1991).

NOTE: Trend growth has been computed using a semi-logarithmic linear trend equation fitted to the time-series data based on the least square method.

boro. All species of aus and boro rice, except for the species called *pajam,* are generally regarded as coarse because of their short and bulky shape. *Pajam* is a medium-variety rice. Diverse qualities of rice are produced mainly in the aman season. Rice produced in this season can be classified as special aromatic, fine, medium, or coarse.

Two sets of prices for Thai rice, export parity and import parity, have been compared with wholesale rice prices in Bangladesh.[1] Thai free on board (FOB) prices for the grades involved have been multiplied by a factor of 0.85 to arrive at the export parity prices, which are estimates of wholesale prices for those Thai grades plus any export levy charged by the Thai government. An assumed zero export levy for Bangladesh posits the prices on a par with one other. For the aromatic varieties, only export parity prices for Pakistani basmati rice have been used for the comparison.

1. The relevant price for gauging self-sufficiency is the export parity price, but determining this price for a country that is not yet a consistent exporter involves problems of matching comparable quality and grade. This is particularly true for the world rice market, which is thin and fragmented. Perhaps rice price in India might be an appropriate export parity price for Bangladesh. The fixed price assumption in the simulation exercise does not provide a precise estimate of exportable surplus; rather, it demonstrates a rough order of magnitude of surplus or deficit under alternate scenarios of productivity and demand and their implication for price itself. The fixed price assumption seems reasonable for this purpose.

For computing import parity prices, a shipping cost of $20 per ton has been added across the board to obtain estimates of cost and freight (C&F) prices for the same Thai varieties.[2] Then the C&F prices have been multiplied by a factor of 1.15 to determine their import parity prices, which are estimates of wholesale prices for those grades in Bangladesh markets when imported. The purpose is to bring the Thai FOB prices on equal terms with Bangladeshi prices for the selected grades.

Export Parity and Import Parity vis-à-vis Domestic Wholesale Prices

By comparing prices of fine aman variety with Thai 5 percent broken rice (see Table 13.5), one can see that during the 17 years between 1975 and 1991 domestic prices have exceeded export prices by 27 percent. A similar pattern holds for prices of high-yielding varieties of rice (HYVs, generally considered coarse rice), which have been compared with the Thai 25 percent super.

The prices of *kalizira* and *kataribhog,* two of the best aromatic rice varieties, have been compared with export parity prices for Pakistani basmati rice. Both are slender, but *kalizira* is short whereas *kataribhog* is long. The ratios for these special varieties of aromatic rice appear to be more encouraging than do the ratios for any of the regular varieties. For most of the years the prices were below the export parity prices for basmati rice. *Kataribhog* rice presents the most promising picture. Better ratios for this variety are explained by the relatively low price it commands in the domestic market. Although *kataribhog* is a long variety, its price is lower because it has less aroma than *kalizira* does.

It is apparent that only the two aromatic varieties have immediate prospects in the international market. Prices for ordinary varieties are not presently competitive with international market prices for comparable varieties. The comparison between the fine aman rice domestic prices and the Thai 5 percent broken import parity price shows that during most of 1975–90 the ratio of domestic wholesale to import parity prices was below 100 percent, implying that imports were not commercially feasible. In the comparison of Bangladeshi HYV, which is coarse rice, and Thai 25 percent super rice, the results of the analysis are similar to that for aman rice, showing that commercial trade in rice was not viable during this period (Table 13.6).

A Case for Rice Exports: Swapping Rice for Wheat

In the good harvest years of the 1990s, an excess rice supply has persisted with excess wheat demand. Thus, it is plausible to consider swapping rice for wheat in international markets as a way to improve food security (Chowdhury and Aziz 1989). In such a scenario, what are the effects of rice exports on produc-

2. All references to dollars indicate U.S. dollars.

TABLE 13.5 Average domestic, international, and export parity prices of various rice varieties

Period	Domestic Wholesale Price	International Market Price	Export Parity Price	Domestic Price as Percent of Export Parity Price
		(taka per metric ton)		
Fine rice				
1975–91	8,205	7,622	6,478	127
1975–80	4,821	5,455	4,637	108
1981–86	8,240	7,734	6,574	132
1987–91	12,225	10,086	8,573	145
HYV coarse rice				
1975–91	6,723	6,739	5,728	119
1975–80	4,067	4,869	4,138	103
1981–86	6,845	6,971	5,926	121
1987–91	9,763	8,703	7,398	134
Aromatic *kalizira* rice				
1975–91	12,089	16,856	14,327	87
1975–80	7,102	9,907	8,421	92
1981–86	12,140	18,464	15,694	78
1987–91	18,011	23,264	19,775	91
Aromatic *kataribhog* rice				
1975–91	10,699	16,856	14,327	77
1975–80	6,286	9,907	8,421	81
1981–86	10,745	18,464	15,694	69
1987–91	15,941	23,264	19,775	81

SOURCES: Hamid (1991), Directorate of Agricultural Marketing, IRRI. *Kalizira* and *khataribhog* are based on 1991 wholesale prices collected from eight dealers based at Badamtali market in Dhaka. We extrapolated prices from previous years by using factors in interyear fluctuations in fine aman rice prices. International prices for basmati rice are from the Rice Export Corporation of Pakistan.

NOTES: Domestic prices for fine rice are for fine-variety aman. International fine prices are FOB for Thai 5 percent broken. International prices comparable to domestic HYV are FOB for Thai 25 percent super. International prices comparable to the special aromatic varieties are for Pakistani basmati rice. Export parity prices have been obtained by multiplying international market prices by a factor of 0.85. The remaining 0.15 accounts for the cost and profit margin of the exporter.

tion, consumption, and prices? To address this question, our simple trade model incorporates various rice qualities and cross-price elasticities for both demand and supply. There are three goods: high-quality rice, low-quality rice, and wheat. Demand and supply depend on the prices of the three goods.

Some of the parameters needed to implement the model empirically are not readily available; hence, an informed guess is required. Sensitivity analysis

TABLE 13.6 Average domestic, international, and import parity prices of various rice varieties

Period	Domestic			Price As Percent of Import Parity Price
	Domestic Wholesale Price	International Market Price	Import Parity Price	
		(taka per metric ton)		
Fine rice				
1975–91	8,205	7,622	9,355	88
1975–80	4,821	5,455	6,642	75
1981–86	8,240	7,734	9,534	90
1987–91	12,225	10,087	12,396	100
HYV coarse rice				
1975–91	6,723	6,739	8,340	81
1975–80	4,067	4,869	5,968	71
1981–86	6,845	6,971	8,657	82
1987–91	9,763	8,703	10,806	91

SOURCES: Hamid (1991), Department of Agricultural Marketing, IRRI. 1990–91 data are from IRRI.

NOTES: Domestic prices for fine rice are for fine variety aman; international fine rice prices are FOB for Thai 5 percent broken. International prices comparable to domestic HYV coarse rice are FOB for Thai 25 percent super. For computing import parity prices, we first added a freight cost of $20 per metric ton across the board to derive an estimated C&F price for the concerned Thai grade. Then C&F prices were multiplied by 1.15 to obtain the import parity prices.

with respect to these parameters helps one to understand the robustness of the results. In the case of demand elasticities for high-quality rice, educated guesses take into account the parameters of the higher urban income groups. Similarly, for low-quality rice the parameters of the lower rural income groups have been taken into account. For supply elasticities the major effects are assumed to move from rice price to wheat production and not vice versa, at least when aggregate rice is considered. The baseline of the exercises uses the 1989/90 level of production, availability, and prices. The model assumes that all foreign exchange earned from the export of rice will be spent to import wheat.

Once cross-price elasticities for wheat and rice are taken into account, there is a tendency for the aggregate foodgrain price to go up, which is most evident for wheat and high-quality rice (Table 13.7). The reason is that the demand for wheat increases as a result of higher rice prices and high cross-price elasticities with respect to rice price. Therefore, even though the domestic aggregate price of foodgrains may go up, total foodgrain consumption increases as a result of rice-for-wheat swaps in the international market. With the export of 200,000 tons of rice, total foodgrain consumption goes up by approx-

TABLE 13.7 Simulation of rice export swap

	Demand Elasticities			Supply Elasticities				Percent Change				Percent Change
	H	L	W	H	L	W		H	L	W		
H	–0.50	0.00	0.00	0.20	0.00	0.00	Price	11.71	0.00	–12.87	Total foodgrains	0.78
L	0.00	–0.60	0.00	0.00	0.05	0.00	Demand	–5.39	0.00	14.77	Total rice production	–0.02
W	0.00	0.00	–1.00	0.00	0.00	0.60	Production	2.24	0.00	–7.93	Aggregate rice price	1.75
H	–0.50	0.10	0.00	0.20	–0.50	0.10	Price	12.95	5.28	6.19	Total foodgrains	0.62
L	0.20	–0.60	0.00	–0.05	0.05	–0.05	Demand	–5.42	–0.65	17.89	Total rice production	–0.19
W	1.00	2.00	–1.00	0.00	–0.60	0.60	Production	2.20	–0.65	0.52	Aggregate rice price	6.48
H	–0.50	0.10	0.00	0.10	–0.03	0.00	Price	8.93	1.85	3.09	Total foodgrains	0.56
L	0.20	–0.60	0.00	–0.03	0.01	–0.03	Demand	–6.25	–0.54	17.74	Total rice production	–0.25
W	1.00	2.00	–1.00	0.00	–0.04	0.04	Production	1.27	–0.54	0.13	Aggregate rice price	7.14
H	–0.80	0.40	0.00	0.20	–0.05	0.00	Price	8.93	1.85	3.09	Total foodgrains	0.68
L	0.20	–1.20	0.00	–0.05	0.05	–0.05	Demand	–5.93	–0.49	17.96	Total rice production	–0.13
W	2.00	3.00	–2.00	0.00	–0.60	0.60	Production	1.63	–0.49	0.73	Aggregate rice	2.94
H	–0.20	0.10	0.00	0.20	–0.05	0.00	Price	25.14	7.93	8.94	Total foodgrains	0.50
L	0.05	–0.30	0.00	–0.05	0.05	–0.05	Demand	–3.65	–1.16	17.90	Total rice production	–0.32
W	0.50	1.25	–0.50	0.00	–0.60	0.60	Production	4.19	–1.16	0.56	Aggregate rice price	10.57

SOURCE: Authors' calculations.

NOTES: H = high-quality rice.

L = low-quality rice.

W = wheat.

Export of high-quality rice = 200,000 metric tons.

imately 0.8 percent—that is, by 147,000 tons compared to the baseline case of no exports.

Higher foodgrain prices affect the distribution of food consumption among various income groups. High-income groups are most likely to consume high-quality rice; therefore, they will be penalized for the most part. Low-income consumers will not be affected negatively by higher prices of foodgrains as long as they consume mostly lower-quality rice. The reason is that consumption of wheat will more than compensate for any loss in rice consumption. Note also that foodgrain consumption increases with the magnitude of supply and demand elasticities. As the commercialization of rice production increases, supply elasticities are also expected to go up, implying that bigger gains in total foodgrain consumption are expected from similar swap arrangements. In summary, the export of moderate quantities of high-quality rice will have a positive effect on aggregate foodgrain consumption without compromising the food security of the poor.

Preconditions for Rice Exports

A rice surplus and favorable international price conditions do not guarantee that the net surplus will be automatically translated into export. In addition to price competitiveness, export success requires research on fine rice varieties, marketing infrastructure, quality, and grading.

Research on Fine Varieties of Rice

As noted, the aromatic varieties are more likely to be tradable, given both the tastes of consumers in importing countries and comparative advantage. Until recently, Bangladesh directed all rice production efforts toward self-sufficiency. Thus, research primarily confined itself to generating HYVs without much concern for consumer priorities. Today, however, the domestic market for improved varieties seems to be increasing, as reflected in the relative stability of prices of fine varieties of rice in 1992, when prices of coarse rice plummeted. With a view to stabilizing their income, farmers are now willing to switch to improved varieties. It is therefore necessary to put research efforts into developing new rice varieties that will fetch better prices for farmers through export. As a prerequisite, such research should examine the tastes of rice consumers in potential export markets and experiment with the feasibility of producing suitable rice varieties in Bangladesh.

Marketing Infrastructure: Storage, Milling, and Transportation

The storage facilities presently available in the private sector are unsuitable for long-term storage of foodgrains. At best they are useful for short-term storage after procurement at different points in surplus-producing areas (Jahangir and Goletti 1992). Renting government-owned warehouses may mitigate immediate space and quality problems, but in the long run construction of standardized warehouses is necessary to ensure delivery of quality rice to the world market. The government may encourage the process by amending and simplifying banking regulations for private sector entrepreneurs who are seeking credit for warehouse construction.

Most existing rice milling facilities are incapable of producing internationally acceptable rice. The mills in Bangladesh are generally classified into three categories: husking, major, and automatic. Husking mills, mostly found in rural areas, can only separate the husk from the paddy; bran is separated manually to obtain the final product. Because there is no polishing process, such rice retains part of the bran, meaning that translucency (an important quality criterion) suffers. These mills also use stone hullers, resulting in a higher percentage of broken grains, another important criterion.

Major rice mills use a two-stage process: (1) the husk is separated from the paddy, and (2) the bran is separated and the rice polished to obtain clean rice. Some of these mills specialize in special varieties of aromatic rice, mostly in areas where production is concentrated. Although they do a fairly decent job, the mills still have much room for improvement. For example, simply by switching from a stone huller to a rubber huller they could minimize the percentage of broken rice. Some modernization may also be necessary to improve their polishing quality.

In the automatic rice mills, parboiling, drying, milling, and polishing are all done by machine with minimal human contact. Most of these mills were set up in the late 1970s and early 1980s and therefore have modern machinery capable of producing internationally acceptable rice. In 1988 Bangladesh had 77 such mills (BBS 1989). Their capacity ranges between 16 to 24 tons per eight-hour shift. A conservative estimate, which uses the lower end of the mills' capacity range, puts their annual total capacity at 1.2 million tons in three shifts over 330 operational days per year. Because of higher milling costs and the limited demand for bulk milling, these mills are presently underused because it is economically unfeasible for them to process a small quantity of rice in one run. Once export of rice becomes a viable venture, they will no longer need to stand idle.

Adequate facilities are already available for moving rice from producing areas to ports. Trucks, boats, and trains are all used for transporting foodgrains, although trucks are most popular because they are fastest and least open to pilferage. Boats, the next most popular means, have limited use because many of the traditional routes are not navigable in the dry season. Country boats, however, are cheap and the only means of transportation in remote riverine areas. Railroads are unpopular because of their high rate of pilferage and problems of misplaced wagons.

Carrying costs could be minimized by improving the management of railway and water transport networks. Transportation, however, encompasses far more than foodgrains and should be addressed as part of the overall economic development of the country. Movement of foodgrains, including rice, will benefit in the process.

Quality and Grading

As Bangladesh shifts to a marginal surplus in rice production, it must pay more attention to improving its quality of rice for the world market (Kaosa-ard and Juliano 1991). The international rice market is skeptical about the ability of temporary or new exporters to deliver rice of specified quality (Siamwalla and Haykin 1983). Because such exporters may have great difficulty in disposing of their surplus stock, they should carefully consider overall quality control before undertaking export.

It is difficult, however, to generalize about consumer preferences for cooking quality, shape, and length of rice. Such preferences vary from country to country and even among different types of consumers within a country. For example, high-income consumers in Bangladesh prefer fine-grade rice with a soft, nonsticky texture, while low-income consumers prefer coarse rice with a hard, nonsticky texture (Toquero 1991). Before entering the world market, countries with fine- to special-quality rice should focus on developing intermediate amylose (20–23 percent) rices with a high recovery rate of head rice (whole grain). Intermediate amylose with medium gel consistency (41–60 millimeters) guarantees nonsticky, soft texture. Chalkiness and shape are two other quality aspects that researchers and breeders can improve upon through varietal developments.

At present there is no standard grading system for milled rice in Bangladesh, and the country must establish one before it undertakes export. The grades need not match perfectly with Thai or American standards, and some latitude can be used in determining the physical features of standardizing rice based on the varietal and milling features of rice produced in Bangladesh. For example, stipulated grain composition for Thai 5 percent broken rice is 25 percent of extra-long grain (with a tolerance of 5 percent more), 35 percent of long grain (with a tolerance of 5 percent more or less), with the remainder composed of medium grain in which not more than 10 percent of short grain is allowed (SGS 1982). For fine-variety Bangladeshi rice, which has been compared with Thai 5 percent broken rice, almost 100 percent long grain can easily be guaranteed because it is processed, milled, and sold by generic variety. Absence of extra-long grain in such a standardization is likely to be more than compensated for by uniform size and shape of the grain.

Two other Bangladeshi varieties, medium and coarse, have similar advantages over Thai grades. As for special aromatic varieties, compared with Pakistani basmati rice, *kalizira* is short and slender but highly fragrant, and *kataribhog* is long. They are not comparable in length to basmati, which is extra-long. Nevertheless, their chemical properties, or genotypes, which determine cooking quality and aroma, may be superior. A large proportion of the market for basmati rice is in the Middle East, where consumers prefer pilaf prepared with butter and vegetable oil (Eve 1973). Both the Bangladeshi aromatic varieties (*kalizira,* in particular) have all the qualities of ideal pilaf rice. As a matter of fact, Bangladeshi consumers use *kalizira* and white *kataribhog* as pilaf in special dishes. Therefore, while standardizing the aromatic varieties of rice, potential exporters should emphasize the properties that make them ideal fragrant pilaf rice.

Conclusions

Achieving self-sufficiency in rice production has been a long-cherished dream of policymakers in Bangladesh. But attaining that objective may give rise to a new set of problems, as the experience of 1992 (when there was an excessive buildup of foodgrain stock, a sudden decline in rice price, and a consequent dilemma over rice procurement) illustrates. Recent deficits in rice may soon be left behind only to give rise to a new situation similar to those of the early 1990s.

With a surplus of rice and an accompanying wheat deficit, policymakers must explore in the coming years the possibility of exporting Bangladeshi rice in international markets. Quality will be one of the main factors affecting competitiveness. By analyzing import and export parity prices compared to domestic prices of different qualities of rice, one can see that there is scope for exporting aromatic varieties. Cross-price effects among different varieties of rice and wheat are important determinants of the impact of swapping rice exports for wheat imports. Rice swaps increase foodgrain consumption through increased consumption of wheat, and rice exports increase the domestic prices of foodgrains, including wheat. As long as the level of exports is low (less than 200,000 tons), the overall price and consumption effects are small. Bangladesh is unlikely to emerge as a large exporter in the near future without significant improvements in productivity.

The feasibility of exporting rice depends on a set of policy measures. First, policy should create favorable conditions for the development of export markets; here, recent abolition of anti-hoarding laws and trade restrictions are positive steps. In addition, the process of export should be kept simple to avoid inordinate delays in completing paperwork. Second, existing infrastructure and equipment affecting transportation, storage, and milling should be updated and expanded. Third, a grading system should be introduced to raise the average quality of rice consumed domestically and to enhance the likelihood of exporting successfully in the international market. Fourth, research to continuously improve productivity, with a particular focus on quality, should be strengthened. Finally, the international market should be opened gradually so that negative effects can be absorbed smoothly. Tax and subsidy policies at the point of external trade may be effective in handling the instability of prices arising from this step.

References

Bangladesh Bureau of Statistics (BBS). 1989. *Statistical yearbook 1988.* Dhaka: Bangladesh Bureau of Statistics.

Chowdhury, N. N., and A. Aziz. 1989. Feasibility of export of rice for import of wheat by Bangladesh. Working Paper. Dhaka: Bangladesh Ministry of Food. Mimeo.

Eve, P. 1973. *Coo King with rice.* New York: Farrar, Straus, and Giroux.

Food and Agriculture Organization (FAO). Faostat data base (www. faostat.fao.org).

Goletti, F. 1994. *The changing public role in a rice economy moving toward self-sufficiency: The case of Bangladesh.* Research Report 98. Washington, D.C.: International Food Policy Research Institute.

Hamid, M. A. (1991). A data base on agriculture and foodgrains in agriculture (1947/48–1989/90). Dhaka.

Jahangir, A. S. M., and F. Goletti. 1992. Prospects and preconditions of rice export by Bangladesh. Washington, D.C.: International Food Policy Research Institute. Mimeo.

Kaosa-ard, M., and B. O. Juliano. 1991. Assessing rice quality characteristics and prices in selected international markets. In *Rice grain marketing and quality issues: Selected papers from the International Rice Research Conference.* Manila: International Rice Research Institute.

Mahmud, W., Rahman S. H., and S. Zohir. 1993. Agricultural growth through crop diversification in Bangladesh. IFPRI-BIDS Agricultural Diversification Study. Washington, D.C.: International Food Policy Research Institute. Mimeo.

SGS Far East Limited. 1982. Export standards for Thai agricultural products. Bangkok: SGS Far East Limited. Mimeo.

Siamwalla, A., and S. Haykin. 1983. *The world rice market: Structure, conduct, and performance.* Research Report 39. Washington, D.C.: International Food Policy Research Institute.

Toquero, Z. F. 1991. Consumer demand for rice grain quality. In *Rice grain marketing and quality issues: Selected papers from the International Rice Research Conference.* Manila: International Rice Research Institute.

U.S. Department of Agriculture (USDA), Economic Research Service (ERS). 1991. *Rice situation and outlook report.* Washington, D.C.: U.S. Department of Agriculture, October.

World Bank. 1992. *Bangladesh food policy review: Adjusting to the Green Revolution.* Report 9641-BD (vols. 1 and 2). Washington, D.C.: World Bank.

14 Conclusion: Old Lessons and New Directions in Food Policy

STEVEN HAGGBLADE AND RAISUDDIN AHMED

Ghosts from the Past

Two gruesome famines visited Bengal—in 1943 and 1974—on the heels of two great wars. The first descended amid the terrors of World War II, while the second followed in the wake of Bangladesh's brutal war of liberation. Wrenching images from these famines have haunted the nation for two generations—visions of hungry masses, pressed in the crush of extraordinary times, knocking at the doors of the rich, who seldom opened; people dying in hordes, not in the warfields but on apparently peaceful and idle compounds, on roadsides destroyed by war, on barren rice fields and in empty markets. Vivid memories of these famines linger in the minds of the elders who have steered economic policies in postwar periods and peacetime. Haunted by these ghosts from the past, policymakers have persistently erred on the side of intervention in food markets through direct public distribution of foodgrains and tight market regulation.

Distrust of traders emerged as an article of faith among citizens and decision makers alike. They perceived traders as hoarders, colluders, and profiteers bent on raising market prices to reap a rich harvest of profits from the misfortunes of the poor. In the emotionally charged aftermath of these two painful episodes, public opinion branded the traders as its most prominent scapegoats; government stood out as the savior. But with the benefit of hindsight, as the pain of personal sufferings subsides, reflection suggests a far more complex story (Knight 1954; Sen 1981; Alamgir 1978). The skyrocketing rice prices of 1943, which priced the poor out of the market and triggered widespread starvation, stemmed from a variety of causes. Government confiscation of all river transport, in accordance with the rice-denial policy against the invading Japanese army, severely disrupted normal transport routes. The British army cordoned northern Bengal districts in a futile attempt to procure surplus foodgrains. Wartime monetary policies contributed to high price inflation. In short, by destroying river transport, cordoning off surplus zones, and printing money, the public's perceived savior, the government, exacerbated a dangerous situation. Nevertheless, traders continue to shoulder the bulk of the blame for the sufferings endured.[1]

With the wars now over, is it not rational to assume that interventions in food markets, introduced during wartime, are no longer required? The Government of Pakistan (with Bangladesh as its eastern province) thought so in 1955, when it abolished the Civil Supplies Department, the public marketing organization set up during World War II to ensure direct public food distribution and market regulation. Yet the government backtracked quickly, resuscitating the department in 1956 to handle a serious food shortage arising from a weather-induced production shortfall. Then, as in subsequent years, natural calamities replaced wars as a rationale for continued public control and presence in food markets.

Public interventions after independence, fueled by steadily growing inflows of food aid, grew gradually into a huge mechanism for distributing subsidized foodgrains to large employers, public employees, and schoolteachers. Stabilizing prices, and holding large public foodstocks for that purpose, became explicit objectives of the growing government food system. The government instituted a rural rationing system and, later, in-kind distribution programs for the poor, who in early years benefited only episodically from government food programs.

Emerging also from famine experiences has been the dominance of foodgrain self-sufficiency in almost all agricultural planning and policies since the beginning of the 1960s. Because bitter memories die hard, faith in the supply side of the food equation has reigned supreme in all plans and programs meant to prevent hunger and alleviate poverty. In 1974, before the onset of famine, the government desperately tried to import foodgrains to meet already-known shortages in public warehouses. But owing to a worldwide crisis in foodgrains and lack of access to American food aid because of Bangladesh's trade relations with Cuba, the government was unable to meet the challenges of the 1974 famine. This experience left a lasting impression on politicians and policymakers, who became convinced that foodgrain self-sufficiency was a necessary component of economic and political sovereignty. Motivated by this belief, policymakers introduced voluntary paddy procurement at support prices to complement technology-based input supply programs for foodgrain self-sufficiency.

Memories of past famines fade gradually. In this process, slowly but perceptibly, public opinion has also changed. Citizens of all ranks increasingly recognize signs of the broad-based maturing of foodgrain markets over the past 50 years. Widespread availability of new high-yielding varieties (HYVs) has increased productivity for farms of all sizes. The resulting surge in marketed

1. Traders naturally form expectations about future prices and stock foodgrains to maximize profit. Nevertheless, in crisis situations this behavior is often erroneously perceived as the primary cause of the problem.

volumes has opened competition so intense among itinerant traders that more than half of even small farmers now prefer to sell paddy from their homesteads at prices comparable to those in local markets. Onerous tied production credit has diminished in regions with high HYV adoption as production and incomes have risen. In these areas villagers see that the tables have turned, with prosperous farmers now lending to the traders. On-farm paddy stocks have roughly doubled per capita since the 1960s. As a result, lean-season farm stocks now outweigh private trade stocks by a factor of three. In these golden mounds, villagers see tangible evidence of a counterbalancing market power that is whittling away at old perceptions of omnipotent traders. Seasonal price movements, wildly volatile in past decades, have moderated substantially since the 1970s. With the advent of a large-scale, dry-season, irrigated boro rice crop, farmers are now able to compensate for shortfalls in one crop by increasing output midyear in the next crop season. Twelve million farmers, rather than one government, provide built-in price stabilization and a clear reduction in interyear price fluctuation. Even the hated traders visibly moderate price swings as they rush to cushion domestic production shortfalls through private import. Since the liberalization of foodgrain imports in 1992, private imports have surged in response to rising prices during the production shortfalls of 1994/95 and 1995/96 and the major dislocations of 1997/98 and 1998/99.

Government, the perceived savior of yore, has watched its image tarnish over time even as traders and farmers have proven their ability to boost supply and moderate price volatility. The massive volume of public foodgrain distribution (2.9 million metric tons per year at its peak in the late 1980s), with its large outside contributions, has inspired well-recognized creativity in graft. An increasingly wary public has seen how early public distribution channels clearly intended to benefit the urban middle class. Later, as the public food system began to direct substantial volumes to rural and low-income consumers, leakage grew to startling proportions—30 to 90 percent in the largest channels. Thus, the public's growing confidence in private markets has coincided with increased disappointment in government's ability to intervene efficiently.

Policymakers, too, have gained gradual confidence in private trader responsiveness and in the growing competitiveness of Bangladesh's expanding grain markets. Like the general public, they have become increasingly weary of bearing the steep cost of public food interventions. By the early 1990s heightened confidence in private markets, by both the general public and policymakers, set the stage for major change in the food policies that had been introduced much earlier, in times of crisis.

Recent Reforms

In the long run Bangladesh's food markets and food policy have been buffeted by two powerful and often unpredictable exogenous forces: the weather and food-aid donors. Floods and poor harvests have scuttled major reform—for instance, the aborted abolition of the Food Department in 1955. In other cases meteorological forces have stimulated a surge in public distribution, as with the floods of 1987 and 1988 and the drought of 1979. Donors, because they supplied 50 to 75 percent of public food resources, were a driving force in the buildup of the ration system. Later they played a key role in reorienting offtake to rural-focused targeted distribution. Ultimately, through their long-term policy conditions, donors helped erode ration subsidies as they plotted the demise of the very system their early inflows had nourished and sustained through its formative years.

In the early 1990s, as so often in the past, these forces played a key role in initiating and sustaining reform. But surprisingly, given past history, these reforms took place immediately after Bangladesh's worst flood in 100 years, the 1988 flood.[2] In this case well-functioning grain markets, an immediate bounce in boro season production, and timely targeted public food distribution contained what in earlier decades would have been a major natural calamity. Close on the heels of this flood was abnormally low rainfall in 1992. This situation raised serious concern because, historically, droughts have proven more devastating than floods: insufficient rainfall compromises Bangladesh's largest rice crop, rainfed aman. But recently expanded HYV technology provided unanticipated drought insurance when late-season irrigation of the aman crop converted a potentially devastating drought into an all-time record aman harvest. Containment of these natural shocks inspired confidence in the growing flexibility and responsiveness of foodgrain markets. Donors likewise helped set the stage for reform by adhering to their long-term plan to reduce ration subsidies.

Rapid structural change in Bangladesh's foodgrain production and markets laid the foundation for a major restructuring of government food policy in the early 1990s. New HYV foodgrain technology, for both rice and wheat, became available in Bangladesh in the mid-1970s. After 10 years of steady expansion, adoption surged perceptibly in the second half of the 1980s following liberalization in key agricultural input markets—fertilizer and irrigation equipment. The sudden widespread availability of these inputs triggered a dramatic boost in the use of irrigated HYVs in foodgrain production, particularly in dry-season irrigated rice. Coupled with sustained investment in key rural infrastructure, such as electricity, telephones, and roads, this buildup of foodgrain production made possible a marketing revolution of far greater scale. While foodgrain production increased from 8 million tons in 1962 to 18 million tons in 1992, quantities marketed increased by a factor of six. This increased

2. In 1998 another devastating flood hit Bangladesh, one as severe as the 1988 "flood of the century." In spite of early media speculation that another famine was unavoidable, large-scale private rice imports from India of more than 2 million tons, together with increased public offtake, ensured foodgrain availabilities and avoided any death from starvation.

production was realized almost entirely through increased productivity without substantial increase in the planted area under rice, particularly after 1975/76. Due to sequential, patchwork adoption, regional trade flows and price seasonality changed. In addition, the number of private rice traders mushroomed. Increased foodgrain production in excess of population growth, growing urbanization, shifting preferences for wheat, and intractable poverty all contributed to a steady softening in real rice prices.

Simultaneously, sustained by long-term donor conditions, gradually rising offtake prices from government ration channels climbed upward to meet the falling market price. By eroding the incentives of millions of ration cardholders to draw rations, the fall in rice prices in the early 1990s played a key role in making rapid downsizing possible. Like the twin blades of a pair of scissors, the falling market price combined with a rising ration price to cut the ration subsidy from the system (Chapter 6). This subsidy erosion, gradual at first and then dramatic in the late 1980s and early 1990s, effectively neutralized 15 million ration recipients, the largest potential opposition to downsizing the enormous public food distribution system.

Spurred by reduced government resources and a softening foreign aid environment, an opportunistic coalition of government reformers seized this favorable moment to launch a series of rapid downsizing moves. In short order, from December 1991 through August 1993, they abolished the major ration channels, reduced domestic rice procurement, and liberalized foreign trade in foodgrains. Even with a change in government, two subsequent bad harvests (1994/95 and 1995/96), and two major crises (the drought of 1997 and the flood of 1998), downsizing and liberalization have been sustained.

Today, Bangladesh's public food system looks considerably different from the way it looked a decade ago. Ration channels, the centerpiece of the system since the 1950s, have been dismantled. Only essential priorities, the outlet serving the army and police, continues to draw rations of any significance. Instead, the system focuses on a small open market sales outlet and a tightly targeted set of distribution programs aimed at vulnerable groups. Government procurement has shrunk apace. Moreover, the rapid private sector response to import liberalization means that, for the first time in five decades, private sector foodgrain imports exceeded the government's imports.

Implications Abroad

Governments elsewhere have also attempted to downsize large-scale government food distribution programs and reduce heavy food subsidy costs. In doing so, they have often aroused lethal opposition and been forced to backtrack. Yet where others have faltered, Bangladesh has succeeded in executing and maintaining its food policy reforms. What can other countries learn from Bangladesh?

Probably the most important lesson is timing—recognizing and selecting an opportune moment for change. The productivity-led foodgrain production surge of the late 1980s and early 1990s, along with declining rates of population growth and softening demand parameters, led to falling market prices, which coincided with gradually eroding ration subsidies. By taking action at this juncture, the government and its donor allies effectively neutralized the most common opponent of food policy reform, the urban ration cardholders. Gradual reform proved necessary in Bangladesh. The slow erosion of ration subsidies over a decade was instrumental in defusing the country's 15 million ration cardholders, the policy's largest potential opposition group.

Although change came gradually at first, the government moved quickly toward the end game by selecting as its first major move the abolition of rural rationing, the largest rice outlet in the food distribution system. Its overnight disappearance forced a rapid series of adjustments to restore the balance between procurement and the substantially reduced volume of offtake. This experience suggests that selecting a strategically positioned first domino may facilitate further action and forestall efforts to derail the reformers' momentum.

Finally, the importance of external allies cannot be overstated. To face internal opposition from idealists and rent seekers, reformers in the Ministries of Finance, Agriculture, and Food benefited from the support of the major food-aid donors—particularly the U.S. Agency for International Development (USAID), the World Bank, and Canada. Their long-term commitment to reform and their steadfast maintenance of policy conditions helped to sustain the pace of change. They also redirected heat from internal to external agencies, thus providing cover for the government's internal advocates of change.

Implications for the Future

The Macroeconomic Perspective

No longer a basket case, Bangladesh has begun to demonstrate that its economic growth can outrace its population, that the country can materially improve its ability to feed itself, and that it might even attain a level of relative prosperity sufficient to accord basic dignity to its vast population. Fulfilling this prospect, however, depends on the country's ability to accelerate the momentum of progress. The final outcome will be influenced by how policymakers and politicians formulate and implement policies that balance short-run exigencies with long-run developmental needs, make most productive use of the nation's huge labor force and natural resources (such as fertile land, ample water supply for agriculture, and natural gas), and foster entrepreneurial growth. A market-oriented approach to development, in both rhetoric and practice, will play a crucial role in shaping the future of Bangladesh. This emphasis does not require indiscriminate preaching of the free-market gospel, as is often the case. Rather, it must stem from a pragmatic recognition of the present needs facing Bangladesh.

Why is a market-oriented approach to development so important for Bangladesh? First, it is clear the country will have to accelerate its current 12 percent rate of investment to achieve faster growth in production, income, and poverty alleviation. Because of dwindling official foreign aid and low domestic savings, the investment rate cannot be increased without a substantial boost in direct foreign investment—supplemented, if possible, by growing domestic savings. Yet direct foreign investment is unlikely to increase without a liberal market environment. Likewise, domestic private savings are most likely to increase only when opportunities for profitable investments are plentiful and unshackled.

Second, if Bangladesh is to grow faster than it has in the past, it must increase efforts to exploit foreign demand for its products. Indeed, the fastest-growing segments of the economy since the 1980s—particularly garments, leather goods, and shrimp—have depended on external markets. Even for foodgrains, which have led growth within domestic agriculture, shifting demand patterns suggest that continued growth will require export outlets. Because of current low levels of income, domestic demand cannot support a robust rate of growth in national income. To be able to exploit foreign demand, the economy must be allowed to make use of its comparative advantage by responding to international price signals and the play of market forces. The necessary growth of entrepreneurship, which is needed to scout world markets and exploit market niches, depends on open market policies and practices.

Third, imports of modern cost-reducing technology and its adaptation to conditions in Bangladesh will take place most effectively through pluralistic forms of trading regimes. In the past, import liberalization of key agricultural inputs (irrigation equipment, pesticides, seeds, and others) has proven crucial to expanded HYV adoption and increased yields and output in foodgrains. In the future, continued access to new agricultural, manufacturing, and information technology will provide vital inputs for an increasingly productive economy.

Fourth, as nations race toward greater economic integration, the gains from trade will be best harvested by those nations that can adjust quickly to a rapidly changing world environment. Such adjustment is possible only when markets operate freely but fairly with up-to-date global information.

Finally, studies on the economic, cultural, and anthropological history of the area now known as Bangladesh demonstrate that the people are strong individualists (Khan 1996). Thus, instilling corporate behavior and organizing effective collective groups may be relatively difficult. Although market institutions seem a more natural fit, a nation cannot sustain itself or even prosper without some form of collective organization and drive.

Market-oriented growth, however, does not mean a passive role for government in economic development. On the contrary, success depends on a proactive government role in a number of strategic areas:

- Macropolicy environment
- Provision of public goods
- Risk-reducing legal, financial, and institutional arrangements
- Monitoring and regulation of monopoly and oligopoly
- Food policy and food security for vulnerable groups

This book has focused primarily, although not exclusively, on the food policy and food security issues that remain so critical in Bangladesh. Despite modest improvements beginning in the 1980s, massive poverty remains a serious threat to human welfare and social and political stability. Rural poverty, the most pervasive and severe, lays the foundation for accelerating urban poverty in years to come. The production side of food policy—stimulating agricultural growth of the labor-intensive HYV variant adopted in Bangladesh—will remain key to the solution because it fosters greater employment and higher incomes for the poor as well as moderating food prices. The nation's history of painful famines and recent threats leaves us with little doubt that healthy food markets and food policy remain essential for political stability as well as for the welfare of the poor.

The Role of Government in Short-Run Food Management and Policy

In the future, several long-standing structural constraints will continue to affect the room for food policy maneuver in Bangladesh. Among them are recurring high levels of extreme poverty that have resisted modest improvements in economic conditions. Growing landlessness continues to drive an increasingly skewed distribution of assets and income, permanently condemning 25 percent of the population to a painful and precarious existence. Likewise, unpredictable weather, including periodic cyclones and floods, will remain a constant.

But the future will be different from the past in several important respects. Built-in stabilizers such as multiple foodgrain crops and the rapid production response of one crop to shortfalls in another will continue to grow. Despite recent increases, farmers have brought only about 30 percent of potentially irrigated area under dry-season irrigation, and they plant only 37 percent of the aman rice crop in HYVs (see Chapter 2). As these proportions continue to grow, farmers' ability to respond rapidly to midyear production shortfalls can only improve. Further, recent experience with private foodgrain imports suggests that commercial import channels will remain poised to relieve temporary supply shortfalls.

Probably more important, the future will usher in an era of declining food aid and falling overall aid resources. Compared with the past, fewer external funds will be available to subsidize costly food market interventions. Therefore, government decisionmakers will have to choose more carefully as they set priorities among the three classic objectives of short-run food policy: targeted distribution to vulnerable groups, emergency stocks, and price stabilization.

TARGETED DISTRIBUTION. Given persistent high levels of extreme poverty, the need for strategic targeting to vulnerable groups will remain undiminished, particularly in the September/October lean season. In the face of declining external resources, this need will continue to swamp available funds. As a result, the government will have to monitor and evaluate more rigorously and to evaluate and improve targeting of these diminished resources. In the past, the government has shown considerable creativity and willingness to experiment and adjust: dropping nonperforming ration channels, trying to reform them, experimenting with new programs (such as Rural Public Works and Food-for-Education), and subjecting them to critical outside evaluation (see Chapter 11). This willingness to monitor, fine-tune, redesign, and redeploy will become even more important in the new era of diminished resources.

EMERGENCY STOCKS. Continued unpredictable weather and periodic emergencies, coupled with opportunistic political opposition (regardless of who is in power), suggest that some level of security stocks will be required for the foreseeable future. But government-held emergency stocks can be much lower than in the past, for several reasons. Multiple cropping and nearly year-round rice harvests make domestic foodgrain supply response faster than ever before. Similarly, recently legalized private imports now respond effectively with increased foodgrain shipments in years of domestic production shortfall. Witness the 0.5 to 0.6 million tons of private rice imports in 1994/95 and 1995/96, two years of bad aman harvest. With the increase in aman production in 1996/97, private imports fell off sharply. Then, following the drought-induced shortfall in the 1997/98 aman harvest, private traders again imported heavily, bringing in more than 1 million tons of foodgrains, mainly rice coming overland from India. The following year, the flood of 1998/99 proved even more devastating to the aman harvest, and it triggered an even greater response from private traders, who brought in 2.6 million tons of private rice imports, again primarily from India. As they have proven repeatedly, private traders can and do respond, tempering the need for public intervention.

Moreover, as the private import and export trade grows, alternate trade-based instruments will become available to guarantee foodgrain availability in times of crisis. Options on forward import contracts may prove a cheaper alternative for lining up supply in periods of stress. Here the government can take a leading role, demonstrating to private traders the potentially effective use of international futures markets as a financial substitute for perishable physical grainstocks held in humid Bangladesh.

How low can government emergency stocks prudently go? Although no precise answer exists, estimates for foodgrains range between 600,000 tons

(World Bank 1979) and 300,000 tons (Chowdhury 1994). For political reasons at the very least, some physical government-held stocks will probably be required for years to come. In the past, working stocks required to lubricate the large-scale ration system provided a cushion and effectively obviated the need for a separate government emergency stock. But as the overall scale of public offtake declines, the cushion provided by these working stocks will diminish and may raise the need for an explicit emergency stock.

Estimating the optimal level of total stocks (for emergency, targeted distribution, and other objectives) is always complex in a dynamic environment. Even so, it seems probable that the Bangladeshi government will need to maintain a total stock of foodgrains (primarily wheat) in the range of 700,000 to 800,000 tons, a substantial reduction from the 1.2 to 1.5 million tons recommended in the past (see Chapter 10).

PRICE STABILIZATION. The need for government intervention to stabilize seasonal price movements has been diminished by falling seasonal price spreads and diminished time intervals between major harvests. In fact, attempts at price intervention can inadvertently generate pernicious side effects. Available studies of private foodgrain stocks indicate that high levels of government stock necessary to manage price interventions drive out private trade stocks by as much as 0.8 to 1 (Chowdhury 1993). Government attempts at price intervention also dampen domestic production responses and diminish incentives for private import, which has proven highly responsive to domestic price increases in the years since 1992, when private foodgrain imports became legal.

Food managers introduced an open market sales channel and an explicit price stabilization mandate in 1978. The latest inductee in the government's roster of short-run food policy objectives, the open market sale program warrants a fresh examination in the light of the emerging role of private import. The case for continued government attempts to influence seasonal or interannual price variation has weakened considerably since the 1970s. These efforts have proven costly and have failed to reach the most vulnerable households, the extreme poor. Seasonally targeted distribution to vulnerable groups appears more feasible, less costly, and more effective in focusing shrinking resources on the truly vulnerable (see Chapter 11). In a new era of strengthened markets and lower resource availability, seasonal and interyear price stabilization appears to be the most expendable of Bangladesh's short-run food policy objectives.

Long-Run Growth in Agriculture and Food

For two generations foodgrains have received highest priority in public investment and research budgets, and they have led agricultural growth since independence. But rice and wheat may not continue to lead in the future. Sluggish domestic demand seems likely given growing urbanization, growing demand for wheat-based convenience foods, and resultant changes in consumption patterns away from domestically produced rice toward imported wheat.

Among prosperous segments of the population, this leads to falling income elasticities of demand for rice. Among the extreme poor, stagnant earnings prevent them from exercising high unrealized demand for basic foodgrains. As a result, the aggregate national income elasticity of demand for rice is low, probably in the range of 0.10 to 0.20. Thus, growth in rice production based on domestic demand will stagnate unless economic growth biased in favor of the poor can be made a reality.

Historically, even though the growth rate in foodgrain production has exceeded population growth, the growth rate in agricultural production has remained low, at about 2 percent per year. To accelerate agricultural income growth, policymakers must first recognize the importance of promoting agricultural products that have the highest potential to contribute to value added in agriculture. This implies abandoning the old dogma of foodgrain self-sufficiency and diversifying agriculture from foodgrains to high-value and high-value-added crops in which Bangladesh discerns a comparative advantage—for example, fruits, vegetables, spices, cotton, jute, and some superior varieties of rice.[3] While foodgrains will continue to be the backbone of Bangladeshi agriculture for many years to come, non-foodgrains may prove to be the legs necessary for accelerating agricultural growth in the future. The second requirement for accelerating agricultural growth is the recognition that sluggish demand for agricultural products can be a serious constraint to increased production but that this constraint can be overcome by exploiting foreign demand. Export of a product does not imply only earnings of foreign exchange; it also implies the export of abundant Bangladeshi labor services underlying the production of exportables. Once these two general principles are recognized, policymakers can identify a number of specific and strategic policies with the potential for boosting agricultural production, rural income, and employment.

OPEN TRADE FOR AGRICULTURE. Elements of agricultural diversification policies are embedded in an open trade policy for agriculture. According to many traders, if all restrictions on the export and import of rice are removed (Chapter 13), the export of better-quality rice will soon attract foreign markets. This will initiate a chain reaction in the production of rice in which farmers will switch to high-quality rice, often associated with aman varieties, and will lead to reduced demand for irrigation water. Rice millers will then have incentives to introduce new machinery for processing so that currently ungraded local rice can be upgraded into higher-valued export-quality rice. The process will require adoption among rice traders of a system of grades and

3. We have not included the potential in the livestock and fisheries subsectors. This exclusion does not imply that they are unimportant for agricultural growth and diversification in Bangladesh. On the contrary, they are the two fastest-growing subsectors in agriculture and deserve close scrutiny. Our omission is primarily due to our inability to conduct the comprehensive investigations that we did for the crop subsector.

standards consistent with those used in the world market. Such open trade policies are likely to result in the import of wheat and cheap, low-quality rice and export of high-quality rice (see Chapters 12 and 13). Given the entrepreneurship of Bangladeshi farmers and traders and the inherent quality of grains in Bangladesh, which are not inferior to the grains that form the bulk of rice exports from India, Thailand, and Vietnam, there is no apparent reason why Bangladesh traders would not be able to follow the same process.

The open trade policy in foodgrains does not imply a passive role for the government. On the contrary, its agencies will need to encourage proactively modernization of the rice industry by helping to establish a system of grades and standards and the certification procedure essential to a competitive export industry. Government action will be required to maintain stable export incentives and procedures and to maintain newly found credit access for the foodgrain trade. Access to new milling technology, with color sorters and polishers, will also be required. A careful watch on the import and export trade in foodgrains is vital to remaining ahead of any potential crisis that may arise due to unforeseen turmoil in domestic and international markets for rice.

EXPLOITING COMPARATIVE ADVANTAGE. In Bangladesh, crops such as jute, cotton, tobacco, pulses, and various vegetables generate high net economic returns (see Chapter 12). Yet oilseeds and sugarcane produce negative value added. Consequently, shifting production resources to higher-value crops can accelerate agricultural growth. To facilitate this reorientation, government will need to play an active role, particularly in withdrawing the protection given to sugarcane and oilseeds. In the case of jute, global concern about protecting the environment has put pressure on the polluting polypropylene industry, which is likely to result in expanded world demand for jute products (Boyce 1997). To exploit this opportunity, Bangladeshi policies on jute milling and the distribution of jute seeds warrant a fresh look.

With vegetables, farmers appear reluctant to expand production despite high net economic returns, probably because most of these products are perishable and their markets are seasonal, thin, and uncertain. Here, government can contribute by maintaining open trade policies and export incentives, providing assistance in locating export markets, and investing in appropriate infrastructure for handling, transportation, and storage. The production growth of potatoes since the establishment of a cold-storage infrastructure shows how strategic public investment can enable crop diversification.

Rice Production

While agricultural diversification is a long-term process likely to respond to a changing incentive structure in agriculture, rice production warrants specific policy attention in the medium term to strengthen the accumulated momentum of growth and impart greater stability in production. Rice will remain the centerpiece of Bangladeshi agriculture, which shelters most of the country's rural poor. As Chapter 2 has shown, year-to-year variations, although diminished significantly by irrigated rice production, can still create short-term crises that distract attention from long-term problems. An increase in productivity and a reduction in instability in rice production call for a strategy that will increase the share of irrigated boro rice from its present 42 percent to 60–65 percent of total rice production. Under current HYV technology, this implies a commensurate increase in the use of balanced doses of fertilizers. Its overall impact, however, could be substantially enhanced if a technologically potent superior seed variety (for example, super rice or hybrid rice seeds) could complement the area expansion under irrigated boro. Such superior varieties are being used in China, India, and Vietnam (Pingali, Hossain, and Gerpacio 1997), making the prospect realistic indeed. Nevertheless, problems with seed production and distribution are complicated, and adaptive trials are essential.

In a tight land situation for growing a wide variety of crops, increasing the area under irrigated boro rice appears to be a formidable challenge. The most scope lies in the expansion of irrigated boro in areas that border F2 and F3 classes of land, where about 2 million acres (about 800,000 hectares) are currently planted with local variety transplanted aman rice and other crops under high risk of flood. For now, irrigated boro is not possible in such areas because of their unsuitability for shallow tubewells (water tables are deeper) and exposure to the high risk of early flood. To make such areas suitable, flood protection devices (such as embankments and drainage) and installation of deep tubewells would be necessary; and public investment might be unavoidable.

Agricultural Technology

Access to new production technology can be a potent stimulus for agricultural growth. In Bangladesh's changing environment, several new opportunities merit consideration. Within foodgrains, research emphasis could benefit by including improvements in quality as well as with yield. The quality and characteristics demanded in the world market should be an added focus of research. Among crops, the relative research emphasis may need to be reviewed to ensure a higher priority for high-valued, non-foodgrain products than has been accorded under the self-sufficiency–dominated policies of the past. Continued facilitation of the import of new seeds and production technologies will be necessary for Bangladesh to capitalize on research conducted abroad, as in the case of potatoes. Of course, some adaptive research may be required to make minor changes in imported technology.

Although these modifications will require additional resources, public investment in agricultural research in Bangladesh has remained low compared to India, Pakistan, Sri Lanka, and other East Asian countries. Bangladesh spends only about 0.25 percent of its gross domestic product from agriculture on agricultural research compared to 0.50 percent in India; 0.58 percent in

Pakistan; more than 1 percent in Malaysia, Taiwan, and Thailand; and more than 3 percent in high-income countries (Pardey, Roseboom, and Fan 1997). Increased spending on agricultural research appears necessary to the future of Bangladesh, given the importance of agriculture to rural income growth and poverty alleviation (Hossain, Rahman, and Sen 1997). Where will the resources come from? This is a question of priority in resource allocation. The government needs to weigh the relative merits of subsidies involved in fertilizer marketing, public output marketing, and agricultural research spending.

Agricultural Inputs

The supply of adequate inputs for agriculture (such as fertilizers, seeds, pesticides, power tillers, electricity, and so on) is a necessary condition for ensuring the supply of increased agricultural products. Past reforms in the marketing of these inputs have opened up markets and improved availability, and this direction must be continued. Some reverses, however, have taken place—for example, in the distribution of fertilizer. As discussed in Chapter 3, solutions that strengthen rather than strangle competition should have been found because access to modern fertilizers remain crucial to continued high-productivity.

Irrigation is the other key agricultural input. Despite the revolutionary change in rice production brought about by access to private shallow tubewells (see Chapter 3), a change in irrigation policy will probably prove necessary. Irrigation practices in the rice culture of Bangladesh follow a flooding method that benefits rice but excludes other crops, resulting in considerable waste of water because the excess gets drained. Owing to this practice, other crops, even those that offer high returns, cannot be grown in the same project area. In the future, water resources will become increasingly scarce, with competing demand from industries, households, and agriculture. Moreover, no matter how friendly Bangladesh remains with its neighbors, there will be less and less water available from rivers coming from neighboring countries. All these considerations imply that Bangladesh should reevaluate its irrigation policies to include systematic water management considerations both in the design and operation of irrigation projects.

Infrastructure

Although the neglect of rural infrastructure is still common in the developing world, Bangladesh has made remarkable progress in developing rural roads and extending electricity to rural areas. This momentum of development must be sustained by correcting geographical imbalances, strengthening local governments that maintain rural infrastructure, and providing culverts and bridges on rural roads. The time has come, however, when emphasis should be placed on selectivity and investment in strategic elements that complement new directions of the economy, including agriculture. Thus, increasing the capacity of energy supply and developing ports, airline cargo facilities, container facilities in shipping, refrigerated trucking, and cold storage facilities for perishable products are key to the diversification of agriculture and the economy. Many of these areas are suitable for public-private cooperation and collaboration. The challenge is for the public sector to identify projects and enlist appropriate private sector participation before infrastructural constraints become bottlenecks.

A New Role for Government

In light of recent changes in technology, production, and private marketing, the future heralds a new role for government, one that implies modifications in organization, efficiency, and communications to keep it alert and able to address emerging issues within the economy and society. In addressing its short-run food policy objectives, government efforts will probably focus, more narrowly than in the past, on a small public emergency stock and on scaled-back but more rigorously targeted distribution to vulnerable groups and seasons. In the long run, government can play a crucial role as a facilitating, modernizing force in agriculture by maintaining a stable open trade policy, access to modern inputs, access to imports, access to export markets, and continued support for agricultural research and infrastructure.

Given regular external shocks from unpredictable monsoon weather and given the highly visible and politicized role of rice in the Bangladeshi economy, food policy will continue to enjoy close scrutiny at the highest political levels. So in the future, as the nation's food markets continue to mature, so, too, will its food policy.

References

Alamgir, M. 1978. *Bangladesh: A case of below poverty level equilibrium trap.* Dhaka: Bangladesh Institute of Development Studies.

Boyce, J. K. 1997. Jute, polypropylene, and the environment: A study in international trade and market failure. Amherst, Mass., U.S.A.: University of Massachusetts, Department of Economics. Mimeo.

Chowdhury, N. 1993. Interaction between private rice stocks and public stock policy in Bangladesh: Evidence for a crowding out. Bangladesh Food Policy Project Manuscript 37. Washington, D.C.: International Food Policy Research Institute. Mimeo.

———. 1994. National security stocks for Bangladesh. Bangladesh Food Policy Project Manuscript 55. Washington, D.C.: International Food Policy Research Institute. Mimeo.

Hossain, M., H. Z. Rahman, and B. Sen. 1997. Income distribution and poverty in rural Bangladesh, 1987–94. Dhaka: Bangladesh Institute of Development Studies; Manila: International Rice Research Institute. Mimeo.

Khan, A. A. 1996. *Discovery of Bangladesh: Explorations into dynamics of a hidden nation.* Dhaka: University Press.

Knight, H. 1954. *Food administration in India.* Stanford, Calif., U.S.A.: Stanford University Press.

Pardey, P., J. Roseboom, and S. Fan. 1997. Trends in financing Asian agricultural research. Washington, D.C.: International Food Policy Research Institute. Mimeo.

Pingali, P. L., M. Hossain, and R. V. Gerpacio. 1997. *Asian rice bowls: The returning crisis.* New York: CAB International; Manila: in association with the International Rice Research Institute (IRRI).

Sen, A. 1981. *Poverty and famines: An essay in entitlement and deprivation.* Oxford: Clarendon Press.

World Bank. 1979. *Bangladesh food policy issues.* South Asia Department Report 2761-BD. Washington, D.C.: World Bank.

Contributors

Akhter U. Ahmed joined the International Food Policy Research Institute (IFPRI) as a research fellow in 1990 and was posted in his native Bangladesh. Now posted in Cairo, Egypt, he is studying options for restructuring food subsidies, generating employment, and liberalizing grain markets. Before joining IFPRI, he worked with the World Bank and was an agricultural economist for the U.S. Agency for International Development (USAID). He received a Ph.D. in agricultural economics from Colorado State University, an M.S. from Cornell University, and an M.S. and a B.S. from Bangladesh Agricultural University.

A. W. Nuruddin Ahmed received an M.S. from Dhaka University and taught college mathematics for three years. He then joined the civil service, working in several capacities in field administration, including section officer in the central secretariat for 6 years, deputy secretary for 13 years, and joint secretary for 1 year. He has been a consultant for a number of studies conducted by the Bangladesh Ministry of Food, including *The History of the Ministry of Food.*

Raisuddin Ahmed, a native of Bangladesh, joined IFPRI in 1976. Previously, he served as deputy chief of the Agriculture and Water Resources Division of the Bangladesh Planning Commission and as chief agricultural economist in the Ministry of Agriculture. The director of IFPRI's Markets and Structural Studies Division since 1983, he has researched food marketing and pricing policies in Asia and Africa and has examined the effects of infrastructure on agricultural productivity, rural employment, and rural income distribution. He received an M.A. in economics and a Ph.D. in agricultural economics from Michigan State University, an M.S. in agricultural economics from the American University in Beirut, and a B.S. in agricultural sciences from Dhaka University. His many publications include *Agricultural Price Policies for Developing Countries,* edited with John Mellor.

David A. Atwood works for the U.S. Agency for International Development's (USAID) Bureau for Africa in Washington, D.C. Previously, he was the deputy director of USAID/Bangladesh's Office of Food and Agriculture, where he helped manage the Public Law (P.L.) 480 Title III food-aid program and many other agricultural development programs. He has worked for more than 10 years as a development practitioner in developing countries. He received an M.A. in agricultural economics from Michigan State University and a B.A. in anthropology from Brown University.

Lutful Hoque Chowdhury is a professor of public administration at Dhaka University. He is involved in the human aspect of development administration and institution building and was responsible for managing and training civil servants at the National Institute of Public Administration during the 1980s. He received an M.A. in sociology from Dhaka University, an M.S. in public administration from American University in Beirut, and a Ph.D. in public administration from the University of Southern California in Los Angeles. He has published several articles about social change and development administration in South Asia.

Nuimuddin Chowdhury has a Ph.D. in economics from Cambridge University. Before joining IFPRI as a consultant for its food policy project in Bangladesh, he was a senior research fellow at the Bangladesh Institute of Development Studies. He has researched and written widely on food marketing and the public food distribution system in Bangladesh and is currently working as an independent consultant in Canada.

Tawfiq-e-Elahi Chowdhury is the secretary of the Energy Division of the Government of Bangladesh. He began his career in 1966 as a lecturer in economics at Dhaka University. Since joining the Pakistan civil service in 1968, he has held both field and policymaking positions in Bangladesh. Between 1984 and 1993 he spent most of his time in the Ministry of Finance, where he was involved in finding budgetary solutions related to domestic food policy. He later became the secretary of the Ministry of Food, where he played a key role in ongoing reform programs. In 1993 he was appointed secretary to the Government of Bangladesh. Chowdhury earned a postgraduate degree in development administration from Leeds University and a Ph.D. in economics from Harvard University. He has written several research publications and is the coauthor of two books.

Paul Dorosh is a research fellow with IFPRI currently working with the Bangladesh Ministry of Food in Dhaka as chief of party of the Food Management and Research Support Project. Before joining IPFRI in 1997, he worked as a senior research associate and associate professor with the Cornell Food and Nutrition Policy Program. Dorosh is coauthor of *Structural Adjustment Reconsidered: Economic Policy and Poverty in Africa.* He earned a B.A. in applied mathematics from Harvard University and a Ph.D. from the Food Research Institute of Stanford University.

Francesco Goletti joined IFPRI in 1990. An Italian citizen, he was trained in mathematics at Rome University and received a Ph.D. in economics from New York University. As a research fellow, he has studied price stabilization and market integration issues in Bangladesh, Egypt, Malawi, Pakistan, Senegal, Vietnam, and Zambia. He has also designed and delivered training courses on food and agricultural policy analysis in Bangladesh and Vietnam. Currently, he coordinates IFPRI's multicountry research program on the privatization and liberalization of agricultural input markets.

Steven Haggblade was chief of party for IFPRI's Bangladesh Food Policy Project, where for nearly three years he played a pivotal role in guiding food policy research in Bangladesh. During that time he also studied policy directions, marketing, and the political implications of policy changes. Haggblade currently lives in Madagascar, researching African food and agriculture policy as a member of the Cornell University Nutrition Studies Center. He has written numerous research publications, has taught at Syracuse University, and has worked at the World Bank. Haggblade holds a Ph.D. in economics from Michigan State University.

A. S. M. Jahangir helped manage the P.L. 480 Title III program for 17 years, reviewing existing food polices, identifying areas for reform, designing such reforms, and overseeing their implementation. In 1989/90 he worked part time as a consultant to the World Bank Resident Mission in Bangladesh, helping frame a food policy matrix and studying the prospect of rice export. In 1991/92 he spent a six-month sabbatical at IFPRI. Jahangir received an M.B.A. from Dhaka University and worked at IFPRI in Washington, D.C., for a short period as a consultant.

Golam Kabir has worked for USAID/Bangladesh for nearly 18 years, helping manage the P.L. 480 Title II program. A specialist in managing both targeted and developmental food-aid programs, he has successfully implemented them under difficult conditions. He received an M.A. in statistics from Dhaka University.

Wahiduddin Mahmud is a professor of economics at Dhaka University. He has served as a minister for Bangladesh's interim caretaker government, which conducted the country's most recent general election. While working for IFPRI, he researched agricultural diversification and the government's agricultural policy priorities. Mahmud received his Ph.D. in economics from Oxford University.

Shamsur Rahman has a degree in law from Dhaka University. He worked for many years in the Bangladesh Ministry of Law and Parliamentary Affairs, where he reviewed existing laws and advised the government about their implications. He now consults on legal matters.

Sultan Hafeez Rahman was a senior research fellow at the Bangladesh Institute of Development Studies when IFPRI invited the institute to collaborate in a study of agricultural diversification in Bangladesh. He has written several papers on Bangladesh's food and agricultural policy and is currently working for the Asian Development Bank in Manila. He has a Ph.D. in economics from Stanford University.

Herbie Smith was a food for peace officer who managed the P.L. 480 Title II food-aid program in Bangladesh. Before joining USAID/Bangladesh, he worked for USAID's Bureau for Humanitarian Resources in Washington, D.C. A specialist in food-aid management, he has executed targeted and developmental food-aid programs in developing countries and is currently managing the Title II program for USAID/Ethiopia.

Sajjad Zohir has worked at the Bangladesh Institute of Development Studies since 1977. He was promoted to research fellow in 1989 after receiving his Ph.D. in economics from the University of Toronto. In 1992 and 1994 he was a visiting fellow at IFPRI and in 1994/95 a visiting researcher at Manchester University in England. During the past 10 years he has held numerous consultancies, working with the World Bank, the European Union, the United Nations, and IFPRI. His policy research and advisory work focuses on the macroeconomy of Bangladesh—particularly the agricultural sector, agribusiness, program food aid, and the implications of the Uruguay Round.

Index

Page numbers for entries occurring in boxes are followed by a *b;* those for entries occurring in figures, by an *f;* those for entries occurring in notes, by an *n;* and those for entries occurring in tables, by a *t.*

LIBRARY OF CONGRESS CATALOGING-IN-PUBLICATION DATA

Out of the shadow of famine: evolving food markets and food policy in Bangladesh / edited by Raisuddin Ahmed, Steven Haggblade, and Tawfiq-e-Elahi Chowdhury.

p. cm.

"Published for the International Food Policy Research Institute."

Includes bibliographical references and index.

ISBN 0-8018-6333-3 (alk. paper) ISBN 0-8018-6476-3 (pbk. alk. paper)

1. Food industry and trade—Bangladesh. 2. Agriculture—Economic aspects—Bangladesh. 3. Famines—Bangladesh. I. Ahmed, Raisuddin, 1933– . Haggblade, Steven. III. Chowdhury, Tawfiq-e-Elahi. IV. International Food Policy Research Institute.

HD9016.B352095 2000

338.1'95492—dc21 99-41406

CIP